W9-AUQ-278

To my children

**Elizabeth Mary, Kathleen Marie (†),
Teresa Mary, James Joseph III,
Michael Haviland, Daniel Joseph,
Mary Kathleen, Kerry Ellen,
Margaret Mary, and John Paul**

*"Children are really the
supreme gift of marriage
and contribute very
substantially to the welfare
of their parents."*

— Second Vatican Council

CATHOLIC REPLIES 2

Answers to another 800 of the
most often asked questions
about religious and moral issues

JAMES J. DRUMMEY

C.R. Publications Inc.
345 Prospect Street
Norwood, Massachusetts 02062

Copyright 2003 by James J. Drummey
ALL RIGHTS RESERVED

Except for brief excerpts in articles or critical reviews, no part of this book may be reproduced or transmitted in any form or by any means, electronic or mechanical, including photocopying, recording, or by any information storage or retrieval system, without permission in writing from the publisher. Write:

C.R. Publications Inc.
345 Prospect Street
Norwood, MA 02062

English translation of the *Catechism of the Catholic Church* for the United States of America copyright 1994, United States Catholic Conference, Inc. — Libreria Editrice Vaticana. English translation of the *Catechism of the Catholic Church: Modifications from the Editio Typica* copyright 1997, United States Catholic Conference, Inc. — Libreria Editrice Vaticana. Used with permission.

Scripture excerpts are taken from the *New American Bible with Revised New Testament* Copyright 1986, 1970 Confraternity of Christian Doctrine, Inc., Washington, DC. Used with permission. All rights reserved. No part of the *New American Bible* may be reproduced by any means without permission in writing from the copyright owner.

Scripture excerpts are taken from the *New American Bible with Revised New Testament* Copyright 1970 Confraternity of Christian Doctrine, Inc., Washington, DC. Used with permission. All rights reserved. No part of the *New American Bible* may be reproduced by any means without permission in writing from the copyright owner.

Cover by Ariel Design
Printed in the United States of America

ISBN 0-9649087-9-4

Contents

Acknowledgements

On the acknowledgements page of the first *Catholic Replies* book, I expressed gratitude to the readers of my "Catholic Replies" column in *The Wanderer* newspaper for having submitted more than 1,000 questions on an amazing variety of religious beliefs, practices, and topics.

I remain very grateful to the readers of this weekly column because they have continued to send in excellent questions that ought to be of interest to all Catholics, and I have selected another 800 of their queries to appear in *Catholic Replies 2*.

This book contains many questions that were not covered in the first *Catholic Replies*, but it also treats some of the same questions again, only with new information from magisterial and other reliable sources, many of which are listed in the Bibliography. (If you don't find a particular question in this book, you may find it in the first volume.)

This is also the place to express my sincere thanks to those fellow Catholics who so willingly agreed to say some very kind things about *Catholic Replies 2* in the foreword and on the back cover of the book. Special thanks are also extended to my daughter Beth for proofreading the manuscript, and to Msgr. Paul J. Hayes for looking at the manuscript with a critical eye and offering many valuable suggestions.

Any opinions expressed in the replies are entirely those of the author, and I take full responsibility for them.

It is my hope and prayer that the contents of this book will help the reader to know the Catholic faith better so that he or she can explain and defend it in a society that is increasingly hostile to the truth. For it is only the truth, who is Jesus Himself, that can set us free from the slavery of falsehood and sin and lead us to eternal glory in Heaven.

James J. Drummey
March 25, 2003
The Annunciation of the Lord

Foreword

And Still There Is Reason for Our Hope

When James Drummey's *Catholic Replies* first appeared in 1995, his easy-to-read, frank approach to addressing our faith, our Catholic tradition, the whys and wherefores of the Church, and our desire to understand better how to live the Gospel of Our Lord quickly made an impression on many.

And well it should. With questions from American Catholics, and answers — thoroughly researched and grounded in the Magisterium — by an American Catholic with a reputation for honest, direct, and prayerful discussion, *Catholic Replies* was an excellent companion to the then newly published *Catechism of the Catholic Church*.

Volume 2 of *Catholic Replies* is equally welcome, and not just because Jim Drummey continues to offer solid, truthful responses to the concerns of American Catholics about living their faith in today's world. *Catholic Replies 2* is a testament to the desire of America's Catholics to find the deeper meaning and a stronger grounding in their faith, to explore the essence of Catholicism in their lives, and to revolutionize the relevance of the Catholic Church and her teachings.

Just as important, *Catholic Replies 2* reinforces the ability of American Catholics to be true witnesses to the faith at a time when many, both outside and inside the Church, question her traditions and her moral leadership. Rather than offer merely "by-the-book" responses to such challenges, Jim Drummey gives appropriate and important perspective into the reasons why we believe what we do, and stand for what we stand for. Indeed, both volumes empower today's Catholic to be a true Apologist in a time of need.

When I talk with representatives of the media about faith, I often say that I do not think in terms of "left" or "right." I tell them it is my role as a bishop to lead my flock deeper into faith. Through *Catholic Replies 2*, Jim Drummey once again has provided a useful tool for any Catholic wishing to discover this magnificent depth of faith that is Catholicism.

+Most Reverend John J. Myers
Archbishop of Newark

Chapter 1

Father, Son, and Holy Spirit

Q. We believe that God created time, the stars, the planets, animals, and man. But before God created these things, what did He do for trillions of years? — B.A.N., Kentucky

A. There were no years before God created time. Before the creation of the world, God existed as a spiritual, substantial, personal Being who never had a beginning and will never have an end. He testified to His eternal existence when He told Moses: "I am who am" (Exodus 3:14). The *Catechism of the Catholic Church* says that "God created the world to show forth and communicate his glory. That his creatures should share in his truth, goodness, and beauty — this is the glory for which God created them" (n. 319).

Q. Can you give me any logical arguments why there cannot be more than one God (of course there is only one), even if one is considered superior to all others? — R.P., New Hampshire

A. Peter Kreeft and Fr. Ronald Tacelli addressed this question on page 92 of their valuable *Handbook of Christian Apologetics* (InterVarsity Press). Here is their reasoning:

"If God is infinite, can there be many Gods? Obviously not. We have already seen that God must exist without limit. But if he is without limit, there cannot be more than one God. For if there were, there would have to be some difference between them, and this would involve nonbeing; the one could *not* be what or where the other was. But if that were so, then neither one could be the limitless fullness of being. And this would mean that what we call 'God' is not the ultimate answer to our question about finite being after all. But if 'God' is the answer to that question, then he must be the limitless fullness of being and cannot be limited by another God outside himself. So God must be one."

Q. My government teacher is an avowed atheist. What are some simple truths for God's existence that I might present to him? Should I even bother? — V.M., Michigan

A. Yes, you should bother. Who knows what might move your teacher away from his atheism? Offer the material and then pray for him.

Two arguments you can offer are from causality and intelligent design. Everything that exists must have been caused by something or someone else, but you cannot extend the line of causes indefinitely. There must have been a First Cause, or an Uncaused Cause, at the beginning, and that First Cause we call God.

If your teacher believes that it took an intelligent being to design a computer, that this complicated piece of machinery was not just the result of the chance coming together of pieces of plastic and metal, then he ought logically to believe that it took an intelligent being to design our complicated but orderly universe. That Intelligent Designer we call God.

To paraphrase G.K. Chesterton: "Show me a computer without a computer-maker, then I'll take a universe without a universe-maker."

For more about the arguments for the existence of God, see such books as Kreeft's and Tacelli's *Handbook of Christian Apologetics*, Hayes, Hayes and Drummey's *Catholicism & Reason* (C.R. Publications), Fr. Albert Nevins' *Catholicism: The Faith of Our Fathers* (Our Sunday Visitor), and William A. Dembski's *Intelligent Design* (InterVarsity Press).

Q. Would you list for me the five reasons for belief in God given by Thomas Aquinas? — M.K.K., New Hampshire

A. Here are the five famous proofs offered by St. Thomas back in the 13th century:

(1) *The argument from motion* — It is evident to our senses that in the world some things are in motion, but whatever is in motion must be put in motion by something else. But this cannot go on to infinity because then there would be no first mover and, consequently, no other mover. "Therefore it is necessary to arrive at a first mover, put in motion by no other; and this everyone understands to be God."

(2) *The argument from efficient cause* — There is no case known

in the world of sense in which a thing is the efficient cause of itself because it would have to be prior to itself, which is impossible. But if it is possible to go on to infinity in search of the ultimate cause, "there will be no first efficient cause, neither will there be an ultimate effect, nor any intermediate efficient causes; all of which is plainly false. Therefore it is necessary to admit a first efficient cause, to which everyone gives the name of God."

(3) *The argument from possibility and necessity* — We find in nature things that are possible to be and not to be, but it is impossible for these always to have existed, for that which is possible not to be at some time is not. If at one time there could have been nothing in existence, then even now nothing could be in existence, but this is absurd. Since not all beings are merely possible, there must exist some being whose existence is necessary. "Therefore we cannot but postulate the existence of some being having of itself its own necessity, and not receiving it from another, but rather causing in others their necessity. This all men speak of as God."

(4) *The argument from the gradation to be found in things* — There are beings who are more or less good, true, noble, and the like, but these comparisons make sense only if they resemble something which is best, truest, and noblest; in other words, the ultimate or uttermost being. "Now the maximum in any genus is the cause of all in that genus; as fire, which is the maximum heat, is the cause of all hot things. Therefore there must also be something which is to all beings the cause of their being, goodness, and every other perfection; and this we call God."

(5) *The argument from the governance of the world* — We can observe things that lack intelligence, such as natural bodies, acting always, or nearly always, in the same way so as to achieve a certain end. "Now whatever lacks intelligence cannot move toward an end unless it be directed by some being endowed with knowledge and intelligence; as the arrow is shot to its mark by the archer. Therefore some intelligent being exists by whom all natural things are directed to their end, and this being we call God."

Q. Some time ago, I heard a priest make the following statement: "God created the world. God is in control of the world. Whatever happens in the world happens only

because God either wills or permits to happen what does happen." If this is correct, it seems to me that nothing happens by chance. Am I right? — J.M.G., Pennsylvania

A. Yes, you and the priest you quoted are right. God is the Lord of the universe and nothing happens in the world that is not part of His plan. Read sections 268-274 and 302-314 in the *Catechism of the Catholic Church* for more insights into God's omnipotence and divine providence.

For example, article 269 says: "Nothing is impossible with God, who disposes his works according to his will [cf. *Jer* 27:5; 32:17; *Lk* 1:37]. He is the Lord of the universe, whose order he established and which remains wholly subject to him and at his disposal. He is master of history, governing hearts and events in keeping with his will."

Fr. John Hardon, S.J., once offered some additional thoughts:

"Saying that Providence is universal is only another way of affirming that all events taking place in this world, even those apparently fortuitous or casual, are part of God's eternal plan for the universe. With God there is no such thing as chance. Nothing merely 'happens' as far as he is concerned. Everything is meant to serve a purpose, mysteriously foreseen and foreordained by God" (*The Catholic Catechism*, p. 79).

Q. In glancing through the *Catechism*, I noticed in section 412 that it quotes Thomas Aquinas as saying that God permits evil in order to draw good from it. I don't understand how God can permit evil? — G.G., Pennsylvania

A. You are not the only one who does not understand how God can permit evil to exist in the world. It is a mystery that we will not fully understand until the Final Judgment. Here is what the *Catechism* quoted Aquinas as saying [St. Thomas Aquinas, *STh* III, 1, 3, *ad* 3; cf. *Rom* 5:20]:

"There is nothing to prevent human nature's being raised up to something greater, even after sin; God permits evil in order to draw forth some greater good. Thus St. Paul says, 'Where sin increased, grace abounded all the more'; and the Exultet sings, 'O happy fault ... which gained for us so great a Redeemer!' "

The dispositive will of God created us with free will, while His permissive will allows us to exercise that free will even in making disordered choices. To exclude sin, God would have had to create us without free will, i.e., as sub-moral beings incapable of making moral choices. He chose, however, to do otherwise.

This does not mean, of course, that God is responsible for evil. He created the first humans in a state of holiness, but their rebellion against Him, at the urging of Satan, and all the personal sins committed since then, including our own, are the cause of the evil in the world.

That's the bad news. The good news is that God did not turn away from sinful humanity, but sent His only Son to die for our sins and to overcome evil. If Jesus did not die on the cross, we could not get to Heaven. Yes, evil is prevalent in the world, but God's grace is even more prevalent, and God, in His own time, will bring about the ultimate triumph of good over evil.

In the meantime, it is the responsibility of each one of us to resist evil and strive for holiness within our own families, neighborhoods, parishes, and communities. If sin abounds in the circles in which we travel, we have the task of seeing that grace abounds all the more. Surely we can make a difference by leading holy lives ourselves and by influencing others to do likewise.

Q. Recently, my son's fifth-grade religion teacher announced that she would be referring to God as "He/She." When I asked her about it, I got the enclosed reply. I think she is putting another interpretation on the passage from the *Catechism*, but how do I respond? — C.P., Minnesota

A. In the letter from her son's teacher, C.P. was told that "we as a Church are growing in the use of language in referring to God as He/She, being conscious of not limiting God to one sex or the other, but broadening our understanding of God. There are many beliefs we continue to define as we grow in our understanding as a Church, and it is of great importance that our children know those beliefs as they grow in their faith."

The paragraph quoted from the *Catechism* was n. 42, which says that because "God transcends all creatures," we must remove from our language everything that would limit or confuse our image of Him, who remains to us " 'the inexpressible, the incomprehensible, the invisible, the ungraspable' [*Liturgy of St. John Chrysostom*, Anaphora]."

It seems to us that calling God "He/She" would most certainly confuse our image of God, and we don't think that paragraph 42 supports the teacher's point. We call God "He" because Jesus told us to call God "Father" (Matthew 6:9). This was not a declaration that God is male, but rather an analogy to help us understand something about the nature of God.

The *Catechism* explains that calling God "Father" indicates "two main things: that God is the first origin of everything and transcendent authority; and that he is at the same time goodness and loving care for all his children. God's parental tenderness can also be expressed by the image of motherhood [cf. *Isa* 66:13; *Ps* 131.2], which emphasizes God's immanence, the intimacy between Creator and creature" (n. 239).

While drawing on the human experience of parents, who are our first representatives of God, even though they "are fallible and can disfigure the face of fatherhood and motherhood," says the *Catechism* (n. 239), we must remember that "God transcends the human distinction between the sexes. He is neither man nor woman: he is God. He also transcends human fatherhood and motherhood, although he is their origin and standard [cf. *Ps* 27:10; *Eph* 3:14; *Isa* 49:15]: no one is father as God is Father."

Purifying our language of limited and imperfect images of God does not mean adopting inclusive terminology for God. It means, according to the *Catechism*, cleansing our hearts of certain false images drawn from the world since "God our Father transcends the categories of the created world. To impose our own ideas in this area 'upon him' would be to fabricate idols to adore or pull down" (n. 2779).

One of the false images drawn from this world is the notion that God can be called "He/She," but you won't find anything resembling this kind of language in the *Catechism*. So it was incorrect for this teacher to say that "we as a Church are growing in the use of the language in referring to God as 'He/She'."

Q. We often see the initials "IHS" and "INRI". What do they mean? — M.W., Massachusetts

A. IHS is both the first three letters of Jesus in Greek and a Latin inscription found on early Christian monuments. It stands for *Iesus Hominum Salvator*, or "Jesus, Savior of Men." INRI was the Latin inscription at the top of the cross of Christ. It stands for *Iesus Nazarenus Rex Iudaeorum*, or "Jesus of Nazareth, King of the Jews."

Q. As I read through the *Catechism of the Catholic Church*, I found statements to the effect that God became

man so that we might become God (cf. n. 460); that [cf. n. 460] " 'the only begotten Son of God, wanting to make us sharers in his divinity, assumed our nature, so that he, made man, might make men gods' " [St. Thomas Aquinas, *Opusc.* 57: 1-4]; and (n. 795) that we should " 'rejoice then and give thanks that we have become not only Christians, but Christ himself. Do you understand and grasp, brethren, God's grace toward us? Marvel and rejoice: We have become Christ' [St. Augustine, *In Jo. ev.* 21, 8: PL 35, 1568]." Isn't it the Mormon teaching that we can become gods? — K.S., Michigan

A. These statements do not mean that we will become gods in the Mormon sense, or that we will become equal to God, but rather that we will, in the words of St. Peter, "become sharers of the divine nature" (2 Peter 1:4). Or as the priest says at Mass, that we will come to "share in the divinity of Christ, who humbled himself to share in our humanity."

That this meaning has long been part of Catholic tradition can be seen from the footnotes to paragraph 460, which cite the writings of Saints Irenaeus, Athanasius, and Thomas Aquinas.

If you continue reading paragraph 795 of the *Catechism*, you will see that it offers additional insights into the sentences you quoted. For example, it says that if Christ is the head, then we are the members and that Christ is one person with the holy Church whom He has taken to Himself, that " 'head and members form as it were one and the same mystical person' [St. Thomas Aquinas, *STh* III, 48, 2]."

These statements, which are footnoted with references to St. Augustine, Pope St. Gregory the Great, and again Thomas Aquinas, mean that if we unite ourselves completely to Christ, we become one with Him mystically as we share in His divine nature. We have "clothed" ourselves with Christ, in the words of St. Paul (Galatians 3:27), who also said, "Whoever is joined to the Lord becomes one spirit with him" (1 Corinthians 6:17).

Q. I have heard priests say that when Jesus went into the desert, He fasted for 40 days, taking no food or drink. But if Jesus became truly human, He would have died of hunger and thirst. If He used His powers as God to prevent this, then He was not really a man. — B.P.B., Ontario

A. St. Matthew says only that Jesus "fasted 40 days and 40 nights" (Matthew 4:2), while St. Luke's account of the temptation in the desert reads: "Jesus, full of the Holy Spirit, then returned from the Jordan and was conducted by the Spirit into the desert for 40 days where he was tempted by the devil. During that time, he ate nothing, and at the end of it he was hungry" (Luke 4:1-2).

It doesn't say that Jesus did without water, but only without food. As true man, He was subject to the same need for food that we are. So how was it possible for Him to go without this basic necessity for that length of time. Perhaps because He was, in St. Luke's words, "full of the Holy Spirit."

Recall, too, that God made it possible for Moses to go without food, and water, for 40 days on Mt. Sinai (Exodus 34:28), so why not Jesus for the same length of time in the desert? And haven't we read of saints who existed for years when their only food was the Holy Eucharist? All things are possible with God.

Furthermore, modern scientific experiments conducted by the Karolinska Institute in Sweden have shown that a person can go without solid food for 55 days if he keeps taking liquids in a clinically monitored situation.

Q. The enclosed information from a seminar in our parish says that Jesus was "like us in all things, including ignorance (which is not the same as sin), and would live His entire life coming to greater self-consciousness." I thought that Jesus always had an awareness of who He was and what His mission was. Is it possible that the Son of God did not know who He was? — J.M., Massachusetts, and N.J.B., Wisconsin

A. No, it is not possible. The *Catechism* (n. 473) says that Jesus' human nature, through its union with His divine Person, knew everything related to God, especially "the intimate and immediate knowledge that the Son of God made man has of his Father [cf. *Mk* 14:36; *Mt* 11:27; *Jn* 1:18; 8:55; etc.]."

A closer look at two of these footnotes illustrates the point: Mark 14:36 ("He kept saying, '*Abba* (O Father), you have the power to do all things. Take this cup away from me. But let it be as you would have it, not as I'") and Matthew 11:27 ("Everything has been given over to me by my Father. No one knows the Son but the Father, and no one knows the Father but the Son — and anyone to whom the Son wishes to reveal him").

Jesus even demonstrated a knowledge of His divine identity at the age of 12 when He asked Mary and Joseph in the Temple in Jerusalem, "Why did you search for me? Did you not know that I had to be in my Father's house?" (Luke 2:49)

The *Catechism* also tells us that Jesus was fully aware of His mission on earth by virtue of the union of His human knowledge to the divine wisdom that He possessed as the Word incarnate. It says that Christ in His human knowledge fully understood the eternal plans He had come to reveal (cf. n. 474).

To support this statement, the *Catechism* in a footnote cites five passages from the Gospel of Mark: 8:31, 9:31, 10:33-34, 14:18-20, and 14:26-30. The first three passages contain Jesus' prediction of His Passion, death, and Resurrection. The fourth passage is Jesus' prediction of Judas' betrayal, and the fifth is His foretelling of Peter's denial.

Q. In a homily on the Parable of the Mustard Seed, one of our priests pointed out that the mustard seed is not the smallest seed and that Jesus was wrong in saying that it was because He was a carpenter and not a botanist. When I suggested after Mass that Jesus was adapting His teaching to accommodate the knowledge of His listeners, the priest said that while Jesus could not be wrong about matters of faith, He could be wrong about this. What is the correct perspective? — J.T.N., New York

A. The correct perspective is that Jesus was not speaking in absolute terms, but in relative terms regarding the size of the plant that can grow to eight or ten feet from such a tiny seed. He was teaching a religious lesson, not a botanical one. If your priest talked about the beauty of the sun rising that morning, he would technically be in error since the sun does not rise; it's the rotation of the earth that makes the sun appear to be rising.

We often use certain examples or comparisons that all recognize as inexact in order to make a point. That is what Jesus was doing. To say that He was in error is foolish and could lead one to think that our Lord could be wrong on other things.

Q. At Mass on the feast of the Immaculate Conception, the priest said some disturbing things in his homily. For example, that Jesus was an insurrectionist, a lawbreaker, and a hippie. How would you respond to him? — T.M.W., Massachusetts

A. Jesus' enemies called Him an insurrectionist and a lawbreaker, but our Lord never advocated overthrowing the government. In fact, He paid taxes to the government and urged the people on one occasion to "give to Caesar what is Caesar's, but give to God what is God's" (Matthew 22:21).

Christ's "lawbreaking" consisted of curing people on the Sabbath, which violated some ordinances that the Pharisees had tacked onto the law of Moses. Jesus' point was that helping someone in need superseded any law restricting one's activities on the Sabbath.

Using the 20th century term "hippie" to describe a man who lived in first-century Palestine is an anachronism. "Hippie" to most people today means a long-haired, pot-smoking, sexually promiscuous rebel. Jesus may have had long hair, as did most men of His time, but He was a respected teacher and preacher. Thousands were spellbound by His words; soldiers sent to arrest Him came back empty-handed, saying that never had they heard anyone speak like that. Furthermore, Jesus promoted and lived a moral code to which no modern-day Hippie would adhere.

Your priest may have been trying to call attention to the human side of our Lord, which is all right to do, but he was careless in portraying the only perfect Man who ever lived in such mundane and inaccurate human terms.

Q. When our Lord prays "that all may be one even as you and I are one," isn't He praying to Himself? — P.L., Massachusetts

A. These words come from chapter 17 of John's Gospel, which begins with Jesus addressing His Father, and the full statement indicates that He is praying not to Himself but to His Father:

"I do not pray for them [the Apostles] alone./ I pray also for those who will believe in me/ through their word,/ that all may be one/ as you, Father, are in me, and I in you;/ I pray that they may be [one] in us,/ that the world may believe that you sent me" (John 17:20-21).

Q. In St. John's Gospel, verse 15:10, Jesus says, "If you obey my commands you will remain in my love, just as I have obeyed my Father's commands and remain in his love." Another version uses the word "commandments." My question is: Just what was Jesus talking about when He made that statement? What are His commandments? — S.R.L., Iowa

A. Our Lord could be referring either to the Ten Command-ments or to the two great commandments. For instance, in chap-ter 19 of Matthew's Gospel, Jesus was asked by a rich young man, "What good must I do to possess everlasting life?" Jesus replied: "Keep the commandments." "Which ones?" the young man asked, and Jesus answered:

" 'You shall not kill'; 'You shall not commit adultery'; 'You shall not steal'; 'You shall not bear false witness'; 'Honor your father and your mother'; and 'Love your neighbor as yourself.' "

In chapter 10 of Luke, a lawyer asked Jesus the same ques-tion ("What must I do to inherit everlasting life?"), and Jesus answered, "What is written in the law?" The lawyer replied: "You shall love the Lord your God/ with all your heart,/ with all your soul,/ with all your strength,/ and with all your mind;/ and your neighbor as yourself." Jesus said, "You have answered correctly. Do this and you shall live."

For some good reflections on both of these statements of our Lord, see Pope John Paul's encyclical "The Splendor of Truth" (*Veritatis Splendor*), especially sections 12-15. In the words of the Holy Father:

"The commandments of which Jesus reminds the young man are meant to safeguard *the good* of the person, the image of God, by protecting his *goods* .... These negative precepts express with particular force the ever-urgent need to protect human life, the communion of persons in marriage, private property, truthful-ness, and people's good name" (n. 13).

Q. In Luke 18:19, our Lord says to the rich official, "Why dost thou call me good? No one is good but God alone." This is kind of confusing since Jesus is God. — P.D.L., Massachusetts

A. Yes, *we* know that Jesus is God, and that He is good, but the rich official did not know that, so Jesus' first step was to point the man in the direction of God. As Pope John Paul ex-plained in *Veritatis Splendor*, in order to answer the official's other question ("Good teacher, what must I do to inherit eternal life?"), Jesus first noted that eternal life "can only be found by turning one's mind and heart to the 'One' who is good: 'No one is good but God alone' (Mark 10:18; cf. Luke 18:19). *Only God can* *answer the question about what is good, because he is the Good itself."*

The Holy Father's explanation continued:

"To ask about the good, in fact, *ultimately means to turn toward God,* the fullness of goodness. Jesus shows that the young man's question is really a *religious* question, and that the goodness that attracts and at the same time obliges man has its source in God, and indeed is God himself. God alone is worthy of being loved 'with all one's heart, and with all one's soul, and with all one's mind' (Matthew 22:37). He is the source of man's happiness. Jesus brings the question about morally good action back to its religious foundations, to the acknowledgement of God, who alone is goodness, fullness of life, the final end of human activity, and perfect happiness" (n. 9).

Q. During a homily about Jesus' multiplication of the loaves and fishes, the priest said that the miracle actually was getting people to share with one another the food that they had brought with them. When I asked the priest for a clarification, he said it was a matter of which theologian you follow. I wrote to the bishop, but the answer I got did not fit the question I asked. Can you help me? — R.J.S., Wisconsin

A. This anti-miraculous nonsense about the only miracle that appears in all four Gospels has been around for some time. All that is necessary to refute it is to read what St. John says happened after the miracle. "When the people saw the sign he had performed," says John, "they began to say, 'This is undoubtedly the Prophet who is to come into the world.' At that, Jesus realized that they would come and carry him off to make him king, so he fled back to the mountain alone" (John 6:14-15).

Why would the people want to make Jesus king, or why would they think that He was the long-awaited Prophet, if all He did was inspire them to share food they had in their pockets? And why did they follow Him to Capernaum the next day looking for another miracle if all He had done was get them to share their fish sandwiches? The reaction of the crowd makes sense only if Jesus actually did multiply five loaves and two fish and feed more than 5,000 people.

This of course was a prefiguring of the Eucharist, with Jesus promising to feed us with His own body, "the living bread/ come down from heaven" (John 6:51), and belief in this miracle is a matter of following magisterial teaching, not the heretical musings of certain dissident theologians.

Q. Why was the atrocity that was the Passion, Crucifixion, and death of our Lord necessary to achieve the redemption of man from the effects of the Fall when God, of whom we predicate omnipotence and infinite mercy, could have pardoned or forgiven man by a simple act of His will? — F.L., California
A. One answer might be that we can learn so much more about God and His incredible love for us from the Passion and death of Christ than we could ever have learned if God had simply pardoned us. In volume three of their *Radio Replies*, Frs. Leslie Rumble and Charles Carty offer this explanation:

"Had God willed it, Christ could have saved us without undergoing so much suffering. But God willed otherwise, and Jesus undertook to satisfy for human nature in human nature, and in generous measure indeed. Nor was his long-drawn-out and intense passion superfluous. He thus made superabundant satisfaction for our sins, gave an extreme manifestation of his love for us, set us an example of almost every virtue in almost every possible trial, and intensified the motives why those who profess to believe in him should refrain from further sin. Thus Christ made essential reparation by his death, and circumstantial reparation by enduring all types of penalties deserved by the various sins of men" (p. 173).

For further insights, see also paragraphs 599-623 of the *Catechism of the Catholic Church*, along with the cross-references in the margins next to these paragraphs.

Q. A priest on our local diocesan TV channel stated that the Romans were responsible for the crucifixion of Christ because it was a Roman form of punishment. I thought that the Roman governor, Pontius Pilate, had asked the crowd whom he should release, Christ or Barabbas. They chose Barabbas. I don't understand the priest's explanation. Please elucidate. — M.K., New York
A. First of all, the manner in which Jesus died was dictated by the Romans, who crucified people for crimes against the state.

If the Jewish leaders had had the authority to execute Christ, they would have stoned Him to death for allegedly committing the crime of blasphemy. But since they lacked the power to execute anyone, they accused the Lord of being a revolutionary and an enemy of Caesar, political crimes that led Pilate to order Jesus crucified, even though the Roman governor knew that Christ was innocent.

While the degree of sin of the participants in the death of Jesus (Judas, the Sanhedrin, Pilate) is known to God alone, bear in mind three things: (1) We cannot blame all Jews or Romans, either those present then or those born later, for the crucifixion of our Lord. (2) Jesus Himself forgave His executors, along with those who shouted for Barabbas, because they were ignorant of what they were doing. (3) All of us bear responsibility for the cruel torments inflicted on Christ because of our own sins.

As St. Francis of Assisi said: "It is you who have crucified Him and crucify Him still, when you delight in your vices and sins."

For more on this, see paragraphs 595-598 of the *Catechism of the Catholic Church*.

Q. In the Apostles' Creed, it says that Jesus "descended to the dead," that is, to all the good people who had died previously. Did He take them to Heaven and when? — R.E., Arizona

A. The *Catechism of the Catholic Church* (n. 632) says that Jesus descended to the dead to proclaim "the Good News to the spirits imprisoned there [cf. 1 *Pet* 3:18-19]." It says that it was these spirits in prison whom Christ released when He descended not into the Hell of the damned, but rather to what has been called the "bosom of Abraham," where all the souls of the good people who had lived before the time of Christ had been waiting for His atoning death on the cross (cf. n. 633).

Jesus did eventually take these holy souls to Heaven, but we don't know when. It may have been before His appearance to Mary Magadalene on Easter Sunday, when He told her not to cling to Him "for I have not yet ascended to the Father" (John 20:17), or maybe He took these souls with Him when He ascended to the Father's right hand. Some have suggested that this ascension took place immediately after His conversation with Magadalene, while the ascension forty days later brought an official end to His public appearances on earth.

**Q. As Easter approaches again, I will have trouble with
"He has been raised." By whom? He who said, "Before
Abraham was, I am" — He has to be raised? The One who
is true God and true man? This has become an obsession
with me. — J.M.M., Maryland, and M.T., Ohio**

A. It is precisely because Jesus is true God and true man that
we can talk about Him being raised from the dead (by His Father) or rising on His own (by His own power). Noting that the
Resurrection is the work of the three divine Persons of the Holy
Trinity, the *Catechism* says that "the Father's power" raised up
Jesus and "perfectly introduced his Son's humanity, including
his body, into the Trinity" (n. 648).

As for the Son, the *Catechism* (n. 649) says that Jesus "effects
his own Resurrection by virtue of his divine power. Jesus an-
nounces that the Son of man will have to suffer much, die, and
then rise [cf. *Mk* 8:31; 9:9-31; 10:34]. Elsewhere he affirms explicitly: 'I lay down my life that I may take it [up] again.... I have
power to lay it down, and I have power to take it [up] again' [*Jn*
10:17-18]."

**Q. Would you please comment on the enclosed article
("Finding the Historical Jesus") from the *St. Anthony
Messenger*? It seems to deny the truth of Christ's Resur-
rection. — V.Y., Arizona**

A. The article in the December 1997 issue consists largely of
an interview with Fr. John P. Meier, then a professor in the biblical studies department at the Catholic University of America
and the author of a four-volume work entitled *A Marginal Jew:
Rethinking the Historical Jesus*. Asked if historians could address the Resurrection, Fr. Meier responded:

"We can verify as historians that Jesus existed and that certain events reported in the Gospels happened in history, yet historians can never prove the Resurrection in the same way ....
The Resurrection of Jesus is certainly supremely real. However,
not everything that is real either exists in time and space or is
empirically verifiable by historical means."

Perhaps there is a sense in which Fr. Meier understands these
words that would conform with the Catholic understanding of
the Resurrection, but we can see why V.Y. might think Meier is
denying the truth of Christ's Resurrection. A much clearer state-

ment about the reality of this "historical and transcendent event" can be found in article 639 of the *Catechism*, which says that "the mystery of Christ's Resurrection is a real event, with manifestations that were historically verified, as the New Testament bears witness."

The *Catechism* then refers to St. Paul's words, written about A.D. 56 to the Christians of Corinth:

"I handed on to you first of all what I myself received, that Christ died for our sins in accordance with the Scriptures; that he was buried and, in accordance with the Scriptures, rose on the third day; that he was seen by Cephas, then by the Twelve. After that he was seen by five hundred brothers at once, most of whom are still alive, although some have fallen asleep. Next he was seen by James; then by all the apostles. Last of all he was seen by me, as one born out of the normal course" (1 Corinthians 15:3-8).

"Given all these testimonies," the *Catechism* says that "Christ's Resurrection cannot be interpreted as something outside the physical order, and it is impossible not to acknowledge it as an historical fact" (n. 643).

Q. Can you explain why the Creed says that Jesus rose "again" from the dead? The word "again" implies that He rose at least once before, yet the *Catechism* insists that this is not the meaning. Can you explain this? — J.L.S., California, G.H.L., Louisiana, and B.Z., California

A. There was no previous Resurrection; Jesus rose from the dead only once, on the first Easter. Like many words, "again" can be understood in different ways. One common meaning, as suggested above, implies that a certain action occurred at least once before and is now happening a second time. But that is not the meaning of "again" when we talk about the Resurrection.

According to *Webster's New World Dictionary*, another meaning of "again" is "back into a former position or condition [he is well again]." This is the correct understanding of the word as it appears in the Creed: Jesus died but now is alive again after rising from the dead.

Q. Do you know anything about the enclosed "True Letter of Our Savior Jesus Christ"? I recall having seen it

many years ago, so it has been around for quite a while.
— A.J.L., California

A. The letter was allegedly found in the Holy Sepulcher after the death of Jesus and preserved until this day. We are going to quote at some length from the letter to show that the statements attributed to our Lord are farfetched and even bizarre. If this "True Letter" were really authentic, it would long ago have been made a part of Revelation. We would advise against believing it or disseminating it.

Among other things, Christ is quoted as saying that people who "cast slurs on this sacred letter shall be forsaken by me. On the contrary, those people who shall carry a copy of this letter with them shall be free from death by drowning and from sudden death. They shall be free from all contagious diseases and lightning; they shall not die without Confession, and shall be free from their enemies and from the hand of wrongful authority and from all their slanderers and false witnesses."

The letter then quotes Jesus as giving this bizarre account of His sufferings during His Passion:

"The blows received on my head were 150; those on my stomach, 108; kicks on my shoulders, 80. I was led, bound with cords by the hair, 24 times. Spits in the face were 180. I was beaten on the body 6,666 times; beaten on the head 110 times. I was roughly pushed and, at 12 o'clock, was lifted up by the hair, pricked with thorns, and pulled by the beard 23 times; received 20 wounds on the head; thorns of marine junks, 72; pricks of thorns in the head, 110; mortal thorns in the forehead, 3.

"I was afterward flogged and dressed as a mocked king; wounds in the body, 1,000. The soldiers who led me to Calvary were 608; those who watched me were 3, and those who mocked me were 1,008; the drops of blood which I lost were 28,430."

Q. What is the significance of the Transfiguration of our Lord? Also, I have seen the dove in many churches, sometimes with the head up and other times with the head down. What does the different position signify? — J.F.M., New York

A. Taking the latter question first, the dove is the universal symbol of the Holy Spirit (see the *Catechism*, n. 701). This symbol stems from the Spirit's descent on Jesus in the form of a dove at the time of our Lord's baptism in the River Jordan (Matthew

3:16). The dove is usually placed on sanctuary ceilings or shown hovering. Whether the head is up or down might depend on the observer's angle of vision.

The Transfiguration of Jesus in the presence of Peter, James, and John (Matthew 17:1-8 and Luke 9:28-36) is a foretaste of Christ's coming in glory at the end of the world. The *Catechism* (cf. n. 555) says that Jesus disclosed His divine glory, thus confirming Peter's statement that He was the Messiah, while at the same time revealing that before entering His glory, He would have to die on the cross in Jerusalem.

According to the *Catechism*, Moses and Elijah were present because they had announced the suffering of the Messiah, the bright cloud that overshadowed them indicated the presence of the Holy Spirit; in fact, " 'the whole Trinity appeared: the Father in the voice; the Son in the man; the Spirit in the shining cloud' [St. Thomas Aquinas, *STh* III, 45, 4, *ad* 2]."

A prayer from the Byzantine liturgy explains this well:

"You were transfigured on the mountain, and your disciples, as much as they were capable of it, beheld your glory, O Christ our God, so that when they should see you crucified they would understand that your Passion was voluntary, and proclaim to the world that you truly are the splendor of the Father."

Q. In my daily missal for the Thursday after Pentecost, the following is said: "We believe that the Holy Spirit works in a very special way in the hierarchical priesthood. That is why we respect, love, and obey the apostolic office in the Church." Is the Holy Spirit male, part of the Father and the Son? — C.M., California

A. First of all, the Holy Spirit is not male. According to the *Catechism*, "God transcends the human distinction between the sexes. He is neither man nor woman: he is God" (n. 239).

Second, the Holy Spirit is not "part" of the Father and the Son either, but the third Person of the Trinity, distinct from the other two Persons. The *Catechism* quotes the Council of Florence (1438) as having said:

"The Holy Spirit is eternally from Father and Son; he has his nature and subsistence at once (*simul*) from the Father and the Son. He proceeds eternally from both as from one principle and through one spiration" (n. 246).

Editor's Note: To T.F.G. of Texas, who requested information about prayers to the Holy Spirit, several readers have recommended sources of information. The sources include *Following the Holy Spirit* (Catholic Book Publishing Company), *The Holy Spirit: Our Greatest Friend* (TAN Books), *Devotion to the Holy Spirit* (Lumen Christi Press), and Antonio Royo Martin's *The Great Unknown: The Holy Ghost and His Gifts* (Western Hemisphere Cultural Society).

Those with older Bibles will also remember the prayer to the Holy Spirit before reading the Scriptures:

"Come, Holy Spirit, fill the hearts of your faithful and enkindle in them the fire of your love. Send forth your Spirit, and they shall be created, and you shall renew the face of the earth. Let us pray. O God, you who have taught the hearts of your faithful by the light of the Holy Spirit, grant us by that Spirit himself to know what is right and ever to rejoice in his help, through Christ our Lord. Amen."

Chapter 2

Sacred Scripture

Q. According to an article in the *Catholic Encyclopedia*, Stephen Langton, a 13th century Archbishop of Canterbury, put the Bible into chapters. Three centuries later, an Italian priest and a printer put the chapters into verses. Where can I get more information about this? — E.T.D., New York

A. One good source of this information is Henry G. Graham's book *Where We Got the Bible*, which has been reprinted by Catholic Answers. Here is what Bishop Graham said:

"Originally, I need hardly say, there was no such thing in the mss. as divisions into chapters and verses, and no points or full stops or commas, to let you know where one sentence began and the next finished; hence the reading of one of these ancient records is a matter of some difficulty to the unscholarly. The division into chapters so familiar to us in our modern Bibles was the invention either of Cardinal Hugo, a Dominican, in 1248, or more probably of Stephen Langton, Archbishop of Canterbury (d. 1227); and it is no calumny upon the reputation of either of these great men to say that the division is not very satisfactory.

"He is not happy in his method of splitting up the page of Scripture; the chapters are of very unequal length, and frequently interrupt a narrative or argument or an incident in an inconvenient way, as anyone may see for himself by looking up such passages as Acts 21:40; or Acts 4 and 5; or 1 Corinthians 12 and 13.

"The division again into verses was the work of one Robert Stephens, and the first English version in which it appeared was the Geneva Bible, 1560. This gentleman seems to have completed his performance on a journey between Paris and Lyons ... probably while stopping overnight in inns and hostels. 'I think,' an old commentator quaintly remarks, 'it had been better done on his knees in the closet.' To this I would venture to add that his achievement must share the same criticism of inappropriateness as the arrangement into chapters" (p. 38).

Q. How many books are there in the Jewish Bible? In what year did the Pharisees of Jerusalem form the canon of books that were originally written in Hebrew in Palestine before the time of Esdras? What about the books in Greek that were accepted by the Jews of Alexandria? Did not our Lord Jesus read from scrolls which would have been part of those books accepted by the Jews of Alexandria? — R.L., New York

A. There are 39 books in the Jewish or Hebrew Bible and 46 books in the Old Testament section of the Greek Bible, also known as the Septuagint, a Latin word meaning "70." It refers to the 70 men who reportedly translated the Bible from Hebrew to Greek in Alexandria a century or two before Christ.

When Jesus read from a scroll in the synagogue at Nazareth (cf. Luke 4:17), He would have been reading a Hebrew version of the Book of Isaiah. However, the Septuagint enjoyed wide acceptance in the first Christian generation, according to John L. McKenzie's *Dictionary of the Bible* (Simon & Schuster), which says that 300 of the 350 citations from the Old Testament that are found in the New Testament are quoted according to the Septuagint translation.

Around the end of the second century before Christ, rabbis in Palestine drew up a canon of Scripture that did not include seven books found in the Septuagint: Judith, Tobit, Wisdom, Ecclesiasticus (Sirach), Baruch, and 1 and 2 Maccabees, along with parts of Esther and Daniel. These books are an official part of Catholic Bibles, and are included in some Protestant Bibles in a separate section know as the Apocrypha, which to them means that the books were not divinely authored and do not belong to the canon of Scripture.

For more information on the history of the Old Testament books, see Fr. Michael Duggan's book *The Consuming Fire* (Ignatius Press).

Q. A friend says that his theology professor at a Catholic college stated that the Douay-Rheims version of the Bible was identical to the King James version. I find this impossible to believe. What say you? — B.M.K., Ohio

A. It depends on what version of the King James you are talking about. Some translations of this Protestant Bible do not carry the seven books mentioned in the previous reply, but others, including the original edition, published in 1611, do. When these books appear in a King James translation, they are called apocryphal, which means of questionable origin. Catholics call them deuterocanonical, which means that their divine inspiration was challenged at one time, but they were later included in the canon of inspired books, including the Douay-Rheims and other Catholic translations.

A.E.F. of Chicago, a convert from the Episcopal Church, was good enough to send along the following helpful comments on this matter:

"The original Authorized Version of 1611 contained the Apocrypha. Under Cromwell's commonwealth, in the 1640s, the publication of the Apocrypha was banned. The immediate result of the ban was the publication of certain Bibles with a gap in the page numbering between the Old and New Testaments. This led to the custom, now almost universally followed in both Catholic and Protestant Bibles, of starting the page numbers over again in the New Testament.

"After the Restoration, Bible publishers realized that it was cheaper to publish Bibles without the Apocrypha, and only very high-quality editions included it. Over the years, the 'Maccabee Bible,' as a Bible containing the Apocrypha is often called, became something of a rarity, and even Episcopalians who wished to follow the daily prayer outlined in the Book of Common Prayer (which has always required readings from the Apocrypha) as often as not used an edition of the Apocrypha which was bound separately from the rest of the Bible."

In that connection, says G.P.R., also of Chicago, "the *full* KJV Bible was recently reprinted by some traditional Anglicans and bound together with the Episcopal Church's 1928 edition of the Book of Common Prayer in order to facilitate recitation of their version of the daily office."

Q. In a reply some time ago, you said that Catholics do not speak of the Bible as being "dictated" by God; only fundamentalists use such language. However, "dictated" has been used frequently by the early Fathers, doctors, Popes, and councils, and is a key part of authentic doctrine. See the enclosed quotation from *Providentissimus Deus*, the 1893 encyclical of Pope Leo XIII. — R.P.G. and F.G.G, Ohio

A. Here is what Pope Leo XIII had to say in his encyclical on Sacred Scripture:

"For all the books which the Church receives as sacred and canonical are written wholly and entirely, with all their parts, at the dictation of the Holy Spirit; and so far is it from being possible that any error can coexist with inspiration, that inspiration not only is essentially incompatible with error, but excludes and rejects it as absolutely and necessarily as it is impossible that God Himself, the supreme Truth, can utter that which is not true. This is the ancient and unchanging faith of the Church, solemnly defined in the Councils of Florence and of Trent, and finally confirmed and more expressly formulated by the [First] Council of the Vatican."

The Holy Father then quoted Vatican I as having said that the Church holds the books of the Bible to be "sacred and canonical not because, having been composed by human industry, they were afterward approved by her authority; nor only because they contain Revelation without errors, but because, having been written under the inspiration of the Holy Spirit, they have God for their Author."

By exerting "supernatural power" on the human writers, the Pope explained, the Holy Spirit "so moved and impelled them to write — He so assisted them when writing — that the things which He ordered, and those only, they, first, rightly understood, then willed faithfully to write down, and finally expressed in apt words and with infallible truth. Otherwise, it could not be said that He was the Author of the entire Scripture."

Virtually the same words can be found in Vatican II's *Dogmatic Constitution on Divine Revelation* (n. 11), which footnotes the above-mentioned passage from *Providentissimus Deus*, and in paragraphs 105 and 106 of the *Catechism of the Catholic Church.*

In light of what has been said thus far, we don't think that the word "dictation," as used by some Church Fathers and by Pope Leo XIII, should be understood to mean verbal dictation, as one would dictate a letter into a recorder to be transcribed later. Rather, it should be understood in the sense of divine inspiration, which Fr. John Hardon's *Modern Catholic Dictionary* (Doubleday) defines as:

"The special influence of the Holy Spirit on the writers of Sacred Scripture in virtue of which God himself becomes the principal author of the books written and the sacred writer is the subordinate author. In using human beings as the instruments in the composition, God does so in harmony with the person's nature and temperament, and with no violence to the free, natural activity of his or her human faculties."

Q. Can you please inform me if the Sacred Scripture readings from the Old Testament at the Mass are the result of Vatican II? Is there a precedent for these readings in the early Church? — J.B.G., Connecticut

A. Readings from the Old Testament, particularly from the law, the prophets, and the psalms, have been part of the Catholic Mass from the Church's earliest days. However, what we now call the first reading was called the epistle at Sunday Mass prior to Vatican II and was usually taken from one of St. Paul's letters; the first reading at daily Mass before Vatican II was usually taken from the Old Testament.

What Vatican II called for was "more reading from Holy Scripture, and it is to be more varied and suitable" (*Constitution on the Sacred Liturgy*, n. 35). As a result of this call to make more of the Bible accessible to the average church-going Catholic, a Catholic who attends Mass every Sunday over a three-year period will hear more than 7,000 verses from Sacred Scripture, including many more passages from the Old Testament. One who attends daily Mass over a two-year cycle will be exposed to more than 14,000 Bible verses.

For additional information on this matter, see two books by Fr. Peter Stravinskas: *The Catholic Church & the Bible* (Ignatius) and *The Mass: A Biblical Prayer* (Our Sunday Visitor).

Q. I have two Catholic friends who go to Bible classes in a Protestant church. I feel strongly that they may be getting the wrong information. — W.P.D., Florida

A. There is no specific Church prohibition against participating in Bible studies with other Christians, but your friends should be careful. If the person conducting the Bible study is honestly trying to develop an appreciation of and love for Holy Scripture, and is not trying to force a particular point of view on the members of the group, then it could be a positive and beneficial experience for your friends.

On the other hand, if the group leader is engaged in disputing the Catholic interpretation of Scripture, or in trying to persuade Catholics to leave their Church, and your friends are not intellectually prepared to defend the Catholic view, then they should get away from that study group.

Q. Can you recommend good Bible study resources that are truly loyal to the magisterium of the Church? I am looking for in-depth commentaries that have sound scholarship. — J.B., Texas, M.L., Arizona, and R.L.D., Ontario

A. For some good books that can be used in studying the background of the Bible, as well as the Bible itself, we would recommend the Navarre Bible commentaries, any of Fr. Alfred McBride's books on Scripture (Our Sunday Visitor), Fr. John L. McKenzie's *Dictionary of the Bible* (Simon & Schuster), Henri Daniel-Rops' *Daily Life in the Time of Jesus* (Servant Books), Fr. Michael Duggan's *The Consuming Fire* (Ignatius), Fr. William Most's *Free From All Error* (Franciscan Marytown Press), Antonio Fuentes' *A Guide to the Bible* (Four Courts Press), Fr. Kenneth Baker's *Inside the Bible* (Ignatius), Henry Graham's *Where We Got the Bible* (Catholic Answers), Steve Kellmeyer's *Bible Basics* (Basilica Press), Fr. Peter Stravinskas' *The Catholic Church & the Bible* (Our Sunday Visitor), Mark Shea's *Making Senses Out of Scripture* (Basilica), Edward Sri's *Mystery of the Kingdom: On the Gospel of Matthew* (Emmaus Road), and Tim Gray's *Mission of the Messiah: On the Gospel of Luke* (Emmaus Road).

Dr. Scott Hahn and Jeff Cavins have put together 13 one-hour videos that give an overview of Bible history from Genesis to the Catholic Church. The series, which first appeared on EWTN, is entitled *Our Father's Plan* and is available from Ignatius Press.

Q. My freshman son has been given the International Student Bible for Catholics in his CCD class. Is this Bible good or bad? — R.G., Michigan

A. This contemporary English version of the New Testament is very good for high school or college students, and you ought to read it and discuss it along with your son. Not only are there paragraphs on every page that explain points of Scripture, but there are also at the beginning of this edition 120 pages of answers to a variety of questions about religion.

The answers are solid and present Church teaching on such topics as where the Bible came from, the existence of God, the divinity of Christ, reasons for believing in the Resurrection, sin and forgiveness, the Commandments and the Beatitudes, Heaven and Hell, why we need to go to Church, Mary and the saints, the seven Sacraments, how to become a better Catholic, sex and chastity, abortion, homosexuality, AIDS, drinking and drugs, the occult, witchcraft, Satanism, the New Age, reincarnation, evolution, and how we can know the will of God.

Q. One of the questions on my granddaughter's test at a local Catholic high school was, "What are the five myths of the Bible?" The answer was the creation, Adam and Eve, Cain and Abel, the Tower of Babel, and Noah's Ark. What does the Church teach about the truth of the Bible? — L.P., Ohio, and R.W., New Hampshire

A. A myth is usually thought to be a fictional, imaginary, or fabricated story that is contrary to actual history. So when certain Old Testament events are described as myths, the implication is that they never happened, that they are just folksy allegories designed to convey religious truths. But what does the Church teach about the so-called myths in the Book of Genesis?

In his 1950 encyclical *Humani Generis*, Pope Pius XII said that the first 11 chapters of Genesis, while "not conforming to the historical method used by the best Greek and Latin writers or by competent authors of our time, do nevertheless pertain to history in a true sense, which, however, must be further studied and determined by exegetes. The same chapters, in simple and metaphorical language adapted to the mentality of a people but little cultured, both state the principal truths which are fundamental for our salvation, and also give a popular description of the origin of the human race and the Chosen People" (n. 38).

The Holy Father then said: "Therefore, whatever of the popular narrations have been inserted into the Sacred Scriptures must in no way be considered on a par with myths or other such things, which are more the product of an extravagant imagination than of that striving for truth and simplicity which in the Sacred Books, also of the Old Testament, is so apparent that our ancient sacred writers must be admitted to be clearly superior to the ancient profane writers" (n. 39).

Applying this to the first chapters of Genesis, said Fr. William Most in his book *Catholic Apologetics Today* (TAN), we can say that "they are historical in that they report things that really happened. Chiefly, that God made the world by a word; that He in some special way made man, and gave him grace and privileges, and that He gave a command to the first pair which they disobeyed, and which caused their fall from favor.

"But what the scene was like, whether a garden or something else, and other similar details, are not *asserted*. Nor did the sacred author *assert* that God made everything in six spans of 24 hours each. Such was the nature of Genesis. It is historical in that it reported things that actually happened; but not in precisely our genre of history writing" (pp. 173-174).

In *Free From All Error* (Prow Books), his book on the authorship, inerrancy, and historicity of Scripture, Fr. Most points out that scholars who describe the genre of Genesis as "myth" do not mean what most people think of when hearing the word *myth*. He referred to Pope John Paul's audience on November 7, 1979, in which the Holy Father said that "the term 'myth' does not designate a fabulous content, but merely an archaic way of expressing a deeper content" (p. 64).

We would like to think that in the Bible classes referred to by our questioners, the high schoolers are being given the understanding of "myth" that is approved by the Church, but knowing the deplorable state of much religious education today, we fear that is not the case.

Q. My ninth grader was told that she did not have to believe there was an actual first man or woman or a place of paradise or that these specific individuals had a relationship with God. She was told that the whole Adam/Eve story was primitive man's way of explaining the presence of sin in the world, that the particulars were unimportant, and that it was one of the myths of the Bible. Is this theologically sound? — W.M., Pennsylvania

Q. I received a card from a friend who is attending an adult Bible study. She told me that there were no such people as Adam and Eve. What is the best way to answer her? — M.B., New Jersey

A. The teachers of these two classes are the real myth-makers here. If you read paragraphs 355-421 of the *Catechism*, you will see that there were indeed a first man and woman in paradise and they had a relationship with God that was damaged by original sin. Under the subhead "Man in Paradise," the *Catechism* says that "the first man was not only created good, but was also established in friendship with his Creator and in harmony with himself and with the creation around him" (n. 374). It says (n. 375) that "the Church, interpreting the symbolism of biblical language in an authentic way, in the light of the New Testament and Tradition, teaches that our first parents, Adam and Eve, were constituted in an original 'state of holiness and justice' [cf. Council of Trent (1546): DS 1511]. This grace of original holiness was to 'share in ... divine life' [cf. *LG* 2]."

The *Catechism* (n. 390) also says that while the account of the fall in chapter 3 of Genesis uses "figurative language," it "affirms a primeval event that took place *at the beginning of the history of man* [cf. GS 13 § 1]."

And the *Catechism* says in paragraph 417 that "Adam and Eve transmitted to their descendants human nature wounded by their own first sin and hence deprived of original holiness and justice; this deprivation is called 'original sin.'"

Q. Did God actually take Adam's rib to make Eve? If so, why a rib? Even if the Bible is divinely inspired, isn't it just a collection of stories to teach us how to lead better lives? — P.E., Missouri

A. The Genesis account of creation is to be read as religious history in which figurative language and popular descriptions are used to teach fundamental religious truths. Some of these truths are that God created the universe out of nothing, that He created the first human pair in some special way and gave them a command that they disobeyed and lost their right to Heaven, that the human race suffers from the consequences of their sin, and that one day God will send a Redeemer for fallen humanity.

God could have created Eve from Adam's rib, but we are not required to accept that description literally. What is more important is the symbolism of the closeness of the rib to the heart, which shows that woman is equal in dignity to man and is meant to be at man's side as a companion through all the joys and sorrows of life.

As for the other question, the Bible is not just a collection of stories that teach us how to lead better lives, although it does do that. The Bible also includes information about the history of the Jewish people and historical material about a man named Jesus, who claimed to be God, who proved His claim by performing spectacular miracles, including His own resurrection from the dead, and who said that He was the Way, the Truth, and the Life that would make it possible for us to get to Heaven.

We pay attention to the Bible because, in the words of St. Paul: "All Scripture is inspired of God and is useful for teaching — for reproof, correction, and training in holiness" (2 Timothy 3:16).

Q. How can I justify the biblical situation in Genesis where we read that Adam and Eve had other children besides Cain and Abel? Their children married among themselves, which amounts to incest. Incest is generally considered a sin against nature, so how can I answer a non-Catholic friend's arguments against God's wisdom? — P.P., California

A. You can point out that this *is* an example of God's wisdom since He permitted the marriage of brothers and sisters for a limited time in order to propagate the human race. He protected the earliest human beings from the evils usually associated with intermarriage in families and, when these special circumstances were no longer necessary, God forbade such intermarriage.

Q. Your reply that God permitted intermarriage among the children of Adam and Eve for a limited time in order to propagate the human race does not suffice. The rest of the answer can be found in chapter five of Genesis, which lists Adam's descendants from his own time to that of Noah. — M.E.B., Maryland

A. Here are the pertinent lines from chapter five: "Adam was one hundred and thirty years old when he begot a son in his likeness, after his image; and he named him Seth. Adam lived eight hundred years after the birth of Seth, and he had other sons and daughters. The whole lifetime of Adam was nine hundred and thirty years; then he died."

Genesis says that Seth lived nine hundred and twelve years and had a son Enosh and other sons and daughters, and that Enosh lived nine hundred and five years and had a son Kenan and other sons and daughters, and so forth down to the time of Noah.

Did our earliest ancestors really live that long? It's certainly possible that God could have allowed them such longevity in order to facilitate the growth of the human race. Just as it is possible that God allowed intermarriage among brothers and sisters for the same reason. Look at chapter four in Genesis and notice that Cain, after leaving the Lord's presence and settling in the Land of Nod, "had relations with his wife, and she conceived and bore Enoch."

Where did Cain get a wife? She couldn't have come from someone not related to Adam since that would undermine the Church's teaching on original sin, which we inherit from Adam, the father of the human race. So she probably was one of Cain's sisters.

Q. I would be very grateful if you would please answer this question which was presented by a child: "If Adam and Eve were white, how is it we have black, yellow, and red races?" — J.C.C., Louisiana

A. In his book *The World Book of Peoples* (Our Sunday Visitor), Fr. Albert J. Nevins said that while no one knows for sure what color Adam and Eve were, "the best scientific theory believes that our earliest ancestors were brown people — between white and black" (p. 33). He explained further:

"As men multiplied, they began to spread out, seeking new areas for food. Gradually over the long centuries, those groups took on special characteristics, due in part to intermarriage within each group. Climate, environment, and diet were also factors.

"The people who were in northern Europe became lighter in color because of the loss of pigmentation. The people who were in the tropical zones became darker. Among some groups, inbreeding produced a majority of people with curly hair; among others, the majority had straight hair. Inbreeding made some groups grow tall, and others grow smaller. Because children inherited the characteristics of parents, certain qualities, passed on through generation after generation, tended to become very strong.

"In this manner were the various races of the world developed. Actually all mankind was (and is) still one, springing from the one common pair of ancestors. The differences that have come among men were accidental differences. In all basic essentials, they were (and are) still the same" (p. 17).

Q. In older translations of the Bible, Genesis 3:15 reads: "I will put enmity between thee and the woman, and thy

seed and her seed: she shall crush thy head, and thou shalt lie in wait for her heel." However, recent translations say: "I will put enmity between you and the woman, and between your offspring and hers; he will strike at your head, while you strike at his heel." Why the change in gender? — S.S., New York, J.L.N., New Jersey, B.N., Florida, and G.W.J., Kentucky

A. The words of course are those of God spoken to the serpent after Adam and Eve had succumbed to his temptation to eat the forbidden fruit. The reason for the change in gender is to make clear that the offspring or seed of the woman, traditionally understood to refer to Jesus, will crush the power of the devil. Here is how the *Catechism* explains the passage:

"After his fall, man was not abandoned by God. On the contrary, God calls him and in a mysterious way heralds the coming victory over evil and his restoration from his fall [cf. *Gen* 3:9, 15]. This passage in Genesis is called the *Protoevangelium* ("first gospel"): the first announcement of the Messiah and Redeemer, of a battle between the serpent and the Woman, and of the final victory of a descendant of hers" (n. 410).

Jesus was always the one who came to destroy the works of the devil (cf. 1 John 3:8), and the modern translation more accurately reflects this fact.

Q. Where can I find information to reply to those who claim that evolution is a well-established scientific fact? My question is precipitated by Pope John Paul II's statement that "evolution is no longer just a hypothesis." — T.M.F., New York, and R.H., Saskatchewan

A. First of all, anyone looking for some sound resources to illustrate the serious problems faced by advocates of the Darwinian theory of evolution should consult the following books: Phillip Johnson's *Darwin on Trial* (Regnery Gateway) and *Defeating Darwinism by Opening Minds* (InterVarsity Press), Michael Denton's *Evolution: A Theory in Crisis* (Adler & Adler), Michael Behe's *Darwin's Black Box* (The Free Press), George Sim Johnston's *Did Darwin Get It Right?* (Our Sunday Visitor), and Jonathan Wells' *Icons of Evolution* (Regnery Publishing).

Also worth consulting are William Demski's *Intelligent Design* (InterVarsity Press), *Mere Creation* (InterVarsity Press), which was edited by Demski, and *Science and Evidence for Design in the Universe* (Ignatius Press), a series of papers presented at a conference sponsored by the Wethersfield Institute.

Second, there was a mistranslation of the Pope's statement when it first appeared in print in the fall of 1996. What he actually said was that "new knowledge leads to the recognition of the theory of evolution as more than a hypothesis." It must be understood that in science a hypothesis is just an intelligent guess. When some evidence is collected that gives support to the hypothesis, it becomes a theory. But a theory is not necessarily true unless it can be verified by a preponderance of evidence.

As John Paul said in his speech to the Pontifical Academy of Sciences on October 22, 1996:

"A theory's validity depends on whether or not it can be verified; it is constantly tested against the facts; wherever it can no longer explain the latter, it shows its limitations and unsuitability. It must then be rethought."

Furthermore, the Holy Father said, "rather than *the* theory of evolution, we should speak of *several* theories of evolution," which plurality has to do "with the different explanations advanced for the mechanism of evolution" and "with the various philosophies on which it is based. Hence the existence of materialist, reductionist, and spiritualist interpretations."

Recalling that one of his predecessors, Pope Pius XII, had said in *Humani Generis* that, even if the human body takes its origin from pre-existing living matter, the spiritual soul is immediately created by God, John Paul said:

"Consequently, theories of evolution which, in accordance with the philosophies inspiring them, consider the spirit as emerging from the forces of living matter or as a mere epiphenomenon of this matter are incompatible with Catholic teaching. Nor are they able to ground the dignity of the person."

In other words, any theory of evolution that excludes God, or that insists that the mind and spirit of man come from the forces of living matter and not from God, is incompatible with Catholic teaching. But that is the prevailing sentiment among evolutionists. Here is how the National Association of Biology Teachers defined evolution in 1995 (they later abandoned this definition):

"The diversity of life on earth is the outcome of evolution: an unsupervised, impersonal, unpredictable, and natural process of temporal descent with genetic modification that is affected by natural selection, chance, historical contingencies, and changing environments."

No room for God there! So if anyone asks if you believe in evolution, you had better find out what the questioner means by evolution. If he means an unguided, purposeless, random process of natural selection, which is what Darwin was talking about, no believer in God (or no one with common sense) can subscribe to such an explanation for the origin and development of the incredibly diverse and complex universe in which we live.

As Michael Behe demonstrates in *Darwin's Black Box*, the complicated molecular mechanisms involved in such processes as seeing or blood-clotting could only have been designed by a higher intelligence.

What diehard evolutionists are really promoting is ideology masquerading as science. Darwinism holds sway over many scientists and educators, says George Sim Johnston, because "it is an effective club with which to beat religion." Try to suggest that neither the historical evidence nor scientific experimentation has confirmed the theory of evolution and you will be termed a creationist or a fundamentalist or a religious fanatic.

But don't be intimidated by such epithets from the "anything-but-God" crowd. More than a century after Charles Darwin published *The Origin of the Species*, evolution is still a theory, not a fact (as Pope John Paul said), despite imaginative textbook drawings and bogus museum exhibits that purport to show, with no corroborating scientific evidence, a protozoan turning into a human. As Phillip Johnson says in *Defeating Darwinism* (p. 81):

"Evolution is not a fact, it's a philosophy. The materialism comes first (*a priori*), and the evidence is interpreted in light of that unchangeable philosophical commitment. If the evidence seems to go against the philosophy, so much the worse for the evidence. To a materialist, putting up with any amount of bad practice in science is better than to let that Divine Foot in the door!"

Q. Has the Bible or the Church ever explained the reason or the meaning behind circumcision for the Jews of the Old Testament? — F.S., Pennsylvania

A. The circumcision of every male when he was eight days old was a sign of the covenant or "everlasting pact" between God and Abraham (Genesis 17:10-14). This requirement was not continued under the new covenant, and Gentiles were not obligated to undergo circumcision in order to join the Church founded by Jesus (Acts 15:28).

Q. I have been studying up on Jacob's acquiring (with the help of his mother) of the birthright of his twin Esau (Genesis 27:1-40). Wasn't Jacob already owner of the birthright by virtue of the contract agreed to by Esau (Genesis 25:29-34)? — P.D.C., Louisiana

A. Esau preceded Jacob from their mother's womb, which entitled him as firstborn son to a position of honor in the family and to a double share in the possessions inherited from his father Isaac. But Esau sold his birthright to Jacob for a plate of stew and Jacob later tricked his dying father into giving him the special blessing that should have gone to Esau.

The rivalry between the two brothers, with the elder serving the younger, was a preview of the historical conflicts between the descendants of Jacob, the Israelites, and the descendants of Esau, the Edomites, with Israel having superiority over Edom even though Edom was older. It also illustrates that God is not bound by customs in carrying out His divine plan, that He can bestow His favor on, or withhold it from, whomever He wishes, as St. Paul explains:

"When Rebekah had conceived twin children by one man, our father Isaac — while they were yet unborn and had done neither good nor evil, in order that God's decree might stand fast, 'not by works but by the favor of him who calls' — God said to her, 'The older shall serve the younger' .... What are we to say, then? That God is unjust? Not at all! He says to Moses: 'I will show mercy to whomever I choose; I will have pity on whomever I wish' " (Romans 9:10-15).

Yes, Jacob was already the owner of the birthright, but his manner of obtaining it, and his deception of his father, were wrong and would be condemned by Jeremiah (9:3) and Hosea (12:4), both of whom would also take Israel to task for its infidelity to the Lord.

Q. In Genesis 35:10, God appeared to Jacob and changed his name to Israel. Jacob had 12 sons. But in Exodus, chapter one, it says that "these are the names of the sons of Israel who, accompanied by their households, migrated with Jacob into Egypt," and then it gives the names of Jacob's children. It seems to me that Israel and Jacob are the same person, but Exodus seems to say that they are two different people. Can you help me with this? — T.C., Virginia

A. The change of Jacob's name to Israel is recorded first in Genesis 32:29 after his struggle with an angel. "You shall no longer be spoken of as Jacob, but as Israel," the angel said, "because you have contended with divine and human beings and have prevailed." So Jacob and Israel are the same person.

The phrase "sons of Israel" in chapter one of Exodus refers at first to Jacob's immediate family, his 12 sons, but then in verse 7 to his more remote descendants and ultimately to the Israelite people, whom the verse calls "fruitful and prolific. They became so numerous and strong that the land was filled with them."

Q. I have come to a bit of a stumbling block in the Bible. Genesis 11:10-14 states that Shem begat Arpachshad, who begat Shelah, who begat Eber. But Luke 3:35-36 says that Eber was the son of Shelah, who was the son of Cainan, who was the son of Arphaxad, who was the son of Shem. Who then is Shelah's father, Cainan or Arphaxad (Arpachshad)? Does this imply an error in transcription? How does one explain this discrepancy? — C.K., Pennsylvania

A. The purpose of the many genealogies in the Bible is to show historical connections among nations, tribes, individuals, and geographical areas. Thus, Matthew 1:1-17 traces the genealogy of Jesus back to Abraham and lists 42 names, while Luke 3:23-38 goes back to Adam, listing 56 names for the period covered by Matthew and 76 names in all. These listings do differ in some details, as does the listing in Genesis 11 with that in Luke 3, but they are substantially the same.

The discrepancies have never been satisfactorily explained, although they may have something to do with the fact that Old Testament family lines were based not only on blood ties but also on adoptive and legal relationships. It also seems clear that the lists were not meant to be exhaustive, but were only to show some of the major connecting figures through the centuries.

In a similar vein, if two different persons were asked to trace the historical connection between George Washington and the current President of the United States, and did not think it necessary to list every President since 1789, they might come up with different lists of Chief Executives based on their impact on the history of the country.

The lists would be substantially the same, but some occupants of the White House might be left out. This wouldn't mean that either list contained errors, but only that the compiler of each list thought it more important to mention some names rather than others.

Q. In his book *Characters of the Inquisition*, William Thomas Walsh quotes from the Book of Exodus (chapter 32, verses 27-28) that the number of Israelites slain for idolatry numbered three and twenty thousand. But the Douay-Challoner Bible, 1950 edition, and the Ignatius Bible, Revised Standard Version, put the number slain at about three thousand. Which number is correct and why the disparity? — G.M., Florida

A. Two readers of this column have offered explanations for the disparity. C.B.M. of Ohio, who has taught biblical languages and text transmission at Franciscan University in Steubenville, says that both figures "are accurate translations — but of two differing ancient sources. Greek manuscript tradition is solidly in the 3,000 camp; St. Jerome's Latin Vulgate clearly holds for 'about 23,000.' Modern scholarship sides with the Greek (and Hebrew), as it certainly should: reconstructing the 'original' text is everyone's goal. But lightly dismissing St. Jerome is never smart. His scholarship is awe-inspiring, he had access to manuscripts now long-gone, and he had a reason for writing 'about 23,000.' "

C.B.M. adds that there are many manuscript problems like this one and says that "it's helpful to remind ourselves that there is no 'original' biblical manuscript. Everything we have is fragmentary, and a copy of a copy of a copy. This realization can rock the faith of *sola scriptura* fundamentalists; it strengthens the faith of those who believe in the teaching authority of a divinely guided Church."

S.K.O. of the International Society of Bible Collectors in Houston says that "the original Douay Version of 1609-1610, which was based on the Vulgate but did not always follow it precisely, uses the phrase 'about three thousand.' In his 1750 revision, Bishop Challoner changed the rendering to 'about three and twenty thousand' based on a more exact translation of the Vulgate text: *viginti tria milia hominum*. Challoner's rendering persisted since his revision was the basis for nearly all subsequent Catholic Bibles in English until the 1950s.

"Father George Leo Haydock comments in his 19th century edition: 'The Heb[rew] letter 'c' means about, and stands also for twenty.' In his 1927 commentary on Exodus, Father Henry J. Grimmelsman states: 'The smaller number is better attested. No resistance was offered the Levites.' As your response to the query indicates, 3,000 appears to be the more correct rendering, despite the Vulgate text."

Q. Why do the Jewish people avoid pork? — P.L., Massachusetts

A. The pig was considered an impure animal after the Lord told Moses to tell the Israelites not to eat the pig, "which does indeed have hoofs and is cloven-footed, but does not chew the cud and is therefore unclean for you" (Leviticus 11:7 and Deuteronomy 14:8).

Q. Can you identify the source of the Old Testament story about a Jewish priest who refused a king's order to eat pork and was condemned to death? A group of his friends urged him to bring meat that Jewish law permitted him to eat and pretend to be eating the king's fare so as to save his life. In refusing to dissemble, the priest pointed out that while the king would be fooled, his eating of the pork would scandalize the people into idolatry. He then suffered martyrdom. — R. D., New York

A. You will find this story about the martyrdom of Eleazar in chapter six of Second Maccabees, verses 18-31. Before undergoing torture and death, the elderly Jewish scribe delivered this courageous statement:

"At our age it would be unbecoming to make such a pretense; many young men would think the ninety-year-old Eleazar had gone over to an alien religion. Should I thus dissimulate for the sake of a brief moment of life, they would be led astray by me, while I would bring shame and dishonor on my old age. Even if, for the time being, I avoid the punishment of men, I shall never, whether alive or dead, escape the hands of the Almighty. Therefore, by manfully giving up my life now, I will prove myself worthy of my old age, and I will leave to the young a noble example of how to die willingly and generously for the revered and holy laws."

Q. I would like to know the interpretation of 2 Kings 2:11, where Elijah went up to Heaven in a whirlwind, with "a flaming chariot and flaming horses." Some have interpreted the chariot to be a UFO. — J.D.S., Vermont
A. The interpretation of 2 Kings 2:11 is precisely that Elijah was taken up to Heaven in a flaming chariot after he had passed on his mantle and a double portion of his spirit of prophecy to Elisha. There is no reason to suggest any other interpretation of this verse, most especially one about ancient UFOs. Elijah was one of the great figures of the Old Testament and was subsequently chosen by Jesus, along with Moses, as a witness to His transfiguration (cf. Matthew 17:3).

Q. From time to time I have seen in secular material the terms C.E. (Common Era) in place of A.D. and B.C.E. (Before the Common Era) in place of B.C. I thought this was another attempt to avoid mention of Christ, but now I find it being used in the *Collegeville Bible Commentary* and I wonder. Also, would you comment on the same *Commentary's* statement that "critical scholarship" has cast doubt on the Christian belief that the Book of Isaiah makes predictions about Christ? — P.D., Illinois
A. Whenever you see the words "critical scholarship," know that you are about to read opinions that are contrary to the teaching of the magisterium of the Catholic Church. It remains the official position of the Church, "critical scholars" to the contrary notwithstanding, that the Book of Isaiah, particularly the "suffering servant" of chapter 53, refers to Christ ("it was our infirmities that he bore,/ our sufferings that he endured ..../ He was pierced for our offenses,/ crushed for our sins/ ... by his stripes we were healed").

We're not sure when or where the abbreviations C.E. or B.C.E. came into vogue (they are often used in Christian-Jewish dialogue), but they do put Christ in the background. It is no surprise, however, that a Bible commentary which can find no references to Christ in Isaiah has adopted these abbreviations.

The mind of the Church on this matter was expressed by Archbishop Daniel Buechlein, chairman of the Ad Hoc Committee to Oversee the Use of the Catechism, in a report to U.S. Bishops at their meeting in Washington on November 15, 1999. Summing up guidelines that the Ad Hoc Committee had given to publishers of religion books, Archbishop Buechlein said:

"Third, when citing dates, publishers were asked to use B.C. and A.D. instead of the designations B.C.E. and C.E. Since the materials involved are catechetical in nature, they should reflect that — for followers of Christ — even time has a Christological significance. The use of the designations B.C. and A.D. is part of the common language of faith."

Q. What is the theological basis for Vatican II (in the Constitution on the Liturgy) to say that Christ is present in the Scriptures? Unfortunately, this statement is causing some to say that Christ is "just as present in the Scriptures as He is in the Eucharist." This statement is theologically incorrect, but unfortunately it is said on occasion. — V.Y., Kansas

A. There are also people going even further and saying that Christ is just as present in the "assembly" of people gathered in the church as He is in the Eucharist. However, here is what Vatican II said in article seven of the Constitution on the Sacred Liturgy:

"Christ is always present in His Church, especially in her liturgical celebrations. He is present in the sacrifice of the Mass, not only in the person of His minister, 'the same one now offering, through the ministry of priests, who formerly offered Himself on the cross,' but especially under the Eucharistic species. By His power He is present in the sacraments, so that when a man baptizes it is really Christ Himself who baptizes. He is present in His word, since it is He Himself who speaks when the holy Scriptures are read in the church. He is present, finally, when the Church prays and sings, for He promised: 'Where two or three are gathered together for my sake, there am I in the midst of them' (Mt. 18:20)."

This paragraph is substantially repeated in the *Catechism* (n. 1373) and, in article 1374, the *Catechism* says that "the mode of Christ's presence under the Eucharistic species is unique. It raises the Eucharist above all the sacraments as 'the perfection of the spiritual life and the end to which all the sacraments tend' [St. Thomas Aquinas, *STh* III, 73, 3c]."

We are not sure about the precise theological basis for saying that Christ is present in the Scriptures, but since the Bible is the word of God, and since John, in the prologue to his Gospel, personifies "the Word" as Jesus Himself, we may say that when we hear the readings from Scripture, we are hearing Christ Himself. "Through all the words of Sacred Scripture," says the *Catechism* (n. 102), "God speaks only one single Word, his one Utterance in whom he expresses himself completely [cf. *Heb* 1:1-3]." The *Catechism* then quotes this from St. Augustine [St. Augustine, *En in Ps.* 103, 4, 1: PL 37, 1378; cf. *Ps* 104; *Jn* 1:1]:

"You recall that one and the same Word of God extends throughout Scripture, that it is one and the same Utterance that resounds in the mouths of all the sacred writers, since he who was in the beginning God with God has no need of separate syllables; for he is not subject to time."

Q. I always thought that the Gospel of Matthew was written before the Gospel of Mark, but my wife heard in a Catholic Bible class that Mark was written before Matthew. Can you tell me the correct order of the Gospels? — C.R., Pennsylvania, D.T., Idaho, and V.F.M., Minnesota

A. Up until the 20th century, Catholic Bible scholars favored the traditional order of the Gospels, i.e., Matthew, Mark, Luke, and John, and all Catholic Bibles still list the Gospels in that order. The historical evidence for this arrangement can be traced back to *Against Heresies*, the second-century work of St. Irenaeus, who was a pupil of St. Polycarp, who knew St. John, the Apostle and Evangelist.

In the past century, however, many Catholic Bible scholars have accepted the theory that Mark came first and that Matthew and Luke are based on Mark and on a collection of Christ's sayings known as the "Q" document (from the German word *quelle*, meaning "source"). No one has ever seen this document and there is no external evidence that it ever existed.

Many of these same scholars have also argued for dating the

composition of the Gospels from around A.D. 70 (Mark) to A.D. 100 (John). In recent years, however, a few scholars have argued for a much earlier dating, i.e., before the fall of Jerusalem in A.D. 70. See, for example, *Redating the New Testament* by John A.T. Robinson (Westminster), *The Hebrew Christ* by Claude Tresmontant (Franciscan Herald), *The Birth of the Synoptics* by Jean Carmignac (Franciscan Herald), and *Eyewitness to Jesus* by Carsten Peter Thiede and Matthew D'Ancona (Doubleday).

In the latter work, Thiede, a papyrologist, says that three papyrus scraps belonging to Magdalen College in England contain phrases from the 26th chapter of Matthew about the anointing of Jesus at the house of Simon the leper in Bethany. Thiede contends that the scraps were written no later than the year 60, which means that Matthew's Gospel could have been written by an actual eyewitness of the things Jesus said and did.

Not surprisingly, these challenges to the conventional biblical wisdom of the day are not being enthusiastically welcomed by those who have based their entire careers on Markan priority and later dating of the Gospels. But we may soon witness a sea change in biblical scholarship as new studies and findings confirm the ancient tradition expressed by Irenaeus and the Church herself.

Q. In a conversation with a Jewish lady, she said that the Gospel of Matthew contains "many mistakes," including the statement that Nazareth was the hometown of the Messiah. Can you please comment on the inerrancy of the Gospels and, specifically, on the thorny issue of Nazareth? — R.P., New York

A. All the evangelists, not just Matthew, indicate that Jesus came from Nazareth, so there is solid evidence that He grew up there. Perhaps the Jewish lady is confusing Bethlehem, the town where Jesus was born, with Nazareth, the town where He grew up, because the Old Testament says that the Messiah would be born in Bethlehem-Ephrathah (Micah 5:1). Jesus was born there, and not in Nazareth, because Mary and Joseph had to travel to Bethlehem for the Roman census.

This same confusion about the identity of the Messiah existed at the time of Jesus, when some of His listeners said that He couldn't possibly be the Christ because He was from Nazareth in Galilee (John 7:41-43). They were unaware that He had been born in Bethlehem of Judea.

In any case, after the flight into Egypt, it is clear that the Holy Family settled in Nazareth (Matthew 2:23) and that Jesus grew to maturity there (Luke 2:51). Mark (1:9) says that when Jesus began His public life, He "came from Nazareth to Galilee and was baptized in the Jordan by John."

The three synoptic Gospels also place the childhood of Jesus in Nazareth when they tell of His rejection years later by some citizens of His hometown (Matthew 13:54-58, Mark 6:1-6, and Luke 4:16-30). In recounting that incident, Matthew calls Nazareth the "native place" of Jesus and says that His former neighbors "found him altogether too much for them." Mark refers to Nazareth as Jesus' "own part of the country" and quotes the inhabitants there as recognizing Jesus as "the carpenter, the son of Mary." Luke says that when Jesus appeared in the synagogue at Nazareth, "where he had been reared," some of those present tried to do violence to Him because their lack of faith dissuaded Him from performing the kinds of miracles He had performed in Capernaum. Recall that Jesus told His critics on that occasion that "no prophet gains acceptance in his native place."

Also confirming Nazareth as the Lord's hometown, strangely enough, was Pontius Pilate, the Roman governor, who ordered that the inscription "Jesus the Nazorean the King of the Jews" be placed in three languages (Hebrew, Latin, and Greek) on the cross (John 19:19).

To those who object to Matthew (2:23) quoting the prophets as having said that Jesus "shall be called a Nazorean," Fr. John McKenzie, in his *Dictionary of the Bible*, concedes that this verse is not found in the Old Testament, but suggests that "it is a play on the word neser, 'shoot' (of Jesse) in Is. 11:1. This illustrates the biblical conception of the significance of the word by assonance."

As for the inerrancy of Scripture, the *Catechism of the Catholic Church* (n. 107), quoting from Vatican II's *Dogmatic Constitution on Divine Revelation*, says this:

"The inspired books teach the truth. 'Since therefore all that the inspired authors or sacred writers affirm should be regarded as affirmed by the Holy Spirit, we must acknowledge that the books of Scripture firmly, faithfully, and without error teach that truth which God, for the sake of our salvation, wished to see confided to the Sacred Scriptures' [*DV* 11]."

The *Constitution on Divine Revelation* also stated that "Holy Mother Church has firmly and with absolute constancy held, and continues to hold, that the four Gospels just named, whose historical character the Church unhesitatingly asserts, faithfully hand on what Jesus Christ, while living among men, really did and taught for their eternal salvation until the day he was taken up into heaven" (n. 19).

Q. I have difficulty with Luke 12:35-48. Could those ignorant of their master's will be non-Christians or non-converted Christians? And are the words about "severe beatings" and lesser punishments references to Hell and Purgatory? — R.D., Texas

A. This section of Luke contains the parable of three kinds of servants: one who remains faithful and vigilant while his master is away and will be rewarded when the master returns, one who knows his master's wishes but takes advantage of his absence to abuse the servant girls and get drunk and who will get "a severe beating," and one who does not know his master's wishes but who nevertheless deserves some punishment and who will "get off with fewer stripes."

While Jesus used this parable to teach at least a couple of lessons, one of which was that we should constantly "be on guard" since "the Son of Man [the master in the parable] will come when you least expect him," it is the other lesson that the questioner asked about, which Jesus summed up by saying: "When much has been given a man, much will be required of him. More will be asked of a man to whom more has been entrusted."

Those ignorant of their master's will could refer to non-Christians or non-practicing Christians, and the two types of punishment could refer to Hell and Purgatory, but the words of St. Peter ("Do you intend this parable for us, Lord, or do you mean it for everyone?") indicate that Jesus, first of all, was reminding the Apostles of their serious responsibility to care for the spiritual needs of their flocks. If they carried out those responsibilities diligently, they would receive places of honor in Heaven.

Second, the words of Jesus could also be applied to the successors of the Apostles, bishops and priests down through the centuries who would be expected to remain vigilant and faithful in leading those dependent on them to Heaven.

But third, the parable could also be applied to all members of the Church, who are called to holiness and who receive graces from God to live holy lives. If one deliberately does not employ those gifts wisely for the benefit of himself and others, if one is not a faithful steward of God's gifts, then one risks severe punishment since to those whom much has been given much is required. So, too, one who fails to use God's gifts well out of laziness may still deserve some punishment, but not to the degree of the person who obstinately rejects God's will.

Q. Please comment on the enclosed article, which says that modern Scripture scholars do not believe that St. John was the "disciple whom Jesus loved" (John 13:23, 19:26, 21:20) or that he wrote the fourth Gospel. — V.E.T., New York

A. There is an ancient tradition that John the Apostle was the author of the fourth Gospel and the person referred to as the "disciple whom Jesus loved." The earliest historical evidence comes from St. Irenaeus in his second-century work *Against Heresies*. Referring to the authorship of the last Gospel, Irenaeus writes: "Afterwards, John, the disciple of the Lord who reclined at His bosom, also published a Gospel while he was residing at Ephesus in Asia." Since Irenaeus was a pupil of St. Polycarp, who had known John, he is considered to be a very reliable source.

However, "modern critical analysis" of the Gospel's literary style and "highly developed theology," say the editors of the New American Bible, "makes it difficult to accept the idea that the Gospel as it now stands was written by one man." This theory contends that one of John's disciples was the real evangelist and that, later, another person, "often called the disciple-redactor," added more information and arranged all the material into what we now know as the fourth Gospel.

It's an interesting but highly speculative and unprovable theory. As for us, we'll stick with Irenaeus and hope that we never hear at Mass, "A reading from the holy Gospel according to the disciple-redactor of John."

Q. A couple of things occurred to me during the readings of the Passion in Holy Week. Was Judas present at the Last Supper when the Eucharist was instituted, and is he in Hell? — M.H.D., New York

A. Taking the second question first, we don't know whether Judas is in Hell. Certainly his betrayal of the Lord and the despair that led him to take his life would seem to point in that direction. As would Christ's words to His Father about keeping "careful watch" over the Apostles, "and not one of them was lost,/ none but him who was destined to be lost —/ in fulfillment of Scripture" (John 17:12). And as would this chilling statement of Jesus: "Woe to that man by whom the Son of Man is betrayed. Better for him if he had never been born" (Matthew 26:24). But Pope John Paul has said that these words of our Lord "do not allude for certain to eternal damnation" (*Crossing the Threshold of Hope*, p. 178).

Perhaps the Holy Father was recalling that after Jesus was condemned to death, Judas "began to regret his action deeply. He took the thirty pieces of silver back to the chief priests and elders and said, 'I did wrong to deliver up an innocent man!' They retorted, 'What is that to us? It is your affair!' So Judas flung the money into the temple and left. He went off and hanged himself" (Matthew 27:3-5).

What prompted this deep regret of Judas? Did he expect that the plot against Jesus would not go so far as to include killing the Lord? Or did he think that Christ, who had performed so many miracles, would perform still another one and prevail over his enemies? Or was there still some spark of love for Jesus that, for the moment at least, outweighed Judas' love for money? We won't know the answers to these questions this side of Heaven, just as we will not know until the next life the ultimate fate of the man whose name is synonymous with treachery.

As for the question of whether Judas was present for the institution of the Holy Eucharist, that has also been the topic of scholarly debate from the earliest days of the Church because the Gospels do not give us a clear answer. Matthew and Mark both place the prayer of institution after Jesus had said that His betrayer was the one "who has dipped his hand into the dish with me" (Matthew 26:23).

John, who does not mention the institution narrative at all, says that as soon as Jesus gave Judas the morsel of food that had been dipped into the dish, he went out to finish making plans with the enemies of the Lord (John 13:30). So it would seem from these three Evangelists that Judas was not there when Christ changed bread and wine into His body and blood.

Luke, on the other hand, reverses the order of the betrayal and the institution. Immediately after he has Jesus pronouncing the words of institution, the evangelist quotes this statement from Christ: "And yet the hand of my betrayer is with me at this table" (Luke 22:21). So what are we to think? Was Judas there or is there some truth to the aphorism that says, "Judas was the first person to leave Mass early"?

One thing that needs to be noted is that the evangelists were not so much concerned with the order in which things happened, as with setting forth what did happen. They tell us what was said and what was done, but not necessarily in the precise chronological sequence that a modern-day historian would consider important. Anyone who has tried to piece together from all four Gospels an accurate, hour-by-hour account of the Passion of the Lord can appreciate what we are saying.

For instance, if you read Matthew's and Mark's Gospels, you would think that Jesus spoke only once from the cross; you must read Luke and John for the other six sayings. And Mark differs from the other evangelists in having the crucifixion begin at nine o'clock in the morning instead of noon. So the fact that Luke places Judas at the Last Supper after Jesus gave us the Holy Eucharist does not mean that it actually happened that way.

However, since Scripture itself offers evidence for both sides of the argument, we can only theorize about how long Judas remained at the Last Supper, and our speculation really comes down to whether we think Christ would give the Eucharist to a person into whose heart Satan had already entered (John 13:27). For hadn't Jesus just said, during the washing of the feet, that not all of the Apostles were entirely cleansed? "The reason he said, 'Not all are washed clean,' " John tells us, "was that he knew his betrayer" (John 13:10-11).

Opinion has always been divided on this subject and, with no official statement from the magisterium, Catholics are free to hold either opinion. Personally, we side with those who think that Judas had already left the Last Supper before the institution of the Eucharist.

Q. In Acts 8, it says that Peter and John went to Samaria and prayed that the people there "might receive the Holy Spirit. It had not as yet come down upon any of them since they had only been baptized in the name of the Lord Jesus. The pair upon arriving imposed hands on them and they received the Holy Spirit." It is evident that Peter and John conferred the Sacrament of Confirmation, but the passage implies that the Holy Spirit is not conferred at Baptism. Please explain. — W.C.S., Connecticut

A. Yes, we do receive the Holy Spirit initially at Baptism, and again in Confirmation. Recall that Jesus told the Apostles to baptize "in the name/ 'of the Father,/ and of the Son,/ and of the Holy Spirit' " (Matthew 28:19). And Peter said as much in Acts 2:38, when he told the crowd, "You must reform and be baptized, each one of you, in the name of Jesus Christ, that your sins may be forgiven; then you will receive the gift of the Holy Spirit."

So how do we explain Acts 8:14-15? Some commentators have suggested that St. Luke, the author of Acts, made this distinction between reception of Baptism and reception of the Holy Spirit as a literary device to emphasize that the Spirit comes through the Church and its bishops, i.e., Peter and John.

The separation of Baptism from the outpouring of the Holy Spirit, says *The Jerome Biblical Commentary*, "should not be over-stressed; for Luke the all-important thing which incorporates men into the Christian community is the gift of the Spirit, which comes through the representatives of the apostolic college and the early institutional Church. He is aware of the necessity of Baptism, but he does not correlate the two elements as closely as they were later understood, or even as Paul understood them" (p. 189).

Q. In our duty to the poor, are we to treat all poor alike, regardless of circumstances? While many are poor through no fault of their own, it seems that some are poor because of choices they have made and continue to make, such as drug use, alcohol abuse, gambling, pursuing luxuries or entertainment, dropping out of school, having children outside of marriage, and even sloth. I refer to St. Paul in 2 Thessalonians 3:10: "Indeed, when we were with you we used to lay down the rule that anyone who would not work should not eat." Are we to use discernment, or is our duty to everyone who is poor?— R.J.M., Wisconsin

A. When St. Paul spoke of those who would not work, he was referring to members of the community who were able to work but who thought that work was useless because they expected the Second Coming of Christ at any moment. They depended upon others for their sustenance, which caused a problem for those in the community who were charitably inclined.

St. Paul's solution was to urge the slackers to work quietly to earn their food and, if they refused to do so, he said that others should exclude such persons from the community in the hope of shaming them into changing their conduct. He added, however, that the non-workers should not be treated like enemies, but rather should be corrected as one would correct a brother.

What about meeting the needs of the poor today? First, love for the poor is part of the Church's long tradition and is "inspired by the Gospel of the Beatitudes, of the poverty of Jesus, and of his concern for the poor" (*Catechism*, n. 2444 [*CA* 57; cf. *Lk* 6:20-22, *Mt* 8:20; *Mk* 12:41-44]). The *Catechism* (n. 2443) says that "God blesses those who come to the aid of the poor and rebukes those who turn away from them," and adds that "it is by what they have done for the poor that Jesus Christ will recognize his chosen ones [cf. *Mt* 25:31-36]."

But are we to treat all the poor alike, regardless of how they came to their situation? Yes, we are obliged to help all those in poverty, regardless of how they got there, because they are our brothers and sisters in Christ. Whether it was bad choices or unfortunate circumstances that brought people to their indigent state, they still deserve our assistance.

Discernment comes in deciding what kind of assistance to provide. There are poor people who decline food vouchers and demand cash instead so that they can buy alcohol or drugs. While it would be right to provide food, clothing, or shelter for the homeless or for substance-abusers, it would be wrong to give them money that would be spent on their destructive habits instead of on necessities. Nor are we obliged to support the able-bodied who are unwilling to work. Helping someone who is unable to help himself is one thing; facilitating a lazy or immoral lifestyle is quite another.

The bottom line, then, is that we are to help all the poor with the necessities of life, that we are to encourage and assist those who are able to earn a living to do so, but that we are to limit to the basic necessities our support to those who take advantage of the charitably inclined, while at the same time seeking to correct them as brothers and sisters and not as enemies.

Q. In First Corinthians 5:1-13, St. Paul lays down some seemingly harsh measures for dealing with "brothers" who are sinning. I firmly believe that the Word of God cannot contradict itself, so could you please help me understand the circumstances in which it would be allowed, either for the Church or in one-on-one relationships with family and friends who are Catholics, to "shun" such

people? My confusion comes from the many other places in Scripture where we are admonished to treat sinners with patience, kindness, and so forth. And would an "immoral" person, as mentioned by Paul, be a fornicator or one who uses artificial birth control? — R.D., Texas

A. In the passage cited, St. Paul is criticizing reports of incestuous conduct among the people of Corinth and the apparent lack of concern about this moral disorder. He tells them not to associate "with anyone who bears the title 'brother' if he is immoral, covetous, an idolater, an abusive person, a drunkard, or a thief. It is clear that you must not eat with such a man. What business is it of mine to judge outsiders? Is it not those inside the community you must judge? God will judge the others. 'Expel the wicked man from your midst' " (1 Corinthians 5:11:13).

Jesus made a similar statement in chapter 18 of Matthew's Gospel: "If your brother should commit some wrong against you, go and point out his fault, but keep it between the two of you. If he listens to you, you have won your brother over. If he does not listen, summon another, so that every case may stand on the word of two or three witnesses. If he ignores them, refer it to the church. If he ignores even the church, then treat him as you would a Gentile or a tax collector."

Both St. Paul and Jesus are talking about a recalcitrant sinner, one who is steeped in sin and who shows no sign of repentance, despite repeated efforts to reach out to him. Such a person does not respond to patience and kindness, and failure to ostracize him or to impose some disciplinary measure on him (such as excommunication) might not only bind him more closely to his sinful ways but could also have a bad effect on others in the local church or community. Like the proverbial bad apple that can spoil a whole barrel of good apples, so an unrepentant and perhaps even arrogant sinner who is not chastised for his wicked ways could lead others into sin or at least promote an unhealthy tolerance for evil conduct.

As for what Paul means by an immoral person, he provides an answer in chapter 6 of First Corinthians when he says: "Do not deceive yourselves: no fornicators, idolaters, or adulterers, no sodomites, thieves, misers, or drunkards, no slanderers or robbers will inherit God's kingdom."

See also chapter 5 of Galatians, where Paul condemns "lewd conduct, impurity, licentiousness, idolatry, sorcery, hostilities, bickering, jealousy, outbursts of rages, selfish rivalries, dissensions, factions, envy, drunkenness, orgies, and the like. I warn you, as I have warned you before: those who do such things will not inherit the kingdom of God!"

Q. Some people think it is morally wrong for a man to have long hair. If so, why do pictures of Jesus show Him with long hair? I am a 14-year-old girl, and nobody has been able to answer this for me. — A.J.K., Minnesota

A. It is not morally wrong for a man to have long hair, but those who think so cite 1 Corinthians 11:14, where St. Paul says: "Does not nature itself teach you that it is dishonorable for a man to wear his hair long?"

There is no indication what Paul meant by "long" hair, but it must be remembered that he was writing to the people of Corinth, which was part of the Greco-Roman world. In that culture, short hair and no beards (except for philosophers) were the norm for men. Palestine, on the other hand, where Jesus and the men of His time wore long hair and beards, had its own cultural norm.

Q. What exactly is the "gift of tongues" so frequently referred to, and why have I never encountered this famous gift? — C.F.M., Michigan

A. The gift of tongues, also known as glossolalia, is the ability to speak so as to be understood by everyone, and also the ability to be able to understand someone speaking in a foreign language. An example of this can be found in the second chapter of the Acts of the Apostles, when on the day of Pentecost devout Jews from many nations of the earth were able to understand, each in his own tongue, the utterances of the Apostles.

In chapter 14 of First Corinthians, St. Paul talks about a different gift of tongues, whereby a person talks in unintelligible speech. The gift can be good, said Paul, if the speaker also has the gift of interpretation and if he uses his gift to build up the Church, not to build up himself. "Thank God, I speak in tongues more than any of you," said Paul, "but in the church I would rather say five intelligible words to instruct others than 10,000 words in a tongue."

The gift of tongues is reportedly prevalent today in charismatic and pentecostal groups, but unless you attend their prayer services, it is not very likely that you would encounter this unusual phenomenon.

Q. I have wondered about verse 15:51 from First Corinthians. In looking at five different Bibles, Protestant and Catholic, the texts are different. Can you tell me which translation is correct? — L.A.P., Pennsylvania

A. The verse in question, which concerns the transformation of our bodies at the resurrection on the last day, says in some translations that "we shall not all be changed," and in others that "we shall all be changed." In the Confraternity of Christian Doctrine Catholic Bible (1961), which says, "we shall not all be changed," we find the following comment in a footnote:

"The reading of most of the Greek MSS is to be preferred: 'We shall not all sleep (die), but we shall all be changed.' The meaning would then be that while those who are living at the last day will not die, they must undergo the change spoken of in the previous verses, from the natural body to the spiritual body."

In the New American Bible Revised New Testament, the verse reads: "We shall not all fall asleep, but we will all be changed." There is then this footnote:

"*We shall not all fall asleep*: Paul expected that some of his contemporaries might still be alive at Christ's return; after the death of Paul and his whole generation, copyists altered this statement in various ways. *We will all be changed*: the statement extends to all Christians, for Paul is not directly speaking of anyone else. Whether they have died before the end or happen still to be alive, all must be transformed."

Q. A little pamphlet that I use when saying the rosary quotes St. Paul as saying, "I have fought the good fight, I ran the good race. From now on a coveted crown awaits me." Is this not presumption, or was Paul privy to information we are not? — D.M., Massachusetts

A. The quotation is from Paul's second letter to Timothy, verses 4:6-8. The apostle is writing from prison in Rome, and he knows that his death by martyrdom is near. Presumption usually means that one expects to receive forgiveness from God and attain salvation without doing anything to deserve it, and even while deliberately enjoying a sinful life.

St. Paul, on the other hand, had lived a very holy life after his conversion on the road to Damascus. He was not being presumptuous since he had indeed "kept the faith" (2 Timothy 4:7) by enduring five floggings, one stoning, three shipwrecks, numerous imprisonments, hunger and thirst, cold and nakedness, before he was finally beheaded.

There are few people, in our estimation, more deserving than Paul of the "merited crown" that awaited him in Heaven because of his heroic fidelity to Christ.

Q. I believe St. Paul said, "With fear and trembling I face God at judgment." I need the exact reference to counteract a Protestant friend's belief in the certainty of salvation rather than "hope" of salvation. — W.C.J., Indiana

A. You are thinking of Philippians 2:12. where Paul said: "So then, my dearly beloved, obedient as always to my urging, work with anxious concern to achieve your salvation." The Douay-Rheims translation says "with fear and trembling."

You might also consider these other statements by Paul as contradicting the theory that one's salvation can be assured merely by accepting Jesus as one's personal Lord and Savior:

• "Consider the kindness and the severity of God — severity toward those who fell, kindness toward you, provided you remain in his kindness; if you do not, you too will be cut off" (Romans 11:22).

• "I do not run like a man who loses sight of the finish line. I do not fight as if I were shadowboxing. What I do is discipline my own body and master it, for fear that after having preached to others I myself should be rejected" (1 Corinthians 9:26-27).

• "Let anyone who thinks he is standing upright watch out lest he fall" (1 Corinthians 10:12).

• "The lives of all of us are to be revealed before the tribunal of Christ so that each one of us may receive his recompense, good or bad, according to his life in the body" (2 Corinthians 5:10).

Q. In the 1986 New American Bible New Testament, there is a line from 1 Peter 2:8 that reads: "They stumble by disobeying the word, as is their destiny." Since the Catholic Church does not believe in predestination, how can we explain this quote? — P.S.C., Massachusetts

A. It depends on what you mean by predestination. If you mean that God from all eternity predestines certain persons to go to Hell, withholds from them the graces that are necessary for salvation, and gives them no freedom of will to choose or reject Him, then that is a form of predestination in which the Catholic Church does not believe.

However, if you mean that God wants every person to be saved (1 Timothy 2:4), that He has "predestined us through Christ Jesus to be his adopted sons" (Ephesians 1:5), that He "wants none to perish but all to come to repentance" (2 Peter 3:9), but that He allows some persons freely to resist His grace, deliberately to refuse to do His will, obstinately to reject His mercy and forgiveness, and willingly to choose eternal separation from Him, then that is a form of predestination in which the Catholic Church does believe.

God does not positively damn souls to Hell; rather, He permits them to be lost because they deliberately and knowingly committed grave evils and persisted in them to the end (*Catechism of the Catholic Church*, n. 1037).

It is also necessary for us to distinguish between God's predestination and His foreknowledge of everything that will happen in human history. Yes, God in His omniscience knows who will be saved and who will be lost, but He does not cause or will anyone to go to Hell. That choice is made by individuals in a free exercise of their will. We are not robots or puppets and God does not force us to choose Him. The God who created us without our cooperation will not save us without our cooperation.

As for the quotation from 1 Peter, it refers to those who found belief in Jesus to be "an obstacle and a stumbling stone." God knew which Israelites would stumble and fall over belief in His Son, but He did not cause them to disbelieve.

Furthermore, St. Paul tells us that God used the unbelief of Israel to pave the way for the Gospel to be preached to the Gentiles (Romans 11:11). Paul also predicted that the blindness would remain upon Israel "until the full number of Gentiles enter in, and then all Israel will be saved" (Romans 11:25).

Chapter 3

Church and Papacy

Q. Some Protestants claim that St. Peter was never in Rome and was not buried there. Is there biblical proof that the papacy under St. Peter was actually in Rome? — W.C.J., Indiana

A. The closest thing to biblical proof that Peter was in Rome can be found in the Apostle's first letter, where he says: "The church that is in Babylon, chosen together with you, sends you greeting, as does Mark my son" (1 Peter 5:13). Babylon was a code word used by the early Christians for Rome. The word is used in the same way six times in the Book of Revelation (cf. chapters 14, 16, 17, 18).

Apart from the Bible, there are plenty of references to Peter's being in Rome in the writings of the early Church. For example, Dionysius of Corinth, writing to Pope Soter around the year 170, said: "You have also, by your very admonition, brought together the planting that was made by Peter and Paul at Rome." And St. Irenaeus, also writing in the second century, said that "Matthew also issued among the Hebrews a written Gospel in their own language, while Peter and Paul were evangelizing in Rome and laying the foundation of the Church."

Furthermore, Pope Paul VI announced in 1968 that the skeletal remains of St. Peter had been found and satisfactorily identified deep under the high altar of St. Peter's Basilica in Rome. For an account of this archaeological investigation, see *The Bones of St. Peter* (Image Books) by John Evangelist Walsh.

For more on this topic, see Patrick Madrid's book *Pope Fiction* (Basilica Press) in which he debunks 30 myths about the papacy.

Q. A recent Gospel reading about Jesus' cure of Peter's mother-in-law of a fever does not mention Peter's wife. Did Peter and his wife have any children? Can we assume that our Blessed Lord did not ask His Apostles to abandon young families? — M.F., California

A. Yes, we can assume that, but we know nothing of St. Peter's wife, or if they had any children. Matthew 8:14 mentions Peter's mother-in-law, and 1 Corinthians 9:5 implies that Peter's wife was still alive when that letter was written, but that is all we know of Peter and his family.

Q. The opening prayer for the feast of the Chair of Peter reads in part: "All-powerful Father, You have built your church on the rock of Saint Peter's confession of faith...." Isn't this Protestant theology? I thought the Catholic Church was built on Peter himself, whose name means "rock." Please comment on this. — W.C.S., Connecticut

A. Like you, we wince every year when we hear those words because that is precisely what Protestants say in an effort to disprove Catholic belief that Jesus founded the Church on Peter. Curiously, the *Catechism of the Catholic Church* refers to this matter twice, once giving the so-called Protestant slant on it, and the other time the more traditional Catholic position. For instance, in paragraph 424, the *Catechism* says: "Moved by the grace of the Holy Spirit and drawn by the Father, we believe in Jesus and confess: 'You are the Christ, the Son of the living God' [*Mt* 16:16]." It was on the rock of this faith confessed by St. Peter, the *Catechism* says, that Christ built His Church.

In paragraph 552, however, the *Catechism* says: "Because of the faith he confessed Peter will remain the unshakable rock of the Church. His mission will be to keep this faith from every lapse and to strengthen his brothers in it [*cf. Lk* 22:32]."

We prefer the latter way of stating Peter's place in the founding of the Catholic Church.

Q. We all know that our Blessed Lord Himself made St. Peter the first Pope, but I would like to know how the second Pope was chosen. — C.L., Texas

A. According to St. Irenaeus, the second Pope was St. Linus, and he reigned from A.D. 67 to 76. Little is known about him, but he is thought to be the same Linus who is listed as a companion of St. Paul in 2 Timothy 4:21. It is possible that Peter himself designated Linus as his successor.

Q. I am interested in a complete history of the Papacy. Can you make any suggestions? — C.A., Pennsylvania

A. Yes, try J.N.D. Kelly's book *The Oxford Dictionary of the*

Popes (Oxford University Press), Eric John's *The Popes: A Concise Biographical History* (Roman Catholic Books), and Our Sunday Visitor's *Encyclopedia of Catholic History*, edited by Matthew Bunson.

For a superb and scholarly but readable handbook on the scriptural origins of the Papacy, with scores of quotations from Church Councils and Fathers in support of the primacy of the Pope, see *Jesus, Peter & the Keys* (Queenship Publishing), which was authored by Scott Butler, Norman Dahlgren, and David Hess.

Q. It is deplorable that in order to boost the stature of the Pope, the term "Holy Father" is used in most Catholic publications. Only God, Christ, and the Holy Spirit deserve that exalted status, according to the Bible. — L.J.M., North Carolina

A. Referring to the Pope as "Holy Father" is not a slight against God the Father, nor a canonization of the man sitting in the Chair of Peter. It is a title that signifies the Pope's position as spiritual father of all the Christian faithful. The title is used not to boost the stature of the Pope — the stature of Pope John Paul II, for example, could hardly have been higher than it was during his pontificate — but to acknowledge that the Supreme Pontiff is Christ's Vicar on earth and that his task, like that of Christ Himself, is to call people to holiness by his words and actions.

As for the claim that only the three Persons of the Trinity are called "holy" in the Bible, we disagree. The Bible not only calls some human beings holy (e.g., John the Baptist in Mark 6:20, brothers in Hebrews 3:1, women in 1 Peter 3:5, and prophets in Acts 3:21), but it also applies the adjective to oil (Psalm 89:21), the temple (Isaiah 64:10), cities (Isaiah 64:9), and a mountain (Isaiah 27:13). In fact, we are all called to be holy: "For I, the LORD, am your God; and you shall make and keep yourselves holy, because I am holy" (Leviticus 11:44).

Q. I always believed that the Popes, no matter how personally immoral they were, never compromised doctrine, but I recently came across an account written by a Church Father, St. Hippolytus (170-235), in which he shows that Pope St. Callistus (217-222) taught that the Father, Son, and Holy Spirit were not three Persons, but one Person. He also said that Callistus approved of unwed women being sexually promiscuous, and he called the Pope and

his followers heretics. Can you shed some light on this disturbing pontificate? — R.S., Massachusetts

A. The first thing to note is that most of what we know of Pope Callistus comes from the writings of Hippolytus, who became the Pope's enemy after being passed over for the Papacy and seeing Callistus elected Pope in 217. Hippolytus then allowed his followers to elect him the first antipope in the Church's history, precipitating a schism that lasted almost two decades. However, he was reconciled with the Church and died a martyr's death along with Pope St. Pontian in 235 while in exile.

As for the charges of heresy raised by Hippolytus in his work *Refutation of All Heresies*, there is some evidence that Callistus, while serving as archdeacon to Pope Zephyrinus, gave some support to a man named Sabellius, whose followers advocated several false theories about the Trinity, including the heresy that the one Person of God had three modes of manifesting Himself, as Creator, Redeemer, and Sanctifier. As Pope, however, as even Hippolytus admits, Callistus excommunicated Sabellius.

Hippolytus also protested what he considered Callistus' moral laxity, in that he allowed fornicators and adulterers to be reconciled with the Church after receiving the Sacrament of Penance. Such lenience, though not wrong, was considered unusual at that time in the Church's history, and reading the biased words of Hippolytus today makes it sound worse than it was.

This is also true of Hippolytus' charge that Callistus "even permitted women, if they were unmarried and burning up at an unsuitable time of life, or if they did not wish to lose their own dignity by a lawful marriage, to take a man of their own choosing as bedfellow, whether slave or free, and to regard such a one as husband, though not lawfully married."

"Stripped of vituperative rhetoric," says William A. Jurgens in volume one of *The Faith of the Early Fathers* (Liturgical Press), "the charge which Hippolytus is making is simply that Callistus had permitted free women to marry slaves, in spite of civil legislation to the contrary" (p. 174n).

So there is nothing in the pontificate of Pope Callistus, saint and martyr, that supports the charge that he compromised Catholic doctrine.

Q. I recently heard the "Bible Answer Man" on radio claim that Pope St. Gelasius I (492-496) had pronounced an anathema on anyone believing in the bodily assumption of the Virgin Mary into Heaven. He cited this as a solid refutation of papal infallibility. What are the facts? — F.C., Virginia

A. We were not able to find any historical evidence that Pope St. Gelasius I, during his brief pontificate, anathematized anyone for believing in the bodily assumption of Mary into Heaven at the end of her life. He is best known for defending the rights of the Church against the state in a letter to Emperor Anastasius, for causing the revived pagan feast of Lupercalia to be abandoned in Rome, and for mandating reception of Holy Communion under both species in response to Manichaean teaching that wine was impure and sinful.

But even if Gelasius had anathematized someone for believing in the Assumption, that would have been a disciplinary action, not a dogmatic statement. It would not have undermined the Church's belief in papal infallibility unless he had used his charism of infallibility to proclaim that no bodily assumption of Mary had ever occurred, only to be contradicted in 1950 by Pope Pius XII, who infallibly defined the Assumption as a dogma of faith. But Pope Gelasius made no such infallible pronouncement about the Assumption, and we challenge the "Bible Answer Man" to prove that he did.

Editor's Note: Regarding a recent column about Pope St. Gelasius, R.L.G. of Oregon writes to say that the Pontiff was also known for his opposition to women priests. According to Manfred Hauke's book *Women in the Priesthood* (Ignatius Press), the Pontiff in A.D. 494 issued the following statement:

"As we have noted with vexation, contempt for divine truths has reached such a level that even women, it is reported, serve at holy altars; and everything that is entrusted exclusively to the service of men is performed by the sex that has no right to do so" (p. 423).

Q. In an interview in a local newspaper, a person from our diocesan Office of the Black Apostolate said that there have been black Popes, including St. Victor I, St. Miltiades, and Gelasius I. I was not aware of this and want to know if it is correct. — Z.F., New Jersey

A. According to the biographical sketches we read, these three Popes were probably from Africa, but we don't know if they were black or not. St. Victor I reigned from 189 to 198, St. Miltiades (also Melchiades) from 311 to 314, and Gelasius I from 492-496.

Q. Donna Woolfolk Cross goes around to schools and colleges talking about a "Pope Joan." Was there ever a Pope Joan? — C.N.Y., New York

A. No, there never was an occupant of the Papacy named Pope Joan. In his book *Pope Fiction*, Patrick Madrid disposed of this myth, although he predicted that the myth will grow if a movie is made of *Pope Joan*, Donna Woolfolk Cross' 1996 novel.

But there is no historical evidence of any kind from the ninth century (when Pope Joan is alleged to have reigned) to the present that would give credence to this legend, said Madrid. He quoted in his book the following comment from Church historian J.P. Kirsch in the 1913 edition of the *Catholic Encyclopedia*:

"Not one contemporaneous historical source among the papal histories knows anything about her; also, no mention is made of her until the middle of the 13th century. Now it is an incredible fact that the appearance of a 'popess,' if it was a historical fact, would be noticed by none of the numerous historians from the 10th to the 13th century. In the history of the popes, there is no place where this legendary figure will fit in. Between Leo IV and Benedict III, where Martinus Polonus places her, she cannot be inserted...." (pp. 171-172).

Q. On the enclosed list of Popes and the dates of their reigns, there is a two-year gap between Pope Gregory XII (1406-1415) and Pope Martin V (1417-1431). Was the Papacy vacant for those two years? — W.C.S., Connecticut

A. Yes, it was because Gregory had resigned in 1415 to help bring an end to the Great Western Schism (1378-1417) that saw three simultaneous claimants to the Papacy. The Council of Constance (1414-1418) had been called to straighten out this confusion, and Gregory abdicated so that antipopes Benedict XIII and John XXIII could be deposed and Martin V could be elected as the first Pontiff of a unified Church in 39 years. The Council, by the way, made Gregory the cardinal of Porto.

Q. Was Pope Benedict XIII (Pedro de Luna) an antipope from 1394 to 1423? — D.R., Pennsylvania

A. Yes, he was. A supporter of antipope Clement VII, Cardinal de Luna was elected as Pope Benedict XIII at Avignon upon the death of Clement in 1394. He clung to his post until his death in 1423, despite being deposed by the Council of Pisa in 1409 and the Council of Constance in 1417. It was that latter Council that brought an end to the Great Western Schism that had divided the Church since 1378 by electing Martin V as Pope.

De Luna, by the way, is not to be confused with the legitimate Pope Benedict XIII, born Pierfrancesco Orsini, who reigned from 1724 to 1730.

Q. Enclosed is a clipping from the *Las Vegas Review Journal*. I realize that Catholic-bashing is prevalent, but the gratuitous nature of this example caught my eye. I realize that not every attack can be easily answered, but if there was some way you could do it, I and perhaps other readers would be interested. — J.P.B., California

A. The article, written by one Dr. James S. Tate Jr., who is identified as the executive director of the National Alliance Against Racist and Political Oppression, says that "it was Pope Nicholas IX who decided that there were three races: black, yellow, and white. Blacks were on the bottom, ostensibly because they were the furthest away from Christianity, but in reality because they had land that the Europeans coveted. Asians were in the middle because they were not Christians, but they were vital trade links and could not be disregarded. Of course, whites were on top as the Christian species with the obligation to 'bring Christianity to the rest of the world.' "

Actually, this charge can be easily answered by pointing out that there never was a Pope Nicholas IX. The last Pope to take that name was Nicholas V (1447-1455).

Q. I recently attended a Catholic-Jewish interfaith meeting which included a discussion of the proposed canonization of several Popes, especially that of Pius IX. One person claimed that Pius IX deserves no credit for releasing the Jews from the ghettos in Rome and Bologna since he was paid to do so by the Rothschilds. Can you shed any light on this? — L.V.P., New York

A. It's so easy to toss out statements like that and never offer any evidence to back them up. The person who made the allegation should have been asked to prove it. The little that we know about this comes from a monograph prepared by Robert P.

Lockwood for the Catholic League for Religious and Civil Rights. Here is what Lockwood, relying in part on the 1998 book *A History of the Popes, 1830-1914*, by Owen Chadwick, has to say about the Holy Father who reigned from 1846 to 1878:

"Pius IX was considered a friend and protector of the Jews during the early years of his pontificate. Rome had its own Jewish ghetto in 1846, established in the late 16th century. (Most other cities in Europe with Jewish populations had similar ghettos.) The ghettos existed both to 'protect' Christians from possible apostasy in contact with Jews, and to protect Jews from mob attack. Jews were allowed outside the ghetto during the day, but were expected to return in the evening. Four synagogues existed within the Jewish ghetto in Rome, the only non-Catholic religious facilities allowed to function within Rome.

"Upon becoming Pope, Pius IX ordered the end to various insulting traditions aimed at the Jewish community in Rome: anti-Jewish comedies, parading of rabbis in costume during Carnival, and the necessity that representatives of the community be forced to hear sermons once a year exhorting them to conversion. The walls enclosing the ghetto were torn down. To the Jews, 'the liberal regime of Pius IX felt to them like a miracle' [Chadwick, p. 129].

"After the revolt in Rome in 1848, Pius IX initially withdrew these liberal statutes, angered at Jewish participation in the revolt (three Jews served on the Roman municipal council during the revolt). It was alleged — and doubtful — that Jews had robbed churches during the uprising. But though the restrictions were back on the books, and the insulting conversion sermon was reestablished, most of the anti-Jewish laws were no longer enforced and Jews were no longer confined to the ghetto. In different areas within the Papal States, the Jews could generally live, work, and move about freely, such as in Bologna."

In conclusion, says Lockwood, "Pius was not an anti-Semite, though he certainly was a man of his times in regard to the question of religous tolerance."

Q. Can you tell us what Pope St. Pius X's encyclical *Pascendi Dominici Gregis* (1907) is about? — Name Withheld, Pennsylvania
A. The encyclical and its companion decree *Lamentabili Sane*

condemned some 65 errors of Modernism, which the Holy Father called the "synthesis of all heresies." Among other things, Modernists hold that the existence of a personal God cannot be demonstrated, that the Bible was not inspired by God, that Christ was not divine, and that He did not establish either the Church or the Sacraments. One would not be wrong, said St. Pius X, in regarding the Modernists "as the most pernicious of all the adversaries of the Church."

He said that not only do they work from within the Church, but "they lay the ax not to the branches and shoots, but to the very root, that is, to the faith and its deepest fibers. And once having struck at this root of immortality, they proceed to diffuse poison through the whole tree, so that there is no part of Catholic truth which they leave untouched, none that they do not strive to corrupt" (n. 3).

Pauline Books has combined *Pascendi* and *Lamentabili* into one booklet, which should be available at any Catholic bookstore.

Q. I recall reading something about the chief rabbi of Rome converting to the Catholic faith. When did this happen and what was his name? — H.S., New Jersey

A. The conversion of Rabbi Israel Zolli took place on February 13, 1945, and the story is recounted in his book *Why I Became a Catholic*. He took the baptismal name Eugenio to show his gratitude to Pope Pius XII for all the Pontiff had done to help the Jewish people during the Nazi persecution. On July 25, 1944, then-Rabbi Zolli had visited Pius XII "to officially thank him for all he, personally and through the Catholics in Rome, had done in favor of the Jews, opening convents and monasteries, dispensing with papal cloister as stated in canon law, so that Jews could be received even in female monasteries and protected from the fury of the Nazis."

Other books which refute the lie that Pius XII did little or nothing to help the Jews during the war include two by Dr. Margherita Marchione: *Yours Is a Precious Witness* (Paulist Press) and *Pope Pius XII: Architect for Peace* (Paulist Press), Ronald Rychlak's *Hitler, the War and the Pope* (Our Sunday Visitor), Ralph McInerny's *The Defamation of Pius XII* (St. Augustine's Press) and Pinchas Lapide's *Three Popes and the Jews* (Hawthorne Books).

Lapide, a former Israeli diplomat, credited Pius XII with saving the lives of at least 860,000 Jews.

Also worth noting is a statement from Jewish scientist Albert Einstein that appeared in *Time* magazine on December 23, 1940. After pointing out that the newspapers and universities in Germany had been silenced during Hitler's assault on freedom and truth, Einstein offered this praise of the Catholic Church:

"Only the Church stood squarely across the path of Hitler's campaign for suppressing truth. I had never any special interest in the Church before, but now I feel a great affection and admiration because the Church alone has had the courage and persistence to stand for intellectual truth and moral freedom. I am forced thus to confess that what I once despised I now praise unreservedly."

Q. We saw a program that mentioned that the United Nations had received a papal tiara from Pope Paul VI. Knowing what we do about the UN, this disturbs us. Can you confirm this report? — R.G., Iowa

A. During a visit to the United Nations in October 1965, Pope Paul gave the Secretary General a diamond pectoral cross and bishop's ring, valued then at about $150,000. The Holy Father asked that the two items be sold and that the proceeds be used to start a United Nations Freedom From Hunger Campaign. The papal tiara he wore during his pontificate was given to the Shrine of the Immaculate Conception in Washington, DC, and is on display there today.

Q. I have learned that among the poems written by Pope John Paul II (probably before he became Pope) was one on Simon the Cyrenian, who helped Jesus carry His cross. Do you know where I could get a copy of this poem? — M.K., Massachusetts

A. The poem, one of many written by Karol Wojtyla under the pen name Andrzej Jawien between 1950 and 1966, can be found in a book entitled *The Place Within: The Poetry of Pope John Paul II*, published by Random House in 1979 and 1982.

Q. Please find enclosed a copy of *101 Heresies of Anti-Pope John Paul II*. I would like you to comment on this tract. — W.E.V., California

A. Our first comment is to pray for the poor misguided (at least we hope he is misguided and not malicious) soul who dreamed up this tract. Our second comment is to say that no Pope in history has ever fallen into heresy because the man in the office enjoys the protection of the Holy Spirit. If Pope John Paul II were guilty of even one heresy, let alone 101, it would mean that the gates of Hell had prevailed against the Church and that Jesus was a liar when He promised that such a thing would never happen since He would be with His Church until the end of the world.

As is so often true of wild charges, it would take a book to respond to all of the 101 allegations, most of which have to do with efforts to bring about unity among Christians, a goal for which Christ specifically prayed at the Last Supper. We have neither the time nor the space to engage in such a massive rebuttal; it is always easier to make outrageous statements than to refute them. But let us address some of the alleged "heresies" to show how unsubstantiated they are and why no intelligent person should pay attention to them.

No. 13. Jews are our elder brothers in the faith. The source cited is *Crossing the Threshold of Hope*, p. 99 (the statement is on p. 95 in the large-print edition). If Abraham is spiritual father to Jews and Christians (the Roman Canon at Mass calls Abraham "our father in faith"), and Jesus and the Apostles were Jews, how is it heretical to say that Jews are our elder brothers in the faith?

No. 18. All inter-religious marriages are good. The source cited is *Familiaris Consortio*, but there is no specific paragraph mentioned, perhaps because John Paul never said that all inter-religious marriages are good. What he did say in paragraph 78 was that the growing number of mixed marriages calls for "special pastoral attention" to make sure that the Catholic party recognizes his or her obligation to have children baptized and brought up in the Catholic Church. "It is of the greatest importance that, through the support of the community, the Catholic party should be strengthened in faith and positively helped to mature in understanding and practicing that faith," the Holy Father said, "so as to become a credible witness within the family through his or her own life and through the quality of love shown to the other spouse and the children."

No. 30. Heretics can be Christian martyrs outside the Church.

The source cited is *Ut Unum Sint*, n. 84, where the Pope paid tribute to all Christians who have shed their blood for Christ. Can the person who calls this statement heresy really believe that only Catholics can be martyrs? That Protestants who willingly give their lives for the Gospel are not martyrs? What nonsense!

No. 48. The plan of salvation includes the Muslims. The source cited is the *Catechism of the Catholic Church*, n. 841. Since St. Paul tells us that God "wants all men to be saved" (1 Timothy 2:4), how can it be heresy to say that God's plan of salvation includes Muslims?

No. 75. Goodness and truth are found in false religions. The source cited is the *Catechism of the Catholic Church*, n. 843. In saying that goodness and truth are found in other religions, the *Catechism* is not saying that those religions have the fullness of truth that only the Catholic Church possesses, but rather that what goodness and truth they do have are " 'a preparation for the Gospel and given by him who enlightens all men that they may at length have life' [*LG* 16; cf. *NA* 2; *EN* 53]."

No. 90. Unbaptized catechumens are members of the Church. The source cited is Vatican II's *Lumen Gentium*, n. 14, which was promulgated in 1964, fourteen years before Karol Wojtyla became Pope John Paul II. Here is the precise sentence: "Catechumens who, moved by the Holy Spirit, seek with explicit intention to be incorporated into the Church are by that very intention joined to her." These catechumens explicitly intend to become Catholics and, barring any harm that might befall them, will be baptized into the Catholic Church. How is it heretical to say that their explicit intention to join the Church already has joined them to the Church?

Q. I would like to know how many encyclicals Pope John Paul II has written and how many countries he has visited. — M.G.M., Wisconsin

A. As of December 2002, Pope John Paul had written 13 encylical letters, beginning with *The Redeemer of Man* in 1979 and ending with *Faith and Reason* in 1998. He had also written 11 apostolic constitutions, 41 apostolic letters, 15 other particular letters (to women, to families, to children, etc.), nine post-synodal apostolic exhortations, and the book *Crossing the Threshold of Hope* (edited by Vittorio Messori).

The Holy Father had delivered over 600 ad limina addresses to bishops, thousands of talks to general and special audiences, and several thousand more addresses and homilies to hundreds of millions of men, women, and children during some 100 pilgrimages to foreign countries. We're not sure exactly how many countries since he visited some countries more than once, e.g., his native Poland seven times, but it's more than 130.

He had also promulgated two codes of canon law and the *Catechism*, beatified more than 1,300 men and women, canonized nearly 500 saints, created some 200 new cardinals, and named over 2,600 of the Church's 4,200 bishops.

Q. How much of the papal writing is actually that of Pope John Paul, and how much is the work of papal theologians? Does he write out his thoughts and then have theologians develop and complete them and submit them to him for approval before publication? It seems to me that the Vatican hierarchy and/or papal theologians are the ventriloquists and the Pope is the dummy. — Supercurious, California

A. Pope John Paul is not some shallow politician with a team of speechwriters; he is a brilliant thinker and writer who has been composing his own material — including poetry, plays, speeches, letters, and encyclicals — for all of his adult life. He surely consults experts in various fields when preparing an important address or document, but the content is very much his own, as are most of the words. To suggest that one of the greatest minds of the past century is merely a ventriloquist's dummy is nonsense.

We recommend that you read *Witness to Hope*, George Weigel's biography of the Pontiff, for some insights into the abilities of this intellectual giant. Note, for example, how the Holy Father's international bestseller *Crossing the Threshold of Hope* was written (cf. pp. 735-737) in collaboration with Italian journalist Vittorio Messori. Messori submitted the questions and John Paul composed the answers and sent the manuscript to Messori, who hardly edited the material before sending it back to the Pope for his approval.

To those who viewed Karol Wojtyla "as an authoritarian seeking to impose a rigorous Polish form of Catholicism on the universal Church, *Threshold* was a revelation," said Weigel. "Emphatically and unmistakably, this was a Pope in conversation ....

"His descriptions of his own struggles in prayer; his autobiographical reflections on the fate of his Jewish schoolmates in Wadowice, on his vocational discernment, on learning 'to love human love' through his first experiences as a young priest with those preparing for marriage; his deep ecumenical hopes; his profound sense of the 20th century as a century of martyrs; his passion to reinstill hope into humanism in the face of modern fear — all this bespoke a richly human and humane sensibility, not the cast of mind of a doctrinaire scold" (p. 736).

Q. Would you know of any book that deals with the history of social justice teachings in the Catholic Church? — N.R.G., Florida

A. We have heard that Pope John Paul II has called for publication of a catechism that would contain all the social justice teachings of the Church, but we don't know when to expect to see such a compilation in print. In the meantime, you could read Vatican II's *Pastoral Constitution on the Church in the Modern World*, paragraphs 2401-2463 of the *Catechism of the Catholic Church*, and the papal encyclicals of Leo XIII (*Rerum Novarum*), Pius XI (*Quadragesimo Anno*), John XXIII (*Mater et Magistra* and *Pacem in Terris*), Paul VI (*Populorum Progressio*), and John Paul II (*Laborem Exercens, Sollicitudo Rei Socialis,* and *Centesimus Annus*).

Q. Can you explain the various papal decrees, such as encyclicals, apostolic constitutions, apostolic letters, papal bulls, decretals? Is it a sin not to follow them? Must bishops follow them under pain of sin? — J.D., New York

A. The writings of the Popes are published in a variety of forms, such as the ones mentioned in the question, and they acquire their force by publication in the *Acta Apostolicae Sedis*, the official journal of the Apostolic See. This journal contains not only papal writings but also the decisions of Roman congregations and notices of ecclesiastical appointments.

Since these writings are the official pronouncements of the magisterium or teaching office of the Church, Catholics are not free to disregard them, especially if the Holy Father is speaking about faith or morals. In that case, said the Second Vatican Council, a "religious submission of will and of mind must be shown in a special way to the authentic teaching authority of the Roman Pontiff, even when he is not speaking *ex cathedra* [infallibly].

"That is, it must be shown in such a way that his supreme magisterium is acknowledged with reverence, the judgments made by him are sincerely adhered to, according to his manifest mind and will. His mind and will in the matter may be known chiefly either from the character of the documents, from his frequent repetition of the same doctrine, or from his manner of speaking" (*Constitution on the Church*, n. 25).

Regarding the character of the documents, let us consider each of the categories mentioned by J.D., as well as a few others:

• **Apostolic Letters** — Generally speaking, all documents issued by the Holy See.

• **Briefs** — Papal documents less formal than a bull and signed by the Secretary of State and stamped with the Pope's ring.

• **Bulls** — The most solemn and weighty documents signed by a Pope and sealed with a disk of lead called a *bulla*. Bulls are used in the appointment of bishops.

• **Constitutions** — Documents issued either by an ecumenical council and approved by the Pope, or by a Pope in his own name to implement the decisions of a council.

• **Decrees** — Usually legislative enactments of the Pope, a Council of the Church, or a congregation of the Vatican, these can be found in constitutions, apostolic letters, and *motu proprios*.

• **Decretals** — Letters carrying authoritative decisions on matters of discipline, or the Pope's reply when he has been asked to rule on a disciplinary matter.

• **Encyclicals** — Letters written by the Pope that may be addressed to bishops, to the whole Church, or, as in the case of John XXIII's *Pacem in Terris*, to "all men of good will." Although not necessarily infallible documents, encyclicals generally contain pronouncements on faith and morals that are infallible because they express the ordinary teaching of the Church. Catholics are to give interior and exterior assent to such documents.

• **Motu Proprios** — Papal documents issued by the Pope on his own accord that can be instructive, administrative, or confer special favor. One example is Pope John Paul's 2002 apostolic letter *Misericordia Dei* on revitalizing the Sacrament of Penance and ending abuses of general absolution.

• **Rescripts** — Written replies of a Pope to questions, petitions, or reports generally made through curial channels. These usually affect only individuals, such as a priest requesting to be laicized.

Q. Can you tell me why the "Dark Ages" are called by that name? — V.M., Michigan
A. In Our Sunday Visitor's *Catholic Encyclopedia*, it says that Dark Ages is "a somewhat inaccurate term used in the past by some historians to describe the centuries following the collapse of the Roman Empire, usually given as from the middle of the 5th century to the 11th century. Although the social and political upheaval brought on by the advances of the barbarians and the destruction of the stability of the Roman Empire did indeed cause some intellectual and cultural stagnation, the heritage of Western civilization was guarded and fostered by the monasteries and some towering figures, e.g., Pope St. Gregory the Great. The flourishing of art and education in the Middle Ages was only possible because of the protection of learning — under the most adverse of circumstances — characteristic of these so-called Dark Ages."
A good history of this period is Henri Daniel-Rops' two-volume work *The Church in the Dark Ages* (Image Books).

Q. I recently read a book published in 1994 that stated "during the 600 years it was in session, the Inquisition killed an average of over 100,000 people a year?" What is the truth about this accusation? — J.D., New Jersey
A. The charge is certainly false that the Inquisition killed some 60 million people over a period of 600 years. One thing wrong with this accusation is that the wildly exaggerated death toll is greater than the population of Europe during those centuries. Victims of these ecclesiastical tribunals may have totaled in the few thousands, but certainly not in the million or tens of millions.
Secondly, there was no single Inquisition. There were in fact

three main Inquisitions that functioned at various times from the 13th to the 19th centuries in southern France, Italy, and Spain, and a few parts of the Holy Roman Empire. The first phase began in 1233 when Pope Gregory IX appointed papal inquisitors to curb the heretical doctrines of the Albigensians and Cathars in southern France, Italy, and Germany. The penalties imposed by these tribunals were spiritual at first, including excommunication, but later violence and torture were condoned because heresy was seen as a threat not only to the Church, but also to the state.

In 1542, Pope Paul III created the Congregation for the Inquisition in Rome to preserve doctrinal integrity. This was the least active and the mildest of the Inquisitions, and it retained that title until 1908 when Pope St. Pius X changed its name to the Congregation for the Holy Office. In 1965, Pope Paul VI gave it its current name of the Sacred Congregation for the Doctrine of the Faith.

The most notorious of these tribunals was the Spanish Inquisition, which was established in Spain in 1478 by Pope Sixtus IV to root out Jews and Moors who had converted to Christianity for political or social rather than spiritual reasons. Its first head was Tomas de Torquemada, a Dominican with the title of grand inquisitor. This tribunal subsequently protected Spanish Catholicism from the Reformation and prevented Protestantism from gaining a foothold in Spain.

The Spanish Inquisition was suppressed in 1834, but its reputation for cruelty, including torture, imprisonment, and execution, had led to claims of death tolls that far exceed the number of people who would have been within its reach. If one accepts the estimate that 100,000 prisoners passed before Torquemada's tribunals during his reign as grand inquisitor (1483-1498), says historian William Thomas Walsh in his book *Characters of the Inquisition* (TAN Books), "hardly more than one percent of all the prisoners in Spain, during Torquemada's term of office, could have been executed" (p. 175).

He offers as an illustration the tribunal in Barcelona, which heard 888 accusations between 1488 and 1498. Of that number, 38 were executed by strangling and/or burning, 430 escaped, 116 were given prison sentences, and 304 were told to go and sin no more. Thus, less than five percent of those accused were punished by death.

Those who claim that Torquemada killed more than 100,000

people rely on a report written in 1817 by Juan Antonio Llorente, who claimed to have consulted official documents but, when challenged on his figures, said that he had burned the documents. This hardly qualifies him as a reputable historian.

A balanced discussion of the Inquisition can be found on pages 290-300 of Karl Keating's book *Catholicism and Fundamentalism* (Ignatius). Keating also offers some good advice on how to respond to charges about the Inquisition: Don't deny that it happened or attempt to defend its excesses, but don't accept every Fundamentalist slander or exaggerated figure either. Try to put the matter into perspective and don't let the critic imply or state that the Inquisition proves that the Catholic Church is not the Church of Christ; this is often the reason why Fundamentalists raise the issue in the first place.

"Far better than wasting time arguing about statistics that can only be roughly approximated or about numbers taken out of a magician's hat," says Keating, "the Catholic should ask the Fundamentalist what he thinks the existence of the Inquisition demonstrates .... That the Church contains sinners? Guilty as charged. That at times sinners have reached positions of authority? Ditto. That even otherwise good Catholics, afire with zeal, sometimes lose their balance? True, all true, but such charges could be made and verified even if the Inquisition never existed" (p. 297).

To use the Inquisition to call into question the Catholic claim to be the Church founded by Christ does not prove the claim false, says Keating. He says that "the Church has not been false to its commission. Individual Catholics, yes — it has always been that way, since the denials of Peter, and it will continue that way until the end — but no degree of unsaintliness on the part of Catholics proves the Church to be other than what it claims to be, even though that unsaintliness puts grave obstacles in the path of people outside and inside the Church" (*Ibid.*).

Q. The 1983 Code of Canon Law is not the same as that of 1917. How can I find the exact differences? Is there some book that compares both and points out the differences? — W.R.G., California

A. There are tables of corresponding canons from both codes at the back of the 1983 version (Paulist Press), but these only show the correlation, or lack thereof, between the canon numbers themselves. However, the commentary that follows each canon in the 1983 Code usually tells the reader how the new canon compares with the old one, so that's one way of determining the differences. Another way is to get a copy of the 1917 and 1983 versions and check out the differences yourself. *The 1917 Pio-Benedictine Code of Canon Law*, translated into English by Dr. Edward N. Peters, is available from Ignatius Press.

A reader, J.L.T.G. of New Jersey, has also recommended the British-produced 1983 *Code of Canon Law Annotated*, which is published by Wilson & Lafleur Limited of Montreal, because it contains the original Latin text of each canon with the authorized English translation in parallel columns with commentary below and seems more faithful to the Latin than the version produced by the Canon Law Society of America.

Q. At a diocesan seminar on the *Catechism of the Catholic Church*, Fr. Berard L. Marthaler of the Catholic University of America did an excellent job of explaining the content of the *Catechism*, but his personal opinions and interjections, in general, were derogatory to the *Catechism* and to the Church. He certainly did not encourage its use, he said that the original version submitted to Rome was "bushwhacked," and he speculated that the *Catechism* would shortly be replaced by one written in inclusive language. His comments made me very uncomfortable, and I feel that our diocese missed an opportunity to increase interest in the *Catechism*. — W.J.M., Ohio

A. Having long been an influential member of the catechetical establishment and a dissenter from Church teachings, it is not surprising that Fr. Marthaler would portray in a negative way the clear and authoritative presentation of Catholic teaching that appears in the *Catechism*.

In 1990, he and 14 other dissenters took part in a symposium designed to discredit the *Catechism* before it even came out. The papers from the symposium were subsequently published in *The Universal Catechism Reader*. In his contribution to that work, Marthaler said that "more is required of Christian education than the handing on of shopworn formulas, tired customs, and trite devotions."

It is a sad commentary on the Church in the United States today when a person who has publicly ridiculed the *Catechism* as a collection of shopworn formulas, tired customs, and trite devotions is sent to a diocesan seminar supposedly designed to show catechists how to implement the *Catechism* in their religious education classes!

Q. A news item I saw quoted a Fr. Lawrence DiNardo as having said that the *Catechism of the Catholic Church* was not intended for the Catholic population at all, but was written for the bishops. Is that true? — R.G., Virginia

A. No, it is not true. The prologue to the *Catechism* says that "this work is intended primarily for those responsible for catechesis: first of all the bishops, as teachers of the faith and pastors of the Church. It is offered to them as an instrument in fulfilling their responsibility of teaching the People of God. Through the bishops, it is addressed to redactors of catechisms, to priests, and to catechists. It will also be useful reading for all other Christian faithful" (n. 12).

In his apostolic constitution *Fidei Depositum*, which accompanied publication of the *Catechism*, Pope John Paul said that this compendium of the Church's teachings is not only for those whose mission is "proclaiming the faith and calling people to the Gospel life," but "it is also offered to all the faithful who wish to deepen their knowledge of the unfathomable riches of salvation (cf. Ephesians 3:8)," as well as "to every individual who asks us to give an account of the hope that is in us (cf. 1 Peter 3:15) and who wants to know what the Catholic Church believes" (n. 3).

Q. An anti-Catholic fundamentalist (Bart Brewer of Mission to Catholics International) sent me a copy of a speech by Bishop Josip Strossmayer attacking papal infallibility at the First Vatican Council in 1870. Is it true that the 1913 *Catholic Encyclopedia* gives an account of Bishop Strossmayer's speech? — J.M., Wisconsin

A. Yes, but only to expose it as a forgery. Bishop Strossmayer never delivered any such speech. It was invented by a former Augustinian priest named Jose Augustin de Escudero. But Bart Brewer, who is also a former priest, doesn't tell his audience that part of the story.

By the way, Strossmayer was opposed to having the Council proclaim the dogma of papal infallibility, but only because he had tried for years to bring about a reconciliation between the Eastern Orthodox churches and the Catholic Church and was afraid that promulgation of the doctrine would hurt his ecumenical efforts. For more on this, see the *Catholic Encyclopedia* or pages 34 and 35 of Karl Keating's book *Catholicism and Fundamentalism* (Ignatius Press).

Q. I have been taught that the Pope is infallible when he teaches *ex cathedra* with the full weight of his supreme apostolic authority with the intention of deciding finally a teaching of faith or morals, and that most of the doctrinal expressions made by the Popes in their encyclicals are not decisions *ex cathedra*. Isn't it Catholic teaching that a pope's private opinions and sermons or speeches, when he does not use his full authority, could be subject to error? Should we put such statements in the same category as private revelations? What should our attitude be towards encyclicals and the *Catechism of the Catholic Church*, if they are not infallible? — T.E.F., Minnesota

A. You are correct in stating that the Holy Spirit protects the Pope from teaching error when he speaks in an extraordinary way on a matter of faith or morals with his full authority "from the chair" (*ex cathedra*) of St. Peter. This does not mean, however, that a Catholic is free to disregard those doctrinal statements of the Holy Father which are presented in the ordinary exercise of his universal magisterium but which do not meet the conditions for infallibility. Those who dissented from *Humanae Vitae* in 1968, argued, falsely, that since Pope Paul VI had not reaffirmed the Church's prohibition against artificial contraception in an infallible manner, Catholics could ignore this encyclical and its teaching.

In point of fact, however, Catholics are obliged to assent to all doctrinal and moral pronouncements of the Pope, whether he is speaking with his extraordinary charism of infallibility or with his ordinary teaching authority, because even in the latter instance he is still teaching with divine assistance and with that special power that belongs to him as the Vicar of Christ on earth.

Pope Pius XII explained it this way in his 1950 encyclical *Humani Generis*:

"Nor must it be thought that what is expounded in encyclical letters does not of itself demand consent, since in writing such letters the Popes do not exercise the supreme power of their teaching authority. For these matters are taught with the ordinary teaching authority, of which it is true to say: 'He who heareth you, heareth me' [Luke 10:16]; and generally what is expounded and inculcated in encyclical letters already for other reasons appertains to Catholic doctrine. But if the Supreme Pontiffs in their official documents purposely pass judgment on a matter up to that time under dispute, it is obvious that that matter, according to the mind and will of the same Pontiffs, cannot be any longer considered a question open to discussion among theologians" (n. 20).

Fourteen years later, the Second Vatican Council said much the same thing in paragraph 25 of the *Dogmatic Constitution on the Church*, and so did the *Catechism of the Catholic Church* (n. 892) when it was promulgated in 1992.

In 1998, Pope John Paul issued an apostolic letter (*Ad Tuendam Fidem*) in which he announced that he had added a section to canon 750 of the Code of Canon Law in an effort "to protect the Catholic faith against errors arising on the part of some of the Christian faithful, in particular among those who studiously dedicate themselves to the discipline of sacred theology." The new section said that Catholics must firmly embrace and hold "each and every proposition stated definitively by the magisterium of the Church concerning the doctrine of the faith or morals" (n. 4).

Commenting on this addition to canon law, Joseph Cardinal Ratzinger of the Sacred Congregation for the Doctrine of the Faith pointed out that doctrines never infallibly defined can still be taught infallibly by the Church's ordinary and universal magisterium because they belong to the deposit of faith.

"When there has not been a judgment on a doctrine in the solemn form of a definition," said Cardinal Ratzinger, "but this doctrine, belonging to the inheritance of the *depositum fidei*, is taught by the ordinary and universal magisterium, which necessarily includes the Pope, such a doctrine is to be understood as having been set forth infallibly. The declaration of confirmation or reaffirmation by the Roman Pontiff in this case is not a new dogmatic definition, but a formal attestation of a truth already possessed and infallibly transmitted by the Church" (n. 9).

Ratzinger gave as examples of such doctrines the illicitness of euthanasia, prostitution, and fornication, and he cited the *Catechism* as his source for saying this. The *Catechism*, by the way, is a sure and certain compendium of infallible Catholic doctrine, even though it was not promulgated in an infallible manner, and Catholics are obliged to assent to what it teaches.

In summary, then, the Pope does not have to invoke his full authority in an extraordinary way to reiterate a doctrine that has been infallibly taught by the Church from the beginning. Whether he transmits that doctrine in an encyclical, a book, a general audience, or in a sermon at Mass in some faraway country, Catholics are still bound to accept the doctrine, not because of the forum in which it was presented, but because the doctrine is part of the deposit of faith.

Is the Pope protected from error when he is not speaking infallibly? Strictly speaking, no. But he still receives divine assistance when he exercises his ordinary authority and affirms, in the words of Cardinal Ratzinger, "a truth already possessed and infallibly transmitted by the Church." Or as Pius XII said, when what he expounds "already for other reasons appertains to Catholic doctrine."

Read the numerous encyclicals, apostolic letters, and speeches of Pope John Paul and you will not see him breaking new doctrinal ground, but rather reaffirming doctrines already set forth infallibly by popes and general councils of the Church (cf. especially *Veritatis Splendor* and *Evangelium Vitae*).

Q. My pastor tells me that *The Truth and Meaning of Human Sexuality*, which was issued by the Pontifical Council for the Family and signed by Alfonso Cardinal Lopez Trujillo, is merely advisory to the Pope, and that he, my pastor, is within his rights to "strongly disagree with parts of it." My pastor says that the views of the Pontifical Council "are in no way magisterial in nature" and "are completely non-binding on local bishops and the faithful." Is this true? — L.G.S., Arkansas

A. In no way magisterial or binding? Tell your pastor to take at look at the footnotes to this Vatican document. Of the 176 footnotes listed, there are some 90 references to statements of Pope John Paul II, 19 to the documents of Vatican II, 15 to the *Catechism of the Catholic Church*, and 30 to other Vatican documents, such as *Educational Guidance in Human Love*, the *Charter of the Rights of the Family*, the *Declaration on Certain Questions Concerning Sexual Ethics*, and the *Letter to Bishops of the Catholic Church on the Pastoral Care of Homosexual Persons*.

When more than 90 percent of the footnotes cited in a Vatican document are taken from magisterial sources, we think it is safe to say that we are dealing with a magisterial document whose conclusions are most certainly binding on bishops and faithful alike. Rome doesn't issue such documents as an academic exercise. It issues them because some Catholic bishops, pastors, and religious educators are promoting or allowing sex education programs that disturb the innocence, deform the consciences, and undermine the decency, modesty, and chastity of children exposed to these programs.

Q. Can you give us a theological definition of indefectibility? Do the Mass of Pope Paul VI and the new sacramental forms fall under this category? If a future Pope gives us another "New Mass," would that be indefectible? Are all the disciplinary and administrative decrees of the Pope indefectible? — Name Withheld, Rhode Island

A. Indefectibility refers to the institution of the Church herself and not to any liturgical, disciplinary, or administrative changes made by Popes. In his *Modern Catholic Dictionary* (Doubleday), Fr. John A. Hardon, S.J., defines the term as meaning that the Catholic Church "now is and will always remain the institution of salvation, founded by Christ. This affirms that the Church is essentially unchangeable in her teaching, her constitution, and her liturgy. It does not exclude modifications that do not affect her substance, nor does it exclude the decay of individual local churches or even whole dioceses."

Thus, the Church's essential role as the institution of salvation founded by Christ cannot be nullified by any modifications of the Mass or the Sacraments that do not change the substance of her teaching, constitution, or liturgy. Nor can the personal misconduct or sinful actions of popes, bishops, and priests adversely affect the Church's immutability until the end of time.

In brief, says Fr. Albert Nevins in his *Maryknoll Catholic Dictionary*, indefectibility is "a quality possessed by the Church which makes it not liable to failure" because Christ promised "to be with the Church until the end of time" (Matthew 28:20).

Q. I have been told that we are having so much dissension in the Church today because, back around 1965, bishops were given the same authority as the Pope and, therefore, bishops do not have to obey the Pope. Is this true? — C.M.B., Florida

A. No, it is not true. The Second Vatican Council ended in 1965, so perhaps whoever said this thinks that Vatican II put bishops on the same level as the Holy Father. But if you read the Council documents, particularly the *Dogmatic Constitution on the Church* and the *Decree on the Bishops' Pastoral Office in the Church*, you will find no evidence for such a claim. In fact, you will find evidence that just the opposite is true in paragraph 22 of the *Constitution on the Church*:

"The college or body of bishops has no authority unless it is simultaneously conceived of in terms of its head, the Roman Pontiff, Peter's successor, and without any lessening of his power of primacy over all, pastors as well as general faithful. For in virtue of his office, that is, as Vicar of Christ and pastor of the whole Church, the Roman Pontiff has full, supreme, and universal power over the Church. And he can always exercise this power freely.

"The order of bishops is the successor to the college of the Apostles in teaching authority and pastoral rule; or, rather, in the episcopal order the apostolic body continues without a break. Together with its head, the Roman Pontiff, and never without this head, the episcopal order is the subject of supreme and full power over the universal Church. But this power can be exercised only with the consent of the Roman Pontiff. For our Lord made Simon Peter alone the rock and key-bearer of the Church (cf. Mark 16:18-19), and appointed him shepherd of the whole flock (cf. John 21:15ff.)."

Q. In a recent column, you quoted Vatican II as stating that "the body of the faithful as a whole [from the bishops down to the last member of the laity], anointed as they are by the Holy One (cf. John 2:20, 27), cannot err in matters of faith and morals" (n. 12). But John 2:20 refers to the Jews' reply that the temple took 46 years to build, and there is no John 2:27.

Also, only the Pope is protected from error in matters of faith and morals. Baptism of itself does not confer this power. You need look no further than the existing bishops, priests, and theologians who dissent from the doctrines of the Roman Catholic Church. I haven't as yet met anyone free from error in regard to mundane things, let alone faith and morals. Please explain to this poor old sinner where you are coming from? — J.A.F., California

A. First of all, you are correct about the Scripture references quoted from Vatican II. The *Dogmatic Constitution on the Church* should have cited the First Letter of John, chapter 2, verses 20 and 27, not the Gospel of John. The verses from 1 John have to do with "the anointing that comes from the Holy One," not with the infallibility of the whole body of the faithful in matters of faith and morals.

That concept is known as the "sense of the faithful," which, according to the *Catechism* (cf. n. 92) means that because all the faithful have received the anointing of the Holy Spirit, who in-structs them and guides them into all truth, the whole body of the faithful cannot err in matters of belief. This *sensus fidei* is recognizable "on the part of the whole people, when, 'from the bishops to the last of the faithful,' they manifest a universal con-sent in matters of faith and morals' [*LG* 12; cf. St. Augustine, *De praed. sanct.* 14, 27: PL 44, 980]."

When this sense of the faithful is aroused and sustained by the Holy Spirit, and guided by the sacred teaching authority of the Church, the *Catechism* continues, the People of God will un-failingly adhere to this faith and apply it more fully in daily life (cf. n. 93).

Dissenting bishops, priests, and theologians, as well as ordi-nary Catholics, are not part of the *sensus fidei* if they are dis-loyal to the Church's magisterium and do not "manifest a uni-versal consent in matters of faith and morals."

Some dissenters have tried to justify their rejection of funda-mental Catholic beliefs by appealing to the sense of the faithful, but there can be no sense of the faithful that is divorced from the "sacred teaching authority" of the Holy Father and those bish-ops, priests, theologians, and laity who are in communion with him.

Q. In Vatican II's definition of the Church as the "People of God," as opposed to the traditional definition as the "Mystical Body of Christ," do we have a meaning now that includes all Christians? — W.E.N., Rhode Island

Q. Would you explain the Mystical Body of Christ? Do all Christians qualify as members? — J.H., Florida

A. The Second Vatican Council used many biblical images to describe the Church — a sheepfold, a flock, a tract of land to be cultivated, a vineyard, the edifice of God, our mother, the spot-less spouse of the spotless Lamb, the Mystical Body of Christ, and the People of God (cf. the *Constitution on the Church*, nn. 6-

9, and the *Catechism*, nn. 753-757). But whatever image you use, the Council clearly stated:

"This is the unique Church of Christ which in the Creed we avow as one, holy, catholic, and apostolic. After His Resurrection, our Savior handed her over to Peter to be shepherded (John 21:17), commissioning him and the other Apostles to propagate and govern her (cf. Matthew 28:18 ff.). Her He erected for all ages as 'the pillar and mainstay of the truth' (1 Timothy 3:15). This Church, constituted and organized in the world as a society, subsists in the Catholic Church, which is governed by the successor of Peter and by the bishops in union with that successor, although many elements of sanctification and of truth can be found outside of her visible structure" (*Constitution on the Church*, n. 8).

As for the Mystical Body of Christ, that refers only to those Christians who are faithful members of the Catholic Church, whether of the Latin or Eastern rites. In the words of the Second Vatican Council:

"That Church, holy and catholic, which is the Mystical Body of Christ, is made up of the faithful who are organically united in the Holy Spirit through the same faith, the same sacraments, and the same government, and who, combining into various groups held together by a hierarchy, form separate churches or rites. Between these there flourishes such an admirable brotherhood that this variety within the Church in no way harms her unity, but rather manifests it" (*Decree on Eastern Catholic Churches*, n. 2)

To be fully incorporated into the Mystical Body of Christ, or Catholic Church, the Council said, persons must "accept her entire system and all the means of salvation given to her, and through union with her visible structure are joined to Christ, who rules her through the Supreme Pontiff and the bishops. This union is effected through the bonds of professed faith, of the sacraments, of ecclesiastical government, and of communion" (*Constitution on the Church*, n. 14).

These statements, which are reaffirmed in the *Catechism of the Catholic Church* (cf. n. 837), reflect what Pope Pius XII said in his 1943 encyclical on the Mystical Body (*Mystici Corporis*):

"Only those are to be included as real members of the Church who have been baptized and profess the true faith and have not been so unfortunate as to separate themselves from the unity of the Body or been excluded from it by legitimate authority for serious faults" (n. 29).

In summary then, all Christian religions do not qualify as members of the Mystical Body, although they are linked to the Body in an imperfect way by virtue of Baptism.

Q. My brother-in-law and his wife have become "traditionalists" and often angrily criticize our Holy Father. Their arguments (Vatican II and the *Novus Ordo* are Protestant inventions, it is accursed to teach that Heaven, Hell, and Purgatory are not "places" but "states," and Pope John Paul has no business apologizing for the Church without demanding an apology from the Freemasons, Muslims, and Jews) are like a broken record, as is "the gates of Hell not prevailing" argument. How can I respond to them? It is no exaggeration to label this a serious issue in my family. — Name and State Withheld

A. It's a serious issue in other families as well, and there is no easy way to deal with those whose minds are made up and who don't want to be confused with any historical or theological facts. Their attitude reminds us of St. Paul's warning to Timothy, which can be applied not only to "cafeteria" Catholics, but also to "traditional" Catholics:

"For the time will come when people will not tolerate sound doctrine, but, following their own desires, will surround themselves with teachers who tickle their ears. They will stop listening to the truth and will wander off to fables" (2 Timothy 4:3-4).

The "gates of Hell not prevailing" argument is a good one; it sounds like a broken record only to those who have come up with their own private interpretation of "truth" and refuse to listen to the One who said, "I am ... the truth" (John 14:6). They won't listen either to the Holy Father, who is the only person given the authority by Christ Himself to bind and loose on earth, but would rather follow their own desires and listen to very fallible mini-popes spread their own unsound version of truth.

To accept these fables promoted by your traditionalist relatives, one would have to believe that Jesus lied when He promised to be with His Church "always, until the end of the world" (Matthew 28:20), that Jesus lied when He promised to send "the Spirit of truth" to guide the Church (John 14:17), and that St. Paul lied when he called the Church "the pillar and bulwark of truth" (1 Timothy 3:15).

It is virtually impossible to reason with those Catholics, not to mention Protestants and Mormons, who think that the Church founded and sustained by Christ and the Holy Spirit could fall into error. One can only pray for them and ask the Lord to enlighten their minds and change their hearts so that they may become faithful and humble followers of the one, true Church of Christ on earth, the Catholic Church headquartered in Rome and presided over by the Supreme Pontiff.

Q. I call your attention to a web site entitled www.true catholic.org. This site claims to be the web site of the Roman Catholic Church. It claims that the only true pope is Pius XIII, who was elected in 1998, thus ending 40 years when the Church had no Pope. Most of the information is presented by a Fr. Lucian Pulvermacher, and almost all of what he espouses is what existed prior to Vatican II. There is enough of the truth in this web site to easily lead even "cradle Catholics" astray. I would appreciate it if you could look at the site and evaluate it. — T.A., Texas

A. Your concern that this web site could lead some Catholics astray is justified, although one would have to be quite ill-informed about the Catholic faith to believe the following comments on the home page of the site:

"It is likely that most of you think that the 'Catholic Church' now centered in Rome, in the Vatican, is the Catholic Church. Since 1958 (after the death of Pope Pius XII on October 9, 1958), the holders of offices there have usurped the name of the Catholic Church from which they of their own free will departed. They left the faith, and therefore they left the Church that was founded by Christ on the apostles with Peter at its head. Their defection from the faith is something we must prove and that is the burden of much of the literature that you will find in this web site.

"The deception into which you have been drawn by bogus Council Vatican II (1962-1965) is extremely acute. Why? Because those leaders, all the Fathers of the bogus Council Vatican II plus their leaders (John XXIII, Paul VI, John Paul I, and now John Paul II) kept not only the name Catholic Church, but they also kept their position in the community that continues to call itself the Catholic Church. The only way that one can prove this truth is to examine the teachings of the Catholic Church before bogus Council Vatican II and then compare those earlier teachings with the ones now taught by that unfortunate and diabolical Council Vatican II. The immense truth that will strike you is that there is a great difference between the doctrines of the pre-Vatican II Catholic Church and those of the post-Vatican II 'Catholic Church.' "

The most charitable thing one can say about such statements is that they are nonsense. There is no difference between the doctrines the Church taught prior to Vatican II and the doctrines she teaches now. Any alleged differences that do exist are in the minds of these sedevacantists, who have tried to put their own private, and erroneous, spin on the meaning of certain doctrines, such as "Outside the Church there is no salvation," instead of humbly submitting to the magisterium of the Church, which is incapable of teaching error in matters of faith and morals.

To say that Vatican II was "diabolical" is to say that the gates of Hell have prevailed against the Church, something which Jesus said would never happen. To say that the last four Popes were not really the Bishops of Rome and true successors of St. Peter flies in the face of history and sacred Tradition.

What St. Ignatius of Antioch said in A.D. 107 is just as true today as it was then: "Where Peter is, there is the Catholic Church." Peter, in the person of the current Pope, is in Rome today and not wherever the so-called Pius XIII resides.

Perhaps we could ask Blessed John XXIII (1958-1963), the Pontiff who convened the Second Vatican Council in 1962, and whose exhumed body was discovered to be incorrupt after 38 years in the grave, to pray for these misguided people who have placed their eternal salvation in jeopardy by separating themselves from the one, holy, catholic, and apostolic Church headquartered in Rome.

Q. My husband attends Mass each Sunday at a Society of St. Pius X church, but I prefer our *Novus Ordo* parish Mass. He has also insisted that our three children be baptized at the Pius X church. I have read conflicting stories

about the validity of this Mass. Is my husband fulfilling his obligation, and are the baptisms valid? — T.C., Texas

A. The Masses of the Society of St. Pius X are valid if they are celebrated by validly ordained priests. However, these Masses are illicit, i.e., contrary to Church law, and one who attends them with the intention of manifesting a desire to separate himself from communion with the Pope, and those in communion with the Supreme Pontiff, would be guilty of grave sin.

Attendance at such a Mass would not be a sin if the primary reason for participating were to manifest one's desire to take part in a Mass according to the 1962 *Roman Missal* for the sake of devotion. Your husband would have to be careful, however, not to get caught up in the schismatic mentality of some members of the Society of St. Pius X.

If T.C.'s children were baptized with water and the trinitarian formula, they were validly, but illicitly, baptized.

Q. Is it true that a canon law trial is required to officially condemn the Society of St. Pius X on charges of schism? Why has there been no trial? — M.S., California

A. Because canons 1364 and 1382 provide for automatic excommunication of schismatics and those who consecrate bishops without a mandate from the Pope. These canons were cited by Bernardin Cardinal Gantin on July 1, 1988, when he issued a decree excommunicating Archbishop Marcel Lefebvre, and by Pope John Paul II on July 11, 1988, when he reaffirmed what Cardinal Gantin had said.

In his apostolic letter *Ecclesia Dei*, the Holy Father made a solemn appeal "to all those who until now have been linked in various ways to the movement of Archbishop Lefebvre, that they may fulfill the grave duty of remaining united to the Vicar of Christ in the unity of the Catholic Church, and of ceasing their support in any way for that movement. Everyone should be aware that formal adherence to the schism is a grave offense against God and carries the penalty of excommunication decreed by the Church's law."

Q. Can a schismatic person who did not accept Catholic dogmas during his lifetime and still feels that way on his deathbed go to Heaven? — M.G., Arizona

A. Canon 751 of the Code of Canon Law defines schism as "the refusal of submission to the Roman Pontiff or of communion with the members of the Church subject to him." Without knowing more details, it sounds to us as if the person in question might be guilty instead of either heresy, which canon 751 defines as "the obstinate post-baptismal denial of some truth which must be believed with divine and catholic faith," or apostasy, which the same canon defines as "the total repudiation of the Christian faith."

To be guilty of these grave offenses, a baptized Catholic must be acting in bad faith and must knowingly, consciously, and intentionally reject Catholic teachings or the authority of the Pope.

If the person in question obstinately and persistently clings to this position on his deathbed, fully aware of what he is doing and the consequences of his actions, then he will not go to Heaven. Vatican II may have been thinking of such a person when it warned: "Whosoever, therefore, knowing that the Catholic Church was made necessary by God through Jesus Christ, would refuse to enter her or to remain in her could not be saved" (*Constitution on the Church*, n. 14).

Q. Could you please answer the following questions about Masses and sacraments celebrated by an excommunicated priest or bishop? — M.M., Wisconsin

A. Before answering the specific questions, let us mention that, according to canon 1331 of the Code of Canon Law, "an excommunicated person is forbidden: (1) to have any ministerial participation in celebrating the Eucharistic Sacrifice or in any other ceremonies whatsoever of public worship; (2) to celebrate the sacraments and sacramentals and to receive the sacraments."

Consider also the following statements from Fr. Nicholas Halligan's book *The Sacraments and Their Celebration*:

"The lawfulness of a sacramental celebration requires the minister to be free from serious sin and from ecclesiastical prohibitions [such as excommunication], and that he be properly deputed .... To celebrate a sacrament without necessary and proper permission or legitimate presumption, outside of necessity, is unlawful and sinful, being a violation of another's right" (p. 7).

Now to the questions: (1) Are the Masses of an excommunicated priest or bishop valid? Yes, they are valid because of the sacrament of Holy Orders, but they are not licit or lawful. (2) If one goes to him on Sunday, does it fulfill one's obligation? Canon

1248 says that "the precept of participating in the Mass is satisfied by assistance at a Mass which is celebrated anywhere in a Catholic rite either on the holy day or on the evening of the preceding day." So, yes, the obligation is fulfilled, but knowing and deliberate attendance at an unlawful Mass could be sinful.

Referring to canon 1335, which says that a member of the faithful in danger of death, or for "any just cause whatsoever," can request a sacrament from a penalized cleric, Fr. Halligan says that "without sufficient reason it is forbidden to request a sacrament for oneself or others from an unworthy minister, i.e., one who it is foreseen will sin in celebrating or conferring it." He says that "the request would be a serious or light sin in the measure of the unworthiness of the minister, of offering the occasion for another to sin, of cooperating in it or perhaps risking scandal or the danger of perversion" (p. 20).

(3) Are his First Communions, Confirmations, marriages, and Baptisms valid? Not the marriages because he must be properly deputed. (4) Will those who receive these sacraments from him have to receive them again from someone else? No. (5) Is it a mortal sin for him to continue saying Masses and giving sacraments after he has been excommunicated? Yes.

(6) Is it a mortal sin for people to continue going to this priest or bishop if they know he has been excommunicated? Yes. (7) Isn't a priest required to have a bishop? Yes. That's what Fr. Halligan means above when he says that the minister of a sacrament must be "properly deputed."

Q. Can an archbishop change the Sabbath? Ours has granted permission for a Saturday morning Mass that is supposed to take care of the Sunday obligation. — D.L.M., Washington

A. The Christian Sabbath is Sunday, and no archbishop can change it to Saturday. Vigil Masses are permitted on Saturday evenings, usually after 4:00, but we have never heard of a Sunday Mass on Saturday morning.

Q. In our diocese, the bishop has changed the feast of the Ascension from Thursday to Sunday so that more people will attend the Masses. Does the bishop have the authority to do this? — R.K., Indiana

A. Yes, he does. The Vatican has given bishops the authority to observe the solemnity of the Ascension of the Lord on the Sunday after Ascension Thursday. Some bishops have moved the feast to Sunday, but others have kept it on Thursday. Personally, we think it should be kept on Thursday since that will bring millions of additional Catholics to Mass on a weekday.

Q. I would be interested in your opinion as to whether or not what is printed in the diocesan paper reflects the views of the bishop. — S.A.M., Maryland

A. We would say that everything in a diocesan paper does not necessarily have to reflect the views of the bishop, but it certainly ought to reflect the teaching of the Church. For example, there can be differing viewpoints on the best way to oppose abortion, e.g., prayer, education, political action, street demonstrations, etc., but there can be no disagreement on the evil of abortion itself. So a bishop, who is usually the publisher of, and often a columnist in, his diocesan paper, could allow articles or editorials that he personally disagrees with as long as they do not contain anything contrary to faith or morals.

But he would fail in his responsibility as chief teacher of the faithful in his diocese were he to allow in his newspaper priests or lay people, no matter their reputed expertise or however widely their columns are syndicated, whose writings cause confusion about what Catholics are to believe. For example, many diocesan papers have for years given dissenting theologian Fr. Richard McBrien a forum for his heterodox opinions and his snide attacks on Pope John Paul II, but recently some bishops have dropped McBrien's column precisely because it often distorts or undermines those Catholic teachings that the bishop is obliged to uphold.

The questionable content that fills too many diocesan papers has long been a source of concern and frustration to faithful Catholics. The time has come for bishops to make sure that diocesan publications give their readers the solid food of Catholic truth instead of the watery gruel of misinformation and even falsehood.

Q. When priests and bishops have a duty to preach and don't, allowing parishioners to err seriously, there must be some guilt accruing to those clergy. You seemed to write that they have no guilt if through their fault their flock sinned, albeit out of ignorance. Sins of contraception and abortion are an offense against God. — M.T.C., Ireland

A. We can't recall ever having written that clergy bear no guilt for having allowed their flocks to err seriously, and we would strongly disagree with such a statement. We believe that all Catholics, but especially priests and bishops as teachers and shepherds of the faith, are called to carry out such spiritual works of mercy as instructing the ignorant, counseling the doubtful, and admonishing the sinner. In its *Decree on the Ministry and Life of Priests*, Vatican II was very insistent on this:

"Toward all men, therefore, priests have the duty of sharing the gospel truth in which they themselves rejoice in the Lord. And so, whether by honorable behavior among the nations they lead them to glorify God, whether by openly preaching they proclaim the mystery of Christ to unbelievers, whether they hand on the Christian faith or explain the Church's teaching, or whether in the light of Christ they strive to deal with contemporary problems, the task of priests is not to teach their own wisdom but God's Word, and to summon all men urgently to conversion and to holiness" (n. 4).

"In achieving this goal [building up the Church], priests must treat all with outstanding humanity, in imitation of the Lord. They should act toward men, not as seeking to win their favor but in accord with the demands of Christian doctrine and life. They should teach and admonish men as dearly beloved sons, according to the words of the Apostle: 'Be urgent in season, out of season; reprove, entreat, rebuke with all patience and teaching' (2 Tim. 4:2)" (n. 6).

"Priests are defenders of the common good, with which they are charged in the name of the bishop. At the same time, they are strenuous defenders of the truth, lest the faithful be tossed about by every wind of opinion. To their special concern are committed those who have fallen away from the use of the sacraments, or perhaps even from the faith. As good shepherds, they should not cease from going after them" (n. 9).

Regarding an issue such as contraception, Pope Paul VI, in *Humanae Vitae*, declared that the first task of priests "is to expound the Church's teaching on marriage without ambiguity. Be the first to give, in the exercise of your ministry, the example of loyal internal and external obedience to the teaching authority of the Church .... You know, too, that it is of the utmost importance, for peace of consciences and for the unity of the Christian people, that in the field of morals as well as in that of dogma, all should attend to the magisterium of the Church, and all should speak the same language" (n. 28).

The Holy Father said that "to diminish in no way the saving teaching of Christ constitutes an eminent form of charity for souls. But this must ever be accompanied by patience and goodness, such as the Lord himself gave example of in dealing with men. Having come not to condemn but to save, he was intransigent with evil, but merciful toward individuals. In their difficulties, may married couples always find, in the words and in the heart of a priest, the echo of the voice and the love of the Redeemer" (n. 29).

Q. After reading about Bishop Fabian W. Bruskewitz and the excommunications, I went to *Our Sunday Visitor's Catholic Encyclopedia* and read about the two ways excommunication can be incurred. Under canon 1425, one must have a judicial trial. The other is for automatic excommunication, which is the penalty for seven specific offenses. What are the grounds for the excommunications threatened by Bishop Bruskewitz? — B.J., Colorado

A. According to Msgr. Timothy J. Thorburn, chancellor of the Diocese of Lincoln, Nebraska, Bishop Bruskewitz relied on 30 canons in the Code of Canon Law in warning members of his flock that they face excommunication unless they sever all ties with organizations whose principles and policies are "totally incompatible with the Catholic faith."

The proscribed organizations include Call to Action and Call to Action Nebraska, Catholics for a Free Choice, Planned Parenthood, the Hemlock Society, the Society of St. Pius X and its St. Michael the Archangel Chapel, and the Freemasons and its affiliates, DeMolay, Eastern Star, and Rainbow Girls.

The following provisions of canon law were cited by Msgr. Thorburn: 208-210, 212, 221, 223, 375, 381, 383, 386, 391-392, 749, 752-754, 1311, 1313-1320, 1369, 1373-1375, and 1399. Excerpts from several of these canons will demonstrate that Bishop Bruskewitz is on firm canonical ground.

Canon 212 — "The Christian faithful, conscious of their own responsibility, are bound by Christian obedience to follow what the sacred pastors, as representatives of Christ, declare as teachers of the faith or determine as leaders of the Church."

Canon 386 — "The diocesan bishop is bound to present and explain to the faithful the truths of the faith which are to be believed and applied to moral issues .... Through suitable means he is strongly to safeguard the integrity and unity of the faith to be believed while nevertheless acknowledging a rightful freedom in the further investigation of its truths."

Canon 391 — "The diocesan bishop is to rule the particular church committed to him with legislative, executive, and judicial power in accord with the norm of law."

Canon 753 — "Although they do not enjoy infallible teaching authority, the bishops in communion with the head and members of the college [of bishops], whether as individuals or gathered in conferences of bishops or in particular councils, are authentic teachers and instructors of the faith for the faithful entrusted to their care; the faithful must adhere to the authentic teaching of their own bishops with a religious assent of soul."

Canon 1311 — "The Church has an innate and proper right to coerce offending members of the Christian faithful by means of penal sanctions."

Canon 1318 — "A legislator is not to threaten automatic penalties (*latae sententiae*) unless perhaps against certain particularly treacherous offenses which either can result in more serious scandal or cannot be effectively punished by means of inflicted penalties (*ferendae sententiae*); a legislator is not to establish censures, especially excommunication, except with the greatest moderation and only for more serious offenses."

Canon 1369 — "A person who uses a public show or speech, published writings, or other media of social communications to blaspheme, seriously damage good morals, express wrongs against religion or against the Church, or stir up hatred or contempt against religion or the Church is to be punished with a just penalty."

Canon 1373 — "One who publicly either stirs up hostilities or hatred among subjects against the Apostolic See or against an Ordinary on account of some act of ecclesiastical power or ministry, or incites subjects to disobey them, is to be punished by an interdict or by other just penalties."

Canon 1374 — "One who joins an association which plots against the Church is to be punished with a just penalty; one who promotes or moderates such an association, however, is to be punished with an interdict."

Because Bishop Bruskewitz clearly has the right to make laws, and because no *judicial* act has taken place, there is no judicial trial under canon 1425. Those who have been affected by the excommunication can appeal to Rome on the grounds that the law established by the Bishop of Lincoln is unjust, but Msgr. Thorburn thinks that they would have a "most difficult time" demonstrating that they have been treated unjustly, "given the various reprehensible activities of the groups involved."

Q. Are members of proscribed groups who are visiting Lincoln, Nebraska, prohibited from receiving the sacraments there even though they may be members in good standing in their own dioceses? Would this prohibition extend to visiting priests, indeed bishops, who are admitted members of Call to Action? Would such priests be allowed to say Mass or administer sacraments in Lincoln? — Name and State Withheld

A. We contacted Msgr. Timothy Thorburn again, and we thank him for his assistance. Regarding whether members of the proscribed groups visiting Lincoln are prohibited from receiving the sacraments, he said:

"They are not, because of diocesan legislation, prohibited from receiving the sacraments since only subjects of the Diocese of Lincoln would be affected directly by that legislation. However, there may be other reasons, for example, their adherence to schismatic or heretical beliefs, which would prohibit them from receiving the sacraments."

Would visiting priests or bishops who are members of Call to Action be covered by the legislation? No, said Msgr. Thorburn, since they are not subjects of the Diocese of Lincoln. He added, however, that "any Catholic, cleric or lay person, member of Call to Action or not, whose beliefs would conform to the categories of canon 751 [which defines heresy, apostasy, and schism] would incur an automatic (*latae sententiae*) excommunication, as is noted in canon 1364."

He also said that canon 1373 (see the previous question) "would also likely apply to clergy, laity, or religious who come from outside a diocese and engage in the kinds of activities which Call to Action engages in."

Finally, the chancellor said, "priests or bishops who come to the Diocese of Lincoln to participate in activities of any of the groups affected by the extra-synodal legislation of March 19, 1996, would be prohibited from celebrating any sacraments or public acts of worship sponsored by one of those groups."

Q. It has been almost a year since Bishop Fabian Bruskewitz threatened with excommunication those who belong to dissenting groups in the Diocese of Lincoln. How is this situation progressing? — B.G., Utah

A. Diocesan Chancellor Msgr. Timothy Thorburn says that "those Catholics in and of the Diocese of Lincoln, who were aware of the penalty of the ipso facto, *latae sententiae* excommunication which went into effect on May 15, 1996, and nevertheless did not sever ties with the organizations listed as incompatible with the Catholic faith, would have incurred the penalty. Because the penalty is automatic, there is no way to know who had incurred it or who has had the penalty removed by later severing ties with the organizations and receiving absolution from the sin and the censure which was incurred. Please God, many of them have."

Q. What are the proper actions of a Catholic who is unable to move away from a diocese where the bishop appears to be acting contrary to the wishes of the Vatican? Must he or she just grin and bear it? Must they wait for the U.S. Bishops Conference to take some action? Will God's actions provide the only relief? Are they justified in staying away from church when the Mass is plainly not being conducted in accord with Church teaching? — P.A.L., Illinois

A. It is very frustrating and disheartening for faithful Catholics when bishops do not follow the lead of the Holy Father and the magisterium, and our first step must be to pray constantly for the bishop — and for all bishops — that he will be a faithful shepherd. You shouldn't "grin and bear it," but you may have to pray and bear it, remembering that one of the spiritual works of mercy is to bear wrongs patiently.

God will find a way to straighten out the situation, but it may take a long time, and enduring this situation may be a heavy cross for you to carry. Try joining your cross with the one our Savior carried and He will give you the patience and perseverance to bear your cross.

Second, write to your bishop and ask him, in a charitable manner, why he appears to be doing things that are not sanctioned by the Pope and the magisterium. Make sure you have your facts straight. If no satisfactory explanation is given, and the aberrations continue, then take your concerns to the apostolic pro-nuncio in Washington (his address is 3339 Massachusetts Ave., N.W., Washington, DC 20008).

Or you could write to the appropriate congregation in Rome, say, the Congregation for Bishops (Piazza Pio XII 10, 00193 Rome, Italy), or the Congregation for the Doctrine of the Faith (Piazza del S. Uffizio 11, 00193 Rome, Italy), or the Congregation for Divine Worship and the Discipline of the Sacraments (10 Piazza Pio XII 10, 00193 Rome, Italy).

Third, do not stay away from church because the Mass is not being conducted in accord with Church teaching, unless there is clear evidence that the Mass might be invalid, for example, due to invalid matter or form or the lack of a properly deputed priest. Masses that are celebrated illicitly, i.e, contrary to the Church's liturgical rules, are still valid, and you should not deprive yourself of the opportunity to receive our Lord in the Holy Eucharist. Offer up your Holy Communions for a return to sound and reverent liturgies.

Q. What is the current status of the imprimatur? Does it mean that a book contains solid Catholic doctrine? Does it mean its contents are aligned to the teaching of the Pope and the magisterium? Has the Pope made any recent statements about it? — D.P., Wisconsin

A. The word "imprimatur" is Latin for "let it be printed." This is what a bishop says after the person assigned to read a book (the Censor Deputatus or Censor Librorum) has declared that "nothing stands in the way" (*nihil obstat*) of publication of this book.

Canon law (c. 827) says that the approval of the local Ordinary is necessary for the publication of "catechisms and other writings dealing with catechetical formation"; for textbooks dealing with "sacred Scripture, theology, canon law, church history, or which deal with religious or moral disciplines" and are used in elementary, middle, or higher schools; and for "books and other writings which treat of questions of religion or morals" and that are "exhibited, sold, or distributed in churches or oratories."

So an imprimatur is still required in the cases mentioned in canon 827, and we are not aware of the Holy Father having made any statements about this requirement. Is the listing of an imprimatur at the front of a book a certain indication that the book in question is free of doctrinal or moral error? Not always. In fact, there was a situation in New Jersey in 1983 where the Vatican's Sacred Congregation for the Doctrine of the Faith told the Archbishop of Newark to remove the imprimatur from a book because it contained theologically inaccurate teachings. And readers of this reply have undoubtedly found very questionable statements in their children's religion books even though those books had imprimaturs.

However, there has been an encouraging trend in religious education in recent years whereby the bishops of this country have established an Ad Hoc Committee to review catechetical books to make sure that they are in conformity with the *Catechism of the Catholic Church*. The committee's stamp of approval for a series is actually better than an imprimatur since it guarantees that the books in the series contain the major elements of the Catholic faith.

Prior to this time, a book that had received an imprimatur might not contain doctrinal errors, but it might have left out or treated very inadequately such key doctrines as the divinity of Christ and the existence of original sin and actual sin.

As the publisher of the *Catholicism Series*, this writer knows the process well since we went through a very rigorous review of our series and, we are happy to say, obtained the approval of the Ad Hoc Committee, as well as its commendation for our strong emphasis on doctrine and our outstanding fidelity to the teaching office of the Church.

Archbishop Daniel Buechlein of Indianapolis, when he was chairman of the Ad Hoc Committee, spelled out ten of the doctrinal deficiencies found in most of the religion series used in this country since Vatican II (see the 10/8/98 issue of *Origins* for the text of his remarks), and he told religion publishers not to submit any textbooks containing those deficiencies or the books would be sent right back for revision.

In a letter to the publishers, dated December 16, 1998, Archbishop Buechlein also listed "certain terms and usages" that must be eliminated to insure approval of a catechetical work:

"1. *The systematic avoidance of personal pronouns in reference to God.* This often leads to an artificial and awkward repetition of the word God in sentences. It can also lead to circumlocutions that tend to depersonalize God. This is a change required by the necessity to assure Trinitarian theology permeates as much as possible all catechetical materials.

"2. *The use of the term "Hebrew Scriptures" when referring to the Old Testament.* From a Christian perspective there are two testaments which have been traditionally referred to as Old and New. The use of the term Old Testament, as cited in the *Catechism of the Catholic Church*, must be preserved as part of the common language of our faith.

"3. *The use of BCE and CE rather than BC and AD.* Since the materials involved are catechetical in nature, they should reflect that even time has a Christological significance for followers of Jesus. The use of the designations BC and AD are, in our judgment, part of our common language of faith. [BCE means Before the Common Era, and CE the Common Era.]

"4. *The order of reception of first sacraments.* In texts which deal with preparation for First Reconciliation and First Eucharist, it should always be clear what the proper sequence is for the celebration of these first sacraments. This is clearly referenced in paragraph 1457 in the *Catechism*." [That paragraph says that children must go to the Sacrament of Penance before receiving Holy Communion for the first time.]

Q. Some persons think that churches should pay taxes like everyone else. Would you please explain why churches do not pay taxes? — G.A.K., South Dakota

A. There are a lot of entities in our society besides churches that do not pay taxes. For example, schools, colleges, hospitals, and charitable institutions are exempt because they help prepare people to lead productive lives, or assist those in need, or provide a healthy environment for the citizens of a country.

Since churches and other religious institutions are also an asset to society if they help to produce citizens with the moral and spiritual values that will contribute to the well-being of a nation, they too have traditionally been exempt from taxes. This exemption also helps to preserve religious freedom since the power to tax is the power to destroy.

Q. Some of us parishioners strongly suspect mismanagement of church funds. We are given no financial data regarding income, expenditures, etc. What rights do

Catholics have to inspect and even audit the books at the parish office? Is there anything we can do to counter the evasiveness of our pastor? — R.A., New York

A. The Code of Canon Law requires the administrators of parishes, whether clerics or laypersons, to "keep well-ordered books of receipts and expenditures" (canon 1284.7) and to "draw up a report on their administration at the end of each year" (canon 1284.8). Both clerical and lay administrators of parishes are also required "to present the local Ordinary with an annual report" (canon 1287.1) and to "render an account to the faithful" of the money they contribute to the parish (canon 1287.2). Each parish is also required to have a finance council to aid the pastor in the administration of the parish goods (canon 537).

We are not aware of any law giving parishioners the right to inspect or audit the parish books; only the Ordinary of the diocese has that right. The usual process of finding out about parish finances would be to contact the pastor and his finance council, although a good steward should report to his parishioners at least on an annual basis.

If one suspects mismanagement of parish funds, then one ought to bring this first to the attention of the regional vicar or bishop, then to the Ordinary, and then, if the problem is not satisfactorily resolved, to the apostolic pro-nuncio in Washington.

Q. What is the obligation of a Catholic to provide financial support to a parish where the politics and theology of the principal forced my wife and I to remove our children from the parish school? Could this obligation be discharged, at least in part, by financial support for organizations that are faithful to the Holy Father ? What should I say to a priest who, when children told him that only two weeks had elapsed since their last Confession, said that they were "abusing the sacrament" and had "no business being there"? — T.B., Wisconsin

A. While one of the precepts or commandments of the Church says that the faithful are obliged to assist with the material needs of the Church, each according to his own ability (cf. *Catechism of the Catholic Church*, n. 2043), that does not mean that one should give financial support to a parish or school or other Catholic institution whose policies and personnel are not faithful to Church teaching. If withholding financial contributions is the only way to express one's opposition to theological dissent or liturgical abuses or even misuse of funds, then one ought to do precisely that and, as T.B. suggested, channel the contributions to other places and organizations that are truly Catholic.

As for frequent Confession being an "abuse" of the sacrament, we suggest that you politely inform this priest that his opinion is very much contrary to the Church's strong encouragement of frequent recourse to the Sacrament of Penance.

The *Catechism* says that while confession of everyday faults is not strictly necessary, it is "strongly recommended by the Church" [cf. Council of Trent: DS 1680; CIC, can. 988 § 2] because it helps the faithful to form their consciences, "fight against evil tendencies," and let themselves be "healed by Christ and progress in the life of the Spirit" (n. 1458).

Q. I am enclosing an article by our bishop in regard to the "pastoral administrator" of a parish. The article seems to conflict with the Vatican's 1997 *Instruction on Certain Questions Regarding Collaboration of the Non-Ordained Faithful in the Sacred Ministry of Priests*. Also, is a deacon a priest? I don't understand their job potential, and I am confused about the sentence in the instruction that says "deacons cannot be overlooked" in providing pastoral care to a parish with no priest. — B.H., Kansas

A. First of all, deacons are not priests and the reference to them in the Vatican *Instruction* means that they should be the first choice as parish administrators if a priest is not available since they are ordained members of the clergy who have gone through years of study and formation. In addition to transitional deacons, i.e., men who are preparing for the priesthood, there are more than 12,000 men, many of them married, serving as permanent deacons in the United States.

Second, your bishop has defined a pastoral administrator as "a person who is appointed by the bishop to assume the pastoral care of a parish. In such a parish situation, a sacramental/canonical pastor is a priest who would be appointed to assist the pastoral administrator in that particular parish. The priest would be available for the celebration of the sacraments and any other canonical procedures."

In his article in the diocesan paper, the bishop said that the pastoral administrator would have charge of the administration, education, and liturgical schedules of the parish; would attend meetings of various parish councils and committees; and could hire a religious education coordinator, RCIA director, liturgical facilitator, and other persons necessary for the administration of the parish.

The authority cited by the bishop for this administrative position is paragraph two of canon 517 of the Code of Canon Law, which reads as follows:

"If the diocesan bishop should decide that due to a dearth of priests a participation in the exercise of the pastoral care of a parish is to be entrusted to a deacon or to some other person who is not a priest or to a community of persons, he is to appoint some priest endowed with the powers and faculties of a pastor to supervise the pastoral care."

The Vatican *Instruction* also cites canon 517.2, calls it an "exceptional provision," and says that it is to be used "only with strict adherence to conditions contained in it." These conditions are (1) that the provision be invoked where there is a true need and "not for reasons of convenience or ambiguous 'advancement of the laity,' etc.," and (2) that those involved in such collaboration be seen as exercising pastoral care "and not directing, coordinating, moderating, or governing the parish; these competencies, according to the canon, are the competencies of a priest alone."

The *Instruction* says that "because these are exceptional cases, before employing them other possibilities should be availed of, such as using the services of retired priests still capable of such service or entrusting several parishes to one priest or to a *coetus sacerdotum*. In any event, the preference which this canon gives to deacons cannot be overlooked. The same canon, however, reaffirms that these forms of participation in the pastoral care of parishes cannot in any way replace the office of parish priest."

In his article, your bishop also listed the names of five pastoral administrators currently serving in his diocese, along with the names of five priests who are the sacramental/canonical pastors of those parishes. So based on the information you sent to us, we would say that your bishop is following canon law, and we see no apparent conflict with the Vatican *Instruction*.

Q. I was told by the nun who is the pastoral coordinator of our church that her job is not administrator, but spiritual director/shepherd. She said that the priest who

"presides" over the Mass is only there to consecrate the bread and wine and that she will be giving most of the homilies, with the priest giving them occasionally. We see the priest sitting quietly in a chair for most of the Mass. Is she correct? — L.S., Virginia

A. No, she is most certainly not correct, and your priest is very wrong to allow her to usurp his liturgical functions. To deal with just these kinds of abuses, eight Vatican offices, on August 15, 1997, issued the *Instruction* mentioned in the previous reply. Regarding the situation mentioned by L.S., the Vatican document had this to say:

• "For a community of the faithful to be called a church, and indeed to truly be a church, it cannot be guided according to political criteria or those of human organizations. Every particular church owes its guidance to Christ since it was he who fundamentally linked apostolic mission to the Church, and hence no community has the power to grant that mission to itself, or to delegate it .... The ministerial priesthood is therefore necessary for a community to exist as 'church' .... Indeed, were a community to lack a priest, it would be deprived of the exercise and sacramental action of Christ, the head and pastor, which are essential for the very life of every ecclesial community. Thus the ordained priesthood is absolutely irreplaceable."

• "It is unlawful for the non-ordained faithful to assume such titles as *pastor, chaplain, coordinator, moderator,* or other such similar titles which can confuse their role and that of the pastor, who is always a bishop or priest."

• "The homily, being an eminent form of preaching ... also forms part of the liturgy. The homily, therefore, during the celebration of the Holy Eucharist must be reserved to the sacred minister, priest or deacon, to the exclusion of the non-ordained faithful, even if these should have responsibilities as 'pastoral assistants' or catechists in whatever type of community or group. This exclusion is not based on the preaching ability of sacred ministers nor their theological preparation, but on that function which is reserved to them in virtue of having received the Sacrament of Holy Orders."

• "It is a grave abuse for any member of the non-ordained faithful to 'quasi preside' at the Mass while leaving only that minimal participation to the priest which is necessary to secure validity."

Q. At a local hospital, we have a married ex-priest acting as chaplain. Is this allowed? — D.J.B., Michigan

Q. I thought only ordained persons could be chaplains. Is this another of the regulations that has been cancelled by the wannabees? — D.M., Massachusetts

A. Technically speaking, there is no such thing as an "expriest" since the permanent character conferred by the Sacrament of Holy Orders can never be taken away. It would be more accurate to say that a priest has been returned to the lay state, after which process he is prohibited from celebrating Mass or confecting the sacraments, although he could hear the Confession of a person in danger of death.

To answer the specific questions, neither a laicized priest nor a non-ordained person is allowed to act as a chaplain because a chaplain must be a priest in possession of all the faculties of a priest. According to canon 564 of the Code of Canon Law, "a chaplain is a priest to whom is entrusted in a stable manner the pastoral care, at least in part, of some community or particular group of the Christian faithful, to be exercised in accord with universal and particular law."

The reason why a chaplain must be a priest is spelled out in canon 566, which says that "a chaplain in virtue of his office enjoys the faculty to hear the Confessions of the faithful entrusted to his care, to preach the word of God to them, to administer Viaticum and the Anointing of the Sick, and to confer the Sacrament of Confirmation on those who are in danger of death."

Chapter 4

Salvation and Ecumenism

Q. The husband of my niece will be converting to the Catholic faith this fall. Could you list some well-known authors who have also converted to Catholicism, along with specific titles of their books that might show the rationale for their conversion? — C.R.M., Minnesota

A. Gladly. Such books would include Scott and Kimberly Hahn's *Rome Sweet Home* (Ignatius Press), Martin Barrack's *Second Exodus* (Magnificat Institute Press), Thomas Howard's *Evangelical Is Not Enough* (Ignatius), David Currie's *Born Fundamentalist, Born Again Catholic* (Ignatius), Stephen Ray's *Crossing the Tiber* (Ignatius), *Surprised by Truth* (Basilica Press) and *Surprised by Truth 2* (Sophia Institute Press), 26 conversion stories edited by Patrick Madrid, and Timothy Drake's *There We Stood, Here We Stand* (1st Books Library), the stories of 11 converts from Lutheranism.

Q. How does any Catholic or non-Catholic benefit from ecumenism? Since the Church has always exhorted us to promote the Catholic faith among non-Catholics, and they have always been welcome in the Catholic Church, what new thing does ecumenism add? Do you have a good definition of ecumenism? — C.J.K., California

A. Ecumenism, said the Second Vatican Council, "means those activities and enterprises which, according to various needs of the Church and opportune occasions, are started and organized for the fostering of unity among Christians. These are: first, every effort to eliminate words, judgments, and actions which do not respond to the condition of separated brethren with truth and fairness and so make mutual relations between them more difficult; then, 'dialogue' between competent experts from different churches and communities" (*Decree on Ecumenism*, n. 4).

Simply stated, then, the specific aim of ecumenism is to overcome the obstacles that stand in the way of unity among Christians. The restoration of complete Christian unity is the will of

Christ Himself, who prayed at the Last Supper "that all may be one as you, Father, are in me and I in you; I pray that they may be [one] in us, that the world may believe that you sent me" (John 17:21).

Q. In his encyclical *Ut Unum Sint*, Pope John Paul reminds Catholics engaged in theological dialogue that: (1) there is a "hierarchy of truths," that is, not all doctrines have equal relationship to the foundations of Christian belief, and (2) there is a difference between doctrine and the formulation of doctrine. I find this disconcerting since I was reared to accept the totality of the Deposit of Faith as given through the magisterium. To question one aspect was to question the very authority which was the basis for all other aspects of our faith.

Is the current pick-and-choose Catholicism so prevalent today among those suffering from *acedia* [indifference to God and to the practice of one's religion] to be the norm once ecumenism has achieved its goal? Have I been a compliant fool all these years? Can you provide me with a list of this hierarchy of truths?

The second point is also rather scary. Is old doctrine to be reformulated so vaguely that all participants in the dialogue can leave the table satisfied that their differing beliefs find expression therein? — J.R.D., New York

A. We have read *Ut Unum Sint* ("That All May Be One") and don't find anything in that papal document to justify your concerns. In fact, we find statements there that should put your fears to rest. But before getting to those statements, let's make it clear what is meant by a "hierarchy of truths." This phrase *does not mean* that some doctrines are truer than others or that we may ignore certain doctrines or pay little attention to them. What it does mean was explained by the Vatican's Sacred Congregation for the Clergy in its 1971 *General Catechetical Directory*:

"In the message of salvation there is a certain hierarchy of truths which the Church has always recognized when it composed creeds or summaries of the truths of faith. This hierarchy does not mean that some truths pertain to faith itself less than others, but rather that some truths are based on others, as to a higher priority, and are illumined by them."

The *Directory* went on to illustrate this explanation by spelling out the hierarchy of doctrines to which Catholics are to give assent:

"These truths may be grouped under four basic heads: the mystery of God the Father, the Son, and the Holy Spirit, Creator of all things; the mystery of Christ the Incarnate Word, who was born of the Virgin Mary, and who suffered, died, and rose for our salvation; the mystery of the Holy Spirit, who is present in the Church, sanctifying it and guiding it until the glorious coming of Christ, our Savior and Judge; and the mystery of the Church, which is Christ's Mystical Body, and in which the Virgin Mary holds the pre-eminent place."

When Pope John Paul used this phrase in *Ut Unum Sint* (n. 37), he was not urging a watering-down of Catholic belief. In the previous paragraph, in fact, he said that Vatican II had envisioned theologians engaged in ecumenical dialogue as "standing fast by the teaching of the Church" and as clearly presenting "the whole body of doctrine."

The Holy Father said that full communion with those of other religions "will have to come about through the acceptance of the whole truth into which the Holy Spirit guides Christ's disciples. Hence all forms of reductionism or facile 'agreement' must be absolutely avoided."

As for your second concern, that old doctrines might be re-worded so vaguely that all participants in the dialogue would come away satisfied, Pope John Paul ruled that out. He said that while "doctrine needs to be presented in a way that makes it understandable to those for whom God himself intends it" (n. 19), this does not mean "altering the Deposit of Faith, changing the meaning of dogmas, eliminating essential words from them, accommodating truth to the preferences of a particular age, or suppressing certain articles of the Creed under the false pretext that they are no longer understood today. The unity willed by God can be attained only by the adherence of all to the content of revealed faith in its entirety" (n. 18).

The Holy Father said that "in matters of faith, compromise is in contradiction with God, who is truth. In the Body of Christ, 'the way, and the truth, and the life' (John 14:6), who could consider legitimate a reconciliation brought about at the expense of the truth?" (*Ibid.*).

Some Catholics, including some theologians, may pick and choose among which truths to accept, but Pope John Paul II is not one of them.

Q. I have read quotations from Popes affirming the necessity of formal adherence to the Catholic Church in order to attain salvation, but what happens to godly non-Catholic Christians who die? — J.A.W., Pennsylvania

Q. Can other people besides Catholics get to Heaven? A Catholic convert friend has asked me what is meant by "there is no salvation outside the Catholic Church." Would you please explain this statement? — G.W., California, L.W., Missouri, and J.G., Arizona

A. We have responded in the past to similar questions by stating official Catholic teaching as expressed by Popes, councils, and the *Catechism of the Catholic Church*, but the questions keep coming up, so it is time to address them again. From previous experience we are well aware that some readers do not agree with the current teaching of the Catholic Church on salvation and believe that it contradicts or waters down previous teaching. What follows is a good-faith effort to outline the doctrine as the Church herself understands it (which is what really counts), not as it is privately interpreted by certain individuals and groups, and to explain the apparent contradictions between the current teaching and expressions of that teaching in centuries gone by.

(1) Who belongs to the Catholic Church? The *Catechism* says that fully incorporated members of the Church are those who possess the spirit of Christ, accept all the means of salvation given to the Church, and are bound together by professing the one faith received from the Apostles, celebrating Mass and the sacraments, and maintaining communion with the Supreme Pontiff and the bishops who constitute the Church's government. The *Catechism* warns in n. 837, however, that one who is fully incorporated but who does not "persevere in charity is not saved. He remains indeed in the bosom of the Church, but in 'body' not in 'heart' [*LG* 14]."

(2) Non-Catholic Christians, who believe in Christ and who have been properly baptized but who do not profess the Catholic faith in its entirety and have not preserved unity or communion with the successor of Peter, says the *Catechism* in n. 838, "are put in a certain, although imperfect, communion with the Catho-

lic Church [*UR* 3]." That is why they don't have to be re-baptized when they become Catholics. They are already related or connected to the Church, albeit in an imperfect way, through a trinitarian Baptism.

(3) According to the *Catechism*, the statement "Outside the Church there is no salvation" means that "all salvation comes from Christ the Head through the Church which is his Body" (n. 846). The *Catechism* says Vatican II taught that "the Church, a pilgrim now on earth, is necessary for salvation [*LG* 14; cf. *Mk* 16:16; *Jn* 3:5]," that Christ is the one mediator and way of salvation, and that He is present to us in His Body which is the Church.

It says that men and women enter the Church through Baptism as one passes through a door, and that a person "could not be saved" if he knew that the Catholic Church was founded as necessary by God through Christ but either refused to enter it or to remain in it.

The *Catechism* makes clear (n. 847) that this does not refer to those who, "through no fault of their own," do not know the Gospel of Christ or His Church, "but who nevertheless seek God with a sincere heart and, moved by grace, try in their actions to do his will as they know it through the dictates of their conscience — those too may achieve eternal salvation [*LG* 16; cf. DS 3866-3872]."

(4) What the *Catechism* is talking about here is when a person is truly ignorant of the necessity of Baptism or the necessity of the Catholic Church for salvation. Since Christ died for everyone, the *Catechism* says, Catholics must believe that the Holy Spirit offers to all the possibility of attaining Heaven.

It says that those who are ignorant of the Gospel of Christ and His Church, but who seek the truth and do the will of God as they understand it, can be saved. The supposition is that such persons would have desired Baptism explicitly if they had known that it was necessary for salvation (cf. n. 1260).

This is not saying that all those who are sincerely ignorant of the Gospel of Christ and His Church are automatically saved. They must still seek the truth and do the will of God as they understand it, and God does put in each person's heart a natural law that calls him to love good and avoid evil.

Such persons might not be culpable for sins against faith (their ignorance of the Gospel), but they might very well be culpable for other sins (abortion, adultery, theft, hatred, racism, etc.) that would keep them out of Heaven.

(5) The teaching that persons not baptized with water can be saved is not some new doctrine that was dreamed up by Vatican II. St. Thomas Aquinas said in the 13th century that "a person can obtain salvation without being actually baptized, on account of the person's desire for Baptism, which desire is the outcome of faith that works through charity, whereby God, whose power is not tied to visible sacraments, sanctifies a person inwardly" (*Summa Theologiae*, III, q. 68, a. 2).

(6) In the 16th century, the Council of Trent said that the transition of a person from being a son of Adam to an adopted son of God "cannot take place without the bath of regeneration or the desire of it (*eius voto*)."

(7) In the 19th century, Blessed Pope Pius IX said that "those who labor in invincible ignorance concerning our most holy religion and who, assiduously observing the natural law and its precepts which God has inscribed in the hearts of all, and being ready to obey God, live an honest and upright life can, through the working of the divine light and grace, attain eternal life, since God, who clearly sees, inspects, and knows the mind, the intentions, the thoughts and habits of all, will, by reason of his supreme goodness and kindness, never allow anyone who has not the guilt of willful sin to be punished by eternal sufferings" (*Quanto Conficiamur Moerore*).

Since "it is also a perfectly well known Catholic dogma that no one can be saved outside the Catholic Church," the Holy Father continued in his 1863 encyclical, "those who are contumacious against the authority and the definitions of that same Church, and who are pertinaciously divided from the unity of that Church and from Peter's successor, the Roman Pontiff, to whom the custody of the vineyard has been committed by the Savior, cannot obtain eternal salvation."

(8) In other words, Pius IX was saying that while salvation is possible for those outside the Church who are not culpable for their ignorance, salvation is not possible for those who are hardened against the Church and who stubbornly and obstinately refuse to submit to the authority of the Roman Pontiff. This warning could also be applied to certain Catholics who are rebelling against the Church's authoritative explanation of outside the Church there is no salvation and who even go so far as to insist that the Chair of Peter is vacant and that Pope John Paul II is a false Pope and a "blatant heretic."

Q. In a recent reply, you said it was "nonsense" to believe that only Catholics can be martyrs. But the Council of Florence in 1442 said that "no one, no matter what alms he may have given, not even if he were to shed his blood for Christ's sake, can be saved unless he abide in the bosom and unity of the Catholic Church." Please explain. — A.B., Illinois

Q. I get the impression from reading paragraphs 839-842 of the *Catechism of the Catholic Church* that Jews and Muslims can be saved without converting and actually being baptized. Isn't it still a Church teaching that these people must convert and be baptized to have any hope of being saved? — B.B., Georgia

Q. I read that the Council of Florence in 1442 infallibly taught that "none of those who are not within the Catholic Church, not only pagans, but Jews, heretics, schismatics, can ever be partakers of eternal life, but are to go into the eternal fire prepared for the devil and his angels." How does one reconcile this in light of the teachings of the Second Vatican Council? — S.G., Ohio

A. Continuing a discussion that began in the previous reply, we will again state the Church's authoritative teaching on the conditions for salvation for those who are not full members of the Church and then offer some background for that teaching.

(1) According to the *Catechism*, "the Church has always held the firm conviction that those who suffer death for the sake of the faith without having received Baptism are baptized by their death for and with Christ. This *Baptism of blood*, like the *desire for Baptism*, brings about the fruits of Baptism without being a sacrament" (n. 1258).

This is not a new teaching. St. Augustine, writing in *City of God* in the fifth century, said:

"Those who, though they have not received the washing of regeneration, die for the confession of Christ — it avails them just as much for the forgiveness of their sins as if they had been washed in the sacred font of Baptism. For He that said, 'If anyone is not reborn of water and the Spirit, he will not enter the kingdom of heaven' [John 3:5], made an exception for them in that other statement in which He says no less generally, 'Whoever confesses me before men, I too will confess him before my Father, who is in heaven' [Matt. 10:32]."

(2) Can this be reconciled with the statement of the Council of Florence? Yes, for that Council was talking about heretics and schismatics who were stubbornly resistant to the unity of the Church, hostile to correction, and therefore culpable for their heresy, schism, or unbelief. But not all heretics are culpable, said Augustine. He explained that if their "false and perverted" views were held "without obstinate ill will" and may have originated not from their own "bold presumption" but "from parents who had been led astray and had lapsed," then they "are not to be rated among heretics" as long as they "seek the truth with careful industry and are ready to be corrected when they have found it."

(3) The impression that B.B. got from reading nn. 839-842 of the *Catechism*, that Jews and Muslims can be saved without being baptized with water, is accurate. That is what the Church teaches, and Catholics are obliged to assent to that teaching. The Jewish people are related to the Catholic Church, the *Catechism* explains, because they were given the covenants and the promises and it was from them that Christ was born " 'according to the flesh' [*Rom* 9:4-5]."

Muslims are also included in God's plan of salvation, says the *Catechism* (n. 841), because they " 'profess to hold the faith of Abraham, and together with us they adore the one, merciful God, mankind's judge on the last day' [*LG* 16; cf. *NA* 3]."

(4) Those who are in heresy or schism because they were brought up from childhood with certain false information and prejudices, have no awareness that they are in heresy and schism, and sincerely seek the truth and try with the grace of God to lead a good and moral life cannot be held blameworthy for their spiritual status.

To put themselves at risk of eternal damnation, such persons must be, in the words of Pope Pius IX in 1863, "contumacious against the authority and the definitions" of the Church and "pertinaciously divided from the unity of that Church and from Peter's successor, the Roman Pontiff" (*Quanto Conficiamur Moerore*).

This also helps to explain the real meaning of the Council of Florence's apparent condemnation of all those who are "not within the Catholic Church." People are connected to the Church in the various ways mentioned above, and it is these connections that make their salvation possible. The *Catechism* is very clear, however, in stating that Catholics still have the duty of evangelizing non-Catholics.

It says (n. 848) that although God, in way ways known only to Him, can lead those who are ignorant of the Gospel, through no fault of their own, to that faith which is necessary to please Him, "the Church still has the obligation and also the sacred right to evangelize all men [*AG* 7; cf. *Heb* 11:6; 1 *Cor* 9:16]."

(5) Another way to help us understand what was said at Florence is to consider the historical conditions in the middle of the 15th century. At the time of that Council, it was thought that all people had heard and had understood the Gospel message and, therefore, those who deliberately refused to respond to that message by joining the Catholic Church couldn't possibly be sincere and must be excluded from Heaven. But that kind of thinking disappeared with the discovery five decades later of the New World, with its millions of inhabitants to whom Christ had not been preached.

That new knowledge changed the Church's understanding of "outside the Church there is no salvation." The dogma didn't change, but the Church's way of explicating it did. That is why there have been no more categorical statements like that of Florence since 1442. In the last 500 years, in the statements of Trent, Pius IX, Vatican II, John Paul II, and the *Catechism*, we have moved from what Fr. Francis Sullivan calls a "presumption of guilt" in the Middle Ages to a "presumption of innocence" today. Those interested in a detailed history of this doctrine should get a copy of Fr. Sullivan's book *Salvation Outside the Church?* (Paulist Press).

(6) As we have tried to make clear in this and the previous reply, the Church has taught for centuries that salvation is possible under certain conditions for those who are not fully incorporated into the Catholic Church. This is an authoritative magisterial teaching of the Church, and all Catholics are bound to accept it or to place themselves in heresy.

(It is ironic that those who are so sure of heresy and schism on the part of others are so oblivious to their own rejection of Church doctrine and their own separation from the Roman Pontiff. Private interpretations of dogma may be typical of some religious denominations, but such private judgments are not open to Catholics.)

(7) In a 1949 letter to Archbishop Richard J. Cushing of Boston, the Vatican's Holy Office issued this warning to those Catholics who continue to call into question the Church's understanding of outside the Church there is no salvation:

"Therefore, let them who in grave peril are ranged against the Church seriously bear in mind that after 'Rome has spoken' they cannot be excused even by reasons of good faith. Certainly, their bond and duty of obedience to the Church is much graver than that of those who as yet are related to the Church 'only by an unconscious desire.'

"Let them realize that they are children of the Church, lovingly nourished by her with the milk of doctrine and the sacraments, and hence, having heard the clear voice of their Mother, they cannot be excused from culpable ignorance and, therefore, to them applies without any restriction that principle: submission to the Catholic Church and to the Sovereign Pontiff is required as necessary for salvation."

Q. Regarding no salvation outside the Catholic Church, can anyone in the West, where the truths of Catholicism have been well taught, claim that they are outside the Church through no fault of their own? — J.S., Illinois

A. In his encyclical *Redemptoris Missio*, Pope John Paul said that it is necessary to keep two truths together, "namely, the real possibility of salvation in Christ for all mankind and the necessity of the Church for salvation" (n. 9).

He went on to explain how those who are not formal members of the Catholic Church can be saved:

"The universality of salvation means that it is granted not only to those who explicitly believe in Christ and have entered the Church. Since salvation is offered to all [cf. 1 Timothy 2:4], it must be made concretely available to all. But it is clear that today, as in the past, many people do not have an opportunity to come to know or accept the Gospel revelation or to enter the Church. The social and cultural conditions in which they live do not permit this, and frequently they have been brought up in other religious traditions.

"For such people salvation in Christ is accessible by virtue of a grace which, while having a mysterious relationship to the Church, does not make them formally part of the Church but enlightens them in a way which is accommodated to their spiritual and material situation. This grace comes from Christ; it is the result of his sacrifice and is communicated by the Holy Spirit. It enables each person to attain salvation through his own free cooperation.

"For this reason, the [Second Vatican] Council, after affirming the centrality of the paschal mystery, went on to declare that 'this applies not only to Christians but to all people of good will in whose hearts grace is secretly at work. Since Christ died for everyone, and since the ultimate calling of each of us comes from God and is therefore a universal one, we are obliged to hold that the Holy Spirit offers everyone the possibility of sharing in this paschal mystery in a manner known to God' " (n. 10).

Can anyone in the Western world today be truly ignorant of the truths of Catholicism and its claims to be the vehicle of salvation? Absolutely, including some nominal Catholics who never learned these truths and claims because of the deplorable state of religious education in the decades after Vatican II.

But this category would also include people who are sincere adherents of other religions or who, in the words of John Paul, have been prevented from knowing these truths by the social and cultural conditions in which they find themselves. But let's let God worry about who is truly ignorant and who isn't because only He knows the inner workings of people's hearts.

Q. In his book *Crossing the Threshold of Hope*, Pope John Paul writes that "men cannot be saved who do not want to enter or remain in the Church, knowing that the Catholic Church was founded by God through Christ as a necessity" (*Lumen Gentium* 14). Does this mean that all Protestants, Jews, Muslims, etc., will go to Hell? — F.C.R., Texas

A. No, that's not what the Holy Father means when he quotes from the Vatican II document *Lumen Gentium*. The key words in the quote are "knowing that the Catholic Church was founded by God through Christ as a necessity." If a person, whether Catholic or non-Catholic, truly knows and understands this and still refuses either to enter the Catholic Church or to remain in her, then that person cannot get to Heaven.

On the other hand, if a person is invincibly ignorant of the necessity of the Catholic Church for salvation, then that person can still be saved. Pope John Paul explained how in his book (p. 136):

"The [Vatican] Council speaks of membership in the Church for Christians and of being related to the Church for non-Christian believers in God, for people of good will (cf. *Lumen Gentium* 15-16). Both these dimensions are important for salvation, and each one possesses varying levels. People are saved *through* the Church, they are saved *in* the Church, but they are always saved *by the grace of Christ*.

"Besides formal membership in the Church, the sphere of salvation can also include other forms of relation to the Church. Paul VI expressed this same teaching in his first encyclical, *Ecclesiam Suam*, when he spoke of the various circles of the dialogue of salvation (cf. *Ecclesiam Suam* 101-117), which are the same as those indicated by the Council as the spheres of membership in and of relation to the Church. This is the authentic meaning of the well-known statement 'Outside the Church there is no salvation.' "

These teachings were reaffirmed on September 5, 2000 by the Sacred Congregation for the Doctrine of the Faith in a document entitled *Dominus Iesus*. Among other things, the document said that the Catholic Church is the "universal sacrament of salvation," and that while the Church accords other religions of the world a "sincere respect," the truth that Christ founded the Catholic Church to be "the instrument for the salvation of all humanity ... rules out in a radical way that mentality of indifferentism characterized by a religious relativism which leads to the belief that 'one religion is as good as another.' If it is true that the followers of other religions can receive divine grace, it is also certain that objectively speaking they are in a gravely deficient situation in comparison with those who, in the Church, have the fullness of the means of salvation" (n. 22).

However, since "God 'desires all men to be saved and come to the knowledge of the truth' (1 Tm. 2:4); that is, God wills the salvation of everyone through the knowledge of the truth," the document says that those outside the Church can find their salvation "in the truth. Those who obey the promptings of the Spirit of truth are already on the way of salvation. But the Church, to whom this truth has been entrusted, must go out to meet their desire so as to bring them the truth. Because she believes in God's universal plan of salvation, the Church must be missionary" (*Ibid.*).

Q. What is the significance of *Dominus Iesus*? How does it differ from the ideas of Feeneyism? — L.R., New York

A. *Dominus Iesus* sets forth Catholic doctrine on the indispensable role of Jesus Christ and the Catholic Church in the salvation of humanity. The declaration was intended to refute current theories that Jesus is only one way of salvation and that "one religion is as good as another."

Thus, the declaration says that "it must be firmly believed that, in the mystery of Jesus Christ, the incarnate Son of God, who is 'the way, and the truth, and the life' (Jn. 14:6), the full revelation of divine truth is given .... Therefore, the theory of the limited, incomplete, or imperfect character of the revelation of Jesus Christ, which would be complementary to that found in other religions, is contrary to the Church's faith" (nn. 5-6).

"Just as there is one Christ," says the declaration, "so there exists a single body of Christ, a single bride of Christ: 'a single Catholic and apostolic Church.' Furthermore, the promises of the Lord that he would not abandon his Church (cf. Mt. 16:18; 28:20) and that he would guide her by his Spirit (cf. Jn. 16:13) mean, according to Catholic faith, that the unicity and the unity of the Church — like everything that belongs to the Church's integrity — will never be lacking" (n. 16).

The document says that " 'the Christian faithful are therefore not permitted to imagine that the Church of Christ is nothing more than a collection — divided, yet in some way one — of churches and ecclesial communities; nor are they free to hold that today the Church of Christ nowhere really exists and must be considered only as a goal which all churches and ecclesial communities must strive to reach.' In fact, 'the elements of this already-given Church exist, joined together in their fullness in the Catholic Church and, without this fullness, in the other communities' " (n. 17).

Dominus Iesus also reiterates the dogma that the Catholic Church "is necessary for salvation" (n. 20). While the late Fr. Leonard Feeney and his followers interpreted this to mean that one must be formally and visibly a member of the Church in order to be saved, the declaration declares that "this doctrine must not be set against the universal salvific will of God (cf. 1 Tm. 2:4); 'it is necessary to keep these two truths together, namely, the real possibility of salvation in Christ for all mankind and the necessity of the Church for this salvation' " (n. 20).

Q. As to the ecumenical movement, why can't Masses be said for the millions of those who have died or who

have left the Catholic faith because of the actions of Martin Luther and Henry VIII? — E.P., California

A. There is no prohibition on having Masses said for any person who has died, whether it occurred centuries ago or last week. In every Mass that is celebrated every day in every part of the world, there are prayers offered for all those who have died "marked with the sign of faith" or "who have gone to their rest in the hope of rising again" or "who have left this world in your friendship" or "who have died in the peace of Christ" and "whose faith is known to you alone." If the person or persons are already in Heaven or, God forbid, in Hell, then the fruits of those Masses will be applied to the souls in Purgatory.

Q. Many good Christians have a conversion, develop a personal relationship with Jesus, and are "baptized in the Holy Spirit." Their lives change, they are admirable Christians, and live happy, effective Christian lives. They seem to have the best of the Christian faith without belonging to the one visible Church founded by Jesus Christ. How is this possible? Doesn't Jesus want everyone to come to the full knowledge of God's revelation and join His Church? — A.D.L., Virginia

A. Certainly Jesus wants everyone to be full members of His Church; after all, He prayed at the Last Supper "that all may be one/ as you, Father, are in me, and I in you;/ I pray that they may be [one] in us,/ that the world may believe that you sent me" (John 17:21). But some Christians come to the Catholic Church by a roundabout route, as described, for example, in Patrick Madrid's books *Surprised by Truth* and *Surprised by Truth 2*, which contain 26 conversion stories that illustrate some of the amazing ways in which the Lord works in our lives.

We have to remember, in the words of the *Catechism* (n. 818), that " 'all who have been justified by faith in Baptism are incorporated into Christ; they therefore have a right to be called Christians, and with good reason are accepted as brothers in the Lord by the children of the Catholic Church' [*UR* 3 § 1]."

The *Catechism* (n. 819) echoes Vatican II in saying that " 'many elements of sanctification and of truth' [*LG* 8 § 2] are found outside the visible confines of the Catholic Church: 'the written Word of God; the life of grace; faith, hope, and charity, with the other interior gifts of the Holy Spirit, as well as visible elements' [*UR* 3 § 2; cf. *LG* 15]."

It points out that the Holy Spirit uses these Christian churches as means of salvation, but adds that their power derives from the "fullness of grace and truth that Christ has entrusted to the Catholic Church" (*Ibid.*).

We have in recent years seen a great many fervent Protestants come into the Catholic Church because they realized that there could be found the fullness of God's truth and the great gift of Christ Himself in the Holy Eucharist. These are not frivolous conversions, but rather ones which were carefully thought out over many years and which, in some cases, caused great hurt to family members and put some former Protestant pastors in considerable economic difficulty. They were willing to make these great sacrifices because they knew they were finally coming to their true home in the Catholic Church.

Q. I am enclosing a short column written in our church bulletin by the permanent deacon of my parish. Would you please comment as to the validity of the Church inviting a non-Catholic spouse to receive the Eucharist on special occasions? The column appeared while our pastor was on vacation, and no follow up has appeared. — P.A.T., Michigan

A. In his column, Deacon Gene said that in order to enrich the faith experience of those in interfaith marriages, "the Catholic Church does invite the non-Catholic to share in the Eucharistic liturgy and receive the Eucharist on special occasions. Those occasions can be a wedding, an anniversary, any Church holy day, a special occasion like a funeral in the family or at Baptisms, Confirmations, and First Communion Masses.

"These occasions for reception of the Eucharist at a Catholic Eucharistic liturgy presuppose that the non-Catholic Christian believes essentially the same as the Catholic regarding the Real Presence of Christ in the Holy Eucharist and that Jesus is really and truly present in the bread and wine and that upon reception has truly received the Body and Blood of Christ."

As we have noted in the past, the reception of Communion by non-Catholic Christians is permitted only in exceptional circumstances, and not on the various occasions mentioned by Deacon Gene. He actually cited just one of the six conditions listed in canon 844 of the 1983 Code of Canon Law — that the person "manifest Catholic faith" in the Eucharist — although he stated that condition in three different ways.

He neglected to mention that the person must be in "danger of death ... or other grave necessity," that he have the permission of the diocesan bishop, that he be unable to approach a minister of his own church, that he ask for the Eucharist on his own initiative, and that he be "properly disposed."

These conditions were reiterated in the *Ecumenical Directory* issued in 1993 by the Pontifical Council for Promoting Christian Unity (cf. nn. 130-131). In a section of the *Directory* dealing with mixed marriages, the Pontifical Council said that "because of the problems concerning Eucharistic sharing which may arise from the presence of non-Catholic witnesses and guests, a mixed marriage celebrated according to the Catholic form ordinarily takes place outside the Eucharistic liturgy."

If the diocesan bishop, "for a just cause," permits the celebration of the Eucharist at a mixed marriage, the *Directory* says, "Eucharistic sharing can only be the exception" and only if the norms mentioned in canon 844 are observed.

Deacon Gene does no service to the cause of ecumenism by ignoring the strict conditions laid down by the Church for sharing the Holy Eucharist.

Q. Does the Old Catholic Church, which separated from Rome over 100 years ago, have valid sacraments? Are Roman Catholics allowed to attend its services and to receive Communion? — Name Withheld, Pennsylvania

A. Old Catholics refers to several sects, including the Church of Utrecht, which broke with Rome in 1724, and the Polish National Catholic Church in the United States, which came into existence about a century ago. They have a valid priesthood and valid sacraments, but they disagree with the Catholic Church on a number of issues, including papal primacy and papal infallibility, clerical celibacy, indulgences, veneration of saints, the use of sacramentals, mixed marriages, and obligatory confession of one's sins to a priest.

For more on Old Catholics, see pages 216-222 of the *Handbook of Denominations in the United States* (Abingdon Press), which was compiled by the late Frank S. Mead and revised by Samuel S. Hill.

As to whether Roman Catholics can attend Old Catholic services and receive Communion, here are the pertinent guidelines that were approved by the National Conference of Catholic Bishops on November 14, 1996:

"Eucharistic sharing in exceptional circumstances by other Christians requires permission according to the directives of the diocesan bishop and the provisions of canon law (canon 844.4). Members of the Orthodox Churches, the Assyrian Church of the East, and the Polish National Catholic Church are urged to respect the discipline of their own churches. According to Roman Catholic discipline, the Code of Canon Law does not object to the reception of Communion by Christians of these churches (canon 844.3)."

Considering the exceptional circumstances mentioned in the previous reply, we think that it would be most unusual for a Roman Catholic to be in the situation of "necessity" or "genuine spiritual advantage" that canon law requires in order for one to receive Communion in a Polish National Catholic church.

Q. My sister who left the Catholic Church and is now a practicing Jew has invited me to take part in a Seder service in her home. When I told her that the Catholic Church does not allow such participation, she accused the Church of anti-Semitism and told me to fax her proof of this prohibition. Can you help me find something about this? — K.D., California

A. As many readers know, a Seder or Passover meal celebrates God's deliverance of the Israelite people from slavery in Egypt. The family ritual includes Scripture readings, music, and food and wine that recall the bitterness of slavery and the sweetness of freedom.

K.D. also posed the same question to Fr. Hugh Barbour, Prior of St. Michael's Abbey in Silverado, California, and Censor Librorum for the Diocese of Orange. Here is what he told K.D. about her decision not to attend the Seder:

"Fr. Barbour confirmed our decision and stated that, as Catholics, we should not actively participate in any Seder (unless it is bishop-approved, as in a Catholic church), and we are even more compelled to not participate because it is the Seder of a convert, and to do so would be to condone her action. He also pointed out that the 'go-but-don't-participate' rule, while still in effect, is basically null and void because a Seder is all about active participation. He recommended not going at all, but attending a dinner party with her another night."

Q. In a column about Christianity and the Holocaust, the writer said that "under the leadership of Pope John Paul II, the Church has repealed its old view of Judaism as a fossil religion, totally supplanted by Christianity, and now recognizes the Jews' continuing covenant with the Almighty." Is this statement true? — J.W.H., Florida

A. No, it is not. The Catholic Church never held the view that Judaism was "a fossil religion" that had been "totally supplanted by Christianity." The Church believes that Jesus established a new and everlasting Covenant, but that the Old Covenant was never repealed because, in the words of St. Paul, "God's gifts and his call are irrevocable" (Romans 11:29). Not only have Jews and Christians always been linked to each other through Abraham, our "father in faith," but we have other spiritual bonds as well, as Vatican II noted in its *Declaration on the Relationship of the Church to Non-Christian Religions* (n. 4):

"For the Church of Christ acknowledges that, according to the mystery of God's saving design, the beginnings of her faith and her election are already found among the patriarchs, Moses, and the prophets. She professes that all who believe in Christ, Abraham's sons according to faith (cf. Gal. 3:7), are included in the same patriarch's call, and likewise that the salvation of the Church was mystically foreshadowed by the chosen people's exodus from the land of bondage.

"The Church, therefore, cannot forget that she received the revelation of the Old Testament through the people with whom God in his inexpressible mercy deigned to establish the Ancient Covenant. Nor can she forget that she draws sustenance from the root of that good olive tree onto which have been grafted the wild olive branches of the Gentiles (cf. Rom. 11:17-24). Indeed, the Church believes that by his cross Christ, our peace, reconciled Jew and Gentile, making them both one in himself (cf. Eph. 2:14-16)."

Not only were Christ and His mother Mary Jews, the Council said, but "the Church recalls too that from the Jewish people sprang the Apostles, her foundation stones and pillars, as well as most of the early disciples who proclaimed Christ to the world. As Holy Scripture testifies, Jerusalem did not recognize the time of her visitation (cf. Lk. 19:44), nor did the Jews in large number accept the gospel; indeed, not a few opposed the spreading of it (cf. Rom. 11:28). Nevertheless, according to the Apostle, the Jews still remain most dear to God because of their fathers, for he does not repent of the gifts he makes nor of the calls he issues (cf. Rom. 11:28-29).

"In company with the prophets and the same Apostle, the Church awaits that day, known to God alone, on which all peoples will address the Lord in a single voice and 'serve him with one accord' (Soph. 3:9; cf. Is. 66:23; Ps. 65:4; Rom. 11:11-32)."

For more insights on Catholic-Jewish relations, see Martin K. Barrack's book *Second Exodus* (Magnificat Institute Press). Mr. Barrack is a convert from Judaism to Catholicism.

Q. My Catholic niece married a Jewish man at an ecumenical service that was presided over by a rabbi and a priest. The husband had promised before marriage to respect his wife's wishes to raise their children as Catholics, but had a change of heart when a son was born and did not attend the Baptism. At the ceremony, which was attended only by Catholics, the priest, apparently thinking that some Jews were present, never used words like "Jesus," "Christ," or "Catholic," but used the word "Lord" throughout.

He did baptize the infant in the name of the Father, Son, and Spirit. Were the wedding and baptismal ceremonies in conformity with the Church's understanding of ecumenism? Do we avoid acknowledging Jesus Christ so as not to offend our Jewish brethren? Is a baptism valid where belief in Jesus is not professed? — J.R.D., New York

A. It is possible for a Catholic and a Jew to be married in an ecumenical service presided over by a priest and a rabbi, provided that the proper dispensations have been obtained by the Catholic party. Baptism into the Catholic Church is valid if there is the pouring of water and recitation of the words, "I baptize you in the name of the Father, and of the Son, and of the Holy Spirit." So from what you have told us the wedding and the Baptism were valid.

However, the priest had to perform some major liturgical gymnastics — and he was dead wrong in doing so — to avoid using the words, "Jesus," "Christ," and "Catholic" in the baptismal ceremony. In point of fact, he would have had to omit most of the ceremony to keep Christ out of it.

For example, the priest is supposed to welcome the child and claim him "for Christ our Savior by the sign of his cross." He begins the intercessions by asking "our Lord Jesus Christ to look lovingly on this child." He anoints the child "with the oil of salvation in the name of Christ our Savior."

The priest also asks the parents and godparents to profess their faith in "Jesus Christ" and in "the Holy Catholic Church," and concludes: "This is our faith. This is the faith of the Church. We are proud to profess it, in Christ Jesus our Lord." The priest anoints the child with chrism "as Christ was anointed Priest, Prophet, and King," clothes him with a white garment signifying that he has been "clothed in Christ," and presents the parents and godparents with a lighted candle as a sign that "this child of yours has been enlightened by Christ."

It is one thing to be ecumenically sensitive at a wedding, where representatives of two faiths are present and presiding, but it is very wrong to emasculate the rite of initiation of a child into the Catholic Church. This priest's actions remind us of Christ's warning: "If anyone in this faithless and corrupt age is ashamed of me and my doctrine, the Son of Man will be ashamed of him when he comes with the holy angels in his Father's glory" (Mark 8:38).

Q. I have difficulty understanding n. 841 of the *Catechism of the Catholic Church*. I thought that Islam's belief centered around the God Allah and not the God of the Bible. Can you help explain this? — J.H.G., Florida

Q. I read the statements you quoted from Vatican II and the *Catechism* about the monotheism of Islam and efforts to reach an understanding with Muslims, but I still have difficulty grasping this. Can you direct me to a book or tract that would help? — B.A.L., Florida

A. The *Catechism* section says that the plan of salvation "'also includes those who acknowledge the Creator, in the first place amongst whom are the Muslims; these profess to hold the faith of Abraham, and together with us they adore the one, merciful God, mankind's judge on the last day' [*LG 16*; cf. *NA 3*]."

The Muslims are a monotheistic religion. They call their Supreme Being Allah and believe that their sacred book, the Koran, contains revelations from God to the prophet Muhammad (or Mohammed), who lived from 570 to 632.

A book that would be helpful in understanding the Muslims

is *Answering Islam* by Norman L. Geisler and Abdul Saleeb (Baker Books). This 336-page book discusses the history and beliefs of Islam and provides the Christian response.

Also helpful would be the chapter on Muhammad in Pope John Paul II's book *Crossing the Threshold of Hope* (Random House). While noting that the situation of Christians in Muslim-controlled countries "is sometimes terribly disturbing," and that the "fundamentalist attitudes" of Islam "make reciprocal contacts very difficult," the Holy Father nevertheless said that "the Church remains always open to dialogue and cooperation."

He made clear, however, that there is a huge abyss between Islam and Christianity:

"Whoever knows the Old and New Testaments, and then reads the Koran, clearly sees the process by which it completely reduces Divine Revelation. It is impossible not to note the movement away from what God said about himself, first in the Old Testament through the Prophets, and then finally in the New Testament through his Son. In Islam all the richness of God's self-revelation, which constitutes the heritage of the Old and New Testaments, has definitely been set aside.

"Some of the most beautiful names in the human language are given to the God of the Koran, but he is ultimately a God outside of the world, a God who is only Majesty, never Emmanuel, God-with-us. Islam is not a religion of redemption. There is no room for the Cross and the Resurrection. Jesus is mentioned, but only as a prophet who prepares for the last prophet, Muhammad. There is also mention of Mary, his Virgin Mother, but the tragedy of redemption is completely absent. For this reason not only the theology but also the anthropology of Islam is very distant from Christianity" (p. 89 of large-print edition).

In spite of this great divide, the Pope still paid tribute to the Muslims' fidelity to prayer. He said that "the image of believers in Allah who, without caring about time or place, fall to their knees and immerse themselves in prayer remains a model for all those who invoke the true God, in particular for those Christians who, having deserted their magnificent cathedrals, pray only a little or not at all" (p. 90).

Q. Why should we Roman Catholics be called Christians like all the Protestants who do not believe all that

we do, but may have attributes that are Christian? Luther, Calvin, Henry VIII were heretics against Christ's teachings. They contradicted transubstantiation, indulgences, Confession, male priests only, divorce, abortion, *ad infinitum.* Why can't we be identified as the true Church and follower of all Christ's teachings? — J.M., Portugal

A. First of all, the word "Christian" was originally applied to those Catholics living in Antioch shortly after the time of Christ (cf. Acts of the Apostles 11:26), so Catholics have the oldest and most legitimate claim to the word. Second, Catholics were the only Christians until the Orthodox Church split with Rome in the 11th century and Protestants began forming their churches in the 16th century. Third, persons who are baptized, believe in Jesus Christ as Lord and Savior, and accept the essential beliefs of the Christian faith are entitled to be called Christians.

Finally, both the Second Vatican Council and the *Catechism of the Catholic Church* have declared the Catholic Church to be the true Church. For example, the *Catechism* says that the only Church of Christ is that Church which Jesus founded on Peter and commissioned him and the other apostles to rule (cf. n. 816).

It says that Christ's Church, " 'constituted and organized as a society in the present world, subsists in (*subsistit in*) the Catholic Church, which is governed by the successor of Peter and by the bishops in communion with him' [*LG* 8 § 2]."

Q. At an ecumenical service, a Lutheran minister asked, "If Jesus said, 'This is my body' and 'This is my blood,' isn't it?" Does this mean that Lutherans believe in the Real Presence? — C.R., Pennsylvania

A. Lutherans believe in *consubstantiation*, which means that Christ is really present in the bread and wine, but they believe that the substance of the bread and wine also remains on the altar. Catholics, on the other hand, believe in *transubstantiation*, which means that the whole substance of the bread is changed into the Body of Christ, and the whole substance of the wine is changed into the Blood of Christ.

While the accidents of bread and wine are still visible to the senses, Catholics believe that the bread and wine have ceased to exist and no longer remain on the altar.

Q. I have heard recently that the Pope has admitted that the Catholic Church was wrong all these years about

justification and the Church now agrees with the Lutherans that salvation is by faith alone. Has the Vatican come out with any such statement and, if so, where can I get a copy? — Name Withheld, Nebraska

Q. I am confused about the news that the Roman Catholic Church and the Lutheran Church resolved many of the major issues that led to Martin Luther's break from the Catholic Church. What critical issues were resolved, and what issues remain contentious? — D.M., New York

Q. Several weeks ago, the news was that Catholics and Lutherans finally agreed on the meaning of justification. Looks like Luther was right all along, and we were wrong. In the enclosed newspaper article, Fr. Raniero Cantalamessa, who preaches to the Pope and the papal household, says that salvation comes from faith alone. This is in total opposition to what St. Paul and St. James say. Sure is getting tougher to remain a true Roman Catholic. — B.P.B., Ontario

A. Regarding the centuries-old controversy over justification, the Catholic Church (represented by the Sacred Congregation for the Doctrine of the Faith and the Pontifical Council for Promoting Christian Unity) and the Lutheran World Federation announced on June 25, 1998, that they had reached "a consensus on basic truths concerning the doctrine of justification." Paragraph 15 of the declaration said that "together we confess: By grace alone, in faith in Christ's saving work and not because of any merit on our part, we are accepted by God and receive the Holy Spirit, who renews our hearts while equipping and calling us to good works."

Notice it says that we are saved by "grace alone," not by "faith alone" And we think that B.P.B. misread Fr. Cantalamessa, for he was quoted as saying that "we are justified freely by the blood of Christ alone, and not by our own accomplishments." This is the Catholic understanding of justification (cf. *Catechism of the Catholic Church*, nn. 1987-1995).

It must also be pointed out that reaching a consensus on fundamental truths regarding justification does not mean that Catholics and Lutherans agreed on everything or that they have eliminated all differences. At a press conference following publication of the declaration, Edward Cardinal Cassidy of the Pontifical Council said that there are still "major difficulties ... concerning the justified person as sinner," the understanding of baptism as taking away all sin, and "the interior transformation that takes place in the justified person."

Furthermore, he said, there are also other "questions of varying importance which need further clarification." The Cardinal mentioned in particular "the relationship between the word of God and Church doctrine, as well as ecclesiology, authority in the Church, ministry, the sacraments, and the relation between justification and social ethics."

So the theological dialogue between Catholics and Lutherans that began in 1967 continues, and will continue until the two sides reach precise agreement, and not just a consensus, on the basic truths of Christianity. The joint declaration is not the final word, said Cardinal Cassidy, but rather "an outstanding achievement of the ecumenical movement and a milestone on the way to the restoration of full, visible unity among the disciples of the one Lord and Savior Jesus Christ."

For the text of the joint declaration, along with the transcript of Cassidy's press conference and the official Catholic response to the joint declaration, see the July 16, 1998 issue of *Origins*. The issue is available by writing to the Catholic News Service, 3211 4th St., N.E., Washington, DC 20017.

Q. When my brother approached his pastor on whether it was okay to marry in a Lutheran church, he was told that there was little difference between our two religions on marriage. Since then, he has been taking instructions there. Can you recommend any books that might help to bring him back to the Catholic Church? — M.S., Michigan

A. First of all, it was very wrong for your brother's pastor to tell him that there is little difference between the two religions on marriage, when in fact there are major differences on this and many other issues, as noted in the previous reply.

Since your brother presumably knows a lot more about the Lutheran Church now than he did before, and presumably didn't know very much about the Catholic Church when he started taking Lutheran instructions, see if you can get him to read the *Catechism of the Catholic Church*. Perhaps if he studied that excellent and comprehensive summary of Catholic beliefs, he would recognize that the fullness of God's truth resides in the Catholic Church and come to realize that he will miss out on a lot in the Lutheran Church, including the opportunity truly to receive Jesus in the Holy Eucharist.

As for books that might dissuade him from joining the Lutheran Church, you could recommend several books on Martin Luther and the origins of Lutheranism: two by Philip Hughes: *A Popular History of the Catholic Church* and *A Popular History of the Reformation*, the *Facts About Luther* by Msgr. Patrick O'Hare, and *Roots of the Reformation* by Karl Adam.

Most helpful of all, however, might be Timothy Drake's *There We Stood, Here We Stand* (1st Books Library). This book contains the testimonies of 11 former Lutherans who converted to the Catholic Church and the reasons for their conversions.

Q. A long while back I heard that when Martin Luther's mother was dying, she asked him if she should die as a Lutheran or as a Catholic. He reportedly replied: "It's nice to live as a Lutheran, but better to die as a Catholic." Is this story based on fact? — C.P., California

A. When we asked a knowledgeable friend, C.J.H. of Massachusetts, about this, he expressed doubt that Luther ever made such a statement because of his hatred of all things Catholic once he had launched his revolution. Another reason to doubt that Luther had such a conversation with his mother, says C.J.H., is that Luther once described his mother's brutality to him as a child in these terms:

"On account of an insignificant nut, [she] beat me till the blood flowed, and it was this harshness and severity of life I led with [my parents] that forced me subsequently to run away to a monastery and become a monk" (Luther's *Tabletalk*, A.D. 1567, fol. 314a).

C.J.H. also suggested that the alleged statement may in fact have been made not by Luther, but by Theodore de Beze, John Calvin's successor as the head of Protestant Geneva. He cited as evidence three anecdotes taken from a book by Fr. Edouard Hugon entitled *Hors de l'Eglise point de salut?* ("Outside the Church No Salvation?"):

(1) When de Beze's mother was approaching death, she asked him: "In which Church may I truly be saved?" He replied: "The Protestant Church is the easiest, but the Catholic Church is the most secure."

(2) When St. Francis de Sales visited de Beze, he asked him:

"Can one be saved in the Catholic Church?" De Beze left the room for 15 minutes to think about the question and then returned saying, "I answer you affirmatively. One can be saved in the Catholic Church and there is no doubt that she is the Mother Church."

(3) A few days before his own death, one of his maidservants asked de Beze which religion she ought to follow in order to be saved. The Protestant leader responded, weeping, that the faith of the Catholic Church was the best.

Q. Can a Lutheran minister be a celebrant at a Catholic Mass? — D.P.B., Wisconsin

Q. Is it proper to have a Lutheran minister preach at a Sunday Mass after the Gospel, while a Catholic bishop is preaching at a Lutheran church? — G.S., California

A. No to both questions. Only a Catholic priest can celebrate the Holy Sacrifice of the Mass and, while ministers of other Christian communities may preach at a *non-sacramental* liturgical service in a Catholic church, and may "on exceptional occasions and for a just cause" read from the Scriptures during a Catholic Mass, they may not preach after the Gospel.

Q. I recently attended a Mass of Christian Burial for a non-Catholic who had attended Mass with his Catholic wife and children. Two priests officiated and a Lutheran minister did the readings and gave a talk after Communion. The minister said that the deceased was a member of his Lutheran parish and that "it is not important where you worship, but who you worship." Is it now allowed for a Catholic priest to offer a Mass of Christian Burial for non-Catholics? It is possible for the bishop of the diocese to grant a dispensation for this? — W.G., North Dakota

A. Yes to both questions. Canon 1183 of the 1983 Code of Canon Law says: "In the prudent judgment of the local ordinary, ecclesiastical funeral rites can be granted to baptized members of some non-Catholic church or ecclesial community, unless it is evidently contrary to their will and provided their own minister is unavailable."

In the situation described by W.G., it would appear that the deceased was a baptized member of a Christian community and that he was not opposed to burial from a Catholic church. So the first two conditions of canon law were apparently satisfied. However, canon 1183.3 says that such a funeral Mass cannot occur unless the person's own minister is unavailable. But not only was the person's minister available, he took an active part in the Mass! So we would conclude that permission for a Mass for this man should not have been granted, if indeed such permission was sought from the bishop.

It should also be noted that the revised *Ecumenical Directory* of 1993, also known as *Principles and Norms of Ecumenism*, states that "the reading of Scripture during a Eucharistic celebration in the Catholic Church is to be done by members of that Church. On exceptional occasions and for a just cause, the bishop of the diocese may permit a member of another church or ecclesial community to take on the task of reader."

Was this Mass the "exceptional occasion" envisioned by the *Directory*, or was there a "just cause" to have a Lutheran minister proclaim the readings? It doesn't seem so.

The dangers of this kind of misguided ecumenism were further illustrated when the Lutheran minister was given the opportunity to state that it really doesn't matter where you worship. Of course it matters, since Jesus is really and truly present, Body and Blood, Soul and Divinity, only in a church where a Catholic priest has the power to confect the Eucharist.

Q. What are the major differences between Catholics and Congregationalists? — V.F.M., Minnesota

A. According to William J. Whalen's book *Separated Brethren* (Our Sunday Visitor), Congregationalism came to America with the Pilgrims and was the established state religion in New Hampshire, Massachusetts, and Connecticut until the early 1800s. It remained primarily a New England institution until 1957 when many of its constituencies merged with the Evangelical and Reformed Church to form the United Church of Christ. However, several hundred Congregational churches refused to take part in the merger and continued their independent existence.

Congregationalists believe that the Bible is the sole rule of faith, and that Christ is the only head of the church. They believe in complete autonomy for the local congregation and refuse to recognize the authority of any bishop, synod, or council over them. They also refuse to bind their members to any particular creed or statement of beliefs.

"A few Congregational churches could be characterized as fundamentalist," said Whalen, "but most taught a mixture of liberalism, modernism, sentimentalism, social gospel, and Unitarianism." He said that their worship service has been shortened from three hours to one and that "an altar, cross, and candles, cassock, surplice, and stole which would have scandalized their Puritan ancestors are accepted by modern Congregationalists."

Q. My wife is a very devout Catholic and, for the sake of unity with her, I left the Orthodox Church last year and became a Catholic. However, I have brought certain aspects of Orthodoxy with me and am unwilling to give them up. Not being in unity with the Catholic Church in a number of doctrines, should I be participating in the supreme act of unity — the Eucharist? I'm physically in the Catholic Church, but my heart is in Orthodoxy and I am uncomfortable. What is your advice? — J.O., Missouri

A. In his letter, J.O. mentioned three specific things about the Catholic Church that he cannot accept. They are matters about which Catholics and Orthodox have disagreed for almost a thousand years, and much greater minds than ours have not been able to work them out despite many years of dialogue. However, we will try to state the Catholic position on these issues.

(1) J.O. finds himself unable to recite the *filioque* clause in the Nicene Creed, which says that the Holy Spirit proceeds from the Father "and the Son." These three words, which J.O. calls "blatant heresy," were not in the original Nicene Creed, but were approved by Pope St. Leo I in 447 and gradually admitted into the Latin Rite liturgy between the eighth and 11th centuries.

The *filioque* clause was affirmed by the Councils of Lyons II (1274) and Florence (1439), but the Orthodox churches do not accept these councils as legitimate and maintain to this day that the Holy Spirit proceeds from the Father *through* the Son. For the reasoning behind the Catholic position, see nn. 246-248 of the *Catechism of the Catholic Church*.

In his 1995 encyclical *Ut Unum Sint*, Pope John Paul said that "the Catholic Church desires nothing less than full communion between East and West," and he said that the task of bringing this about is "equally incumbent" on both the Catholic Church and the Orthodox Church (n. 61).

(2) J.O. cannot accept the supremacy of the Pope, whom he sees as "a leader among the Apostles but not over the Apostles." He says that "at the Council of Jerusalem, James presided and

made the final judgment, not Peter." This James was the immediate leader of the Jerusalem community, but he was not one of the 12 Apostles. And even if he were, a look at chapter 15 of the Acts of the Apostles shows that it was Peter's intervention that ended the lengthy debate over whether Gentile converts ought to be required to undergo the Mosaic rite of circumcision. After Peter had spoken, "the whole assembly fell silent" (Acts 15:12).

Thus was Peter's supreme authority recognized and accepted by the early Church, as also indicated, for example, by Peter's presiding over the election of a successor to Judas (Acts 1:15-26), by his acting as spokesman for the Apostles on Pentecost (Acts 2:14-41), and by his meting out punishment to Ananias and Sapphira (Acts 5:1-10).

That Peter was to be more than just a leader among the Apostles is demonstrated by our Lord's words to him: "Simon, Simon! Remember that Satan has asked for you, to sift you all like wheat. But I have prayed for you that your faith may never fail. You in turn must strengthen your brothers" (Luke 22:31-32). Note that Jesus prays only for Peter. Why? Because on his shoulders alone was to rest the burden of governing the Church. It was to Peter alone that Jesus said, "Feed my lambs .... feed my sheep" (John 21:15-17).

(3) J.O. also contends that when Christ said, "You are Peter, and on this rock I will build my Church," He used a masculine and a feminine for rock, meaning that He was talking about Peter's faith and not about Peter himself as the rock. The explanation is that when Jesus spoke these words to Peter in Aramaic, He said, "You are *Kepha*, and on this *kepha* I will build my Church" (Matthew 16:18).

While you can use *kepha* in both places in Aramaic, the nouns must have masculine and feminine endings when the passage is translated into Greek. It's all right to use *petra* for rock, but since *petra* is feminine, it must be changed to the masculine *Petros* (an already existing Greek word meaning a small stone) for Peter's name. Actually, the common Greek word for a small stone is *lithos*, so those who translated the Bible into Greek should have rendered Matthew 16:18, "You are *Lithos*, and on this *petra* I will build my Church."

But that would have distorted the point Matthew was trying to make, namely, that Peter was the rock or foundation of the Church Jesus was establishing. The French have it correctly, using the word *pierre* both for Peter's name and for the rock.

For a more detailed discussion of this, see chapter 2 of Patrick Madrid's book *Pope Fiction*.

Editor's Note: Regarding the *filioque* dispute, J.L. of New York says that the Catholic Church also professes that "the Holy Spirit proceeds through the Son." He cites as evidence the following statement from Vatican II's *Decree on the Church's Missionary Activity* (n. 2):

"As the principle without principle from whom the Son is generated, and from whom the Spirit proceeds through the Son, God [the Father] in his great and merciful kindness freely creates us and, moreover, graciously calls us to share in his life and glory."

J.L. says further that "the expression 'through the Son,' dear to some of the Eastern Fathers of the Church, is regarded as equivalent to the procession of the Holy Spirit 'from the Son' (*filioque*) used by the Latin Fathers. Moreover, those Eastern Orthodox who still regard the *filioque* as heretical profess the *temporal* mission of the Holy Spirit 'through the Son,' but — and this is the essential point — deny the Holy Spirit *eternal procession* through or from the Son.

"Fortunately, there are Eastern Orthodox theologians who no longer regard Catholic teaching that the Holy Spirit proceeds from or through the Son as a dogmatic barrier to the reunion of the churches."

As to the propriety of including the *filioque* clause in the Latin text of the Nicene-Constantinopolitan Creed recited or sung at Mass, J.L. says that we should not forget the following quotation from the Council of Florence (1439):

"We further define that it was for the purpose of declaring the truth and under stress of necessity at the time that those words 'and the Son' were added to the Creed by way of explanation, both lawfully and with good reason."

For more on this issue, J.L. recommends consulting the Pontifical Council for Promoting Christian Unity's "The Greek and Latin Traditions Regarding the Procession of the Holy Spirit," which appeared in the September 20, 1995 issue of *L'Osservatore Romano*.

Q. A friend of mine, a permanent deacon, told me of a couple, one a devout Catholic and the other a devout Anglican, who were married in the presence of clergy from both faiths. Neither one wants to convert, so they have agreed to attend the Catholic church one Sunday and the Anglican church the next Sunday. When I questioned this arrangement, the deacon said that keeping them together was more important than where they attended church. What do you think? — J.E.E., California

A. We think that this arrangement implies that the Catholic and Anglican churches are equally true and that it doesn't matter which one they attend. However, such religious indifferentism is contrary to Catholic belief. If the Catholic party is truly devout, she would want to attend her own church every week to receive Jesus in the Holy Eucharist. Furthermore, how can she square her absence every other week with the Church's precept requiring attendance at Mass in a Catholic church each Sunday? And we wonder how long a couple with mixed feelings about something as important as religion will be able to stay together.

Q. Is there any difference between the Anglican Church and the Episcopal Church? Henry VIII started the Episcopal Church in England and yet it is referred to as the Anglican Church. Also what is the difference between the High Episcopalian Church and the Low Episcopalian Church? — L.H. Wisconsin

A. The Anglican Church or Church of England was started by King Henry VIII in 1534 when he refused to submit to papal authority. Anglicans who came to America during the colonial period (the first Anglican liturgy was celebrated in Jamestown, VA in 1607) became independent of the Church of England and formed the Protestant Episcopal Church by adopting a new constitution and Book of Common Prayer at a general convention held in 1789. The Episcopal Church is part of the worldwide Anglican Communion.

American Episcopalians reflect the whole spectrum of Anglicanism, ranging from "High Church" to "Low Church" to "Broad Church." A formal liturgy that is quite similar to the Roman Catholic rite and belief in the traditional doctrines of Christianity characterize the "High Church" movement, while "Low Church" resembles evangelical Protestantism in its simple liturgical style and its adherence to morality and doctrine, and

"Broad Church" is often recognized by its rather broad or loose interpretation of doctrine and moral practice.

There are also "Anglo-Catholics" who agree with many Roman Catholic doctrinal beliefs and devotional practices and are moving closer to reunion with Rome. Many have already converted to the Catholic Church in response to the Episcopal Church's ordination of women and public promotion of abortion, divorce, euthanasia, and homosexuality.

Q. Our eldest daughter married a practicing Mormon some 25 years ago, and their four children all were baptized and raised in the LDS-Mormon Church. My daughter says that Mormons do not accept Christ as God, nor do they consider the Holy Spirit as a deity in any way, but a priest told me the Catholic Church recognizes Mormon baptism as valid. I cannot understand, regardless of the proper wording used at the pouring of water or immersion in water, if a religion does not accept the triune God, how this rite could be acceptable by the Catholic Church as valid. — J.C.F., Montana

A. This is not as far-fetched as it seems if you remember that anyone, even a non-believer, can confer baptism in an emergency, provided that they use the proper matter and form and that they intend to do what the Church intends.

But on the question of Mormon beliefs and practices, we recommend two books — *Inside Mormonism: What Mormons Really Believe* and *When Mormons Call: Answering Mormon Missionaries at Your Door* — both published by Catholic Answers and authored by Isaiah Bennett, a Catholic priest who converted to Mormonism and was an active member of the Church of Jesus Christ of Latter-Day Saints for two years before returning to the Catholic Church. He taught at the Mormon Institutes of Religion and knows well from the inside the errors of Mormonism.

First of all, while Catholics believe that the three Persons of the Blessed Trinity are co-equal and co-eternal, and that there never was a point at which one or the other of these Persons did not exist as God, we learn from Bennett's two books that Mormon theology considers Jesus to be God, but a lesser God than the Father, and the Holy Spirit is lower still.

According to the book *Mormon Doctrine*, by Bruce R. McConkie, Jesus was begotten in the flesh through intercourse between God the Father and the Virgin Mary. McConkie says:

"God the Father is a perfected, glorified, holy Man, an immortal Personage. And Christ was born into the world as the literal Son of this Holy Being; he was born in the same personal, real and literal sense that any mortal son is born to a mortal father. There is nothing figurative about his paternity; he was begotten, conceived, and born in the normal and natural course of events, for he is the Son of God, and that designation means what it says" (p. 742).

In his book *The Seer*, Orson Pratt says that "the fleshly body of Jesus required a Mother as well as a Father. Therefore, the Father and Mother of Jesus, according to the flesh, must have been associated together in the capacity of Husband and Wife: hence the Virgin Mary must have been, for the time being, the lawful wife of God the Father" (pp. 158-159).

The Holy Ghost, according to Joseph Fielding Smith, was created at some point in the distant past and "is the third member of the Godhead. He is a Spirit, in the form of a man .... As a spirit personage the Holy Ghost has size and dimensions. He does not fill the immensity of space, and cannot be everywhere present in person at the same time" (*Doctrines of Salvation*, 1:38).

As for the validity of Mormon baptism, the Vatican's Sacred Congregation for the Doctrine of the Faith, in a letter dated March 31, 1992, said that while there may be irregularities in individual cases, and each case should be carefully examined, "there are insufficient grounds to change the current practice" of not contesting the validity of Mormon baptism.

However, in June 2001, the Congregation, with the approval of Pope John Paul II, published a document stating that the Catholic Church does not recognize the validity of Mormon baptism. According to an article in *L'Osservatore Romano*, the Congregation found no problem with the matter of the sacrament — water — since the Mormons baptize by immersion, a practice that the Catholic Church also accepts.

Regarding the form of the sacrament, however, the article said that "the similarities with the formula used by the Catholic Church are, at first glance, evident, but in reality they are only apparent. There is not in fact an underlying doctrinal coincidence. There is not a true invocation of the Trinity because the Father, Son, and Holy Spirit, according to the Church of Jesus Christ of Latter-Day Saints, are not three Persons in which a sole divinity subsists, but three gods who form one divinity."

Furthermore, the article says, the Catholic belief that Baptism remits original sin "is not accepted by the Mormon Church, which denies the existence of this sin and therefore baptizes only people who have the use of reason, who are at least eight years old, excluding the mentally handicapped."

Q. I have Jehovah's Witnesses come frequently to my door, and they distress me with their superficial arguments against the Trinity and the divinity of Jesus. Can you help me in this matter? — M.C., Oregon

A. For information on how to deal with Jehovah's Witnesses, and to answer their arguments, see William Whalen's two books *Faiths for the Few* and *Strange Gods* (both published by Our Sunday Visitor), Fr. Albert Nevins' *Strangers at Your Door* (OSV), Jason Evert's *Answering Jehovah's Witnesses* (Catholic Answers), and *Index of Watchtower Errors*, edited by David A. Reed. This last book is also available from Catholic Answers (P.O. Box 199000, San Diego, CA 92159).

Q. I am a family physician and several of my patients are Jehovah's Witnesses who refuse to receive blood transfusions because of their religious convictions; presumably they would also refuse transfusions for their children should the occasion arise. It has come to my attention that secular courts generally honor adults who, because of religious convictions, refuse to receive medically necessary treatments, but these same courts generally override the rights of parents to refuse treatment for their minor children. What is the Catholic understanding of this ethical dilemma? — J.R.T., New York

A. One of the best places for answers to questions about medical ethics is the National Catholic Bioethics Center, 159 Washington St., Boston, MA 02135 (www.ncbcenter.org). Its monthly publication *Ethics & Medics* offers the Catholic perspective on moral issues in the health and life sciences.

According to the June 1987 issue of this publication, there are over half a million Jehovah's Witnesses in the United States who do not accept blood transfusions because they believe that certain passages in the Bible prohibit such procedures. The courts, as J.R.T. noted, have generally respected the religious convictions of adult Witnesses and have declined to order blood transfusions. But when a minor child is involved, the courts have ordered tranfusions on the grounds that parents have an obligation to promote their child's basic right to life and health.

The position of the Catholic Church on this ethical dilemma is similar to that of the courts. When a J.W. tells a Catholic physician that allowing a blood transfusion would be contrary to religious beliefs, said Msgr. Orville N. Griese, S.T.D., J.C.D, "such an individual must be reminded of the risk involved for herself or himself and family if the transfusion is not given and death ensues. If all efforts at persuasion fail, however, it would be in violation of that person's right to religious freedom if the transfusion nevertheless is administered."

Griese said that "the situation is quite different if that Witness of Jehovah is a pregnant mother, or if the patient in urgent need of a blood transfusion is not the mother, but a young child of a Jehovah's Witness family. In both cases, the protesting Jehovah's Witness parent is in violation of his or her objectively serious obligation to provide ordinary care and protection for the child (born or unborn).

"If all efforts at persuasion fail, and such cases go to court, the contemporary trend is to uphold the Witness of Jehovah's right to religious freedom except in situations where there is conflict with the rights of the unborn infant or an infant after birth. The right to life of such infants takes precedence over the right of the mother to religious freedom."

For additional insights into this matter, see pp. 328-331 and 832-836 of Germain Grisez's book *Difficult Moral Problems* (Franciscan Press).

Q. Are Roman Catholics and Masons in any "degree" compatible? — C.V.M., New Jersey

A. No, they are not compatible. Both the Sacred Congregation for the Doctrine of the Faith, in 1983, and the U.S. Catholic Bishops, in 1985, said that the principles of Freemasonry are "irreconcilable with the Church's doctrine," that those Catholics "who knowingly embrace such principles are committing a serious sin," and that membership in Masonic associations is forbidden to Catholics.

Writing in the September 1996 issue of *Homiletic & Pastoral Review*, Msgr. William B. Smith explained the Church's stand:

"Masons as Masons accept the fatherhood of God, the brotherhood of man, and the immortality of the soul; but the inspiration of the Bible, the unique claims of Jesus Christ, the authority and teaching role of the Church, and the sacraments as means of grace, these are 'particular opinions' they are asked to keep to themselves and not disturb the brothers in the lodge.

"Perhaps a religious naturalism is better than no belief at all, but for the professing Christian this is a retreat from the Gospel. Freemasonry clearly rejects dogma and the possibility of absolute truth. The inspiration of the Bible and the divinity of Christ cannot be periodic lay-asides for believing Catholics. When revealed doctrines are relegated to the harmless status of private opinion, will it or not, one contributes further to the endemic relativism that John Dewey so much fostered in education and Oliver Wendell Holmes advanced in jurisprudence."

For more information on this subject, see William Whalen's book *Christianity and American Freemasonry* (Our Sunday Visitor), Paul Fisher's book *Behind the Lodge Door* (TAN), and Pope Leo XIII's encyclical on Freemasonry entitled *Humanum Genus*.

Q. During the Christmas holidays, TV documentaries try to explain away the Virgin birth, the star, and the Magi by saying that these beliefs are found in ancient pagan cultures. These programs say that the early Christians who wanted to do away with pagan practices spread the version of the Christmas story that we know today and even picked December 25th because it was a pagan holiday. Can you tell me how to answer these allegations? — M.J.A., Florida

A. Just because certain beliefs found in pagan cultures have been given a Christian significance does not mean that they are suspect. It is true that the Catholic Church transformed the Roman feast of Sol Invictus into a celebration of the birth of our Lord, but what's wrong with leading people from worshiping the Unconquered Sun to worshiping the Unconquered Son of God? As John Henry Newman pointed out in his *Essay on the Development of Christian Doctrine*, many things of pagan origin — the use of temples, incense, candles, holy water, processions, blessings, vestments, images, the ring in marriage — were "sanctified by their adoption into the Church" (p. 369).

These examples show, said Karl Keating in *Catholicism and Fundamentalism* (Ignatius Press), that "even paganism had some truth mixed in with its error. Christianity took those elements of truth, removed erroneous associations so that they ceased to be pagan, and made use of the purified truth the better to express Christian notions. Christianity gave new meanings to old things, and in the process the pagan connections ceased" (p. 150).

Keating also said that "we should expect the true religion to be a fulfillment of, but not a complete contradiction of, mankind's earlier stabs at religious truth. After all, each ancient religion had something true in it, even if what was true was buried under much that was false and even pernicious.

"On the positive side, ancient religions were remote preparations for Christ's coming, which occurred in the 'fullness of time,' when mankind had taken itself about as far as it could go on its own. We should expect that the religion that is the fullness of truth, coming in the 'fullness of time,' would incorporate the good points of earlier religions while rejecting their errors" (p. 163).

Q. If a non-Catholic Christian lives in the state of mortal sin, how does this person get back into the state of grace? And if this person dies with mortal sin on his soul, will he go to Hell or Purgatory? Most non-Catholic Christians are ignorant of mortal sin and venial sin, so will God in His infinite mercy let these souls into Purgatory? I have also read that Protestants suffer the most in Purgatory because they have no one to pray for them. Is this true? — M.C.B., Texas

A. The only way that any person, Catholic or non-Catholic, can get back into the state of grace after committing a mortal sin is to tell God that they are truly sorry for that sin, to have a firm intention of not committing that sin in the future, and to make some satisfaction for the sin (what Catholics would call a penance). The normal way for a Catholic to accomplish this is through the Sacrament of Penance, which was given to us by Jesus on that first Easter Sunday night (cf. John 20:22-23).

A Catholic with no access to a priest can obtain forgiveness for mortal sins with an act of perfect contrition (out of love for God), and the same is true for non-Catholics who are truly sorry for their sins and who express that sorrow to God in some way.

Any person, Catholic or non-Catholic, who dies with unforgiven mortal sin on his soul will go to Hell. Those in Purgatory had all their mortal sins forgiven before they died, but they were still in need of purification before they could see the Lord face to face in Heaven.

Every time the Church (or you and I) prays for the souls in Purgatory, those prayers include everyone in Purgatory, not just those who were Catholics in this life. Those who suffer the most in Purgatory are the ones in need of the greatest purification, say, a person who turned back to God at the end of an evil life. But even that suffering is mitigated by the knowledge that they will eventually reach Heaven.

Finally, we don't agree that most non-Catholic Christians are ignorant of mortal and venial sin. If they are Christians, they must have been baptized and must have had some instruction in the moral life, some knowledge of the Ten Commandments or of the moral code preached by Jesus, for example, in the Sermon on the Mount (cf. Matthew 5-7).

Furthermore, God has imprinted on each person's heart a knowledge of right and wrong which his own reason can perceive (cf. Romans 1:18-32). This we call the natural law. Here is how the Second Vatican Council explained that law in the *Pastoral Constitution on the Church in the Modern World* (n. 16):

"In the depths of his conscience, man detects a law which he does not impose on himself, but which holds him to obedience. Always summoning him to love good and avoid evil, the voice of conscience can when necessary speak to his heart more specifically: Do this, shun that. For man has in his heart a law written by God. To obey it is the very dignity of man; according to it he will be judged."

Chapter 5

Catholic Prayers and Practices

Q. I have seen people, particularly those of Italian and Spanish background, kiss their thumb and forefinger after making the Sign of the Cross. What is the origin and meaning of this practice? — P.B., Virginia

A. We don't know where or when the custom began, but those practicing it form a cross with their thumb and forefinger and then kiss that cross as an expression of reverence for the cross of Christ.

Q. Can a parent make the Sign of the Cross on a child's forehead and say, "Jesus, please bless N...."? Also, is it permissible to spray a room with holy water and at the same time bless oneself? — K.M.R., Florida

A. Yes, a parent can make the Sign of the Cross on a child's forehead and ask for the Lord's blessing on the child. The parent is not conferring the blessing, as ordained persons do, but is asking God to do so.

While it is a good idea to have holy water in the home, and perhaps a font at the door so family members can bless themselves when leaving and entering the home, we would think that spraying a room with holy water would be excessive use of a sacramental. Just having the holy water in the room, and blessing oneself with it, ought to be sufficient.

Q. Does a person receive the full benefits of getting ashes on Ash Wednesday when they are given by a Eucharistic minister? Also, can a Eucharistic minister bless throats on St. Blaise Day? Can Eucharistic ministers bless people? — Name Withheld, Michigan

A. Yes to the first two questions, and sometimes to the third. The *Book of Blessings* says that "the blessing of throats may be given by a priest, deacon, or a lay minister who follows the rites and prayers designated for a lay minister" (n. 1626). The book also says that distribution of ashes "may be celebrated by a priest or deacon who may be assisted by lay ministers," although the blessing of the ashes themselves "is reserved to a priest or deacon" (n. 1659).

Since blessings involve "a particular exercise of the priesthood of Christ," they are normally conferred by priests, but the ministry of blessing also belongs to deacons, formally instituted acolytes and readers, and other laymen and laywomen, who because of their Baptism and Confirmation possess the dignity of the universal priesthood. Thus, the laity "may celebrate certain blessings, as indicated in the respective orders of blessings, by one of the rites and formularies designated for a lay minister" (n. 18).

Q. When I received ashes on Ash Wednesday, the woman who distributed them said, "Remember, *woman*, you are dust ...." Legitimate or not? — C.S., New Mexico

A. The woman placing the ashes on your forehead had no right to change the formula, but you still received the graces of this sacramental.

Q. At a friend's church last Ash Wednesday, the priest sprinkled the ashes on top of people's heads instead of the more common way of putting them on the forehead. He explained in his homily that, according to the Gospel of Matthew (6:1-6, 16-18), Christ was telling us not to bring attention to ourselves, and therefore we should receive the ashes in a quiet and humble way. Which is the proper way to receive the ashes, on top of the head or on the forehead? — R.G., Virginia

A. The proper way is to have the priest, deacon, or lay minister make the Sign of the Cross with the ashes on the person's forehead while saying something like, "Remember, man, you are dust and to dust you shall return," or "Turn away from sin and be faithful to the Gospel."

The Scripture passages cited in the question are those where Jesus says, "Be on guard against performing religious acts for people to see," and "When you fast, see to it that you groom your hair and wash your face. In that way no one can see you are fasting but your Father who is hidden; and your Father who sees what is hidden will repay you."

Jesus is not condemning the performance of religious acts and duties in public, but rather the attitude of performing them to impress other people instead of to serve God. Recall that in Matthew 23, He condemned those Pharisees whose "works are performed to be seen. They widen their phylacteries and wear huge tassels. They are fond of places of honor at banquets and the front seats in synagogues, of marks of respect in public and of being called 'Rabbi.' " (Phylacteries were small capsules containing miniature scrolls with Bible verses on them. They were strapped either to the forehead or to the upper left arm and were worn in public.)

If a person today were to get ashes just to impress other people, that would be a phony display of piety instead of the real thing. On the other hand, if one were to display the ashes with an attitude of genuine piety, then the act could give good example to others and perhaps even serve as an actual grace that might change the heart of someone who had fallen away from the faith.

Recall, too, the words of Jesus that present the positive side of this question: "Your light must shine before men so that they may see goodness in your acts and give praise to your heavenly Father" (Matthew 5:16).

Q. The pastor of our church refuses to bless any religious medal or rosary or statue because he says he does not believe in such "superstition." He tells the parishioners from the altar to "bless them yourselves." Any comment? — R.D.C., Texas

A. The blessing of religious objects is an ancient and honorable tradition in the Catholic Church. It is classified as a sacramental — an action that is used to gain God's help by reason of our own devotion plus the prayers of the Church on our behalf.

Among the sacramentals, says the *Catechism*, "*blessings* (of persons, meals, objects, and places) come first. Every blessing praises God and prays for his gifts. In Christ, Christians are blessed by God the Father 'with every spiritual blessing' [*Eph* 1:3]. This is why the Church imparts blessings by invoking the name of Jesus, usually while making the holy sign of the cross of Christ" (n. 1671).

Following the example of Jesus, who blessed the loaves and fishes (Matthew 14:19), little children (Mark 10:16), the bread and wine at the Last Supper (Luke 22:17), and the Apostles (Luke 24:50), the *Roman Ritual* contains some 200 blessings of persons, places, and things.

This is not superstition, which means giving to some object or gesture a power it does not possess, but rather an effort to bring about a religious effect through the power of Christ and by virtue of the prayer of the Church and the devotion of the person involved.

Q. Can we say the rosary with the Blessed Sacrament exposed? It was done for years in our cathedral, but now a new bishop has drastically decreased the hours of adoration and has said that the rosary is not allowed during exposition. Which is correct? — M.C.B., Sasketchewan

A. There is no Church prohibition against saying the rosary during adoration of the Holy Eucharist. Fr. John Hardon answered a similar question this way in the January/February, 1997 issue of *The Catholic Faith* magazine:

"Yes, by all means the rosary not only may but should be said before the Blessed Sacrament exposed upon the altar. This is true for three reasons:

"(1) Except for our Lady, we would not have the Blessed Sacrament. It is she who gave her divine Son the flesh and blood in which Christ is present in the Holy Eucharist.

"(2) The mysteries of the rosary are the mysteries of our faith. We believe the same identical Jesus whose life, Passion, death, and Resurrection we commemorate in the rosary is also present in the Blessed Sacrament.

"(3) Who better than our Lady is the model of our faith in the Real Presence of Christ in the Blessed Sacrament? When we say the rosary we are uniting ourselves with the Blessed Mother, expressing our faith in her divine Son being present in the Holy Eucharist."

Furthermore, the Congregation for Divine Worship in Rome issued the following statement in 1998:

"One should not expose the Eucharist only to recite the rosary. However, among the prayers that are used during adoration, the recitation of the rosary may certainly be included, emphasizing the Christological aspects with biblical readings relating to the mysteries and providing for silent adoration and meditation on them."

Q. Our pastor has started the beautiful Benediction service, but without the Divine Praises. I suggested that the service should include the Litany of the Sacred Heart and the Divine Praises, but Father said these prayers are no longer approved for Benediction. Can you tell me if this is true? — R.R.C., Pennsylvania

A. According to the *Roman Ritual*, after the blessing with the Blessed Sacrament, the priest or deacon "replaces the Blessed Sacrament in the tabernacle and genuflects. Meanwhile, the people may sing or say an acclamation, and the minister then leaves" (n. 100). While the ritual suggests certain songs that may be sung before the Eucharistic blessing (e.g., *Pange Lingua*, *Lauda Sion*, *Adoro Te Devote*, and *Ubi Caritas*) and certain prayers that may be said (cf. nn. 98, 224-229), there is no mention of a litany or of the Divine Praises.

Q. For many years, my mother has said 1,000 Hail Marys on the solemnity of the Annunciation. She got the practice from her Irish mother, but we have inquired in Ireland and found no trace of this practice. Perhaps one of your readers knows something about it. — L.E.C., Illinois

A. Fr. Michael Roach, who teaches Church history at Mt. Saint Mary's Seminary in Emmitsburg, MD, says that "this is an ancient practice among the Irish. With secularization even in holy Ireland, this has disappeared. The 1,000 Hail Marys were prayed not only on the Annunciation, but on all Marian feasts and Christmas Day. I've even seen this noted on the death entry of a pious Irish woman buried from St. Agnes, Catonsville [MD], in the last century."

Q. What can you tell me about a rosary-like article of devotion with nine groups of three beads each? — B.S.C., Florida

A. According to Mrs. D.F. of Texas, the devotion is called the Chaplet of St. Michael, and it consists of one Our Father and three Hail Marys in honor of each of the nine choirs of angels (seraphim, cherubim, thrones, dominations, virtues, powers, principalities, archangels, and angels).

The story behind the devotion is that St. Michael appeared to a holy woman named Antonia d'Astonac and told her that he wished to be honored by nine salutations corresponding to the nine choirs of angels. The first salutation says: "By the intercession of St. Michael and the celestial choir of seraphim, may the Lord make us worthy to burn with the fire of perfect charity. Amen." This and the other salutations are followed by the recitation of one Our Father and three Hail Marys.

Whoever practices this devotion, St. Michael is reported to have said, will have an escort of nine angels when approaching the altar to receive Communion, will have his continuous assistance and that of all the angels throughout life, and will have deliverance from Purgatory for himself and his relatives after death.

Q. When a Catholic who is not in the state of grace prays, are those prayers heard by God before he or she goes to Confession the next time? Or does one have to be in the state of grace in order for his or her prayers to be heard? — F.C.R., Texas

A. God hears all of our prayers, including those of the person in mortal sin. The prayers of that person are the first step on the way back to God and His mercy and forgiveness. The *Catechism* says that while we may forget our Creator or hide far from Him, or we may run after idols or accuse God of having abandoned us, "yet the living and true God tirelessly calls each person to that mysterious encounter known as prayer" (n. 2567).

In prayer, the *Catechism* says, God's initiative of love always comes first and, as God gradually reveals himself and reveals us to ourselves, the drama of this exchange between God and us opens up our hearts to God (cf. n. 2567).

Q. I collect and restring rosaries, especially old or unique ones. Someone is going to give me rosaries blessed by Pope John XXIII, Padre Pio, and Pope Paul VI. If I restring those rosaries, do their blessings still remain? — H.V.A., New York

A. Yes, their blessings remain.

Q. Years ago, I asked about wearing a relic around my neck, and you replied that it would be all right as long as it was done with proper respect. I didn't mention that it was a first-class relic, and this might be why you answered as you did. But I wrote to the Congregation of Saints just to be sure. I am enclosing a copy of their reply. — A.C.G., Illinois

A. Thank you for the information, and here is that reply:

"In reference to your letter of 7th February last, this Congregation for the Causes of Saints wishes to inform you that the distribution of relics for the private veneration of the faithful has been a long-standing tradition. It would seem proper, however, that first-class relics of Saints and Blesseds be kept in a reliquary and in a place, such as a Church, Chapel, or Oratory, that they may be preserved properly and given that particular reverence due to them, as recently indicated by competent authority."

Relics, by the way, are divided into three classes: (1) part of a saint's body, (2) part of the clothing or anything used during the saint's life, and (3) any other object, such as a piece of cloth, that has been touched to a first-class relic.

Q. What is the Church teaching on the selling of blessed objects? I understand a donation toward expenses can be made, but the blessed objects may not be sold. I also understand that selling them makes the blessing null. — M.T.C., Ireland

A. It depends on what you mean by blessed objects. If you mean statues, icons, crucifixes, medals, rosaries, etc., those objects can be sold, although they are usually not blessed until after they are purchased. But one could sell these things even if they were blessed, provided that a fair price was asked and they were not being sold to someone who would profane them. And the sale would not nullify the blessing on an object.

You may be thinking of sacred relics, the sale of which is specifically forbidden by canon law (c. 1190). The reason is to prevent the relics, whether pieces of the true cross or the bones of a saint, from falling into the hands of those who do not appreciate their spiritual value or who might ridicule them or use them in a sacrilegious manner.

Canon law, however, does not forbid the buying of relics for the purpose of redeeming them from, say, a pawnshop or from a person who was misusing them or not showing the proper respect for these holy objects.

Q. Can you explain why most people have dropped the "Amen" after the Our Father? Every prayer book that I have ever looked at has an "Amen" at the end of the Lord's

Prayer, and the *Catechism* shows an "Amen" at the end. It seems incomplete without it. — R.R., Maryland

A. It is correct to conclude the Lord's Prayer with "Amen" when one is saying that prayer apart from Mass, e.g., while reciting the rosary. In the words of the *Catechism* (n. 2856): "'Then, after the prayer is over you say 'Amen,' which means 'So be it,' thus ratifying with our 'Amen' what is contained in the prayer that God has taught us' [St. Cyril of Jerusalem, *Catech.myst.* 5, 18: PG 33, 1124; cf. *Lk* 1:38]."

The reason why many people have stopped saying "Amen" when praying the Our Father apart from Mass, in our opinion, is because they have gotten used to no "Amen" at the end of the Lord's Prayer during Mass.

Instead of "Amen" following "deliver us from evil" at Mass, the priest says a prayer ("Deliver us, Lord, from every evil, and grant us peace in our day....") that is followed by the people's response, "For the kingdom, the pow'r and the glory are yours, now and for ever." Omitting the "Amen" at Mass has caused Catholics to omit it when they recite the Our Father outside Mass.

Q. We say "deliver us from evil" (*sed libera nos a malo*) at the conclusion of the Our Father at Mass, but both early Church writings and the 1970 New American Bible translate the passage from Matthew 6:13 as "deliver us from the evil one." Clearly the missal texts are saying the conceptual *malo* rather than the personal devil. I find no reference to any debate concerning the theological migration from a personal devil ("the evil one") to a conceptual "evil." Did I miss something? — K.C.R., New York

A. We don't think so. It is not a case of one concept or the other, but of both being part of Catholic teaching. Thus, the *Catechism* says that in this final petition of the Our Father, "evil is not an abstraction, but refers to a person, Satan, the Evil One, the angel who opposes God" (n. 2851). But the *Catechism* also says that "when we ask to be delivered from the Evil One, we pray as well to be freed from all evils, present, past, and future, of which he is the author or instigator. In this final petition, the Church brings before the Father all the distress of the world" (n. 2854).

Q. I am an American nun, member of an Italian religious institute, living in Italy. A priest has given me some

scapulars of Our Lady of Mount Carmel (the brown scapular), and I would like to distribute them as gifts, but I would also like to tell them the prayers that the Church has said should accompany the wearing of the scapular if one wishes to obtain the benefit of Our Lady's promises. Can you help? — S.M.R., Italy

A. Scapulars are sacramentals, i.e., holy objects that can bring graces to those who use them correctly. The efficacy of scapulars, or other sacramentals, depends not on the object itself but on the devotion, faith, and love of those who use them. Wearing a scapular will not automatically keep a person out of Hell or ward off the power of the devil; the person must sincerely try to lead a holy life and seek God's mercy and forgiveness if he falls into sin. A person wears a scapular not as some magical piece of cloth, but as a holy reminder that our eternal destination is Heaven and that we have a responsibility to live in such a way as to reach that destination.

The Blessed Mother's promise that those who wear the brown Carmelite scapular "shall not suffer eternal fire" does not mean that one could deliberately lead a sinful life and expect to benefit from this promise. Pope Pius XI put the promise into perspective when he wrote:

"Although it is very true that the Blessed Virgin loves all who love her, nevertheless those who wish to have the Blessed Mother as a helper at the hour of death must in life merit such a signal favor by abstaining from sin and laboring in her honor."

So, Sister, you may tell those to whom you give a scapular that they must lead a holy life, which involves at least weekly Mass attendance and reception of Holy Communion, frequent Confession of one's sins, observance of the Church's laws on fast and abstinence, participation in Eucharistic adoration, Bible reading, works of charity, and constant prayer, including recitation of the rosary, that beautiful devotion that the Blessed Virgin herself has recommended.

Editor's Note: Following up on a recent reply about wearing the brown scapular, several readers have written to say that there is an enrollment ceremony for investing a person in the scapular fraternity. After a priest has blessed the scapular, he says to the person to be invested:

"Receive this blessed scapular and beseech the Blessed Virgin that, through her merits, you may wear it without stain. May it defend you against all adversity and accompany you to eternal life. Amen."

After the ceremony, the priest says:

"I, by the power vested in me, admit you to participate in all the spiritual benefits obtained through the mercy of Jesus Christ by the Religious Order of Mt. Carmel. In the name of the Father, and of the Son, and of the Holy Spirit. Amen.

"May God Almighty, the Creator of Heaven and earth, bless you, He who has deigned to join you to the confraternity of the Blessed Virgin of Mt. Carmel. We beseech her to crush the head of the ancient serpent so that you may enter into possession of your eternal heritage, through Christ our Lord. Amen."

Q. Do you know the history of the Green Scapular? I have heard that it is not worn around the neck, like other scapulars, but is secretly placed in a person's home so that the person in that home will be converted to the Catholic faith. — M.R., Texas, and J.W.W., Texas

A. According to a flyer we have, the Blessed Mother in 1840 entrusted the Green Scapular of the Immaculate Heart to Sister Justine Bisqueyburu, a Daughter of Charity of St. Vincent de Paul in France. The scapular was approved twice by Blessed Pope Pius IX, in 1863 and 1870. On the latter occasion, the Holy Father said: "Write to these good Sisters that I authorize them to make and distribute it."

On one side of the scapular is a full-length picture of our Lady with a sword piercing her Immaculate Heart. Only her pierced heart, dripping with blood, is shown on the other side, and it is encircled by the prayer, "Immaculate Heart of Mary, pray for us sinners now and at the hour of our death."

The flyer says that "the manner of using the scapular was indicated by the Blessed Virgin. Since it is not the badge of a confraternity but simply a double image attached to a piece of cloth and suspended from a cord, investiture is not required. It suffices that it be blessed by a priest and worn by one for whom it is intended. It may be placed in the clothing, on the bed, or simply in the room."

For more information, or for reports of conversions and cures attributed to the Green Scapular, you can contact the Daughters of Charity, Marian Center, St. Joseph's Provincial House, 333 S. Seton Ave., Emmitsburg, MD 21727.

Q. What is the obligation to do penance on the Fridays outside the Lenten season? What exactly is required? How serious is the obligation? — P.J.S., California

A. When Pope Paul VI promulgated his *Apostolic Constitution on Penance* in 1966, he said that abstinence from meat was to be observed on every Friday throughout the year that did not fall on a holy day of obligation, but he allowed the bishop's conferences in each country to "substitute abstinence and fast wholly or in part with other forms of penitence and especially works of charity and the exercises of piety."

That same year the U.S. Bishop's Conference said that "abstinence from flesh meat on all Fridays of the year is especially recommended to individuals and to the Catholic community as a whole."

So while abstinence from meat on the Fridays outside of Lent is not required of Catholics in the United States, but only "especially recommended," the U.S. Bishops said in their 1993 statement *The Challenge of Peace* that Catholics should continue to observe this custom "out of love for Christ crucified," as a reminder that "we must preserve a saving and necessary difference from the spirit of the world," and as "an outward sign of the spiritual values that we cherish."

Q. I have seen a list of holy days of obligation that are not celebrated in the United States. How do we know what a holy day is and what our obligation is? Also, I know folks in California who have fewer holy days than we do in New York. I'm confused. — A.W., New York

A. Welcome to the club. First of all, the Universal Church celebrates ten holy days of obligation, but each country's Conference of Bishops is free to celebrate fewer than that. So in the United States we celebrate eight such days, although two of them — the Epiphany and Corpus Christi — are transferred to Sundays. The six traditional holy days are: the Solemnity of Mary (January 1), the Ascension of the Lord (40 days after Easter), the Assumption of the Blessed Virgin Mary (August 15), All Saints Day (November 1), the Immaculate Conception of Our Lady (December 8), and the Birth of Our Lord (December 25).

(The other two days observed by the Universal Church, by the way, are the feasts of St. Joseph on March 19 and Sts. Peter and Paul on June 29.)

However, the U.S. Bishops decided in 1991 that if certain holy days (e.g., the Solemnity of Mary, the Assumption, and All Saints Day) fall on a Saturday or a Monday, the obligation to attend Mass is abrogated. This has caused considerable confusion among Catholics about whether the traditional holy day obligation binds or not for a particular feast in a particular year. For example, when the Solemnity of Mary fell on a Monday in 2001, one was not obligated to attend Mass. That should also have been true in 2000, when the feast fell on a Saturday, but some bishops kept the obligation in place because it was the Jubilee Year.

Can't we please go back to the former schedule of observing six special days every year in the United States, the only exception being when one falls on a Sunday?

Q. Enclosed is a list of the spiritual works of mercy, which have virtually disappeared in today's Church. The corporal works of mercy are heavily emphasized in the Church today, but it is sad that, along with so much other spirituality, we never hear of these spiritual obligations we must follow. Can you identify the source of both the corporal and spiritual works of mercy and comment on why the latter are seldom mentioned today? — A.M.C., Maine

A. The corporal works of mercy, which originate in Isaiah 58:6-7 and Matthew 25:31-46, refer to the bodily needs of others: to feed the hungry, give drink to the thirsty, clothe the naked, visit the sick, shelter the homeless, visit the imprisoned, and bury the dead. The spiritual works of mercy, which originate in the practice of the Church since the time of Christ, refer to the spiritual needs of others: to admonish the sinner, instruct the ignorant, counsel the doubtful, comfort the sorrowful, bear wrongs patiently, forgive all injuries, and pray for the living and the dead.

Both categories are mentioned in paragraph 2447 of the *Catechism*, but we agree that there is much more emphasis today on the corporal rather than the spiritual needs of others. This is particularly true of the first three spiritual works. Why is this so? We would suggest that it has to do with a loss of a sense of sin and with an unhealthy tolerance for the misdeeds of others.

You know, the attitude that says, "It's okay to live together before marriage so you can find out if this is the person for you." Or, "I would never have an abortion, but it's none of my business if someone else wants to have one."

We don't hear much about admonishing the sinner because that would be "judgmental." We don't talk about instructing the ignorant, except in sex education classes of course, because people have to find out things for themselves. We don't seek to counsel the doubtful because that would be imposing our moral views on someone else.

This is all nonsense, of course, but the deleterious impact of these attitudes on contemporary society can be clearly seen in the actions of our political leaders, our sports and entertainment figures, and even family members and friends who think that they can "do their own thing" without any moral accountability.

Our task, however, is to speak the saving truth to them in charity, to call upon them to "reform your lives and believe in the gospel!" (Mark 1:15). Remember the warning of Jesus that we should "not fear those who deprive the body of life but cannot destroy the soul. Rather, fear him who can destroy both body and soul in Gehenna" (Matthew 10: 28).

And keep in mind the words of St. James, who said that "the person who brings a sinner back from his way will save his soul from death and cancel a multitude of sins" (James 5:20).

Q. Are the indulgences that can be found in old prayer books still valid? One of my favorites is titled "Indulgenced Prayer Before a Crucifix" and has a No. 201 next to it. What does this number indicate? Also, is Benediction of the Blessed Sacrament still permitted? If so, under what circumstances? — A.H., Washington and G.T.Z., Missouri

A. Answering the last question first, yes, Benediction is still permitted, and even encouraged. It brings to a close exposition of the Blessed Sacrament during, say, a holy hour or a longer period of Eucharistic adoration. The rite and prayers for Benediction can be found in paragraphs 97-99 and 224-229 of the decree *Holy Communion and Worship of the Eucharist Outside Mass*, which was approved by the Sacred Congregation for Divine Worship in 1973.

Turning to indulgences, which bring about the remission of the temporal punishment due to sins which have already been forgiven, those that are found in old prayer books are no longer valid. They were suppressed in 1968, when Pope Paul VI approved a new *Enchiridion of Indulgences*. This handbook lists 70 indulgenced works, prayers, or devotions, including No. 22, "Prayer Before a Crucifix" (201 was the number of that particular indulgence on the previous list).

A partial indulgence is granted to a member of the faithful who, after receiving Communion, devoutly recites the following prayer before an image of Jesus Christ crucified (a plenary indulgence is granted on the Fridays of Lent):

"Good and gentle Jesus, I kneel before you. I see and I ponder your five wounds. My eyes behold what David prophesied about you: 'They have pierced my hands and feet; they have counted all my bones.' Engrave on me this image of yourself. Fulfill the yearnings of my heart: give me faith, hope, and love, repentance for my sins, and true conversion of life. Amen."

In addition to the 70 specific grants, there are also three general grants of partial indulgences to those who, "while performing their duties and enduring the difficulties of life, raise their minds in humble trust to God and make, at least mentally, some pious invocation"; to those who, "prompted by a spirit of faith, devote themselves or their goods in compassionate service to their brothers and sisters in need"; and to those who, "in a spirit of penitence, voluntarily abstain from something which is licit for and pleasing to them."

Q. In his Bull of Indiction for the Year 2000 (*The Mystery of the Incarnation*), Pope John Paul stressed the importance of indulgences in the Jubilee Year. Can you explain the doctrine of indulgences and the conditions for obtaining them? — G.F.E., Massachusetts
A. We would be happy to do that, while at the same time recommending that one read the papal document in its entirety.

What is an indulgence? — An indulgence is a remission or taking away of the temporal punishment due to sins that have already been forgiven in the Sacrament of Penance. When we commit a mortal sin, we are subject to eternal punishment. Contritely confessing our sins to a priest takes away the eternal punishment, but the temporal punishment remains and can only be removed by prayer, acts of devotion, and works of charity.

Why do we need indulgences? — Bishop Fulton Sheen once said that sins were like nails driven into a block of wood. Confession removes the nails, but the holes in the wood remain. Prayers, acts of devotion, and works of charity help to fill in those holes. If they are not filled in during this life, the repair work will have to be done in Purgatory. Indulgences provide a repair kit or framework for making up for our sins. We can also apply the indulgences to the souls in Purgatory to help them get to Heaven.

Where do we get the grace for indulgences? — The death of Jesus on the cross and the "virtuous deeds" of the Blessed Mother and the saints (Revelation 19:8) have built up a treasury of grace and merit that the Church can open up to the faithful. Since we are all linked together in the Communion of Saints, those of us pilgrims on earth can pray to the saints in Heaven and for the souls in Purgatory so that one day all of us will be together in Heaven.

How many kinds of indulgences are there? — There are two kinds of indulgences: Plenary, which takes away all temporal punishment due to sin, and partial, which takes away some of the punishment. A person who fulfills all the conditions for an indulgence perfectly will receive a plenary indulgence, but only a partial indulgence if something is lacking. A plenary indulgence can be gained only once a day.

But haven't I heard that indulgences were a bad thing? — Several hundred years ago, some Catholics abused indulgences, saying that they could be obtained by giving money to the Church. This was a misuse by some individuals of a worthwhile source of grace and was never countenanced by the Church herself. Indulgences are a good thing when obtained through the strict set of conditions described below.

Why should I seek indulgences? — To make it possible for you to go directly to Heaven when you die (that's what a plenary indulgence means) or to help a soul in Purgatory get to Heaven.

What are the conditions for getting an indulgence? —
(1) You must worthily celebrate sacramental Confession before performing the indulgenced work and seek true conversion of heart.

(2) You must participate in the Holy Sacrifice of the Mass and receive Holy Communion, preferably on the same day that the indulgenced work is performed.

(3) You must pray for the intentions of the Holy Father by

devoutly reciting one Our Father, one Hail Mary, and a profession of faith (the Apostles' Creed or the Nicene Creed).

(4) Those who are infirm or unable to leave their homes can gain the indulgence by spiritually uniting themselves with those carrying out the prescribed work in the ordinary manner and by offering to God their prayers, sufferings, and discomforts.

Q. Why don't women go up to the altar after Mass anymore to be "churched" after the birth of a baby? — M.C., Massachusetts

A. The rite of "churching," once a common sight at the conclusion of a Sunday Mass, was a liturgical ceremony whereby mothers gave thanks to God for the blessing of motherhood and removed any suspicion that, in giving birth, they incurred a legal defilement, as in ancient Judaism. In imitation of Mary at her purification, the mother was expected to offer a gift to the Church.

This blessing used to take place after Mass because mothers seldom attended the Baptism of their children. Today, however, after the child has been baptized, the priest or deacon says the following prayer over the new mother:

"God the Father, through his Son, the Virgin Mary's Child, has brought joy to all Christian mothers, as they see the hope of eternal life shine on their children. May he bless the mother of this child. She now thanks God for the gift of her child. May she be one with him (her) in thanking him forever in heaven, in Christ Jesus our Lord. Amen."

A similar prayer is said for the father of the child.

Editor's Note: In response to a question about the custom of burying a statue of St. Joseph on the property of a house that's for sale, D.P.H. of Wyoming sent along an article from his local paper. The article quoted a Sr. Anna, who works at St. Paul's Religious Supply in Chicago, as saying that the custom began a century ago with the Little Sisters of the Poor in Europe, who used to bury a statue of St. Joseph when seeking any favor.

"It started through faith and friendship with St. Joseph, but as it has been handed down, people have seen it as more like magic," said Sr. Anna. "These were women of simple faith, bargaining with St. Joseph as they would bargain with family or friends. But the faith is what makes it work, not the burying."

She said that her research turned up no special reason for burying the statue upside down. "You can put him in the window," she said. "You don't have to put him in the ground."

A Little Sister of the Poor in Cleveland said that "we have a strong devotion to St. Joseph, and we pray for his intercession. We may have buried his statue on occasion, but it's hard to see the connection [with those selling their homes]. It seems more popular now than it was 50 or 100 years ago, but I wouldn't want people to get superstitious about it."

Q. Somewhere I saw something negative about "centering prayer." If I remember correctly, this article said that it smacked of New Age religion. Will you please comment? — J.J.H., Arizona

A. Several persons have sent us material that makes a strong case for using centering prayer only in a very prudent and discerning way. We cannot quote all of the material, but we can try to mention the major points and suggest that those seeking additional information consult the sources cited in their entirety.

What Is Centering Prayer (CP)? — Before getting into the problems associated with centering prayer, let us turn to one of its principal promoters to describe what it is.

"Centering prayer is a method designed to facilitate the development of contemplative prayer by preparing our faculties to cooperate with this gift," says Fr. Thomas Keating, O.C.S.O., in a pamphlet entitled *The Method of Centering Prayer*. "It is an attempt to present the teaching of earlier times (e.g., *The Cloud of Unknowing*) in an updated form and to put a certain order and regularity into it.

"It is not meant to replace other kinds of prayer; it simply puts other kinds of prayer into a new and fuller perspective. During the time of prayer we consent to God's presence and action within. At other times our attention moves outward to discover God's presence everywhere."

Fr. Keating recommends taking part in this method of prayer for at least two 20-minute periods each day, and he suggests the following guidelines:

"(1) Choose a sacred word [Lord, Jesus, Abba, Father, Mother, Love, Peace, Shalom] as the symbol of your intention to consent to God's presence and action within.

"(2) Sitting comfortably and with eyes closed, settle briefly and silently introduce the sacred word as the symbol of your consent to God's presence and action within.

"(3) When you become aware of thoughts, return ever so gently to the sacred word.

"(4) At the end of the prayer period, remain in silence with eyes closed for a couple of minutes."

Similarities With Transcendental Meditation (TM) — Fr. Finbarr Flanagan, O.F.M., a former practitioner of both TM and CP, says that "Centering Prayer's similarities to TM are readily apparent. For example, both use 20-minute meditations and rely on the mental repetition of a word, or mantra."

Writing in the May/June, 1991 issue of *Faith & Renewal*, Fr. Flanagan said that "CP is basically similar to TM, adopting TM's Hindu view of God and man and of 'enlightenment.' This 'enlightenment' is not the same as true knowledge of God, but comes from a self-induced altered state of consciousness. Given their lack of discernment about TM and other New Age spiritualities, the proponents of CP are not reliable guides to Christian spirituality."

The Franciscan said that "Eastern meditation does yield, as TM and CP proponents state, a lessening of tension. But this is a purely natural form of psychological rest, not produced by the action of God on the soul." He said that practitioners of TM and CP "make the mistake of equating altered states of consciousness — beautiful as they may be — with God himself. God is not a product of our little minds expanded by anoxia or mantras."

Quoting St. Augustine as having said that "the whole life of a good Christian is a holy desire" and that "this very desire of yours is your prayer. If your desire is continual, your prayer is continual too," Fr. Flanagan concluded:

"It is this kind of prayer — filled with love for God and the truth he has revealed — rather than prayer that empties the mind and loses sight of God's personal being, that we need to practice and teach in the Church."

Fascination With Oriental Religions and Methods — Why the growing interest in methods of prayer and meditation stemming from such religions as Buddhism and Hinduism? In a book entitled *The Church in Dialogue*, Francis Cardinal Arinze of Nigeria, president of the Pontifical Council for Interreligious Dialogue, said that there are many reasons.

They include the ease with which Western Christians can travel to the East, the availability of information about Oriental religions in the media, the search for friendship and security, the attraction of experiencing the spiritual life directly through techniques of prayer and contemplation, a desire to escape from the hubbub of Western society, and deficient formation in the Christian life.

However, there are risks and dangers in using these methods, said Cardinal Arinze. He said that there is a danger of Pelagianism, of believing that we can reach sanctity through our own efforts without the supernatural help of grace; the danger of becoming complacent about the state of our soul, unlike the Christian saints and mystics who were very much "aware of being poor sinners before God, in need of pardon and gratuitous redemption, whereas some gurus who wander around the world make an ostentatious show of having an immaculate and perfect halo"; and the danger that excessive or mistaken use of Oriental techniques "can cause real harm on the deepest level of the person."

The Cardinal cautioned that "no matter how much effort we make on our own, no matter if we follow the latest meditation techniques, we cannot of ourselves win our salvation. We have to take salvation on our knees as a gift of the God of love." He said that "Christian meditation should have Christ for its center; it should have a clear-cut religious character seeking before all a relationship with God; it should be an effort to love God and not a technique; and this God sought for should be a personal God, the Father of our Lord Jesus Christ who allows us to call him Father."

Finally, Cardinal Arinze warned that "Oriental religions and Oriental methods are very complex. We need much prudence and discernment to be able to distinguish the true riches God has placed in the heart of other religious traditions from the negative, obscure, and even sinful elements."

He said that "many Christians who enthusiastically embrace an Oriental method do not escape receiving some wound on their Christian faith. The Christian who wants to follow this road needs a sure guide so as always to do the truth in charity. And, still more important, the Christian must center his own life completely in Jesus Christ, Savior of the world!"

Authentic Christian Prayer — In its 1989 *Letter to the Bishops of the Catholic Church on Some Aspects of Christian Meditation*, the Sacred Congregation for the Doctrine of the Faith (SCDF) said that true Christian prayer is properly defined as "a personal, intimate, and profound dialogue between man and God. It expresses, therefore, the communion of redeemed creatures with the intimate life of the Persons of the Trinity. This communion, based on Baptism and the Eucharist, source and summit of the life of the Church, implies an attitude of conversion, a flight from 'self' to the 'you' of God" (n. 3).

Thus, the letter continued, "Christian prayer is at the same time always authentically personal and communitarian. It flees from impersonal techniques or from concentrating on oneself, which can create a kind of rut, imprisoning the person praying in a spiritual privatism which is incapable of a free openness to the transcendental God. Within the Church, in the legitimate search for new methods of meditation, it must always be borne in mind that the essential element of authentic Christian prayer is the meeting of two freedoms, the infinite freedom of God with the finite freedom of man" (n. 3).

Erroneous Ways of Praying — Attempts to fuse Christian and non-Christian meditation are "not free from dangers and errors," said the SCDF. "Proposals in this direction are numerous and radical to a greater or lesser extent. Some use Eastern methods solely as a psychophysical preparation for a truly Christian contemplation; others go further and, using different techniques, try to generate spiritual experiences similar to those described in the writings of certain Catholic mystics. Still others do not hesitate to place that absolute without image or concept, which is proper to Buddist theory, on the same level as the majesty of God revealed in Christ, which towers above finite reality" (n. 12).

These attempts must be "subjected to a thoroughgoing examination," said the SCDF, because "they propose abandoning not only meditation on the salvific works accomplished in history by the God of the Old and New Covenant, but also the very idea of the One and Triune God, who is love, in favor of an immersion 'in the indeterminate abyss of the divinity' " (n.12).

One can take "what is useful" from other religions as long as the Christian concept of prayer is not obscured, the Sacred Congregation said, mentioning as one example "the humble acceptance of a master who is an expert in the life of prayer, and of the counsels he gives" (n. 16).

However, "one has to interpret correctly the teaching of those masters who recommend 'emptying' the spirit of all sensible representations and of every concept, while remaining lovingly attentive to God. In this way, the person praying creates an empty space which can then be filled by the richness of God" (n. 19).

"The emptiness which God requires," the SCDF stressed, "is that of the renunciation of personal selfishness, not necessarily that of the renunciation of those created things which he has given us and among which he has placed us" (n. 19)

Furthermore, the letter said, while the use of specific bodily postures can be of help to certain people, "not everyone is equally suited to make use of this symbolism" and, if used incorrectly, "the symbolism can even become an idol and thus an obstacle to the raising up of the spirit to God .... It can degenerate into a cult of the body and can lead surreptitiously to considering all bodily sensations as spiritual experiences" (n. 27).

Keeping Our Sights Fixed on Jesus — In conclusion, the SCDF said that "the love of God, the sole object of Christian contemplation, is a reality which cannot be 'mastered' by any method or technique. On the contrary, we must always have our sights fixed on Jesus Christ, in whom God's love went to the cross for us and there he assumed even the condition of estrangement from the Father (cf. Mark 13:34). We therefore should allow God to decide the way he wishes to have us participate in his love. But we can never, in any way, seek to place ourselves on the same level as the object of our contemplation, the free love of God" (n. 31).

Centering Prayer Not for Everyone — Centering prayer, properly conceived, is nothing new, said Fr. Thomas Dubay in *Seeking Spiritual Direction.* He said that St. Teresa of Avila, speaking of it without using the term, "did not propose the simple practice as generally or commonly suitable, but only for certain people at a certain time in their journey to God. Many people are not ready for the approach, while others are beyond it and would be hindered were they to try it as a daily practice."

Noting that the Blessed Mother is "the model of contemplation" who pondered the divine mysteries (Luke 2:19, 51), Fr. Dubay said that "nowhere do we read of emptying the mind as a procedure for encountering God. When the Lord gives a loftier, non-conceptual communion, well and good — and he surely gave it to his Mother. But even then the mind is not empty."

He said that "in our biblical and Catholic tradition, we actively meditate until God takes the initiative and gives us something better on which to focus our attention, that is, the beginnings of infused prayer. For St. Teresa to sit before the Lord with an empty mind is to be a 'ninny,' not exactly a desirable state! It is difficult to see the contrary teaching as anything more than another among fads."

It was St. Teresa who said of such a technique that "the very care taken not to think about anything will arouse the mind to think a great deal," and that the separation of the mystery of Christ from Christian meditation is always a form of "betrayal."

Fr. Dubay found "somewhat unreal the promise that by a centering method one has a quick access to God, a contemplative experience of his presence. Perhaps an Oriental emptying approach may yield some sort of impersonal awareness, but this is not Christic communion; an impersonal awareness is not a contact with the living, Triune God."

In a homily on November 1, 1982, Pope John Paul said that St. Teresa's advocacy of a prayer completely centered on Christ "is valid, even in our day, against some methods of prayer which are not inspired by the Gospel and which in practice tend to set Christ aside in preference for a mental void which makes no sense in Christianity. Any method of prayer is valid insofar as it is inspired by Christ and leads to Christ, who is the Way, and the Truth, and the Life" (cf. John 14:6).

Chapter 6

Mary, Angels, and Saints

Q. I learned "our tainted nature's solitary boast" from my eighth grade teacher. Can you tell me the author of that text about the Virgin Mary? — F.J., Florida

A. It was the English poet William Wordsworth (1770-1850) in Ecclesiastical Sonnet XXV, entitled *The Virgin*. The opening lines are: "Mother! whose virgin bosom was uncrost/With the least shade of thought to sin allied;/ Woman! above all women glorified/Our tainted nature's solitary boast."

Q. At a recent pro-life dinner, I heard a speaker say that we should be sympathetic to unwed mothers since the Blessed Virgin was an unwed mother. Is this true? — W.C.B., Massachusetts, and J.T., New Jersey

A. No, it is not true. The *Catechism* (n. 497) refers to Joseph as Mary's "fiancee" [*Mt* 1:20], and we understand this, and terms like "espousal" and "betrothal," to mean that some kind of a ceremony had taken place and that it would be solemnized later when the bride moved into the groom's house.

Else why would Joseph have decided "to divorce her quietly" (Matthew 1:19) so as not to "expose her to the law" against adultery? How could Mary be thought guilty of adultery if she were not in some way married to Joseph? Or how could Joseph seek a divorce if Mary were not already his wife?

Pope John Paul confirmed this in his 1989 apostolic exhortation *Guardian of the Redeemer*, which deals with the person and mission of St. Joseph in the life of Christ and the Church. For example, the Holy Father said:

"According to Jewish custom, marriage took place in two stages: first, the legal, or true marriage was celebrated, and then, only after a certain period of time, the husband brought the wife into his own house. Thus, before he lived with Mary, Joseph was already her 'husband.' Mary, however, preserved her deep desire to give herself exclusively to God" (n. 18).

Earlier in the same apostolic exhortation, John Paul said that "at the moment of the Annunciation, Mary was 'betrothed to a man whose name was Joseph, of the house of David.' The nature of this 'marriage' is explained indirectly when Mary, after hearing what the messenger says about the birth of the child, asks, 'How can this be, since I do not know man?' (Luke 1:34) The angel responds: 'The Holy Spirit will come upon you, and the power of the Most High will overshadow you; therefore the child to be born will be called holy, the Son of God' (Luke 1:35). Although Mary is already 'wedded' to Joseph, she will remain a virgin because the child conceived in her at the Annunciation was conceived by the power of the Holy Spirit" (n. 2).

One reason why people get the wrong slant on this is because some translations of Luke 1:34 quote our Lady as saying, "How can this be since I have no husband?" This is a faulty translation since Mary indeed did have a husband when she conceived Jesus through the power of the Holy Spirit. The correct translation is, "How can this be since I do not know man?" Mary is not concerned about her marital status, but rather about how she can have a child and maintain her vow of perpetual virginity.

Q. I was so floored by the enclosed article from my local newspaper that I thought I would send it along for your comments. How on earth can one respond to a nationally read columnist who has just spread such an error? — G.R., Tennessee

A. The reference is to a syndicated column by Jeffrey Hart, a convert to the Catholic Church, in which he said that the idea of the Blessed Mother's virginity "is complicated. Essentially, it is a theological deduction. After all, Jesus had a brother, James." Later in the column, Hart said that "Mary gave fully human birth to James."

It has been the constant teaching of the Catholic Church for 2,000 years that Mary had no children other than Jesus; she was a virgin before, during, and after the birth of Christ, which is why we speak of her as "ever-virgin." Search the Scriptures from beginning to end and you will not find Mary identified as the mother of anyone but Jesus. The James mentioned, for example, in Mark 6:3 as a "brother" of our Lord was in fact His cousin. He was the son of Mary of Clopas (Matthew 27:56), who is identified as the Blessed Mother's "sister" (John 19:25), which would make her Jesus' aunt.

It was not uncommon in those days, nor in our own time either, to call close friends or relatives "brothers" (or "sisters"), as Jesus did in John 20:17, when He told Mary Magdalene to "go to my brothers and tell them, 'I am ascending to my Father and your Father, to my God and your God!' "

But Mary Magdalene went not to any blood brothers of Jesus, but "to the disciples" (John 20:18). Surely, if Jesus had brothers, Mary would have gone to them rather than to the disciples. So, too, if our Lord had blood brothers, He would have entrusted the care of His mother to them rather than to the Apostle John (John 19:26-27).

How does one respond to Mr. Hart's article? By writing to the newspaper in which the column appeared and presenting the information above.

Q. *At Home with the Word*, a booklet published by Liturgy Training Publications and recommended for Bible study in our parish, states that "brothers and sisters" of Jesus could have included "stepbrothers and sisters by Joseph from a previous marriage." Was Joseph married before? — D.C.D., South Dakota

Q. Christian popular devotion seems to have a long-held assumption that Joseph was somewhat older than Mary. If that is true, a previous marriage could be one of the reasons. — N.R.F., New Jersey

A. There is no evidence in Scripture or elsewhere that St. Joseph had been married to someone else, and presumably widowed, before he married the Blessed Virgin. Nor is there any evidence that Joseph was much older than Mary. We suspect that some who speculate about a much-older Joseph are trying to account for Joseph's willingness to enter into a celibate marriage. Pope John Paul, however, shed a different light on Mary and Joseph's consecrated virginity at his general audience on August 21, 1996:

"It may be presumed that at the time of their betrothal there was an understanding between Joseph and Mary about the plan to live as a virgin. Moreover, the Holy Spirit, who had inspired Mary to choose virginity in view of the mystery of the Incarnation and who wanted the latter to come about in a family setting suited to the Child's growth, was quite able to instill in Joseph the ideal of virginity as well."

Q. Regarding your recent response about Mary's perpetual virginity, I have highlighted the Gospel reading for Christmas Day. As you can see, the reading implies that after the birth of Jesus, Joseph and Mary had relations. Is this a flaw in the new translation of this passage. — Name Withheld, Illinois

A. The highlighted line from the 1986 NAB New Testament reads: "He [Joseph] had no relations with her until [another translation says "before"] she bore a son, and he named him Jesus." Actually, this translation does not really differ from previous ones. For example, the Douay Rheims version says that "he knew her not till she brought forth her firstborn son."

The problem today is that we interpret the words "until" or "till" to mean that something happened after that. But in the Bible those words only meant that something had not happened up to that point in time. The footnote in the Douay Rheims translation explains:

"From these words Helvidius and other heretics most impiously inferred that the Blessed Virgin Mary had other children besides Christ: but St. Jerome shews, by divers examples, that this expression of the Evangelist was a manner of speaking usual among the Hebrews, to denote by the word *until*, only what is done, without any regard to the future.

"Thus it is said, Genesis 8.6 and 7, that *Noe sent forth a raven, which went forth and did not return* till *the waters were dried up on the earth*. That is, did not return any more. Also Isaias 46.4, God says: *I am* till *you grow old*. Who dare infer that God should then *cease to be*?

"Also in the first book of Machabees 5.54, *And they went up to the mount Sion with joy and gladness, and offered holocausts, because not one of them was slain* till *they had returned in peace*. That is, not one was slain before or after they had returned.— God saith to his divine Son: *Sit on my right hand* till *I make thy enemies thy footstool*. Shall he sit no longer after his enemies are subdued?

"Yea and for all eternity, St. Jerome also proves by Scripture examples, that an *only begotten son*, was also called firstborn, or *first begotten*: because according to the law, the *firstborn* males were to be consecrated to God: *Sanctify unto me*, saith the Lord, *every firstborn that openeth the womb among the children of Israel*, &c. Ex. 13.2."

By the way, if any Protestant friends attempt to cast doubt on Mary's perpetual virginity, tell them that they are out of step with the founders of Protestantism, who shared the Catholic view. For example, Martin Luther said that "Christ our Savior was the real and natural fruit of Mary's virginal womb .... This was without the cooperation of a man, and she remained a virgin after that" (*Luther's Works*, edited by Jaroslav Pelikan, vol. 22, p. 23).

In criticizing the fourth-century heretic Helvidius, John Calvin said that "Helvidius has shown himself too ignorant, in saying that Mary had several sons because mention is made in some passages of the brothers of Christ."

And Ulrich Zwingli, the Swiss Reformation leader, wrote: "I firmly believe according to the words of the Gospel that a pure virgin brought forth for us the Son of God and remained a virgin pure and intact in childbirth and also after the birth, for all eternity."

The Calvin and Zwingli statements can be found in "Protestants and Our Lady" (*Marian Library Studies*, nn. 128/129, January/February, 1967). Another valuable source is the 24-page booklet *Refuting the Attack on Mary* by Fr. Mateo, the pen name of Catholic priest who is a university professor.

Q. A priest told a group of us that Mary did not know that she was truly the Mother of God's Son until the Resurrection. We find it almost impossible to believe this. — Name Withheld, Pennsylvania

A. We also find it almost impossible to believe this because of the words spoken to our Blessed Lady by the angel Gabriel at the time of the Annunciation:

"You shall conceive and bear a son and give him the name Jesus. Great will be his dignity and he will be called Son of the Most High. The Lord God will give him the throne of David his father. He will rule over the house of Jacob forever and his reign will be without end .... 'The Holy Spirit will come upon you and the power of the Most High will overshadow you; hence, the holy offspring to be born will be called Son of God' " (Luke 1:31-35).

After assenting to the angel's words, Mary went to visit her kinswoman Elizabeth, who was thought to be sterile but who had miraculously conceived a child in her old age. "Blest are you among women and blest is the fruit of your womb," Elizabeth said to Mary. "But who am I that the Mother of my Lord should come to me?" (Luke 1:42-43).

The Blessed Virgin then recited her famous canticle of praise, which includes these words: "All ages to come shall call me blessed./ God who is mighty has done great things for me,/ holy is his name" (Luke 1:48-49)

Mary might have been only a teenager, but she was not stupid or naive. She understood what the angel was asking and even inquired about how this could be in light of her vow of virginity. Satisfied with the angel's explanation, she unhesitatingly said yes to God: "Let it be done to me as you say" (Luke 1:38).

If her holy offspring was to be called "Son of the Most High" and "Son of God," and if she was to be the "Mother of my Lord," and if her pregnancy had come about without the cooperation of her husband Joseph, or any other man, then Mary would have to have been particularly dense not to know that something unique was happening and that this Child she was carrying was someone special.

But Mary was not dense or uncertain or confused. There was no original sin to cloud her mind since she had been conceived immaculate in her mother's womb. She heard the holy man Simeon say that her Son was "destined to be the downfall and the rise of many in Israel, a sign that will be opposed — and you yourself shall be pierced with a sword — so that the thoughts of many hearts may be laid bare" (Luke 2:34-35).

So there is no evidence that Mary was ignorant of who Jesus was until after the Resurrection.

Q. St. Paul in his epistles never mentions the fact that the Blessed Virgin Mary lived in Ephesus at one time. Is it true that Mary did indeed live there? — E.W.V., Ohio, and P.M.K., Florida

A. Tradition tells us that John the Apostle lived for a time in Ephesus (modern-day Turkey) and eventually died there. For example, St. Irenaeus (140-202) said in *Against Heresies* that John wrote the fourth Gospel "while he was residing at Ephesus in Asia." And St. Polycrates of Ephesus (125-196), in a letter to Pope St. Victor around A.D. 190, said that the same John who reclined at the bosom of the Lord "fell asleep at Ephesus."

Since Jesus on the cross entrusted the care of His mother to John (John 19:26-27), it is supposed that the Blessed Virgin spent some time with the evangelist in Ephesus before the end of her life. There is in fact a house in that city that has been venerated since ancient times as the place where the Blessed Mother lived. Thousands of pilgrims visit the house every year, and Pope John Paul II prayed there during a visit to Turkey in November 1979.

For more information about this, see pages 177-178 of Joan Carroll Cruz's book *Relics* (Our Sunday Visitor). According to Mrs. Cruz, "the little house is called Panaya Kapulu, the house of the Holy Virgin. It has become the object of so many pilgrimages that the Turkish authorities have built an excellent road to its entrance. It is estimated by one authority that 10,000 people of all faiths visit the shrine each week."

Q. Please tell me the seven sorrows of the Blessed Virgin Mary. — N.G.S., Minnesota, and K.M.D., New York

A. Also known as the Seven Dolors of the Blessed Mother, they are: the prophecy of Simeon that Mary's heart would be pierced by a sword (Luke 2:34-35), the flight into Egypt to escape the murderous wrath of King Herod (Matthew 2:13-23), the three-day separation from Jesus in Jerusalem when He was 12 years old (Luke 2:41-50), the meeting with her Son on the road to Calvary, the crucifixion and death of our Lord, the placing of His body in Mary's arms after it was taken down from the cross, and His burial in the tomb provided by Joseph of Arimathea.

The feast of Our Lady of Sorrows is celebrated on September 15th each year.

Q. Can the Church's teaching on Mary being a filter for our prayers be explained simply in one or two sentences? I have a difficult time trying to explain it. — S.E., Minnesota

A. Without denying the importance of direct prayer to God, e.g., through the Mass, one can make a strong case for going to Jesus through Mary. The Church's teaching on Mary, and her intercessory role, can be found in such sources as paragraphs 52-69 of Vatican II's *Dogmatic Constitution on the Church*, Pope John Paul's encyclical letter *Mother of the Redeemer*, and paragraphs 963-975 of the *Catechism*. We cannot summarize this in one or two sentences, but how about eight sentences?

First, we have to look at Mary's unique place in our salvation. She said yes to becoming the Mother of God; gave us at Cana the important admonition: "Do whatever he tells you" (John

2:5); accepted at the foot of the cross the role of spiritual mother to all of us; and devoted herself in prayer with the leaders of the early Church.

As one who willingly cooperated with her Son's mission of salvation on earth, Mary did not abandon this saving role when she was taken up into Heaven. She is still the Mother of Christ, who showed such a willingness on earth to grant her every request. How better can we ask a favor of Jesus than by presenting it through Mary's hands? As Vatican II said: "By her maternal charity, Mary cares for the brethren of her Son who still journey on earth surrounded by dangers and difficulties, until they are led to their happy fatherland" (*Constitution on the Church,* n. 62).

The Council Fathers urged the faithful to "pour forth persevering prayer to the Mother of God and Mother of men. Let them implore that she who aided the beginnings of the Church by her prayers may now, exalted as she is in Heaven above all the saints and angels, intercede with her Son in the fellowship of all the saints" (*Ibid.*, n. 69).

Q. In a recent reply about how Mary can be a filter between God and us in prayer, I think your answer, while doctrinally sound, does not explain in a way that can be easily understood by those who do not absolutely accept the Church's authority or who are having a difficult time understanding why the Church teaches as she does. When I was stationed in Alaska, I heard the best explanation of Mary's special place in the Church. It was in a sermon by Army Chaplain Fr. Edward Hartmann. Can you please share this story with your readers? — D.A.P., Indiana

A. Yes, we can, and here is Fr. Hartmann's story:

"Once there was a kingdom whose king was beloved by all. Now there was a farmer in the kingdom who had an apple orchard. Because of his great love for the king, every year the farmer picked the best, the reddest, and the biggest apples and presented them as a gift to the king. The king always praised the farmer for his beautiful apples and his generosity.

"It came to pass that one year was especially hot and dry, and pests infested the farmer's orchard. Even the best apples were small and their skin was wrinkled and cracked. The farmer could not find even one apple that did not have a worm, and he was very anxious because he could not give the king such poor apples.

"Then the farmer had an idea. He took his gift of apples to the queen and explained his problem. The queen accepted the apples and carefully cut out every spot and blemish from them. She then cut the apples into beautiful thin wedges, just the way the king liked them for dessert.

"When the time was right, the queen presented the apples to the king on behalf of the farmer. When the king ate one of the wedges, he said: 'By far, these apples are the finest gift this farmer has ever given. May he be greatly blessed.'

"In the same way Mary takes our imperfect and stained human intentions and presents them to the Father, not as we presented them to her, but cleaned and perfected."

Q. I have often wondered about the background and meaning of some of the beautiful invocations to the Blessed Virgin Mary, such as Tower of David, Tower of Ivory, House of Gold, Mystical Rose, Morning Star, Mirror of Justice, Seat of Wisdom, and Star of the Sea. Is there a book that explains these? Also, what is the meaning of the phrase "terrible as an army set in battle array" that appears in the prayer *Catena Legionis* of the Legion of Mary? — S.M.W., Virginia

A. According to Fr. Jovian Lang's *Dictionary of the Liturgy* (Catholic Book Publishing Company), the invocations are taken from the Litany of Loreto, which dates from the 12th century and was approved for public worship in 1587 by Pope Sixtus V. The last five invocations (concerning the Immaculate Conception, Assumption, rosary, peace, and families) were added later by the Holy See. Said Fr. Lang:

"The list of praises to Mary (49 titles) owes much to prayers of the Greek Church, in particular to the Akathist Hymn (translated into Latin and first published in Venice about the year 800). Originally, the litany counted some 15 more invocations, among which were Our Lady of Humility, Mother of Mercy, Temple of the Spirit, Gate of Redemption, and Queen of Disciples.

"The first 20 invocations are Marian praises addressed to Mary as *Mother* and *Virgin*; the next 13 are remarkable descriptions of her *office*, *power*, and *virtues*. Four common titles follow, and then 12 address Mary as *Queen*. The litany concludes with the opening prayer from the common of the Blessed Virgin Mary.

"Although some people have criticized the titles as extravagant, they are based on the writings of the Fathers of the first six centuries."

The phrase "terrible as an army set in battle array" refers to the Blessed Virgin and is part of an antiphon recited by those who belong to the Legion of Mary before and after recitation of the Magnificat. The reason for the metaphor can be found on page 1 of the official handbook of the Legion:

"The Legion of Mary is an association of Catholics who, with the sanction of the Church and under the powerful leadership of Mary Immaculate, Mediatrix of All Graces (who is fair as the moon, bright as the sun, and — to Satan and his legionnaires — terrible as an army set in battle array), have formed themselves into a legion for service in the warfare which is perpetually waged by the Church against the world and its evil powers."

The Legion takes its name from the Roman Legion and seeks to inspire in its members the same spirit of "submission to authority, an unflagging sense of duty, perseverance in the face of obstacles, endurance in hardship, and loyalty to the tiniest details of duty" — only "supernaturalized and tempered and sweetened by contact with her [Mary] who can best teach the secret of loving, gracious service" (p. 271).

Other sources of information about the titles of our Lady include the *Dictionary of Mary* (Catholic Book Publishing), *The Glories of Mary* by St. Alphonsus Liguori (TAN Books), and *Listen! Mother of God* by Msgr. Charles Dollen (Our Sunday Visitor).

Q. Why do we so seldom see pictures or icons of the Blessed Virgin Mary pregnant with Jesus? Wouldn't this be an appropriate symbol for the pro-life movement? — S.S., Mississippi

A. The famous picture of Our Lady of Guadalupe, taken from the cloak of Juan Diego after the Blessed Mother appeared to him in Mexico in 1531, shows a pregnant Virgin Mary. This has led many pro-life groups to place their efforts under the protection of Our Lady of Guadalupe, who is the patroness of the Americas, and to seek her intercession in ending the abortion holocaust. More information on this representation of the Blessed Mother is available from Daniel J. Lynch, The Missionary Society of Our Lady of Guadalupe, St. Albans, VT 05478.

We have also seen a postcard with the figure of the Pregnant Madonna in Poland. According to tradition, in 1790 a pregnant Virgin Mary appeared to save the life of a father lost in the forest. He had gone to get help for his wife, who was experiencing a difficult labor. Mary came to their home and helped with the delivery. Her role as midwife is symbolized by the rolled-up sleeves in the picture.

Q. Some months ago, you mentioned in an almost off-handed manner the earth-shaking news that Our Lady of Guadalupe was pregnant at the time of the apparitions. Now for me this was indeed a most startling bit of information. What is your source? — J.H.G., New Mexico

A. Our source is Daniel Lynch's book *Our Lady of Guadalupe and Her Missionary Image*. On page 16, Lynch writes:

"Our Lady appears on the tilma [the cloak of Juan Diego] as an olive-skinned young woman, four feet eight inches tall. She is clothed in Middle Eastern dress of the time of Christ. However, the colors of the clothing are of an Aztec royal virgin. But she is pregnant, which is physically obvious and which is symbolized by the four-petaled flower (Nahui Ollin) over her womb and the sash which is wrapped around her body and tied above her womb.

"The Nahui Ollin symbolizes the center of the universe, the One True God and Christ Himself who was born through Our Lady. Recent gynecological measurements have determined that Our Lady's image on the tilma has the physical dimensions of a pregnant woman!"

Q. Re Our Lady of Guadalupe being with child, who says besides Daniel Lynch that the petaled flower signifies pregnancy? The worst statement of all was "recent gynecological measurements" on a painting! Why on earth would you print such stuff? — T.W., California

Q. Dr. Charles Wahlig spent many years researching Guadalupe in Mexico City. Statements about the pregnancy of the Blessed Virgin in her portrait are purely imaginary. — E.K.M., Connecticut

Q. You have quoted as your source that the lady on

Juan Diego's tilma is pregnant Daniel Lynch's book *Our Lady and Her Missionary Image*. I am wondering about his source. I have visited the Guadalupe Shrine ten or more times, with and without tour guides. None of those tour guides ever told tourist groups that Mary was pregnant. — E.B., Tennessee

Q. I worked in Mexico from 1959 to 1988 and had two parishes in Mexico City, one with 100,000 parishioners and the other with 80,000. I heard experts talk about the image of Our Lady of Guadalupe, but I never heard any say that the image represents our Lady as pregnant. So I say maybe. Caution. — D.O., Texas

A. We wrote to Mr. Lynch about his statement, and he sent us a copy of *A Handbook on Guadalupe*. This 226-page book, which was published in 1996 by the Franciscan Friars of the Immaculate in New Bedford, MA, contains some 40 essays about Guadalupe, two of which refer to our Lady being pregnant.

In the preface to the book, Bishop Sean P. O'Malley of Fall River, MA says that "it is universally believed that Mary appeared on Tepeyac Hill as the Immaculate Conception, and there is also clear evidence that she is 'with child.' That is the second reason I am pleased to recommend this book which has devoted so much space to Mary as the patroness of the pro-life movement in the United States."

In his essay on "Our Lady of Guadalupe: Protectress of the Unborn," Fr. Paul Marx of Human Life International said this:

"The appropriateness of hailing Our Lady of Guadalupe as patroness of our apostolate is remarkable. Of all the many manifestations of Mary's loving presence among us throughout the centuries, in this apparition alone does she appear to us in the manner of a pregnant mother. She holds within her the unborn Christ, proclaiming the sanctity and blessedness of life within the womb. Her reverence and tenderness communicate to us the joy and awe with which we must approach each nascent life" (p. 147).

In her essay on "Holy Mary of Guadalupe: Pro-life Patron," Dr. Janet Barber, I.H.M., an authority on Guadalupe who has been devoted to the apparition since 1952, made these comments:

"The Blessed Virgin Mary best reveals herself as Patroness

of the Unborn in her advocation of Guadalupe. In her image, which she left us in Advent of 1531, miraculously stamped and conserved on Juan Diego's cloak, she is represented 'with child.' Her pregnancy is recognized by the high position of her sash, from the slight swelling of her abdomen most visible to the right of the sash, and with the four-petaled flower over her womb.

"Until recently, she was judged to be in her first trimester. However, an analysis by a leading gynecologist/obstetrician of Mexico City, Dr. Carlos Fernandez Del Castillo, now suggests that she is very close to giving birth. Dr. Fernandez believes that the Infant is resting vertically, head down, and that the four-petaled flower over her womb, symbolizing life, lies directly over the left shoulder of the Infant, in the best place for listening to his heartbeat.

"The four-petaled flower over her womb is the only one of such design among the 57 flowers and 13 buds on her tunic. This unique flower is the Flower of the Sun, the Nahuatl symbol Nahui Ollin, which announced to the conquered Indians that the Sun of the New Era was about to be born liturgically and in their lives, that is, the great Sun of Justice announced in Malachi, the last book of the Old Testament" (p. 135).

Contrary to what T.W. thinks, we printed this "stuff" not because we had nothing else to put in the column, but because we were asked about it and because some reputable people believe it to be true. This is not dogmatic teaching. One is free to disagree with the statements above, or to accept them with caution, as Fr. D.O. recommends. But one ought to read the *Handbook on Guadalupe* before rejecting them outright. The *Handbook*, by the way, also contains several articles by Dr. Charles Wahlig, whom E.K.M. cited as an authority on Guadalupe.

Q. Some years ago, a theologian told us that Jesus was born in a manner similar to His Resurrection, in that he "appeared" in Mary's arms without passing through her birth canal. Please give us your guidance about this. — C.W., New Jersey, and A. and J. G., Virginia

A. The best analogy we have heard is that the birth of our Lord was like a ray of sunshine passing through a window that leaves the pane of glass undisturbed. Others have compared the birth of Jesus to the coming forth of the glorified Christ from the tomb or His passage through closed doors on Easter Sunday night.

And St. Bernard, referring to our Lady's title "Star of the Sea," wrote:

"There is indeed a wonderful appropriateness in this comparison of her to a star, because as a star sends out its ray without detriment to itself, so did the Virgin Mary bring forth her Child without injury to her integrity. And as the ray emitted does not diminish the brightness of the star, so neither did the Child born of her tarnish the beauty of Mary's virginity."

Q. I have read that St. Thomas Aquinas opposed the doctrine of the Immaculate Conception. If this is true, could you please tell me the reason behind his position? — Name Withheld, Ohio

A. According to Our Sunday Visitor's *Encyclopedia of Catholic Doctrine*, St. Thomas (along with such other devotees of the Blessed Mother as Saints Albert the Great, Bernard of Clairvaux, and Bonaventure) was unable to accept the Immaculate Conception as a revealed truth of faith because the doctrine "seemed to exempt Mary from being redeemed by her Son, the Savior of the whole world (which included his own Mother). The theological breakthrough came chiefly through John Duns Scotus (1266-1308), who was mainly responsible for introducing the notion of 'preservative' redemption into the explicit consciousness of the Church" (pp. 320-321).

Scotus conceded that Mary was a daughter of Adam, but said that she was sanctified when God infused her soul into her body. "Some have been raised up after they have fallen," he said, "but the Virgin Mary was sustained as it were in the very act of falling, and prevented from falling, like the two men who were about to tumble into a pit" (cf. Fr. John Hardon's *The Catholic Catechism*, p. 153).

Dr. Ludwig Ott, in his classic *Fundamentals of Catholic Dogma* (TAN Books), explains Mary's "pre-redemption" this way:

"By reason of her natural origin, she, like all other children of Adam, was subject to the necessity of contracting original sin, but by a special intervention of God she was preserved from stain of original sin. Thus Mary also was redeemed 'by the grace of Christ,' but in a more perfect manner than other human beings.

"While these are freed from original sin present in their souls, Mary, the Mother of the Redeemer, was preserved from the contagion of original sin. Thus the dogma of the Immaculate Conception of Mary in no way contradicts the dogma that all children of Adam are subject to original sin and need redemption" (p. 199).

Q. Could you please explain the underlined sentences in the first reading for the Solemnity of the Assumption of our Blessed Mother into Heaven? — J.C.N., California
A. The sentences, from chapter 12 of the Book of Revelation, are as follows:

"Then another sign appeared in the sky: it was a huge dragon, flaming red, with seven heads and ten horns; on his head were seven diadems. His tail swept a third of the stars from the sky and hurled them down to the earth. Then the dragon stood before the woman about to give birth, ready to devour her child when it should be born. She gave birth to a son — a boy who is destined to shepherd all the nations with an iron rod. Her child was snatched up to God and to his throne."

The Book of Revelation, which is filled with extravagant symbolism and apocalyptic imagery, is not easy to interpret. But the traditional explanation of these verses (cf. the footnotes in most Catholic Bibles) is that the dragon is Satan, the seven diadems symbolize the fullness of the dragon's sovereignty over the kingdoms of this world, the child brought forth is the Messiah, the woman who gave birth to the Messiah is Israel, and the snatching of the child up to Heaven is the Ascension of Jesus.

For more thoughts on these verses, see chapter 12 of Fr. Alfred McBride's book *The Second Coming of Jesus: Meditation and Commentary on the Book of Revelation* (Our Sunday Visitor).

Q. Can you please tell me when and why were the months of May and October designated as months of special devotion to the Blessed Virgin? — R.A.G., New Jersey
A. According to an article by Francis D. Costa, S.S.S., which can be found in volume III of *Mariology*, which was edited by Fr. Juniper B. Carol, O.F.M., and published in 1960 by the Bruce Publishing Company, May was chosen as the month of Mary during the Middle Ages to counteract pagan festivals that were common at that time of year. King Alphonsus X of Spain (died in 1284) appears to have been the first person to link Mary with

the month of May, and the idea gained popularity over the next few centuries.

The practice spread rapidly in the 18th century due to the publication of several handbooks or manuals, such as *The Month of Mary or the Month of May* in 1725, *The Month of Mary* in 1758, and *The Month of May* in 1785, with chapters on the life of the Blessed Mother, her virtues and privileges, and suggestions for decorating her altar or statue, reciting the rosary, and singing her litany.

By the 19th century, May was celebrated as Mary's month throughout Europe and the United States, and Popes Pius VII and Pius IX attached indulgences to the May devotions. Twentieth century Popes also spoke favorably of Marian piety during the month of May, notably Pius XII in *Mediator Dei* (1947) and Paul VI in *Mense Maio* (1965). In the latter, Pope Paul said:

"It is precisely because the month of May is a powerful incentive to more fervent and trusting prayer, and because during it our petitions find their way more easily to the compassionate heart of Our Blessed Lady, that it has been a custom dear to our predecessors to choose this month, dedicated to Mary, for inviting the Christian people to offer up public prayers, whenever the needs of the Church demanded it, or whenever danger hovered menacingly over the world."

While the origins of October as the month dedicated to Our Lady and her rosary go back to the Dominican rosary devotions commemorating the victory at Lepanto in October 1571, and to the institution of the feast of the Holy Rosary on October 7th by Pope Gregory XIII in 1573, it was Pope Leo XIII who was particularly responsible for designating this month as one devoted to the Blessed Virgin.

He ordered all parish churches to celebrate October as Our Lady's month in 1883 and, in 1894, said in one of his many rosary messages that "it is always with joyful expectation and renewed hope that we look forward to the return of the month of October. At our exhortation and by our express order this month has been consecrated to the Blessed Virgin" (*Iucunda Semper*).

Q. Please tell me whatever is known about the beautiful spiral stairway in the Loretto Chapel in Santa Fe, New Mexico. — P.R.B., Michigan

A. According to the information we have, the beautiful chapel, which was the subject of a 1998 CBS television movie ("The Staircase"), was originally built without a way to reach the choir loft. Adding a regular staircase would have taken up too much room, and a ladder wasn't a viable option, so the Loretto nuns at the chapel prayed a nine-day novena to St. Joseph.

On the final day of the novena, an elderly man arrived at the chapel on a donkey and said that he had been sent to build a stairway. Using only a hammer, a T-square, a saw, and some hot water to bend the wood, he completed the work in six to eight months in the year 1878. The spiral stairway makes two 360-degree turns and was built without nails or any visible supports.

When the nuns went to pay the man, he had disappeared. They thought they should at least pay for the wood, but the only lumber yard in town had not sold any lumber to the mysterious carpenter and the wood he had used was not found anywhere in New Mexico, nor had he brought any lumber with him.

The sisters believed that St. Joseph had built the stairway, and some of the details have a religious significance. The 33 curving steps symbolize the years Jesus lived on earth and the seven-foot diameter of the staircase and the seven-inch height of the steps signify the seven Sacraments. A handrail and some metal braces were added several decades later, and the chapel operates today as a private museum that is visited by more than 100,000 people each year.

Q. My friend says that we are not obliged to believe in apparitions. I say we are. If the Church proclaims something to be true, we have an obligation to believe it. Is my friend right or am I? — D.G., Pennsylvania

A. Your friend is correct. We are only obliged to believe in *public* revelation, which ended with the death of the last Apostle, and in what the Church teaches about the revealed truths we find in Sacred Scripture and Tradition. The apparitions of our Lord, the Blessed Virgin Mary, or the saints to certain individuals come under the heading of *private* revelation, and we are not bound to believe in those apparitions since they are not part of the Deposit of Faith.

The *Catechism* tells us that "throughout the ages, there have been so-called 'private' revelations, some of which have been recognized by the authority of the Church. They do not belong, however, to the deposit of faith. It is not their role to improve or complete Christ's definitive Revelation, but to help live more fully by it during a certain period of history." It is up to the magisterium of the Church, the *Catechism* says, to guide "the *sensus fidelium*" in knowing "how to discern and welcome in these revelations whatever constitutes an authentic call of Christ or his saints to the Church" (n. 67).

The *Catechism* says that the "Christian faith cannot accept 'revelations' that claim to surpass or correct the Revelation of which Christ is the fulfillment, as in the case in certain non-Christian religions and also in certain recent sects which base themselves on such 'revelations' " (n. 67).

Catholics may, however, believe in those apparitions which are well-authenticated and have been approved by the Church. "Marian shrines and places of pilgrimage are a kind of 'geography' of faith by which we seek to meet the Mother of God in order to find a strengthening of our Christian life," said Pope John Paul in San Antonio, Texas, on September 13, 1987. "Popular devotion to the Blessed Virgin Mary is rooted in sound doctrine."

Q. I would like to know if the Pope and the bishops consecrated Russia to the Immaculate Heart of Mary in 1984. According to Fr. Nicholas Gruner, the Pope has not consecrated Russia and needs to do so. What am I to believe? — D.L., Illinois

A. There are two schools of thought on the Fatima consecration, that of Fr. Gruner and that of Fr. Robert Fox, who believes that the consecration did take place. We have always found Fr. Fox to be a more reliable commentator on the Fatima events than Fr. Gruner, and we would side with him, especially since Fr. Fox contends that Sister Lucia, the surviving member of the trio to whom the Blessed Mother appeared in 1917, has confirmed that the 1984 consecration was authentic.

Editor's Note: In a recent reply about whether the Holy Father consecrated Russia to the Immaculate Heart of Mary in 1984, we sided with Fr. Robert Fox, who believes that the consecration did take place, This prompted 22 readers of this column to take issue with us.

Before addressing their objections, some background information is in order. During her appearance to Lucia, Francisco, and Jacinta on July 13, 1917, Our Lady said that to prevent God from punishing the world for its crimes by means of war, hunger, and persecution of the Church and of the Holy Father, "I come to ask the consecration of Russia to my Immaculate Heart and the Communion of reparation on the first Saturdays. If they listen to my requests, Russia will be converted and there will be peace.

"If not, she will scatter her errors throughout the world, provoking wars and persecutions of the Church. The good will be martyred, the Holy Father will have much to suffer, various nations will be annihilated. In the end, my Immaculate Heart will triumph. The Holy Father will consecrate Russia to me, and it will be converted and a certain period of peace will be granted to the world."

Twelve years later, on June 13, 1929, the Blessed Mother appeared to Sister Lucia, the surviving member of the trio, and said that "the moment has come when God asks the Holy Father, in union with all the bishops of the world, to make the consecration of Russia to my heart, promising to save it by these means."

Now here are the objections voiced by our readers and our response:

Objection: The consecration of March 25, 1984 was not done as the Blessed Mother had requested since Russia was not specifically mentioned and the consecration was not carried out simultaneously by bishops in their own cathedrals throughout the world.

Response: On December 8, 1983, Pope John Paul had sent a letter to the world's Catholic bishops, along with an Act of Consecration that he asked them to make with him on the feast of the Annunciation, March 25, 1984. The act did not specifically mention Russia, but rather "the whole world" and "especially the peoples for which by reason of their situation you have particular love and solicitude." The Holy Father said that "the power of this consecration lasts for all time and embraces all individuals, peoples, and nations."

Since "all individuals, peoples, and nations" presumably includes Russia, Fr. Fox contends that the consecration was authentic. He concedes that not every bishop in the world joined in the consecration, but agrees with Bishop Alberto Cosme do Amara, the Bishop of Leira-Fatima, that a "moral totality" of the world's bishops participated.

Fr. Gruner disagrees on both counts, insisting that the consecration was not valid since it did not mention Russia by name and the Holy Father was not joined by every bishop in the world in a simultaneous consecration in his own cathedral. Fr. Gruner would appear to have the better of the argument here, but note the words of Sister Lucia at the end of the next response.

Objection: Pope John Paul admitted afterwards that the conditions of the Blessed Mother had not been met, and Sister Lucia has also said that the consecration was not authentic.

Response: Fr. Gruner says that during the consecration, Pope John Paul addressed Our Lady of Fatima in these words: "Enlighten especially the peoples of which you yourself are awaiting our consecration." Gruner contends that the words "are awaiting" mean that the Pope knew that the consecration had not really taken place. We don't think that such an interpretation is credible. It might be credible if those words of the Holy Father were spoken days or weeks later, but they were spoken during the act of consecration and thus before it was completed

What was Lucia's reaction to the 1984 consecration? In the book *Fatima Priest*, Francis Alban's laudatory account of the life and apostolate of Nicholas Gruner, Fr. Gruner offers as evidence that the consecration was not authentic this statement, allegedly from Lucia, that appeared in the September 1985 issue of *Sol de Fatima*: "There was no participation of all the bishops and there was no mention of Russia." When the interviewer then asked, "So the consecration was not done as requested by Our Lady?" Sister Lucia reportedly answered: "No. Many bishops attached no importance to this act."

It is curious that Gruner would cite that 1985 statement as proof of his position since he contends that Lucia has been silenced since 1960!

On the other side, we have Fr. Fox, who has published in his *Fatima Family Messenger* a letter purportedly from Sister Lucia, dated August 29, 1989, in which she said:

"Then this same Supreme Pontiff, His Holiness Pope John Paul II, wrote to all the bishops of the world asking them to unite with him. He sent for the statue of Our Lady of Fatima — the one from the little chapel — to be taken to Rome, and on March 25, 1984 — publicly — with the bishops who wanted to unite with His Holiness, made the consecration as Our Lady requested. They then asked me if it was made as Our Lady requested, and I said 'yes.' Now it was made."

Fr. Gruner says that this letter is a fake, but there is no evidence to support his claim.

Objection: Fr. Fox said on Mother Angelica's EWTN television station that Russia has not been consecrated yet and that the real consecration will take place on October 16, 1999.
Response: We called Fr. Fox and he told us that he had made no such statement on EWTN or anywhere else. He also sent us the April-June 1999 issue of *Fatima Family Messenger* in which he had reiterated his conviction that the 1984 consecration was authentic.

Objection: There has been no conversion of Russia and no peace in the world since 1984, which can only mean that a real consecration did not take place.
Response: The Blessed Mother did not set a timetable for the conversion of Russia or say when the world would be granted a period of peace. The fact that neither has happened yet does not mean that the consecration did not occur. The beginnings of the conversion of Russia are underway — as indicated by the dedication of a shrine to Our Lady of Fatima in St. Petersburg in October 1998 and the presence of 77 Russian students in the Catholic seminary in that city — but we don't know when the Immaculate Heart of Mary will finally triumph.

Objection: If we had read Francis Alban's book, we would know the truth about this matter and would not think that Fr. Fox was a more reliable commentator on the Fatima events than Fr. Gruner.
Response: We have read *Fatima Priest*, and it did not change our evaluation of the two men. For instance, there is Fr. Gruner's disturbing statement that Pope John Paul is in a state of objective mortal sin for not having consecrated Russia according to Our Lady's wishes. "I am not the confessor of the Pope," said Gruner, "so I cannot judge his subjective state of guilt or innocence. I have confined my answers to what the Pope is bound to do in the objective moral order" (p. 266).

If he were the Pope's confessor, said Gruner, "then I would have to tell him he would be bound before God to make such an undertaking [the consecration] and tell him that he was in danger of losing his soul in Hell if he didn't make such an undertaking." Gruner said that "the Pope is most seriously bound to obey

Our Lady of Fatima, even under pain of mortal sin" and, if he didn't obey Our Lady, then his confessor, "if he knows Fatima like I do," would be obligated "to refuse the Pope absolution" (pp. 268-269).

It's one thing to express doubt about whether the consecration has actually taken place, but it's quite another to assert that the Vicar of Christ on earth is in a state of objective mortal sin

In conclusion, we don't pretend to be the last word on this matter, and we are sure that people will continue to disagree on the Fatima consecration. But we believe that there are good reasons for siding with Fr. Fox and that it is unfair and uncharitable to accuse those who agree with him of slandering Fr. Gruner. It is not slander to look at the evidence and to choose one point of view over another.

Q. I recently read that the "third secret of Fatima" was made public by the Vatican in June 2000. What were the three events foretold by the Blessed Mother at Fatima? — J.J.V., Illinois

A. The first secret was the vision of Hell given to the children on July 13, 1917. "You have seen Hell where the souls of poor sinners go," the Blessed Virgin said. "In order to save them, God wishes to establish in the world devotion to my Immaculate Heart." That was part of the second secret, that Lucia would spread devotion to the Immaculate Heart of Mary.

Lucia would also later reveal our Lady's promise "to assist at the hour of death, with all the graces necessary for salvation, all those who, on the first Saturday of five consecutive months, go to Confession and receive Holy Communion, recite five decades of the rosary, and keep me company for a quarter of an hour while meditating on the mysteries of the rosary, with the intention of making reparation to me."

Other parts of the second secret that were revealed by the Blessed Mother during that same appearance on July 13th included the spread of Communism throughout the world, but the eventual conversion of Russia and a period of peace "if my requests are heeded"; the persecution of the Church and much suffering for the Holy Father; and the imminent end of World War I, but also the outbreak during the pontificate of Pope Pius XI (1922-1939) of an even more terrible war if people did not "cease offending God."

In 1944, then-Sister Lucia wrote down a third secret, which was sent to the Holy Father but not revealed to the world until June 26, 2000. That secret involved a vision of "a bishop dressed in white" (presumably the Pope) struggling up a mountain amid many corpses until he reached the top and, while kneeling at the foot of a large cross, "he was killed by a group of soldiers who fired bullets and arrows at him, and in the same way there died one after another the other bishops, priests, men and women religious, and various lay people of different ranks and positions.

"Beneath the two arms of the cross, there were two angels each with a crystal aspersorium in his hand, in which they gathered up the blood of martyrs and with it sprinkled the souls that were making their way to God."

Pope John Paul interpreted the vision as referring to the assassination attempt on his life on May 13, 1981, the anniversary of the Blessed Virgin's first appearance to the children at Fatima 64 years earlier. The reason he was not killed, the Holy Father said later, was that the Blessed Mother's hand guided the bullet away from what would have been a fatal path. That bullet was subsequently set in the crown of the statue of Our Lady of Fatima in Portugal.

Still there are those who do not believe that the whole third secret was revealed, that it may have included predictions of the terrorist attacks on New York City and the Pentagon on September 11, 2001, and that Sister Lucia has revealed new apocalyptic interpretations of the Fatima message. To dispel such rumors, Archbishop Tarcisio Bertone, secretary of the Vatican's Sacred Congregation for the Doctrine of the Faith, met personally for two hours with Sister Lucia on November 17, 2001, at her convent in Coimbra, Portugal.

Asked whether any part of the third secret had not been made known, Lucia replied: "Everything has been published; there are no more secrets. If I had received new revelations, I would not have communicated them to anyone, but I would have told them directly to the Holy Father."

Asked about Fr. Nicholas Gruner's campaign to collect signatures urging that the Holy Father finally consecrate Russia to the Immaculate Heart of Mary, Sister Lucia replied that her religious community "has rejected the forms for the collection of signatures. I have already said that the consecration requested by our Lady was done in 1984, and it has been accepted in Heaven."

Q. Is La Salette an approved apparition? A book I read on it indicated that our Lady said, "Rome will lose faith and become the seat of the Antichrist." But isn't that a contradiction of what our Lord said about the gates of Hell not prevailing against His Church? — E.B., New York

A. Yes, La Salette is an apparition approved by the Church. On November 16, 1851, the bishop of the region, after a five-year investigation, ordered the following statement to be read at every Mass in his diocese: "We give judgment that the apparition of the Blessed Virgin to two herders on September 19, 1846, on the mountain of the Alpine chain situated in the parish of La Salette, in the territory of the archpriest of Corps, bears in itself all the marks of truth, and the faithful have grounds to believe it indubitable and certain."

During her appearance to 14-year-old Melanie Mathieu and 11-year-old Maximin Giraud, the Blessed Mother said that the two things most distressing to her were neglect of the Sunday Mass obligation and the misuse of her Son's name. If people did not stop committing these sins, she said, "I shall be compelled to loose my Son's arm. It is so heavy, so pressing that I can no longer restrain it. How long have I suffered for you! If my Son is not to cast you off, I am obliged to entreat Him without ceasing. But you take no least notice of that. No matter how well you pray in the future, no matter how well you act, you will never be able to make up to me what I have endured for your sake."

Our Lady also revealed a secret to each of the children. This information was later passed on to the Holy Father, but the nature of the secrets has never been made public.

The La Salette accounts that we have read do not include the statement about Rome losing faith and becoming the seat of the Antichrist. While it is possible that the city of Rome could lose faith and become the seat of the Antichrist, this could never happen to the See of Peter (the Catholic Church), since, as you suggest, it would contradict our Lord's promise that His Church would never be overcome by the powers of Hell.

Q. Would you please let your readers know about the phoniness of the Lourdes Research Organization, which sent me the enclosed information? People do get snookered by this kind of nonsense. — D.J.L., Washington

A. The letter from the Lourdes Research Organization, with addresses in New York City and Ontario, Canada and the signature of a "Mathew [sic] Saint Paul," promises miracles to those who buy, for $20, a "Genuine Lady of Lourdes Rosary containing both the Miraculous Water of Lourdes and 59 genuine Aurora Borealis Faceted Crystals." And those who respond within five days will also get "the Miraculous Earth of Fatima, the Miraculous Water of the River Jordan, [and] the Miraculous Earth of Bethlehem."

The letter promises "miracles that make you rich (with wads of big bills to spend as you please); miracles that bring you lasting Love (and the unquestioning faithfulness of those you adore); miracles that deliver you new expensive cars; miracles that let you win at bingo, the lottery, the race track, the casinos (wherever you go, you hit the jackpot!); miracles that put you in a top job with great pay and glamorous vacations; miracles that give you a luxurious new home, where all your family lives the life of joy and happiness."

We hope and pray that nobody, Catholic or otherwise, will fall for this unscrupulous scam.

Q. Recently we received a video from a benefactor on Garabandal. I was deeply impressed, but my confessor says that he thinks Garabandal is disapproved. What is the status of Garabandal? — R.L.F., Alabama

A. Your confessor is right, and here is the background. Garabandal is a town in northern Spain where the Blessed Mother was reported to have appeared to a group of children from 1961 to 1965. After an investigation of the alleged appearances, Bishop Vicente Montis, Ordinary of the diocese in which Garabandal is located, issued this statement:

"There have been no apparitions of the Blessed Virgin, of Michael the Archangel, or of any other celestial person; there have been no messages. All of the reported happenings in that area have a natural explanation."

The following year, this finding was upheld by Bishop Montis' successor, who told priests and laity to stop their pilgrimages to a chapel built at Garabandal "in rebellious resistance to the findings of the Church" concerning the alleged apparitions.

In 1977, the Ordinary of the diocese, Bishop Antonio Del Val Gallo, visited the shrine and met with those said to have been involved in the reported events of 1961. He then said that "I am in agreement with these bishops, my predecessors. I was always open in charity and without prejudice, and will always be willing to consider any occurrence that takes place here. But in the six years I have been bishop of Santander, no new phenomenon has taken place."

Editor's Note: Several readers have taken issue with what they called "inadequate" and "negative" comments on the reported apparitions of the Blessed Virgin Mary in Garabandal, Spain. To show that we were off base, these readers sent along an interview that Bishop Del Val gave in 1992, nine months after he retired as Ordinary.

In the interview, which was reprinted in the October/December, 1993 issue of *Garabandal* magazine, the bishop said that while his predecessors "did not admit that the apparitions were supernatural," they did not condemn them, He said that he decided to reopen the investigation into the matter in the mid-1980s "because I thought something serious had happened in Garabandal. It seemed to me that because it was so serious, I had to find out for myself exactly what happened."

The investigation was completed in April, 1991, Bishop Del Val said, and the results were given to Joseph Cardinal Ratzinger of the Sacred Congregation for the Doctrine of the Faith in Rome. He said, however, that he was not aware that the Congregation had issued any statement, positive or negative, on Garabandal.

Asked in the interview if the reported messages of Garabandal were "found to be theologically correct and in accordance with the teachings of the Catholic Church," Del Val responded:

"Theologically correct, yes. But one of the details bothers me: 'Many bishops and cardinals are walking the path of perdition.' It seems to me to be a bit severe. However, the messages do not say anything that is against the doctrine of the Church."

Without stating that the messages are authentic, the bishop said that "it is important for us Christians to live what the messages of the Blessed Mother are saying, if we consider that she could have said them — but I'm not saying that she did, since this would be admitting that the apparitions are true, and I cannot do that because the Church has not yet said so. The Church is the one that has the last word."

There is nothing in this interview that contradicts what we reported in the previous reply. All we said is what the publishers of *Garabandal* magazine have been saying on their masthead for years, namely, that the original negative determination of the bishop's office "has not been amended by the bishop of Santander or by the Sacred Congregation for the Doctrine of the Faith. The publishers of this magazine hope that the Church's official position will, after further investigation, be amended in the future."

Q. Please tell me if the enclosed statements on Medjugorje attributed to Pope John Paul II are legitimate? — F.V.W., Oregon

A. According to the enclosed bulletin from Apostles of the Holy Spirit in Cincinnati, the Holy Father has reportedly said: "It is good for pilgrims to go to Medjugorje and do penance" (1988), "Medjugorje is a great center of spirituality!" (1990), "Our Lady of Medjugorje will save America!" (1994), and "if I were not Pope, I would be in Medjugorje already" (no date).

There is no credible evidence that Pope John Paul ever made any of these statements. In fact, when inquiries about the alleged 1988 statement were made to the Vatican, then-Apostolic Nuncio Archbishop Pio Laghi replied:

"The statement you cite as a quotation from the Holy Father has never been published or officially verified. Although there have been many observations about Medjugorje attributed to the Holy Father or other officials of the Holy See, none of these have been acknowledged as authentic."

There are other indications that Pope John Paul does not support the alleged apparitions in Medjugorje: (1) In 1993, he appointed as the bishop of the region Msgr. Ratko Peric, who is adamant in his belief that the reported apparitions are not authentic. (2) During a visit to the Croatian capital of Zagreb on September 10-11, 1994, the Holy Father never made any reference to Medjugorje, although he did send greetings to Msgr. Peric and his predecessor, Msgr. Pavao Zanic, who is also a strong critic of those who claim supernatural happenings at the village.

(3) Speaking at the Sacred Heart Cathedral in Sarajevo on April 12, 1997, John Paul again made no mention of Medjugorje, although he did praise pilgrimages to a diocesan-approved Marian shrine, Our Lady Queen of Peace in Hrasno, 25 miles

from Medjugorje. He later praised that shrine as "a true center of Marian devotion" in a letter to Msgr. Peric.

If the Holy Father were truly a supporter of Medjugorje, where the same Blessed Mother to whom he has entrusted his papacy is alleged to have appeared thousands of times since 1981, how likely is it that he would say nothing about it while only a few miles away? And why would he specifically single out instead a virtually unknown shrine, unless perhaps it was his subtle way of telling the faithful to patronize only approved apparition sites?

Is it possible that his true feelings about Medjugorje were expressed in the following statement that appeared in *L'Osservatore Romano* on September 18, 1996 (cf. Michael Davies' book *Medjugorje After Fifteen Years*)?:

"Some members of the People of God are not rooted firmly enough in the faith, so that the sects, with their deceptive proselytism, mislead them to separate themselves from true communion in Christ. Within the Church community, the multiplication of supposed 'apparitions' or 'visions' is sowing confusion and reveals a certain lack of a solid basis to the faith and Christian life among her members."

Q. I have come across a book entitled *My Work With Necedah* by Henry H. Swan. Where can I obtain other books about Mary Ann Van Hoof? — R.V., Arizona

A. Mrs. Van Hoof, who died in 1984, claimed in the 1950s that the Blessed Virgin Mary was appearing to her in Necedah, Wisconsin. People soon flocked to the site, but the Bishop of La Crosse concluded after a five-year investigation that the claims of Mrs. Van Hoof were false.

Another bishop of that diocese came to the same conclusion in 1969 and, in 1975, the bishop placed the leaders of the shrine under personal interdict, which meant that they could not receive the sacraments. When in 1979 Mrs. Van Hoof and her followers brought in a phony "archbishop" to consecrate the shrine, the bishop of La Crosse issued a statement that said, among other things:

"For the guidance of the faithful, it should be noted that this action on the part of Mrs. Mary Ann Van Hoof and her followers joined in 'For My God and Country, Inc.' definitely establishes that they are no longer affiliated with the Roman Catholic Church and acknowledge this separation by this action of approving the celebration of the Holy Sacrifice of the Mass by an unauthorized person."

We not only don't know where you would obtain books about Mrs. Van Hoof, but we see little value in reading about this misguided woman. Pray for her soul.

Q. Regarding your recent column about Mary Ann Van Hoof and her claim that the Blessed Virgin appeared to her in Necedah, Wisconsin, in the 1950s, I visited the Necedah shrine twice this past summer. They have a home for unwed mothers, oppose abortion, and run a Christ-centered orthodox Catholic school. As far as I could tell, they are much more aligned to the Roman Catholic Church than are most of the more liberalized churches I have been to over the years. They say that the bishop considers them disobedient, but could it be that the information released to the public by the bishops of the area was in error? Can you give me any other references about this group of people? They seem to be part of the "remnant" church that could be instrumental in keeping Catholicism alive. — D.H.P., Wisconsin

A. As we noted in the previous reply, the bishops of La Crosse declared on four different occasions, from the mid-1950s to the late 1970s, that there was no validity to the claims that the Blessed Mother had appeared at Necedah. When several bishops, after years of investigation, come to the same conclusion about a reported apparition, a prudent Catholic will heed such authoritative warnings and distance himself from those who would substitute their own authority for that of the Church.

Second, the suggestion that the group in Necedah might be the surviving remnant of the true Church is simply ludicrous. "Where Peter is, there is the Church" is an ancient truism, and Peter (in the person of the reigning Pontiff) is in Rome today, not in Necedah.

Third, we don't doubt for a minute that some devotees of Necedah seem much closer to what the Catholic Church teaches than some other people who call themselves Catholics and then dissent from what the Church holds to be true. But this doesn't excuse their rejection of legitimate Church authority or their establishment of their own magisterium. All salvation comes from

Jesus Christ through the Church which is His Body, and not through private revelations, whether they are true or false. Those who leave the Bark of Peter to pursue some private revelation endanger their salvation.

Q. What can you tell me about a group called St. Michael's World Apostolate in Bayside, NY and a woman named Veronica Lueken to whom the Blessed Mother is supposed to have appeared from 1970 until her death in 1995 and to have given over 300 messages for the Church and the world? I called them and they sent me a rose petal blessed by Jesus and Mary and the enclosed flyer. — D.L., Illinois

A. Two bishops of Brooklyn investigated the reported apparitions to Mrs. Lueken at Bayside and declared, in 1973 and 1986, that they were not worthy of belief and that Catholics should not participate in the Bayside vigils or read or distribute any of the Bayside literature since some of the so-called messages were contrary to the teachings of the Catholic Church and instilled doubt in the minds of the faithful. One message, for example, claimed that Pope Paul VI was replaced by an imposter during his reign (1963-1978) as Supreme Pontiff.

The St. Michael's World Apostolate is apparently a group of people who are trying to keep alive Mrs. Lueken's hoax. Stay away from them.

Q. How many archangels are there? I contend that only three are mentioned in the Bible: Michael, Gabriel, and Raphael. My antagonists have come up with seven — the above three and an additional four which they obtained from a *Funk & Wagnall's Dictionary* and whom I believe are listed in the apocryphal Book of Enoch. Can you shed any light on the above? — H.A.H., New Jersey

A. You are correct that only three archangels (the name means a chief or ruling angel) are named in the Bible: Michael in Jude 9 and Revelation 12:7-9, Gabriel in Luke 1:11-20 and 26-38, and Raphael in Tobit 12:15. Others are named in the Book of Enoch (Uriel or Phanuel), but they are not recognized in Catholic teaching because that book is not considered a work inspired by the Holy Spirit.

According to Fr. John McKenzie's *Dictionary of the Bible* (Simon & Schuster), there are actually two books of Enoch: the Ethiopic

Enoch and the Slavonic Enoch, both of which have much to say about angels. Ethiopic Enoch is even quoted in the Letter of Jude, verses 14-15, but it is not included in the canon of Scripture because it did not have a divine Author.

Q. It is my understanding that some years back a Pope prescribed that the prayer to St. Michael the Archangel be said after each Mass. Do you have the background on this, and the words of the prayer? — R.A.H., Washington

A. It was Pope Leo XIII who, after experiencing a vision of the devil in 1884, composed the prayer to St. Michael, which was recited after Mass until the revision of the Mass in 1964. We know of many people who continue to recite this prayer every day, and we would strongly recommend the practice. Here is the prayer (the words may vary, depending on who is saying it):

"St. Michael, the Archangel, defend us in battle. Be our protection against the wickedness and snares of the devil. May God rebuke him, we humbly beseech you, and may you, O Prince of the Heavenly Host, by the power of God, cast into Hell Satan and all the evil spirits who prowl about the world seeking the ruin of souls. Amen."

Q. The Apostles had to pick a replacement for Judas from two choices. I know that the one selected, Matthias, became a saint. What can you tell me about the one not picked? — M.P., Illinois

A. His name was Joseph Barsabbas, also known as Justus. He was a candidate to replace Judas because, in the words of St. Peter, he "was of our company while the Lord Jesus moved among us, from the baptism of John until the day he was taken up from us" (Acts 1:21-22).

But that's all we know about this disciple, except that, yes, he is a saint and his feast day is July 20th.

Q. I am devoted to St. Jude. Please tell me more about his life and how he came to be honored as the saint of hopeless causes. — M.B.C., Illinois

A. There is very little information about St. Jude. Listed in the Gospels as one of the 12 Apostles, he was also known as Thaddeus. In the first line of the brief New Testament letter that many scholars have attributed to him, Jude calls himself "a servant of Jesus Christ and brother of James," a reference to St. James, the leader of the Christian community in Jerusalem.

Some scholars, however, think that the Apostle Jude and the author of the letter were two different persons. In any case, tradition tells us that Jude and St. Simon preached in Mesopotamia and Persia, and that they were martyred. They share October 28th as their feast day, and Jude is usually depicted in art with a halberd, a battle-ax and pike mounted on a handle about six feet long, because that was the instrument of his death.

We do not know the reason why he is the patron saint of hopeless causes.

Q. Please explain about Santiago de Compostela. Is this in Spain, and is this St. James the Apostle? Also, what can you tell me about San Diego and San Jacinto? — A.H., Washington

A. Tradition tells us that St. James the Greater, one of the 12 Apostles, spread the Gospel in Spain (he is now that country's patron saint) and is buried there at Santiago de Compostela, which has long been one of the major pilgrimage sites in Europe.

As the story goes, the Blessed Mother appeared to James and several of his disciples near Saragossa (now Zaragoza) and left behind a small jasper column on which she had stood. That column or pillar has survived numerous invasions and destructions of chapels and churches in which it was housed and is kept today in the Church of the Virgin of the Pillar, which was declared a national museum in 1904. Pope John Paul II prayed at this shrine in 1982.

For more on the shrine, see Joan Carroll Cruz's book *Relics* (Our Sunday Visitor).

As for the other questions, two readers have provided answers. P.B. of Pennsylvania wrote to say:

"The two Apostles named James are called Santiago el Mayor and Santiago el Menor in Spanish. Santiago de Compostela refers to the city in Spain and thus differentiates it from the cities of Santiago de Cuba and Santiago de Chile in the Americas. San Diego becomes the combined form Santiago, and San Jacinto is Spanish for St. Hyacinth."

And R.S.J. of Virginia, a recent visitor to the pilgrimage site of Santiago de Compostela, said:

"Santiago de Compostela is indeed the city in which St. James the Greater is reputedly buried. Shepherds were supposedly led to the grave-site by stars, supporting the contention that 'compostela' is derived from *campus stellae* (field of stars), although a relatively recent discovery of a necropolis under the massive cathedral makes an alternative explanation possible since 'compostela' is Latin for cemetery.

"Santiago de Compostela is in Galicia, in northwest Spain. This is a Celtic region and the language is Gallego, somewhat akin to Portuguese. 'Santiago' is Gallego and Portuguese spelling for St. James. On the other hand, 'San Diego' is Castillian for St. James. The California city of San Diego was named in 1602 for the Franciscan San Diego de Alcala (although he in turn might have been named for an Apostle, of course).

"There are numerous Santiagos and San Diegos in Spanish-settled areas, named, presumably, for various Saints James or for the Iberian cities already bearing their names."

Q. Please tells us some particulars about the Priscilla who is mentioned in today's Mass reading. (Nice to know my namesake goes back so far. — P.L., Massachusetts

A. Also known by the name Prisca, the Priscilla mentioned in Acts 18:1-3 came to Corinth with her husband Aquila after the Roman Emperor Claudius had ordered all Jews out of Rome. The couple lived with St. Paul in Corinth and they worked as tent makers. The three of them later traveled to Ephesus (Acts 18:18-19) and, after Paul had gone on to Antioch, Aquila and Priscilla instructed the brilliant orator Apollos in "God's new way" (Acts 18:26).

The couple's house in Corinth served as a church, and Paul commended them as "my fellow workers in the service of Christ Jesus," who "even risked their lives for the sake of mine. Not only I but all the churches of the Gentiles are grateful to them. Remember me also to the congregation that meets in their house" (Romans 16:3-5)

They were martyred in Asia Minor, according to the *Roman Martyrology*, but another tradition has them martyred in Rome.

Q. Last night on TV I saw a program that spelled out the procedure for the canonization of a saint. It said that the process changed in 1983, that there is no longer a "devil's advocate," that seven men read the history of the

individual, and they act upon the history and other information in making their decision. Is this now the procedure? — C.E.Z., California, and F.C.S., Michigan

A. Yes, the process for canonization was changed in 1983 when Pope John Paul issued the apostolic constitution *Divinus Perfectionis Magister* and a revised set of procedural steps entitled *Norms to Be Observed in Inquiries Made by Bishops in the Causes of Saints*. There are 36 of these norms, many of them with subsections, so we would recommend getting a copy of Michael Freze's book *The Making of Saints* (Our Sunday Visitor). He lists all of the norms in chapter nine and describes the entire process in subsequent chapters.

There still is a "devil's advocate," though he is not known by that inappropriate title, but rather as the "promoter of justice" during the diocesan phase of the inquiry and as the "promoter of the faith" when the petition reaches Rome. Both promoters must be priests who are experts in theological, historical, and canonical matters.

Their responsibilities include making sure that all norms and procedures are followed to the letter, and that all negative facts, errors, misleading information, and false testimony about the candidate are disclosed. They function much as a prosecutor does in a courtroom, with the postulator or petitioner for the cause acting as a defense counsel.

Once the diocesan inquiry has been satisfactorily completed, the *Acts of the Cause* are sent to Rome, where the Sacred Congregation for the Causes of Saints compiles two documents: a *Position on the Life and Virtues or Martyrdom* of the servant of God, and a *Position on the Miracle*. Both are studied and evaluated by the bishops and cardinals of the congregation, and the final step is when the Holy Father reviews their evaluation and decides whether to beatify the candidate for sainthood.

Q. Does the act of canonization imply that the saint went to Heaven without first going through Purgatory? Would a canonized saint have to go through Purgatory before reaching Heaven? — G.J.L., Louisiana

A. While every person who reaches Heaven becomes a saint, very few members of the human race have been officially proclaimed a saint by the Church, and most of those only after a long and very thorough investigation of their life. Since canonization is the Church's official recognition of a person's extraordinary holiness of life and detachment from the things of this world, such persons have no need of purification in Purgatory and thus go directly to Heaven.

In his book *The Making of Saints*, Michael Freze illustrated what we are saying when he defined a saint as "a privileged or chosen soul who, because of his or her total faith and love for God and neighbor, lived a life of heroic virtue in a constant and persevering manner (or who died a martyr's death through another's hatred of the faith), and who imitated Christ's life and teaching according to the letter of the Gospel" (pp. 18-19).

Freze said that "the saint has lived a life of such singlemindedness and determination that he or she has become totally selfless, completely giving for God and for others .... Another rarity in the quest for sanctity concerns the qualities of humility and purity of heart. Those who truly possess these characteristics have reached a level of wholeness and completeness that only a select number ever achieve.

"To be one with Christ — to be 'in this world but not of this world' — means to be transformed into his very likeness and image, to reflect the divine in an imperfect world riddled with pride, aggression, greed, lust, hate, and oppression. It is to strip oneself naked before others and before God. It is to subdue the weakness of spirit and flesh, and live for love and love alone. And to love God for himself — unconditionally — without expecting anything in return other than his love and sustaining grace" (pp. 20-21).

Q. Is it expensive to have a person canonized as a saint? — Name and State Unknown

A. According to an article published by the Catholic News Service, it cost about $250,000 to bring about the canonization of Elizabeth Ann Seton in 1975, and Fr. Gabriel O'Donnell, the postulator who is promoting the cause of Knights of Columbus founder Fr. Michael J. McGivney, estimates that the fraternal organization will spend about the same amount in pursuing sainthood for Fr. McGivney. He said that the expenses involved in the lengthy process are for such things as:

• Collection, examination, translation, and duplication of testimony from witnesses and documents by and about the candidate for sainthood.

• Exhumation and reburial of the "servant of God's" body.

• Preparation and publication of the position paper summarizing the candidate's life and heroic virtue.

• Investigation of miraculous cures attributed to prayers to the potential saint (two confirmed miracles are required).

• Stipends and expenses for the postulator and others working on the cause.

• Fees for theological, historical, and medical consultants.

• Beatification and canonization ceremonies, which are usually held in Rome.

Q. Do you know of a novena prayer to St. Monica, who prayed for so many years for her son Augustine? — M.J., Minnesota

A. Here is one you can try:

"Eternal and merciful Father, I give you thanks for the gift of your divine Son, who suffered, died, and rose for all people. I thank you also for my Catholic faith and ask your help that I may grow in faithfulness by prayer, by reflection on your word, by works of charity and penance, and by regular participation in the sacraments of Penance and the Holy Eucharist.

"You gave St. Monica a spirit of selfless love manifested in her constant prayer for the conversion of her son, Augustine. Inspired by boundless confidence in your power to move hearts, and by the success of her prayer, I ask the grace to imitate her constancy in my prayer for (N.), who no longer share(s) in the intimate life of your Catholic family.

"Grant through my prayer and witness, that they be open to the promptings of your Holy Spirit to return to loving union with your people. Grant also that my prayer be ever hopeful and that I may never judge another, for you alone can read hearts. I ask this through your Son, Jesus Christ, our Lord. Amen."

Q. Why are some of the Old Testament people who led such holy lives, such as Abraham, Moses, Isaiah, Jeremiah, Ezekiel, Daniel, and Elijah, not referred to as saints? Surely, they must be with God in His Kingdom? — R.L., New York, and P.W.S., California

A. Though these persons are not usually referred to as saints, that is precisely what they are. We know, for example, that Moses and Elijah are in Heaven because they appeared with Jesus during the Transfiguration (cf. Luke 9:28-36) and, in the *Rite of Bap-*

tism for Children, there is a litany of the saints that includes petitions to the prophets and fathers of our faith in general ("Holy patriarchs and prophets, pray for us") and by name ("Abraham, Moses, and Elijah, pray for us"). We also know of a church in a neighboring town that is called St. Jeremiah.

Furthermore, Abel and Abraham are mentioned in the Roman Canon or first Eucharistic Prayer of the Mass, and the *Roman Martyrology* lists as saints, with their feast days, Abdias, Aggaeus, Amos, Anna, Elisha, Gideon, Habacuc, Job, Joel, Jonas, Joshua, Nahum, Samuel, and Zachary. And on the Russian calendar of the Byzantine Catholic Rite, there are liturgical commemorations of Abraham and Lot (October 11), Moses (September 14), Samuel (August 20), Isaiah (May 9), Job (May 6), and the seven Maccabee brothers and their mother (August 1).

Q. Can you tell me anything about Bartolo Longo? Someone gave me a medal with his name stamped on it. — I.B., Connecticut

A. Bartolo Longo (1841-1926) was a young Italian who abandoned the Catholic faith for rationalism and spiritualism while studying law at the University of Naples. He came back to the Church through the efforts of a Dominican priest and joined the Third Order of St. Dominic in 1871, taking the religious name of Fratel Rosario (Brother Rosary) and beginning a crusade against spiritualism. He would attend seances and student parties and hold up a medal of our Lady while saying, "I renounce spiritualism because it is nothing but a maze of error and falsehood."

Arriving in Pompeii in 1872 to help Countess Marianna de Fusco handle some legal problems, Bartolo found a deteriorated parish church and people who were terribly poor and whose religious practice was more superstition than religion. He then dedicated his whole life to spreading devotion to the rosary, organizing a number of activities to accomplish this, and obtaining an image of the Blessed Mother to be used for public veneration.

Bartolo's small shrine to our Lady eventually became a basilica after a number of miracles occurred there, including the cure of Bartolo's dying mother. He also erected a complex of buildings, known as the "City of Mary," that served the poor and the destitute and founded a congregation of Dominican sisters, the Daughters of the Rosary, to educate orphan girls.

When Bartolo was falsely accused of mismanagement of the large complex, Pope Pius X set up a separate administration of the basilica. In 1904, however, the Pope, convinced that Bartolo was innocent, reversed his earlier action. But in 1906, Bartolo turned over everything he had to the Church and worked at the City of Mary as a simple employee until his death at the age of 85. He died praying the rosary and blessing the orphans who had come to keep him company.

On October 26, 1980, Pope John Paul, calling Bartolo the "Man of Mary," proclaimed him Blessed Bartolo Longo.

Q. One of my favorite books is the *Imitation of Christ* by Thomas a Kempis. What can you tell me about him? — P.M.L., Ontario

A. Thomas a Kempis (1380-1471) was born in Kempen, near Cologne, entered a monastery in 1399, and was ordained to the priesthood in 1413. He remained in the monastery for the rest of his life, writing, preaching, copying manuscripts, and serving as a spiritual adviser.

His best-known work is the *Imitation of Christ*, which first appeared in 1418 and is divided into four parts: Useful Admonitions for a Spiritual Life, Admonitions Concerning Spiritual Things, Interior Consolation, and the Blessed Sacrament. His motto is thought to have been: "Everywhere I have sought rest and found it nowhere, save in tiny nooks with tiny books."

Q. Whatever became of the cause of Therese Neumann (1898-1962), the German stigmatist? Was she ever beatified? — T.R.M., New Jersey

A. Thousands of people were impressed when they visited Therese in Germany because of her bleeding wounds, her mystic visions, and her ability to exist for many years on no food at all, except Holy Communion. For a good account of her life, see Albert Paul Schimberg's book *The Story of Therese Neumann* (Roman Catholic Books).

Therese, who was born on Good Friday in 1898, received the sacred wounds of Christ in 1926 and suffered from the stigmata until her death in 1962. Her cause for beatification is currently being pursued.

Therese was miraculously cured at different times from blindness, paralysis, and back ulcers and had not only the five wounds given to most stigmatists, but also the marks of the scourging and the crowning with thorns. Therese also had the gifts of bilocation, visions, apparitions, and prophecy.

More information can be found in Michael Freze's book *They Bore the Wounds of Christ* (Our Sunday Visitor), two books by Johannes Steiner: *The Visions of Therese Neumann* (Alba House) and *Therese Neumann: A Portrait* (Alba House), and one by Albert Vogl: *Therese Neumann: Mystic and Stigmatist* (TAN Books).

Q. I have said the Rosary of the Holy Wounds of our Lord Jesus Christ or Chaplet of Mercy for many years and have received many graces from it. However, I can find almost nothing about Sr. M. Martha Chambon, who was given the mission of making this devotion known. Can you help me? — J.S., Kentucky

A. J.H.H. of Illinois wrote to us and said that Sister Chambon was born in France on May 24, 1844. At the age of nine, during adoration of the cross on Good Friday, she experienced a vivid manifestation of our Lord on the cross, terribly wounded and covered with blood.

Beginning in 1866, four years after Sister had entered the convent of the Visitation Order of Chambery, France, she began to receive frequent visits from Jesus, the Blessed Mother, the angels, and the souls in Purgatory. Jesus crucified granted her nearly daily contemplation of his Holy Wounds, sometimes resplendent and glorious and at other times livid and bleeding. He gave her the power to unite her sufferings with His to bring release to the souls in Purgatory. Here are the Christ's words to Sister Chambon:

"The benefit of the Holy Wounds causes graces to descend from Heaven and the souls in Purgatory to ascend there. Every time you look at the Divine crucified with a pure heart, you will obtain deliverance for five souls from Purgatory, one at each source. If your heart is very pure and well detached, you will also obtain the same favor at each station in making the Way of the Cross, through the merits of each of my wounds. When you offer my Holy Wounds for sinners, you must not forget to do so for the souls in Purgatory, as there are but few who think of their relief. The Holy Wounds are the treasure of treasures for the souls in Purgatory."

Jesus also taught Sister Chambon a rosary chaplet of mercy. On the large beads of the rosary, we are to pray: "Eternal Father, I offer Thee the Wounds of our Lord Jesus Christ to heal the wounds of our souls." And on the small beads: "My Jesus, pardon and mercy through the merits of thy Sacred Wounds."

Q. A friend is looking for a novena prayer to St. Maximilian Kolbe. Do you know of such a prayer? — D.J.S., Ohio
A. Yes, we do, and here it is:

"Merciful God, you made St. Maximilian Kolbe one of the foremost Catholic evangelists of the difficult twentieth century. Through the *Militia Immaculatae* movement which he founded, he implanted the truths of the Immaculate Conception and Your merciful plan for us all in countless hearts, thus moving them to full conversion in faith and hope, to perfect obedience and union with the Heart of Jesus, and to complete observance of the New Covenant.

"You made him fruitful through carrying the cross of suffering with dignity and hope, loving his persecutors and giving up his life for a total stranger. Through his intercession grant us our petitions ... (here mention the requests you have). Give us a like dignity and hope in our sufferings and sacrifices and, if it will glorify You, heal us of all our infirmities, both physical and spiritual.
"Grant to all enrolled in this novena all the great graces St. Maximilian himself desires and asks for them. Enable each of us individually, and the Church as a whole, to follow his example of effective Catholic evangelism with Mary. Finally, grant his ardent prayers for the return to You of every individual person, family, society, nation, and culture of our time and of all time to come. Amen."

For the litany that precedes this novena prayer, write to the St. Maximilian Kolbe Shrine, Conventual Franciscan Friars of Marytown, 1600 W. Park Avenue, Libertyville, IL 60048.

Q. Could you please let me know if there are any books about the life of Katharine Drexel, who was recently canonized? — T.D., Wisconsin
A. P.K.T. of Maryland was kind enough to send the following list: Katherine Burton, *The Golden Door: The Life of Katharine Drexel* (1957), Ellen Tarry, *Katharine Drexel: Friend of the Ne-*

glected (1958), Sr. Consuela Marie Duffy, S.B.S., *Katharine Drexel: A Biography* (1966), and Lou Baldwin, *A Call to Sanctity* (1987).

There are also three youth-oriented biographies — Gerald Francis Muller, *More Than Money Can Buy: A Story of Mother Katherine Drexel* (1959), Katherine Burton, *The Door of Hope* (1963), and Ellen Tarry, *Katharine Drexel: Friend of the Oppressed* (1990) — and one adult condensed booklet by Fr. Salvator Fink, O.F.M., and Fr. John Manning, O.F.M., entitled *A Philadelphia Story* (1986).

The book by Sister Consuela is the official biography and can be obtained from the Mother Katharine Drexel Guild, 1663 Bristol Pike, Bensalem, PA 19020. Also available at the gift shop in Bensalem are the Tarry biography, the Baldwin biography, and the Fink/Manning booklet.

Q. I am interested in your opinion of the beatification of Cardinal Stepinac, who was Archbishop of Zagreb during World War II. I have heard that he collaborated with the pro-Nazi Ustasha regime in Yugoslavia and that he personally blessed the murder of Serbs, Jews, and Gypsies. Is this true? I would greatly appreciate it if you could provide any perspective on Cardinal Stepinac's life. — J.Y., State Unknown

A. Like the slanders which have been heaped on the memory of Pope Pius XII, the allegations against Alojzije Cardinal Stepinac (1898-1960) are just as false and baseless. There is no reason whatsoever for Catholics to wonder about his beatification by Pope John Paul II on October 3, 1998. As the Holy Father said at the ceremony, Stepinac was "one of the outstanding figures of the Catholic Church, having endured in his own body and his own spirit the atrocities of the Communist system."

According to a profile in the August-September 1998 issue of *The Catholic World Report*, Stepinac became the youngest bishop in the world when he was named coadjutor bishop of Zagreb in 1930. He visited all 208 parishes in his diocese over the next three years and, by the time World War II broke out, had founded fourteen new parishes, taken part in many national and international Eucharistic congresses, made a pilgrimage to the Holy Land, helped start a Catholic newspaper, spoken out frequently against abortion, and shepherded plans for celebrating the 1,300th anniversary of Christianity in Croatia.

The Cardinal was a vigorous opponent of Fascism, racism,

and extreme nationalism. "At death," he told a group of university students in 1938, "all racial differences disappear. Therefore, man will not be justified in God's judgment by belonging to this or that race, but by honest life and good deeds. So if love toward a nation crosses the borders of sound reason, then it is no longer love, but passion, and passion is neither of use, nor lasting .... That is why the Church, in the matters of ethnicity, also puts forward this principle: What you do not want to have done to yourself, do not do to others!"

But it was his fierce opposition to Yugoslav Communism, which was personified by Josip Broz (Tito), that led to Stepinac's arrest in 1946, followed by a show trial, conviction on false charges, and imprisonment until his death in 1960 from poison administered by his captors. The Cardinal's "crime" in the eyes of Tito was his refusal to break with Rome and set up a national Catholic church that could be controlled by the Communists.

Yugoslav Communists began the defamation of the Croatian archbishop more than 50 years ago, and the falsehoods that they invented back then are still being circulated today. Let's take a look at some of the lies that have been spread about this good and holy man.

• *Stepinac collaborated with the pro-Nazi Ustasha regime in his country.* — When the Independent State of Croatia was proclaimed in 1941, Stepinac at first welcomed the new government in the hope that it would protect the rights of Croats. But when the regime announced new racial laws and began to persecute ethnic minorities, the Archbishop protested directly to officials of the government and then spoke out openly against the laws, saying that he would oppose them with "my whole being, as a bishop and as a man."

He condemned the racial laws in 1942, saying that "all nations and races come from God. In essence there is only one race: God's race. Its birth certificate is in the Book of Genesis .... Members of that race can be of higher or lower culture, white or black, separated by oceans, live at the North or South Pole, but indeed they remain one race, which comes from God and should serve God .... Every nation and every race, as it is reflected today on earth, has the right to live with dignity and to receive decent treatment."

• *Stepinac blessed the murder of Serbs, Jews, and Gypsies.* — As early as 1935, the Archbishop condemned both Serbian terrorism against Croats and the "exaggerated nationalism" of some Croats. In 1936, he sponsored a committee to help Jewish refugees fleeing Hitler. In 1938, he founded Action for Aid for Jewish Refugees and told wealthy Catholics that it was their "Christian duty" to contribute to the support of Jews in exile. In 1943, he declared that "we cannot allow the innocent to be killed .... We always preach the holy principles of God's law, no matter whether Croats, Serbs, Jews, Gypsies, Catholics, Muslims, Orthodox, or others are involved."

• *Stepinac acquiesced in the forced conversion of Jews and Orthodox Serbs to Catholicism.* — On the contrary, the Archbishop opposed forced conversions, and he issued the following instructions to his priests:

"When people of the Jewish and Orthodox religions come to you and, finding themselves in danger of death, want to convert to Catholicism, receive them to save their lives. Do not ask for any special religious instruction, for the Orthodox are Christians like us, and the Jewish religion is that from which Christianity draws its origins. The role and the duty of Christians are in the first place to save people. When this era of savagery and madness has passed, those who are converted by conviction will remain in the Church, while the others, when the danger is passed, will return to theirs."

When Cardinal Stepinac died on February 10, 1960, his last words were those by which he had lived his whole life: "Thy will be done!" That is why he was beatified by Pope John Paul, who said during the ceremony that "in his human and spiritual journey Blessed Alojzije Stepinac gave his people a sort of compass to serve as an orientation. And these were its cardinal points: faith in God, respect for man, love toward all, even to the offer of forgiveness, and unity with the Church guided by the successor of Peter. He knew well that no bargains can be made with truth because truth is not negotiable. Thus he faced suffering rather than betray his conscience and not abide by the promise given to Christ and the Church....

"He is now in the joy of Heaven, surrounded by all those who, like him, fought the good fight, purifying their faith in the crucible of suffering. Today we look to him with trust and invoke his intercession."

Blessed Alojzije Stepinac, pray for us.

Chapter 7

The Last Things

Q. I have looked at the *Catechism of the Catholic Church* and cannot find predestination treated there. Is it covered in the *Catechism*? — L.C.M., Pennsylvania

A. The word "predestination" did not appear in the index of the English translation of the *Catechism* published in 1994, but the topic was treated in several places (e.g., nn. 600 and 2012). In the 1997 English edition, however, the index entry for "Predestination" refers the reader to paragraphs 257, 600, 1007, 2012, 2782, and 2823.

In paragraph 600, for example, the *Catechism* says that all moments of time are immediately present to God and, "when therefore he establishes his eternal plan of 'predestination,' he includes in it each person's free response to his grace." Regarding, for example, those who plotted Jesus' death, the *Catechism* says that "for the sake of accomplishing his plan of salvation, God permitted the acts that flowed from their blindness [cf. *Mt* 26:54; *Jn* 18:36; 19:11; *Acts* 3:17-18]."

Paragraph 2012 refers to St. Paul in Romans 8:28-30:

"We know that God makes all things work together for the good of those who have been called according to his decree. Those whom he foreknew he predestined to share the image of his Son, that the Son might be the first-born of many brothers. Those he predestined he likewise called; those he called he also justified; and those he justified he in turn glorified."

Q. I have a Catholic friend who believes in reincarnation and denies the doctrine of the bodily resurrection of the dead. We have discussed this so many times, and she has been given the scriptural references about it, yet she persists in her errors. She receives Communion regularly and refuses to confess any of it. Other than prayers, what is my obligation to her? — R.J., Texas

A. While we can see how a person steeped in New Age nonsense could be misled into believing in reincarnation, or even into thinking that such a belief can somehow be compatible with Catholic teaching, we cannot fathom how a practicing Catholic can reject one of the principal tenets of Catholicism, the bodily resurrection of the dead. When this friend attends Mass on Sunday, does she keep silent at the end of the Nicene Creed, when we profess our belief in the resurrection of the dead?

What can you do in addition to praying for this person? Well, for one thing, you must keep emphasizing that for a Catholic to deny the resurrection of the body is to deny a teaching of the Church that all baptized Catholics are required to believe "with divine and catholic faith" (canon 750). If your friend obstinately and defiantly continues to deny the doctrine of bodily resurrection, knowing full well that the position she is taking is contrary to Catholic belief, then she is guilty of heresy and incurs automatic excommunication (canon 1364). Having thus separated herself from the Catholic Church, she is not entitled to receive Holy Communion.

Second, you could get a copy of Edmond Robillard's book *Reincarnation: Illusion or Reality*, which was published in 1982 by Alba House. Fr. Robillard, a Dominican priest, traces the origin of reincarnation, shows how it is incompatible with Catholic belief, explains the Christian doctrine of the resurrection of the body, and provides some good answers to questions about reincarnation that he has gotten on the lecture circuit. After you have read this book, you might want to pass it along to your friend in the hope that it will straighten out her thinking.

Q. What is the Church's position on what happens to our body and soul after death? — G.P., New York

A. After our death, our bodies will decay while our souls will come before Jesus for a particular judgment based on our works and our acceptance or refusal of His grace (cf. *Catechism*, n. 682). That judgment will be followed by either entrance into the glory of Heaven — immediately or after being purified in Purgatory — or by immediate entrance into the eternal punishment of Hell (cf. *Catechism*, n. 1022).

Thus, if we lead holy and saintly lives and die with all our sins forgiven and no attachment to creatures remaining, we will go directly to Heaven. If we have led evil lives and die with unforgiven mortal sin on our soul, we will go directly to Hell. If we die in God's grace and friendship, but with some sins still in need of atonement, we will have to undergo a purification in Purgatory before we can see God face to face in Heaven.

At the end of the world, our bodies will be reunited with our souls to spend all eternity either in Heaven or in Hell. "All the dead will rise," says the *Catechism* (n. 998), " 'those who have done good, to the resurrection of life, and those who have done evil, to the resurrection of judgment' [*Jn* 5:29; cf. *Dan* 12:2]." (For more on this, see nn. 678-682 and 988-1060 of the *Catechism*.

Q. A Protestant friend was asking about the Catholic belief in judgment at death and the final judgment at the end of the world. He feels that souls are in Limbo until the final judgment. Could you explain the Church's teaching on this? — A.K., Massachusetts

A. In addition to what was said in the previous reply, there are a number of places in the New Testament that support the belief of immediate reward or punishment after death rather than languishing in what your friend calls Limbo until the final judgment. For example, there is the story of the rich man and the beggar Lazarus:

"Eventually, the beggar died. He was carried by angels to the bosom of Abraham. The rich man likewise died and was buried. From the abode of the dead where he was in torment, he raised his eyes and saw Abraham afar off, and Lazarus resting in his bosom" (Luke 16:22-23).

There is also the conversion on the cross of the good thief, who said to Jesus: " 'Remember me when you enter upon your reign.' And Jesus replied, 'I assure you: this day you will be with me in paradise' " (Luke 23:42-43).

Q. I believe I have heard that after our departing from this world all things will be made known to us. Can you help me find this? — J.L.S., Alabama

A. You may be thinking of the Last Judgment, about which the *Catechism* says that "only the Father knows the day and the hour" when this will take place. At that time, the Father, through Christ, will bring human history to an end and help us to know "the entire economy of salvation and understand the marvellous ways by which his Providence led everything towards its final end. The Last Judgment will reveal that God's justice triumphs over all the injustices committed by his creatures and that God's love is stronger than death" (n. 1040 [cf. *Song* 8:6]).

Q. What is the Church's position on the rapture, which is popular among some Protestant fundamentalists? — R.H., New York, and M.F., Ohio

A. The notion of the rapture is based on 1 Thessalonians 4:16-17, where St. Paul says that at the Second Coming of Christ, "the Lord himself will come down from heaven at the word of command, at the sound of the archangel's voice and God's trumpet; and those who have died in Christ will rise first. Then we, the living, the survivors, will be caught up with them in the clouds to meet the Lord in the air."

While some fundamentalists picture this as Christ secretly snatching certain people out of homes, cars, and planes to meet the Lord in the air, Catholics believe that Paul was referring in general to the final coming of Christ and the resurrection of the dead (cf. *Catechism of the Catholic Church*, nn. 997-1001).

The notion of a secret rapture has gained many adherents in recent years thanks in large part to the influence of the fictional *Left Behind* books, authored by Protestant evangelicals Tim LaHaye and Jerry Jenkins, and a movie by the same title. Here is how Paul Thigpen summarizes the eccentric beliefs of LaHaye and Jenkins in his valuable book *The Rapture Trap* (Ascension Press):

"These two authors believe that Christ will invisibly snatch true believers and innocent children, both living and dead, up into heaven. Their divine abduction will cause massive, worldwide turmoil, and once they are gone, the Devil will be free to take control of the world through his puppet, the Antichrist.

"Gross horrors will accompany this man's wicked reign. But the rapture will have taken place because, according to the authors, God has promised to spare true believers from the evil by snatching them off the planet before the 'great tribulation' begins. Later, after the tribulation has reached its climax, Christ will come back yet once more, this time publicly in 'a glorious appearing,' to defeat the forces of evil and bring history to a close" (p. 27).

The problem with this fantastic scenario, says Thigpen, is that there is nothing in the Bible to support it. After citing many Scripture passages about the return of Christ (cf. Matthew 24:27

and 30-31, Mark 14:62, 1 Corinthians 15:51-52, 1 Thessalonians 4:14-17, 2 Thessalonians 1:7-8, 10, and Revelation 1:7), he declares that in every biblical account, the Second Coming

"... is not a secret or invisible event. On the contrary, in various accounts it is described as unmistakably public, universally visible, glorious, full of splendor. The Lord returns on magnificent clouds of glory with brilliant angels and saints and a trumpet blast announcing their arrival; the faithful on earth are gathered to Him, while the rest of the world wails at the terrifying sight" (p. 118).

Don't let anyone talk you into exploring the *Left Behind* books or tapes, says Thigpen, because "they are spiritual poison." Their authors "will fill your head with flawed history, faulty theology, and twisted interpretations of Scripture. They will lead you astray in matters of eternal importance.

"These people continue to repeat age-old falsehoods about the Catholic Church, the Church that Jesus Christ Himself founded through His Apostles. And they want to persuade you to leave that Church. They want you to trade its rich spiritual feast for a pot of half-baked spoiled leftovers they call the 'true' faith.

"Don't fall into their trap. Instead take the time to learn more about what the Church teaches so you can avoid that sort of trouble" (p. 240).

Q. Some devout Catholic friends are excited because they think the Pope said that Jesus is coming soon. They are all excited and want to know why priests aren't talking about it in church. They think that Jesus is coming to hang around and straighten out our world, and we will have peace for 1,000 years. I try to tell them that this is a heresy called millennialism, but they do not believe me. Can you suggest some good materials? — R.B., Michigan

A. First of all, Pope John Paul did not say that Jesus is coming soon. He spoke instead of a "springtime for Christianity" in the new millennium and the need for evangelization. "The future of the world and the Church born in this [the 20th] century will reach maturity in the next, the first century of the new millennium," the Holy Father said in *Tertio Mellennio Adveniente*. He said that if the young people of today follow the road which Jesus points out to them, "they will have the joy of making their own contribution to his presence in the next century and in the centuries to come, until the end of time" (n. 58).

The theory of millennialism (or millenarianism) comes from chapter 20 of the Book of Revelation, which talks about a thousand-year peaceful reign of Christ, after which the devil is allowed to spread his evil throughout the world for a time before God crushes him and hurls him into "the pool of burning sulphur" where he and his minions will be "tortured day and night, forever and ever."

The debate revolves around the meaning of the thousand-year reign. Premillennialists hold that Christ and His saints will rule the world for a thousand years before His Second Coming, while Postmillennialists think that the reign of peace will come after the Second Coming of the Lord.

The Catholic view is that of St. Augustine, who said that the thousand years is not a literal number, but rather a symbolic one that refers to the spiritual reign of Christ from the time of His birth in Bethlehem until His Second Coming.

For more on this, see pages 199-208 of *The Rapture Trap* and chapter 20 of Fr. Alfred McBride's book *The Second Coming of Jesus* (Our Sunday Visitor).

Q. Can you tell me what exactly is temporal punishment? — J.S., Kentucky

A. Temporal punishment is a consequence of venial and/or forgiven mortal sins and is the penalty that God in His justice inflicts either on earth or in Purgatory. Unlike eternal punishment in Hell for unforgiven mortal sins, temporal punishment is not everlasting and may be remitted in this life by acts of penance. Temporal punishment not remitted in this life is remitted by suffering in Purgatory.

According to the *Catechism*, every sin we commit entails "an unhealthy attachment to creatures," which must be purified either on earth or in Purgatory. This purification removes the temporal punishment of sin and, if works of "fervent charity" are practiced in this life, there may be no temporal punishment remaining when we die (cf. n. 1472).

Q. Can you tell me if Padre Pio's prophecies about millennium disaster are true? Do you know anything about the "three days of darkness" that are supposed to be coming soon? — A.M., Illinois, and K.D., California

A. Be very cautious about believing in any prophecies attributed to Saint Padre Pio that have anything to do with "three days of darkness," since he firmly denied any involvement with this so-called prophecy and his superiors branded as a forgery a letter allegedly signed by him regarding such a phenomenon.

According to an article ("The Three Days of Darkness") by Fr. John A. Schug, O.F.M.Cap. that appeared in the June 1998 issue of *Homiletic & Pastoral Review*, the phrase "three days of darkness" originated early in the 19th century either with St. Gaspar del Bufalo or Blessed Anna-Maria Taigi and has been popularized in many books written in the past century.

The calamities predicted, says Fr. Schug, include massive earthquakes and history's most ferocious storm; the takeover of the Vatican by Communism; seventy-two hours of absolute darkness, with no light except that provided by blessed candles; and fire over all the earth that will incinerate all the enemies of the Church, i.e., about three-fourth's of the world's population.

The three days of darkness, its believers say, will bring an end to evil on earth, the creation of a new Garden of Eden, and a period of love, joy, and cooperation for the survivors of the predicted calamities.

Padre Pio's name was connected with this prophecy in the late 1940s by the Council of Heroldsbach, a group in Germany that was formed after some children claimed that the Blessed Mother had appeared to them. The Council composed a letter about the three days of darkness and forged Padre Pio's name to it. The letter was declared to be a forgery in 1950 by Padre Pio's superior in San Giovanni Rotondo. In 1951, the Vatican's Holy Office, without mentioning Padre Pio by name, stated that the alleged appearances of the Blessed Virgin in Heroldsbach were not supernatural and warned that "priests who in the future take part in this outlawed cult are automatically suspended from the exercise of their priestly ministry."

On March 31, 1994, the Auxiliary Bishop of Bamberg, Germany, informed Fr. Schug by letter that "Padre Pio had nothing whatsoever to do with Heroldsbach. There is not the slightest connection."

Instead of worrying about three days of darkness, Fr. Schug says that we should be focused on the light of Christ, who came into the world to dispel the darkness (cf. John 1:5), and who has told us: "Stay awake, therefore! You cannot know the day your Lord is coming" (Matthew 24:42).

Q. At a recent funeral, no body was present since the man had been cremated. I was told that cremains are not permitted in church. Why is this so if cremation is permitted by the Church? — A.S., Pennsylvania

A. At their November 1996 meeting, the Catholic Bishops of the United States voted to allow a funeral Mass to be celebrated in the presence of cremated remains. The previous policy required that the body of the deceased be present and that cremation take place after the Mass.

Cremation has for some time been allowed in the Catholic Church provided that it has not been chosen for reasons contrary to Catholic teaching (cf. canon 1176.3). Such reasons would include hatred of the Catholic Church or denial of the doctrine of the resurrection of the body.

Q. I understand that cremation is permitted by the Catholic Church, but that the ashes are not to be scattered over land or sea. So why were John F. Kennedy Jr.'s ashes scattered at sea? How could they have a Mass after this was done against Church teaching? Is this another example of the Church caving in to the Kennedys? — A.J.L., Louisiana; V.T.D., North Dakota; J.J.H., Virginia

A. The Church's *Order of Christian Funerals* says that cremated remains "should be treated with the same respect given to the human body from which they come. The cremated remains should be buried in a grave or entombed in a mausoleum or columbarium (a shallow, sealed, recessed niche for ashes). The practice of scattering cremated remains on the sea, from the air, or on the ground, or keeping cremated remains in the home of a relative or friend of the deceased are not the reverent disposition that the Church requires."

What was the disposition of the ashes of JFK Jr.? Some have said that the ashes were scattered, which would have been a violation of Church law, but others said that his cremated remains were in a sealed urn that was dropped into the sea off the coast of Martha's Vineyard. Only those who were present can confirm the method of disposition.

As is so often the case with the Kennedys, whether it involves funerals, or weddings, or annulments, or worthy reception of Holy Communion, one is never quite sure if they are in conformity with the Church or not, partly because all the facts are not known. Those who speak for the Church in an official capacity seldom issue statements that would clarify the situation for the puzzled Catholic.

In summary, then, if JFK Jr.'s remains were scattered at sea, that was definitely contrary to Church teaching. If the ashes were dropped into the sea in an urn, we would think that would not be a violation of Catholic burial policy for cremated remains.

Q. Given the reality of Heaven, Hell, and Purgatory, how do we explain ghosts? — R.B., New Hampshire

A. A ghost is a disembodied spirit and there is nothing in Catholic teaching that would rule out the possibility that God might permit departed souls to appear in some visible form on earth. Ghostly apparitions or illusions could be caused by the devil, of course, but there is sufficient evidence to indicate that there are ghosts who have appeared on earth for some good purpose, e.g., to help or warn someone or to request prayers from the living.

Q. My son, who recently returned to the Church, heard a priest say that Limbo had been dropped by the Church. My son remembers hearing about Limbo when he was young and is deeply troubled by what the priest said. Please help me explain to him who dropped Limbo and why. — E.S., New Jersey

Q. I found a quote from Pope Pius XII in 1951 in which he said that "an act of love can suffice for an adult to obtain sanctifying grace and supply for the absence of Baptism; for the unborn child or for the newly born, this way is not open." Does this statement contradict the present teaching of the Church, as expressed in the *Catechism of the Catholic Church*, n. 1261? — R.D., Texas

A. The two statements are not contradictory. Pius XII said that he did not know of a way that unborn or newly born children could make up for the absence of Baptism; the *Catechism* says the same thing, but expresses the hope that the mercy of God will in some way make salvation possible for children who die without Baptism.

The *Catechism* bases its hope on "the great mercy of God" and "Jesus' tenderness toward children" (n. 1261), which caused Him to tell the Apostles, "Let the children come to me. Do not hinder them. The kingdom of God belongs to such as these" (Matthew 19:14).

The Limbo of Infants was never a defined teaching of the Catholic Church, and therefore was never "dropped." It was a theological deduction which attempted to reconcile the teaching of Christ that "no one can enter into God's kingdom/ without being begotten of water and Spirit" (John 3:5) with the belief that unbaptized infants did not deserve the punishment of Hell.

So it was reasoned that there might be a special place for these infants called Limbo (from the Latin *limbus* and meaning a place on the perimeter of Heaven). This would be a place of purely natural happiness, where these children would receive all the happiness proportionate to their natural capacity, but without the supernatural happiness of Heaven, where one would enjoy the Beatific Vision of God.

Not being able to figure all this out is no reason for E.S.'s son to leave the Catholic Church. He should pray instead for the wisdom to know God's will and the perseverance to follow it, while putting any doubts and concerns into the hands of our loving and merciful Father in Heaven.

Q. It is my understanding that, being members of the Mystical Body of Christ and Communion of Saints, we can offer our prayers, works, joys, and sufferings to God either as reparation for our own sins or for those of others. I would be happy if *Catholic Replies* would give me some scriptural proof for answering fundamentalists who say it is not biblical to do so. — J.F.M., California

A. As is so often the case when seeking solid, biblically based replies to the objections of fundamentalists, we recommend Karl Keating's masterful book *Catholicism and Fundamentalism* (Ignatius), particularly chapters 16 ("Purgatory") and 21 ("Honoring the Saints"), for help with this question. Also of great help would be Patrick Madrid's excellent book *Any Friend of God's Is a Friend of Mine* (Basilica Press).

However, before getting your hopes of converting fundamentalists too high, we must pass along words of caution from Karl Keating:

"To fundamentalists the term communion of saints and its allied term, the Mystical Body of Christ, mean nothing. They have never heard of them, except for those who once were Catholics, and probably none of *them* ever understood the phrases" (p. 263).

The doctrine of the Mystical Body of Christ was developed by St. Paul in 1 Corinthians when he compared the human body, with its many members all working in harmony, to the Body of Christ, with its many members all linked to each other: "If one member suffers, all the members suffer with it; if one member is honored, all the members share its joy. You, then, are the body of Christ. Every one of you is a member of it" (1 Corinthians 12:26-27).

So, too, in his Letter to the Romans (12:4-5), St. Paul says that "just as each of us has one body with many members, and not all the members have the same function, so too we, though many, are one body in Christ and individually members one of another."

This connection among members of the Mystical Body of Christ applies not only to those on earth (the Church Militant), but also to those in Heaven (the Church Triumphant) and in Purgatory (the Church Suffering), a connection that Catholics refer to as the Communion of Saints. As Pope Paul VI said in his *Credo of the People of God*:

"We believe in the communion of all the faithful of Christ, those who are pilgrims on earth, the dead who are attaining their purification, and the blessed in Heaven, all together forming one Church; and we believe that in this communion the merciful love of God and his saints is ever listening to our prayers, as Jesus told us: Ask and you will receive."

Regarding the offering of one's prayers, works, joys, and sufferings for the living, we have the example of St. Paul begging his brothers in Christ to "join me in the struggle by your prayers to God on my behalf (Romans 15:30), and urging them to use "prayers and petitions of every sort. Pray constantly and attentively for all in the holy company. Pray for me that God may put his word on my lips, that I may courageously make known the mystery of the gospel — that mystery for which I am an ambassador in chains. Pray that I may have courage to proclaim it as I ought" (Ephesians 6:18-20).

If we can offer prayers for the living, thus acting as mediators or intercessors with God for our friends and without diminishing in any way the unique role of Jesus as the Mediator *par excellence*, why can't we intercede for the dead who are undergoing purification in Purgatory? They also are part of the Communion of Saints that encompasses those already in Heaven and those still on the journey on earth.

The saints in heaven are not dead, as some Christians claim. In fact, they are more alive now than they were on earth. The Letter to the Hebrews says that we are surrounded by a "cloud of witnesses" (12:1), the "spirits of just men made perfect" (12:23). These are the ones referred to in the Book of Revelation as the elders falling down before the Lamb of God [Jesus] and offering Him "vessels of gold filled with aromatic spices, which were the prayers of God's holy people" (5:8).

These are the ones who are only too happy to bring our prayers and petitions before the throne of God.

Q. Upon what Scripture passages does the Catholic Church base its teaching on Purgatory? I recently heard an Evangelical preacher spend an hour saying there is no mention of such a place in Scripture. — M.F., Ohio

A. Just because the word "Purgatory" does not appear in the Bible does not mean that the teaching about Purgatory is missing. The word "Trinity" does not appear in Scripture either, but the teaching is there, and so is the teaching about a place of purification after death.

Catholics traditionally point to the Second Book of Maccabees, where Judas Maccabeus, upon learning that some of his soldiers had died in battle while wearing pagan amulets, led his men in praying for the souls of the dead and then took up a collection, which he sent to Jerusalem to provide for an expiatory sacrifice for them.

"In doing this," Scripture says, "he acted in a very excellent and noble way, inasmuch as he had the resurrection of the dead in view; for if he were not expecting the fallen to rise again, it would have been useless and foolish to pray for them in death. But if he did this with a view to the splendid reward that awaits those who had gone to rest in godliness, it was a holy and pious thought. Thus he made atonement for the dead that they might be freed from this sin" (2 Maccabees 12:43-46).

Evangelicals do not accept this passage because they do not accept Second Maccabees as divinely inspired, but there are other biblical passages we can cite that they do recognize. For example, Jesus warns those who do not make peace with their neighbor that they will be thrown into prison, and that they "will not be released until you have paid the last penny" (Matthew 5:26 and

Luke 12:59). These words of Christ refer to the need for complete purification from all attachment to sin before we can enter Heaven.

Then there is Jesus' statement that "every sin, every blasphemy, will be forgiven men, but blasphemy against the Spirit will not be forgiven. Whoever says anything against the Son of Man will be forgiven, but whoever says anything against the Holy Spirit will not be forgiven, either in this age or in the age to come" (Matthew 12:31-32).

This implies that some sins will be forgiven in the age to come. This can't mean Hell, where there is no forgiveness, or Heaven, where there is no need for forgiveness, so it must refer to Purgatory, where we will not be released until we have paid the last penny.

Lastly, there is the passage where St. Paul talks about fire purifying gold and silver (a reference to our good works) while it burns away wood, hay, and straw (our imperfect works). When our lives are tested on the day of judgment, says Paul, each person "will receive his recompense." If the quality of each person's work fails the test, that person will be saved, says Paul, "but only as one fleeing through fire" (1 Corinthians 3:14-15).

Thus, the purgatorial fire burns away all the dross and imperfections that we have accumulated in this life and prepares us for entry into the new and heavenly Jerusalem, where nothing profane or unclean can enter (cf. Revelation 21:27).

Q. When a loved one dies, we direct our thoughts to that person's heading for Heaven and, of course, we offer prayers and Masses to shorten any time in Purgatory. But is there such a thing as disappointment in Heaven when someone is fortunate enough to get there, but then finds some loved ones missing? — G.D.W., Pennsylvania, and B.M., Rhode Island

A. It is virtually impossible for our limited human minds to understand, let alone to explain, what things might be like in Heaven. There are no earthly experiences that can prepare us for the extraordinary wonders of Heaven. As St. Paul said: "Eye has not seen, ear has not heard,/ nor has it so much as dawned on man/ what God has prepared for those who love him" (1 Corinthians 2:9).

However, we might make a stab at an explanation by saying that while here on earth we have a natural love for family members and friends, this natural love will turn into supernatural love for God when we reach Heaven. God will be the focus and the source of all our happiness, and nothing will be able to disturb that happiness, not even the knowledge (if we have such knowledge) that some of our loved ones are in Hell.

We find that hard to fathom from an earthly perspective, but our outlook in Heaven will be entirely different. Experiencing the Beatific Vision will make us so supremely happy that any sadness over the absence of loved ones is impossible. As the Book of Revelation (21:4) tells us, in Heaven God "shall wipe every tear from their eyes, and there shall be no more death or mourning, crying out or pain, for the former world has passed away."

Q. In discussing the resurrection of the "body," you have used the terms "body" and "dead" interchangeably. They are not the same words. I can't believe literally in the resurrection of the "body." It leads to some silly but logical questions: How old will the body be? What will it wear? Where will it be? If it's a body in the normal sense, it would have to be some "where" in space.

In good conscience I recite the Nicene Creed at Mass. It believes in the resurrection of the "dead" (form unspecified). I question your excommunicating me "automatically." Only God knows my mind. I cannot lie to God and say I believe something which I don't and can't. — W.T.O., Pennsylvania

A. In replying to a question about reincarnation, we said that a baptized Catholic who willfully and obstinately denied the doctrine of bodily resurrection was guilty of heresy and incurred automatic excommunication. He would be guilty of heresy because the Catholic Church has from the beginning affirmed that our mortal bodies will be rejoined with our souls at the end of the world and will live forever with the risen Christ.

For example, article 11 (n. 990) of the *Catechism* says that the resurrection of the body "means not only that the immortal soul will live on after death, but that even our 'mortal body' will come to life again [*Rom* 8:11]."

The *Catechism* bases this belief on the words of St. Paul, whose discussion of the resurrection in general and the manner of the resurrection and glorification of the body in particular takes up the entire 15th chapter of First Corinthians. W.T.O. is not the first person to wonder about such questions as "How are the dead to be raised up?" and "What kind of body will they have?" They are legitimate questions and were once posed to St. Paul. Here is how he answered them:

"Not all of us shall fall asleep, but all of us are to be changed — in an instant, in the twinkling of an eye, at the sound of the last trumpet. The trumpet will sound and the dead will be raised incorruptible, and we shall be changed. This corruptible body must be clothed with incorruptibility; this mortal body with immortality" (15:51-53).

How this will happen exceeds our understanding, says the *Catechism* and is accessible only to faith (n. 1000). But it will happen (n. 998): "All the dead will rise, 'those who have done good, to the resurrection of life, and those who have done evil, to the resurrection of judgment' [*Jn* 5:29; cf. *Dan* 12:2]."

How old will we be in Heaven? Some have suggested the prime age of a human life, perhaps in our twenties or thirties, but we don't know for sure. What will our bodies be like? Fr. John Hardon gives this answer in *The Catholic Catechism* (Doubleday):

"Since the Council of Trent, four terms have been officially used to identify the qualities of the risen body: impassibility, or immunity from death and pain; subtility, or freedom from restraint by matter [Jesus was able to pass through closed doors]; agility, or obedience to spirit with relation to movement and space [able to move through space with the speed of thought]; and clarity, or refulgent beauty of the soul manifested in the body [as when Jesus was transfigured on Mount Tabor]" (p. 265).

Fr. Hardon emphasizes, however, that "risen persons are still of the same human species and still the same individuals they were on earth. The word 'mortal' designates no essential property of human nature; it merely denotes a liability to undergo change. When we say that a glorified body is no longer mortal, we do not imply that it ceases to be a body. It becomes, of course, a spiritualized body; but it does not lose its corporeity. It remains truly human, though with an immortality coming from the divine strength, which enables the soul to so dominate the body that corruption can no longer enter what had formerly been subject to decay" (pp. 265-266).

For more information on the resurrection of the body, we would recommend reading articles 988-1019 of the *Catechism* and Peter Kreeft's *Everything You Ever Wanted to Know About Heaven*.

Q. What is the reason that the number 666 has satanic connotations? — P.L., Massachusetts

A. In chapter 13 of the Book of Revelation, Satan, who is portrayed as a dragon, gives two beasts the authority to persecute the Church. Verse 18 says that one with ingenuity "can calculate the number of the beast, for it is a number that stands for a certain man. The man's number is six hundred sixty-six." Since the number 7 was thought to symbolize perfection, and the number 6 imperfection since it falls short of 7, the number 666 symbolizes imperfection in the extreme, that is, total evil.

The first beast is traditionally seen as representing the Roman Empire, with its seven heads representing emperors of Rome, including Nero, who were fierce persecutors of the Church. Each letter of the Hebrew, Latin, and Greek alphabets has a numerical value. If the full name of Emperor Caesar Nero is used, the letters of the Hebrew form of his name add up to 666.

Anti-Catholics have tried to assign the number to the Papacy by contending that the letters in *Vicarius Filii Dei* (Vicar of the Son of God) add up in Latin to 666. The problem, however, is that the Pope's correct title is *Vicarius Christi* (Vicar of Christ), which does not add up to 666. But this has not prevented foes of the Papacy from ascribing a fictitious title to the Pope.

Q. I feel sure that Satan cannot enter into a person without that person's permission. How then can he enter into a small child, as when the woman asked Jesus to heal her little girl who was possessed, or when a man asked Jesus to heal his possessed son, who would often throw himself into fire or water? — V.L., Kansas

A. Actually, Satan can enter into a person without their permission and take full possession of their body, speaking and acting through them without their knowledge or consent. However, he cannot forcibly possess a person's soul, and unwilling victims of diabolical possession are morally blameless.

In his book *The Devil: "… alive and active in our world"* (Alba House), Msgr. Corrado Balducci says that the devil "can have direct and immediate contact only with what is corporeal, namely, the human body and its organs and functions. This means that the devil is able to act upon our external and internal senses and on any organ of the human body. He cannot, however, touch the purely spiritual faculties of intellect and will, except indirectly through some bodily sense or faculty. It follows, therefore, that the power of the devil is not without limitations" (p. 95).

Some people come under Satan's influence through ouija boards, Tarot cards, astrology, seances, witchcraft, and satanic cults. Others, like those mentioned by V.L. as having been freed by Jesus, may have done nothing to expose themselves to the influence of the devil, but God uses them to show forth His works (cf. John 9:2-3). Msgr. Balducci explains how diabolical possession allows God to demonstrate the following divine attributes:

"...divine providence, which restricts and controls the devil's activity and influence so that he can do only what God allows; divine omnipotence, because the devils tremble at His name; divine wisdom, which is able to bring good out of evil; divine justice, which allows sinners to get what their evil deeds seem to be asking for by allowing the devil to take possession of them; divine goodness, because God gave the Church and her ministers power over the evil spirits" (p. 118).

For more on diabolical activity in the world, see Fr. Jeffrey Steffon's book *Satanism: Is It Real?* (Servant Publications) and Fr. Gabrielle Amorth's two books: *An Exorcist Tells His Story* and *An Exorcist: More Stories*, both published by Ignatius Press.

Q. Our monsignor said that "no one is condemned to fire for eternity" and that the Gospel was just written metaphorically. Is he correct or is he preaching heresy? And why would the Blessed Mother have shown the children at Fatima a vision of Hell and taught them the prayer, "O my Jesus, forgive us our sins, save us from the fire of Hell. Lead all souls to Heaven, especially those in most need of your mercy"? — J.A.B., California

A. Your monsignor's opinion that no one is condemned to eternal fire in Hell is not the teaching of the Church. For example, the *Catechism* affirms the existence of Hell and its eternity and says that "immediately after death the souls of those who die in a state of mortal sin descend into Hell, where they suffer the punishment of hell, 'eternal fire' [cf. DS 76; 409; 411; 801; 858; 1002; 1351; 1575; Paul VI, *CPG* § 12]." It says that "the chief punishment of hell is eternal separation from God, in whom alone man can possess the life and happiness for which he was created and for which he longs" (n. 1035).

We do not know the exact nature of the fire of Hell; it can't be a consuming fire, such as we are familiar with, since that would destroy those in Hell. But whether it's an exterior or interior fire, your monsignor ought to be warning parishioners in his homilies to lead holy lives so they never have to experience either kind, especially in view of what Christ Himself, Church Fathers, and saints have told us.

For example, Jesus said that in Hell, "everyone will be salted with fire" (Mark 9:49). When one puts salt on meat and cooks it, the salt permeates the whole piece of meat and does not stay just on the outer layer.

Listen to what some early Church Fathers had to say. St. Augustine said that the fire of Hell "will be a corporeal fire and it will torture the bodies of the damned." Lactantius said that this fire "lives forever of its own accord and keeps strong without any nutriment. Neither does it have any smoke mixed in it. It is pure and liquid, and fluid like water .... The same divine fire, then, by one and the same force and power, will both consume the wicked and recreate them; and as much as it takes away from their bodies, that much also will it replace, while it will be for itself its own supply of eternal food .... Thus, without any wasting of bodies, which constantly regain their substance, it will only burn and inflict with a sense of pain."

St. Teresa, who was mysteriously transported body and soul to the regions of Hell one day while at prayer, said that "I felt within my soul a stinging fire which defies my powers to describe. At the same time my body fell prey to the most terrible pains. I have endured fearful pains in my earthly life, pains which were, according to the testimony of physicians, the most severe one can endure here below .... Yet all these were as nothing in comparison with the tortures I now underwent. But most terrible of all was the thought that these horrible pains were without end, without the possibility of alleviation."

She went on to say, however, that "these awful pains of the body were insignificant as against those of the soul. Oh! these embraced such fear, such oppression, and such agonies of heart that ... never, never could I succeed in describing this internal fire, this sense of despair, the most terrible of all the pains and torments. I could not see who it was that tortured me, and yet I could feel myself being crushed and burned. But the pain of all pains was this interior flame, this despair of the soul. In this terrible place there is no hope of relief."

Q. Pope John Paul has stated that Hell is not a place but rather the state of those who reject God. How can the Pope deny the existence of Hell as an actual place? Please clarify this matter. — J.E.K., Pennsylvania

A. We're not sure we can clarify it because of our limited understanding of what Hell might be like and because it has historically been described both as a place and a state of being.

In his general audience of July 28, 1999, the Holy Father actually mentioned both possibilities. He first said that Scripture frequently refers to Hell as "a place of eternal suffering," but then said that "the images of Hell that Sacred Scripture presents to us must be correctly interpreted. They show the complete frustration and emptiness of life without God. Rather than a place, Hell indicates the state of those who freely and definitively separate themselves from God, the source of all life and joy."

While the magisterium of the Church has affirmed the reality, eternity, and awful pains of Hell over and over again through the centuries, we have been unable to find the Church designating Hell exclusively as a place. For example, Ludwig Ott, in his *Fundamentals of Catholic Dogma* (TAN Books), describes Hell as "a place or state of eternal punishment inhabited by those rejected by God." The dictionary defines "inhabit" as to occupy or live in a place, so one could reasonably see this word as pointing toward Hell as a place.

Similar ambiguity can be found in the *Catechism of the Catholic Church*, which first calls Hell a "state of definitive self-exclusion from communion with God and the blessed" (n. 1033), but then also says that "immediately after death the souls of those who die in a state of mortal sin descend into hell" (n. 1035). To "descend" into Hell, would seem to imply going to a place of terrible punishment.

That was the impression that Fatima visionary Lucia got when the Blessed Mother showed her and her two cousins a vision of Hell on July 13, 1917. When the ground opened up, said Lucia, she saw "a sea of fire. Plunged in this fire were demons and souls in human form ... floating about in the conflagration ... and shrieks and groans of pain and despair which horrified us and made us tremble with fear."

"You have seen Hell where the souls of poor sinners go," the Blessed Virgin told the children. She then taught them the prayer to be said after each decade of the rosary: "O my Jesus, forgive us our sins; save us from the fire of Hell. Lead all souls to Heaven, especially those in most need of your mercy."

In the vision granted years earlier to St. Teresa, the saint told of being transported to the "regions of Hell" and related her horrifying experiences in this "abode of torture." She said that the physical pain was much worse than anything she had suffered in life, but the pain of the body was insignificant compared to the pain of soul she underwent, the interior despair of the soul with no hope of relief. Here we see elements of both place and state of being.

Peter Kreeft, in his book *Everything You Ever Wanted to Know About Heaven*, echoed the words of Pope John Paul quoted above. "The images of Hell in Scripture," Kreeft wrote, "are not to be taken literally, that is, as something other than images. But they are to be taken seriously because they point to something more, not less, horrible than the literal images denote."

He said that "Hell is a state of mind. Nothing on earth has as much potency for good or evil, pleasure or pain, joy or horror, as the mind. Unlike Heaven, Hell is only a state of mind .... Hell is not thrust upon us from without. Hell grows up from within, a spiritual cancer. It emerges from our freedom and eats away that freedom, just as a cancer eats its host."

The widely respected author and lecturer said that "the existence of Hell and the nature of Hell as something other than eternal punishment of fire and brimstone are both confirmed by the medically dead and resuscitated. These 'death-travelers,' especially suicides, often found themselves in a place strikingly similar to the 'grey town' in C.S. Lewis' *Great Divorce* (which none of them, apparently, had read): a dreary place in which all the earthly problems they had tried to escape were merely intensified — naturally, since our problems are never merely outside us but inside us, and we can never escape ourselves" (pp. 229-231).

In the last analysis, however, whether Hell is a place or a state of being doesn't really matter. The point is that we don't want to experience either manifestation and can avoid doing so only by living lives of holiness and dying in the state of grace.

Q. I think your response on the Pope's opinion about Hell leaves something to be desired. He said that "rather

than a place, Hell indicates the state of those who freely
and definitively separate themselves from God, the source
of all life and joy." If he had said "more than a place, Hell
is a state of mind," he would have been absolutely correct, for the essence of Hell is in the mind of the one who
has lost God for all eternity. So perhaps this is a mistranslation of the Pope's actual words. We can only hope so. —
P.A.T., New Jersey

A. The quotations are from Pope John Paul's general audience of July 28, 1999 and, according to a "Faith Fact" published
by Catholics United for the Faith (CUF), the Holy Father's comments, which were given in Italian, were indeed mistranslated.
CUF said that "the original Italian for 'rather than a place' was
piu che un luogo, which means 'more than a place.' In the official
English summary, read by the Pope himself after the initial address, he said, 'More than a physical place, Hell is the state of
those who freely and definitively separate themselves from God,
the source of all life and joy.'"

In conclusion, said CUF, John Paul certainly was not denying that Hell is a place, "but instead was shifting our focus to the
real essence of Hell — what the term 'Hell' truly indicates — the
self-chosen separation from God. The 'place' or 'location' of Hell
is secondary, and consideration of where it is should not deflect
us from our most important concerns: what it is and how to avoid
it."

Q. Would you please comment on Pope John Paul's
statement about Heaven not being a place? If Heaven is
not a place, then to where was Mary taken body and soul
at the end of her life? And what did Jesus mean when He
said, "In my Father's house there are many dwelling
places; otherwise, how could I have told you that I was
going to prepare a place for you?" (John 14:2)? — J.J.W.,
Massachusetts

A. At his general audience on July 21, 1999, the Holy Father
said that Heaven "is not an abstraction nor a physical place amid
the clouds, but a living and personal relationship with the Holy
Trinity. When this world has passed away, those who accepted
God in their lives and were sincerely open to His love, at least at
the moment of death, will enjoy that fullness of communion with
God, which is the goal of human existence."

As noted previously in reference to Hell, the Church, and those who are loyal to her teaching, have also traditionally referred to Heaven as both a place and a state of being. Dr. Ludwig Ott, in his book *Fundamentals of Catholic Dogma*, said that "Heaven is a place and condition of perfect supernatural bliss, which consists in the immediate vision of God and in the perfect love of God associated with it" (p. 476).

In addition to the essential bliss of Heaven which springs from the immediate vision of God, said Ott, there is also an "accidental bliss ... achieved by the blessed in virtue of the community of life with Christ in his human form, with the Mother of God, and with the angels and saints; in virtue of their reunification with families and former friends from their earthly life; in virtue of their knowledge of God's works" (p. 478).

Heaven may not be a place in the earthly sense that we understand the word, but it seems that there must be some kind of space to contain the glorified bodies of Christ, His mother, and all the blessed.

However, the *Catechism*, while saying that God is "in heaven, his dwelling place" (n. 2795), also says that the biblical expression "who art in heaven" does not mean "a place ('space'), but a way of being; it does not mean that God is distant, but majestic. Our Father is not 'elsewhere': he transcends everything we can conceive of his holiness" (n. 2794).

It says that " 'who art in heaven' does not refer to a place but to God's majesty and his presence in the hearts of the just. Heaven, the Father's house, is the true homeland toward which we are heading and to which, already, we belong" (n. 2802).

Try as we might, it is very difficult to describe Heaven in earthly terms. As St. Paul said: "Eye has not seen, ear has not heard,/ nor has it so much as dawned on man/ what God has prepared for those who love him" (1 Corinthians 2:9). So let's give the last word to Frs. Leslie Rumble and Charles Carty of *Radio Replies* fame. Responding in volume two of their three-book set to the question of what Heaven would be like, they said:

"It will be an everlasting experience rendering the complete human being happy, not merely with human happiness, but with divine happiness. Just as the eye now sees the things of this world, so the mind will see God's own personal perfections. Instead of being merely self-conscious, the soul will become God-conscious; and in God we shall find in an ever so much better way all that we have ever found to be good in created things or in self. And, of course, ever so much more besides.

"Heaven, then, is not a place to be described in terms of longitude and latitude, nor by ideas of scenery drawn from this earth. It is a spiritual state of perpetual existence which escapes limitations of time and space concepts. For further knowledge of the conditions that prevail in Heaven, I can only advise you to live in such a way as to go there. Then you will know all" (p. 212).

Chapter 8

The Sacraments

Q. Our pastor has stated that "the sacraments [all] come through the community," and this bothers me. Please settle this for me. — A.C.R., New Jersey

A. We are afraid that your pastor is misinformed. According to the *Catechism*, and the Council of Trent, all seven sacraments were instituted by Christ our Lord Himself (cf. n. 1114). Furthermore, the *Catechism* says that "the ordained priesthood guarantees that it really is Christ who acts in the sacraments through the Holy Spirit for the Church" (n. 1120).

Priests act in the name and person of Jesus and constitute "the sacramental bond that ties the liturgical action to what the apostles said and did and, through them, to the words and actions of Christ, the source and foundation of the sacraments" (*Ibid.*).

Q. My understanding is that a sacrament is valid as long as the celebrant is the valid minister of the sacrament and intends what the Church intends. I also have the understanding that if a sacrament is not valid (e.g., a priest who has lost his faith and is saying a sacrilegious Mass consciously with the intention of not transforming bread and wine into the Body and Blood of Christ), the recipients would incur no personal sin by not attending this invalid Mass because the Church provides for the defect. But is sanctifying grace imparted to the recipients? Also, if a person was confirmed by a bishop whose writings and official actions indicated that he no longer accepted the teachings of the Church, would the grace of the sacrament flow? If the bishop was later deposed by the Holy Father, would the special character of the sacrament of Confirmation have been imprinted on the person confirmed earlier? — Name and State Withheld

A. This is a complicated series of questions and we will try to sort them out with the assistance of Fr. Nicholas Halligan's valuable book *The Sacraments and Their Celebration* (Alba House) and the *Catechism of the Catholic Church.*

First of all, for a sacrament to be valid, the minister or celebrant must be legitimately qualified and he must use the required material and the prescribed formula of the sacrament. The celebrant's lack of faith or lack of sanctity do not prevent the graces from flowing because in the sacraments, says the *Catechism*, "Christ himself is at work: it is he who baptizes, he who acts in his sacraments in order to communicate the grace that each sacrament signifies" (n. 1127).

This is what the Church means when she says that "the sacraments act *ex opere operato* (literally: 'by the very fact of the action's being performed'), i.e., by virtue of the saving work of Christ, accomplished once for all. It follows that 'the sacrament is not wrought by the righteousness of either the celebrant or the recipient, but by the power of God' [St. Thomas Aquinas, *STh* III, 68, 8]." If a sacrament is celebrated in accordance with the intention of the Church, the *Catechism* says, "the power of Christ and his Spirit acts in it and through it, independently of the personal holiness of the minister" (n. 1128).

Whether the sacrament bears fruit in the recipient depends, of course, on the disposition of the person receiving it.

Since the questioner is not talking about the use of invalid matter or the omission of key words in the formula of consecration at Mass, both of which would invalidate the sacrament, but rather about the intention of the celebrant, we will focus on that.

Fr. Halligan says that the valid celebration of a sacrament demands that the minister "have a true and serious intention, not only to perform an external rite but also a sacramental rite, i.e., he must have an internal intention. He thereby wills to do through the means of the sacramental sign that which the Church does. His intention determines what this required material and this formula shall signify sacramentally" (p. 5).

Obviously, therefore, a Mass celebrated by a priest who specifically intended not to consecrate the bread and wine would not be valid and the Church could not supply for this defect. Those attending this so-called Mass would incur no sin if they were unaware that an invalid celebration was taking place, but no graces would flow from this invalid rite.

In the case of the bishop, even if it could be proven that he had apostasized, and even if he were later deposed by the Pope, his lack of faith would not nullify the Confirmation or the imprint of its special character because it is Christ "who acts in his sacraments in order to communicate the grace that each sacrament signifies" (*Catechism*, n. 1127).

For more on this, see the Halligan book, pages 3-20.

Editor's Note: Regarding the question of whether there was baptism of infants in the early Church, R.E.S. of Missouri recommends Stephen K. Ray's book *Crossing the Tiber* (Ignatius) for a comprehensive treatment of the subject. Ray, who was raised a Baptist and entered the Catholic Church in 1994, devotes an entire section of his book (pp. 93-185) to "Baptism in the Scriptures and in the Ancient Church."

Q. My niece was brought up Catholic, is living with a man without benefit of marriage, and has invited us to the baptism of her child in a non-Catholic church. My inclination is not to attend the baptism. What do you think? — T.C., Massachusetts

A. We think your inclination is correct. To attend the baptism would imply that you are indifferent to your niece's sinful situation and hold that it really doesn't matter in what church the child is baptized.

Since you believe just the opposite, you should politely decline the invitation and explain to your niece that your love for her includes concern about her soul. Tell her that your attendance at the baptism would go against your conscience and your commitment to follow Christ and His Church, and that you will keep her and the child in your prayers.

Q. My friend's daughter and her husband have left the Catholic Church and have not had their baby baptized. However, the daughter said they would go through a baptism themselves at home, possibly to make my friend feel better. What are your thoughts on this? — M.J.F., New York

A We would be surprised if the promised "baptism" at home would make your friend feel better. The Catholic Church has certain rules for Baptism, but is it likely that a couple who has left the Church would care about conforming to those rules? Would they use the proper matter and form, or would they just go through the motions?

The Baptism would be valid if done correctly, but it would not be licit if it were in violation of canon law. And, from what you have told us, we think that the couple's promised action would violate canon law in several respects.

For example, canon 857 says that "the proper place for Baptism is a church or oratory," except in cases of necessity, such as danger of death, religious persecution, or serious family disagreement about Baptism. Canon 861 says that "the ordinary minister of Baptism is a bishop, presbyter [priest], or deacon."

And canon 868 says that for the licit Baptism of an infant there must be "a founded hope that the infant will be brought up in the Catholic religion; if such hope is altogether lacking, the Baptism is to be put off according to the prescriptions of particular law and the parents are to be informed of the reason."

Q. Recently my two-year-old niece was baptized in California, and I am a godmother by proxy. She was baptized in a Catholic church, but a priest did not officiate and was not present. A visiting professor from a local college, who is not a Catholic, administered the sacrament. Although holy water and the baptismal candle were used, no holy oil was used and no white garment was given to her. Was this a licit Catholic Baptism? — A.F., Georgia

A. As noted in the previous reply, the ordinary minister of Baptism is a bishop, priest, or deacon. "If the ordinary minister is absent or impeded," says canon 861, "a catechist or other person deputed for this function by the local Ordinary confers Baptism licitly, as does any person with the right intention in case of necessity."

Without knowing all the details, the strange situation described by A.F. doesn't sound like a licit Baptism to us. The visiting professor who attempted to confer the sacrament could not have been deputed by the local bishop because the professor was not a Catholic, and while any person with the right intention can confer Baptism licitly in case of necessity (e.g., a child in danger of death), that does not seem to have been the situation.

We would suggest writing to the pastor of the church where the purported Baptism took place and asking him if your niece was baptized according to the laws of the Catholic Church and, if not, why not.

Q. As you can see from the enclosed notice in our bulletin, there will be no Baptisms during the Lenten season, "except for health emergencies." What can be done

about this when the Code of Canon Law says that babies are to be baptized as soon as possible after birth? — E.C., Minnesota; J.L., New York; K.W.M., Michigan

A. Canon 867 says that infants are to be baptized "within the first weeks after birth," except in the case of an infant in danger of death, who is to be baptized "without any delay." The *Rite of Baptism* goes into greater detail:

"As for the time of Baptism, the first consideration is the welfare of the child, that it may not be deprived of the benefit of the sacrament; then the health of the mother must be considered, so that, if at all possible, she too may be present. Then, as long as they do not interfere with the greater good of the child, there are pastoral considerations, such as allowing sufficient time to prepare the parents and to plan the actual celebration in order to bring out its true character effectively. Accordingly:

"(1) If the child is in danger of death, it is to be baptized without delay; this is permitted even when the parents are opposed and even when the infant is the child of non-Catholic parents....

"(2) In other cases, the parents, or at least one of them or whoever stands in the place of the parents, must consent to the Baptism of the infant....

"(3) An infant should be baptized within the first weeks after birth. In the complete absence of any well-founded hope that the infant will be brought up in the Catholic religion, the Baptism is to be delayed ... and the parents are to be informed of the reason" (n. 8).

Article 9 of the same document says that "to bring out the paschal character of Baptism, it is recommended that the sacrament be celebrated during the Easter Vigil or on Sunday, when the Church commemorates the Lord's Resurrection. On Sunday, Baptism may be celebrated even during Mass, so that the entire community may be present and the relationship between Baptism and Eucharist may be clearly seen; but this should not be done too often."

In light of all this, we cannot see any justification for refusing to baptize infants during Lent. Obviously, if a child were born in the middle of Lent, and the parents were properly prepared, it would make sense to schedule the Baptism for the Easter Vigil or on Easter Sunday.

But if the child were born, say, a week or two before the beginning of Lent, holding off that child's Baptism until the Easter Vigil would mean a delay of some eight or nine weeks. This would, in our opinion, go well beyond "the first weeks after birth" and would contradict the sense of canon 867.

Q. Recently my one-year-old grandchild was baptized sitting in a tub of water up to the waist. The water was carelessly sprinkled on his upper body or shoulder. We have doubts that the baby is baptized. Please inform us as to the proper procedure. — J.C.S., Massachusetts

Q. I attended a Baptism where part of the baby's body was immersed in water while the priest said the words, but the head remained dry. I thought immersion meant putting the whole body under the water. Was this a valid Baptism? — Name and State Withheld

A. The proper procedure for Baptism, according to the *Rite of Baptism for Children* (n. 60), is to immerse the child in the water three times or pour water on the child's head three times while saying, "I baptize you in the name of the Father, and of the Son, and of the Holy Spirit." It is not necessary to submerge a baby's head during the rite of immersion, but water must be made to flow on it.

In his book *The Sacraments and Their Celebration*, Fr. Nicholas Halligan said that whether the Baptism is by total or partial immersion, "there must be in the common estimation of men a true washing or ablution, a flowing of water whereby the whole body or the head is washed ....

"For the validity of a true washing, the water should *flow*, even though there be only some drops (merely one or two drops are doubtfully sufficient). Merely to anoint the person to be baptized, e.g., with a thumb moistened with blessed water, is not sufficient. To draw a wet cloth or sponge or wet fingers across the head or forehead is at least doubtfully valid....

"The water that flows much *touch the skin*, otherwise the Baptism is invalid or at least doubtful and thus is to be conferred again conditionally...." (pp. 27-28).

The Baptisms described by our two questioners seem doubtful, and should be repeated conditionally.

Q. At a recent infant Baptism of my niece, the priest, while pouring the water over her head, said, "I baptize

you in the name of the Father, and of the Son, and of the Holy Spirit. Amen." I always thought that the exact words, excluding "amen," had to be used. Is this correct and, if so, was the Baptism valid? Also, the priest anointed my niece with chrism and said that she would "remain forever a member of Christ who is Priest, Prophet, and King." Kindly explain this and its origins. — W.W., Massachusetts

A. (1) Adding the word "amen," which is not part of the formula of Baptism, would not invalidate the sacrament since nothing essential to the sacrament was changed. It may have been just a slip of the tongue by the priest, since he is used to saying "amen" after blessing himself "in the name of the Father, and of the Son, and of the Holy Spirit." If the priest had said, "I baptize you in the name of the Creator, and of the Redeemer, and of the Sanctifier," as some priests and deacons have done in the interests of using inclusive language, then the Baptism would not be valid since the essential words of the formula had been changed.

(2) In ancient Israel, those consecrated to God for a mission, such as priests, prophets, and kings, were anointed in His name. This was all the more so for the Messiah, whose title "Christ" means "anointed." It was necessary, says the *Catechism*, that the Messiah be anointed by the Spirit of the Lord at once as king and priest, and also as prophet because Jesus fulfilled the messianic hope of Israel in His threefold office of Priest, Prophet, and King (cf. n. 436).

By virtue of the anointing with sacred oil in Baptism, said Vatican II's *Dogmatic Constitution on the Church*, the laity "are in their own way made sharers in the priestly, prophetic, and kingly functions of Christ. They carry out their own part in the mission of the whole Christian people with respect to the Church and the world" (n. 31). How do the laity accomplish this?

They share in Christ's priestly role in union with the "ministerial priest," who "brings about the Eucharistic Sacrifice, and offers it to God in the name of all the people," said the document. "For their part, the faithful join in the offering of the Eucharist by virtue of their royal priesthood. They likewise exercise that priesthood by receiving the sacraments, by prayer and thanksgiving, by the witness of a holy life, and by self-denial and active charity" (n. 10).

The laity exercise their prophetic role by spreading the truth about Christ and acting as a living witness to Him, "especially by means of a life of faith and charity and by offering to God a sacrifice of praise, the tribute of lips which give honor to His name (cf. Heb. 13:15). The body of the faithful as a whole [from bishops down to the last member of the laity], anointed as they are by the Holy One (cf. 1 Jn. 2:20, 27), cannot err in matters of faith and morals" (n. 12).

The laity exercise their kingly role by being ready to serve others, said Pope John Paul in his encyclical *Redemptor Hominis*, "in keeping with the example of Christ, who 'came not to be served but to serve.' If in the light of this attitude of Christ's, 'being a king' is truly possible only by 'being a servant,' then 'being a servant' also demands so much spiritual maturity that it must really be described as 'being a king.' "

The Holy Father said that "in order to be able to serve others worthily and effectively, we must be able to master ourselves, possess the virtues that make this mastery possible. Our sharing in Christ's kingly mission — his kingly function — is closely linked with every sphere of both Christian and human morality" (n. 21).

For more on our sharing in Christ's threefold office, see the *Catechism*, nn. 783-786; the *Constitution on the Church*, nn. 31-42; and *Redemptor Hominis*, nn. 18-21.

Q. My husband and I have been asked to be long-distance godparents to a child who lives in Illinois, and my husband is very uncomfortable with this. He thinks it is too far to really have an effect on the child's religious life. I am willing to compromise and have me be godmother (long-distance) and have my friend choose a man closer by to be godfather. Is it okay to split the godparents like this, and is it okay to have such a long-distance one? — K.D., California

A. Yes, it is, and congratulations for taking this responsibility so seriously. You might bear in mind, though, that your situation is no different from persons who may have lived close by at the time of a child's Baptism and later moved away and became long-distance godparents.

But regardless of when a person achieved this status, he or she can still influence a child's religious life from afar, obviously through prayer for the child, but also by sending religious articles or books or videos on the child's birthday or Baptism anniversary. Or when the child is preparing for First Communion and later for Confirmation (when a godparent would be the most appropriate choice for a sponsor), the long-distance godparent could express encouragement and support for the child by letter or telephone or E-mail and, if possible, attend the child's reception of these two sacraments.

Q. My husband and I are expecting our first child. We recently moved here from Seattle, WA, and have chosen two good practicing Catholics from that state to be the godparents because they have promised a lifelong spiritual commitment to our baby. But we wish to use proxies for the Baptism. What are the Church's rules for the proper use of proxies? — M.M.S., New Jersey

A. Here are the rules for being a godparent by proxy as issued back in 1925 by the Vatican's Sacred Congregation for the Sacraments:

"If the godparent cannot be present in person, he or she may appoint another person to serve as a proxy, but the appointment must be made in such a way that there is certainty as to the person who takes the responsibility as godparent. Ordinarily the appointment of the proxy should be made by the godparent in writing or before two witnesses, in order that there be certainty as to who is the responsible person.

"The custom of leaving the appointment of the proxy to the parent of the infant or to the baptizing priest tends to make sponsorship doubtful, and is to be reprobated. The real godparent must give a mandate directly or indirectly (through the agency of others but with his or her consent) to the proxy. In the record of Baptism, the names of both the godparent and the proxy should be entered."

Q. Is it a sin to refuse to be godmother or godfather at a Baptism for no apparent reason, not once but twice? — Name and State Withheld

A. No one is obligated to be a godparent, so it is not a sin to say no, but we wonder why a person would refuse such an honor. In any case, we have found bigger problems with those who have said yes to being godparents, but who do not meet the Church's conditions.

Those conditions, according to canon 874, are that the person have completed the sixteenth year (although an exception can be made for a "just cause"), have been confirmed and received

Holy Communion, "leads a life in harmony with the faith and the role to be undertaken," is not bound by any canonical penalty, and is not the mother or father of the one to be baptized.

Q. At our parish, our pastor has recently declared that parents will be required to pay $40 for the baptism of a child. This is not to cover materials, nor is it an offering; it is a fee. Is this consistent with Church teaching, or is it simony? — J. and T. B., State Unknown

A. Simony means selling something spiritual, such as a sacrament or a Church office, for money. The word comes from chapter 8 of the Acts of the Apostles, where Simon Magus sought to buy spiritual powers from St. Peter. We think it would be a stretch to say that your pastor is guilty of simony because he is asking a $40 fee for a baptism.

What he is probably doing is trying to get the parishioners to live up to their obligation to support the Church financially. If free-will offerings and donations are not forthcoming for Baptisms, then some pastors have to impose fees, just as they do with weddings and funerals, where there is a charge for the church, singer, and organist.

It's too bad that your pastor has to do this, but surveys show that Catholics are notoriously cheap when it comes to supporting their Church. It is also true that some persons seeking the Baptism of a child have no discernible connection with the parish and feel little if any responsibility to make a donation to the parish. While no child should be refused Baptism because of inability to make a free-will offering — and your pastor would be wrong if he denied Baptism because parents did not come up with the required amount of money — nevertheless it is not unreasonable for pastors to suggest donations, or even fees, to help with the expenses of running a parish.

Q. My daughter received the sacrament of Confirmation this year, but there was no provision made to attend Confession before receiving the sacrament. There was a two-year time line which included many nice activities, but today's preparation seems to be solely based on the gospel of good works and not on receiving God's grace through the Holy Spirit. If the children do not go to Confession before Confirmation, would they receive less sanctifying grace? — G.L., New York

A. According to the *Rite of Confirmation*, "Persons who are to receive Confirmation must already have received Baptism. Moreover, those possessing the use of reason must be in the state of grace, properly instructed, and capable of renewing the baptismal promises" (n. 12).

Obviously, the only way to ensure that the confirmands are in the state of grace is to provide them with the opportunity to receive the sacrament of Penance. Any program that fails to offer this opportunity is not doing what the Church mandates.

If a child were to receive Confirmation in the state of mortal sin, the sacrament would be valid, but the graces would not flow until the child obtained God's forgiveness through Confession.

Q. Our parish bulletin says that "specially designated priests" can confer the sacrament of Confirmation, and paragraph 1313 of the *Catechism of the Catholic Church* says that "the bishop may for grave reasons concede to priests the faculty of administering Confirmation." I should like a definition of the word "grave" as it is used here. Also, there is a second item about the commissioning of a "lay pastoral minister." Hasn't the Vatican issued a letter requesting the bishops of the United States not to commission lay ministers? — V.M., Tennessee

A. (1) Actually, paragraph 1313 does not mention "grave" reasons (although canon 884.2 does), but only says "if the need arises." However, reasons for delegating priests to administer Confirmation would include danger of death of the one to be confirmed, the unavailability of the bishop, and the large number of those to be confirmed.

(2) In November 1997, eight Vatican offices issued an instruction on the collaboration of the non-ordained faithful in the sacred ministry of priests. The purpose of the instruction was to clarify the nature of this collaboration and to put a stop to "abusive practices" where the laity had been assuming roles and titles that belong exclusively to those who have received Holy Orders.

For example, some lay people had unlawfully assumed such titles as pastor, chaplain, coordinator, and moderator, and had gone to such extremes as wearing sacred vestments, quasi-presiding at Mass, reading the Gospel, and preaching the homily.

The Vatican instruction did not forbid the commissioning of the laity in pastoral roles, but sought to specify when and where the non-ordained faithful could collaborate with their pastors while at the same time safeguarding "the integrity of the pastoral ministry of priests."

In affirming that "the ordained priesthood is absolutely irreplaceable," the instruction also said that "when necessity and expediency in the Church require it, the pastors, according to established norms from universal law, can entrust to the lay faithful certain offices and roles that are connected to their pastoral ministry but do not require the character of orders."

Q. What does the Church teach about children receiving Confirmation in the second grade, at the same time as First Holy Communion? — G.M., Michigan

A. Canon law (c. 891) states that "the sacrament of Confirmation is to be conferred on the faithful at about the age of discretion [seven years] unless the conference of bishops determines another age or there is danger of death or in the judgment of the minister a grave cause urges otherwise." However, this is not the case in the United States, where the age of reception ranges from about seven to 16, with most children receiving it as sophomores or juniors in high school, but an increasing number celebrating it along with First Communion.

As canon law indicates, ordinarily a person must have reached the age of reason before receiving Confirmation. Conferring it then would maintain the original order of the sacraments, but the U.S. bishops have decided to continue allowing Confirmation to be conferred at a later age.

Q. In what century did the confessional box start and where did it originate? Why has it been replaced with reconciliation rooms? Could this be part of the reason why there has been a decrease in people going to Confession? I have always felt more comfortable in a confessional box. — J.W., Pennsylvania

Q. Seventy years ago, when there were so many priests, they came to our homes, our picnics, and our games. It was common to ask a priest to hear your confession on those occasions and to walk with him to some quiet spot. It seems unnatural to go to Confession in a church. Can you tell me what is the origin of the confessional box? — W.H., New York

A. For most of the Church's history, there was no special place for the hearing of confessions. It was common until the 16th century for the confessor to sit on a chair or a bench between the altar and the Communion rail, with the penitent seated next to him. But after the Council of Trent in the 16th century, in the interests of secrecy and anonymity, confessional boxes became the norm in the Western Church for four centuries.

They usually had three compartments, the middle one for the priest and the two on the sides for the kneeling penitents. There was a grille separating priest from penitent, and the penitent might either be open to public view or concealed behind a door or a curtain.

In 1974, the U.S. Conference of Catholic Bishops said that it is "considered desirable that small chapels or rooms of reconciliation be provided in which penitents might choose to confess their sins through an informal face-to-face exchange with the priest, with the opportunity for appropriate spiritual counsel."

The Bishops said that "it would also be regarded as desirable that such chapels or rooms be designed to afford the option of the penitents kneeling at the fixed confessional grille in the usual way, but in every case the freedom of the penitent is to be respected" (*Bishops' Committee on the Liturgy NewsLetter 1965-1975* [December, 1974], p. 450).

Notice that, even in reconciliation rooms, the anonymity of the penitent is to be respected by providing the option of a fixed confessional screen between the person and the priest. This requirement was reiterated in canon 964.2 of the 1983 Code of Canon Law, which said that the conference of bishops was to see to it that "confessionals with a fixed grille between penitent and confessor are always located in an open area so that the faithful who wish to make use of them may do so freely."

The decline in the number of people going to the sacrament of Penance might be partly due to the lack of anonymity in some parishes, but we think the main reason is that many Catholics have lost their sense of sin. Too many bishops, priests, and catechists have neglected their obligation to teach the faithful all the truths they need to know to get to Heaven, including the truths that certain thoughts, words, deeds, and acts of omission are contrary to the commandments of God and the Church and to the moral code preached by Jesus and the Apostles.

As for where confessions can be heard, canon 964 says that "the proper place to hear sacramental confessions is a church or an oratory," and that "confessions are not to be heard outside the confessional without a just cause." A just cause for asking a priest to hear one's sins away from the confessional would be the inability to get to a church or an oratory for a variety of reasons, such as confinement to a hospital, nursing home, one's own home, or a prison, or service on a military ship or outpost.

Q. When I expressed to my Protestant wife the Catholic view of forgiveness, she said that "Christ died on the cross and all our sins are forgiven. So Heaven is ours; there is no need for Confession and all that Catholic jargon." What would be a good explanation of why Catholics feel that confession of sins to a priest is necessary for God's forgiveness? — J.E.Y., California

A. Ask your wife to read John 20:22-23, where Jesus said to the Apostles on the night after He rose from the dead: "Receive the Holy Spirit./ If you forgive men's sins,/ they are forgiven them;/ if you hold them bound,/ they are held bound." Notice that Jesus did not say, "If *I* forgive men's sins, they are forgiven them," but rather, "If *you* forgive ... if *you* hold bound."

The early Church Fathers — and the Church herself over the centuries — have understood that passage to mean that the ordinary way for a person to obtain God's forgiveness for sins committed after Baptism is to tell those sins to a priest with sorrorw for them and with the intention of not committing them again.

The Apostles were the first priests of Jesus' Church, and note that our Lord told them that there would be times when they would "hold bound," or not forgive, someone's sins. But how could a priest know whether to forgive or not forgive a person unless the sinner first told the priest his sins? And why would Jesus have given the Apostles the power to hold sins bound if all sins were automatically taken care of on Good Friday?

Yes, Jesus' death on the cross was sufficient to forgive all our sins and, yes, He won Heaven for us. But we can lose Heaven by ignoring Jesus' saving death and by turning our backs on Him by deliberately leading a life that is contrary to the moral code He preached.

It was St. Paul who warned: "Consider the kindness and the severity of God — severity toward those who fell, kindness toward you, provided you remain in his kindness; if you do not, you too will be cut off" (Romans 11:22). And who also said: "The lives of all of us are to be revealed before the tribunal of Christ so that each one may receive his recompense, good or bad, according to his life in the body" (2 Corinthians 5:10).

That doesn't sound to us like Heaven is a sure thing. It sounds as if we will be judged by Christ on the good and bad things we did in this life and will receive our just reward or punishment. Perhaps that is why St. Paul also urges us to "work with anxious concern to achieve your salvation" (Philippians 2:12).

Your wife is compressing into one concept *redemption*, which is accomplished by the Blood of Christ, and *salvation*, which is as yet uncertain for each of us.

Q. Our second grader was instructed by a religious sister to confess two sins (and no more than two!) along with the rest of the classmates preparing for First Reconciliation at the local Catholic school. We believe a penitent having more than the allowable two sins who does not confess the remainder would be making a bad Confession. And the bad Confession would itself have to be confessed. Are we mistaken? — M.M., Iowa

A. The *Rite of Penance*, whether for those receiving the sacrament for the first time, or for any subsequent confessions, says that "the priest helps the penitent to make an integral confession and gives him suitable counsel" (n. 44). The key word is "integral," which means telling all mortal sins of which the penitent is conscious and mentioning any circumstances that would change the quality of a sin. Since it is unlikely, although not impossible, for a child of seven or eight to commit a mortal sin, integral would mean telling any willful thoughts, words, or actions of which the child is aware that show a failure to love God or to love other people.

In preparing children for First Penance, we usually go over with them an examination of conscience that pretty much follows the Ten Commandments, and that examination involves more than two areas where children fall short of holiness. For example, we have them ask themselves:

"Did I neglect my prayers? Did I misuse the name of Jesus or use bad language? Did I miss Mass on purpose or misbehave in church? Did I disobey or show disrespect for my parents, guardians, or teachers? Did I fight with siblings or with schoolmates, or say mean and nasty things to them? Did I use my body or the bodies of others in an impure or immodest way? Did I steal, cheat in school, or damage the property of others? Did I lie or gossip or harm the good name of another person? Did I deliberately keep impure or hateful or jealous thoughts in my mind? Did I fail to do something I should have done?"

In light of this, is it pastorally wise to restrict children to only two sins when there may be more that need to be confessed? Might this approach encourage a child to tell only minor sins and perhaps leave out more serious ones? What kind of a lesson does this teach a child? That it's okay to ignore or conceal certain sins? Those reading this reply can surely think of times when they would very much have preferred not mentioning some sins to the priest, but that would not have been an integral Confession, and forgiveness would not have been received.

Are children who follow Sister's instruction guilty of making a bad Confession? We would say no since they don't know any better. But we would suggest that their parents take the responsibility, outside of school, of getting the children to the sacrament of Penance frequently and catechizing them properly.

Q. Before Christmas, the pastor announced a Penance Service where each person would tell one sin and say three Hail Marys to a priest seated at the altar. I think this was illicit. What do you think? — R.J.C., California

A. This procedure is a violation of the integrity of the sacrament of Penance, and Pope John Paul sternly rejected this approach in his apostolic letter *Misericordia Dei*, which was issued on May 2, 2002 and was to "have full and lasting force and be observed from this day forth." In the course of the letter, which urged bishops and priests "to undertake a vigorous revitalization of the sacrament of Reconciliation," the Holy Father said:

"Since 'the faithful are obliged to confess, according to kind and number, all grave sins committed after Baptism of which they are conscious after careful examination and which have not yet been directly remitted by the Church's power of the keys nor acknowledged in individual Confession,' any practice which restricts Confession to a generic accusation of sin or of only one or two sins judged to be more important is to be reproved. Indeed, in view of the fact that all the faithful are called to holiness, it is recommended that they confess venial sins also."

Q. Can you tell me the correct rule on the Third Rite of Penance or general absolution? I have protested to my

pastor and bishop that grave sin is not absolved by Third Rite but only by one-on-one Confession. I have also suggested that if Third Rite is used, it should be emphasized at the beginning that the penitents should go to individual Confession as soon as possible. — F.V., Australia

A. First of all, grave sin is absolved by general absolution legitimately administered, provided that the penitent "not only be suitably disposed but also at the same time intend to confess individually the serious sins which at present cannot be so confessed" (canon 962), and the priest granting general absolution must instruct the faithful about this essential requirement.

Second, although the questioner is from another country, the rules about general absolution that were stated in the U.S. Bishops' December 1998 *NewsLetter* are the same for the universal Church (cf. Pope John Paul's 2002 apostolic letter *Misericordia Dei*). Here is the statement of the Bishops' Liturgy Committee:

"The third form of the sacrament of Penance, a communal celebration with general absolution, is designed for extreme situations when individuals would be deprived of access to a confessor for a long period of time and would, therefore, be deprived of the grace of the sacrament of Penance or Holy Communion. The National Conference of Catholic Bishops has interpreted a long period of time as one month. Individual confession and absolution remain the 'only ordinary way by which the faithful person who is aware of serious sin is reconciled with God and with the Church' " [Canon 960; *Rite of Penance*, 311; *Catechism of the Catholic Church*, 1484].

The Bishops also said that general absolution may not be given "simply because an insufficient number of confessors" shows up for Penance, that "each penitent must confess all grave sins in private auricular Confession at the earliest possible opportunity" after general absolution has taken place, and that "the bishop is the sole competent authority for determining the appropriateness and conditions which must be met for the celebration of general absolution in a particular diocese."

Q. The communal Penance services that I have seen in the Rochester diocese consist of the congregation reciting a prayer in which we acknowledge our sinfulness and express our repentance. This is followed by the congre-

gation being given absolution by the priest. Doesn't this form require individual confession of one's sins to a priest, and are the sins of those attending a communal service actually forgiven? — G.L., New York

A. On March 20, 2000, the Vatican's Congregation for Divine Worship and the Discipline of the Sacraments reiterated the Church's policy on communal Penance services that feature general absolution in a letter to the bishops of Australia. Noting that communal celebrations of Penance "have not infrequently occasioned an illegitimate use of general absolution," the Congregation said that "this illegitimate use, like other abuses in the administration of the sacrament of Penance, is to be eliminated" (n. 3).

It is the Church's longstanding policy, says the *Catechism*, that "the sacrament of Penance can also take place in the framework of a *communal celebration* in which we prepare ourselves together for confession and give thanks together for the forgiveness received" (n. 1482). It says that "the personal confession of sins and individual absolution are inserted into a liturgy of the word of God with readings and a homily, an examination of conscience conducted in common, a communal request for forgiveness, the Our Father and a thanksgiving in common" (*Ibid.*). Notice that such communal celebrations must include "personal confession of sins and individual absolution."

Only in cases of "grave necessity" can there be a communal celebration with general confession and general absolution, says the *Catechism*. Such cases would include when there is "imminent danger of death without sufficient time for the priest or priests to hear each penitent's confession," or when there are so many penitents and so few priests that "the penitents through no fault of their own would be deprived of sacramental grace or Holy Communion for a long time" (n. 1483).

Furthermore, canon 961.2 says that it is up to the diocesan bishop to decide whether the conditions for general absolution exist, and canon 962.1 says that those in attendance must have the intention of individually confessing their serious sins as soon as possible in order for the absolution to be valid.

Q. Can you answer two questions: (1) If a penitent tells the priest in Confession he is sorry for all his sins and the priest does not ask the type or number or gravity of the sins, but gives him absolution, is the penitent forgiven?

(2) **If after the sins are confessed, the priest says something like, "I'm also going to include all your past sins, those that you have forgotten, those you are ignorant of, etc." can he do this without the penitent actually recalling to mind his own sins? Are they in fact absolved? — A.G.K., Indiana**

A. We turn to canon law for guidance. Canon 988 says that "a member of the Christian faithful is obliged to confess in kind and in number all serious sins committed after Baptism and not yet directly remitted through the keys of the Church nor acknowledged in individual Confession, of which one is conscious after diligent examination of conscience."

Canon 978 says that "in hearing confessions the priest is to remember that he acts as a judge as well as a healer...." Canon 979 says that "the priest in posing questions is to proceed with prudence and discretion, with attention to the condition and age of the penitent...." And the *Rite of Penance* says that the priest, if necessary, "helps the penitent to make an integral confession and gives him suitable counsel" (n. 44).

Since the responsibility for helping a penitent make a good Confession rests with the priest, and since a penitent can reasonably assume that the priest knows what he is doing, a priest who fails to ask the appropriate questions renders the Confession objectively illicit, but not invalid. No guilt attaches to the penitent in this situation, and his sins are forgiven.

In answer to the second question, the priest can include all of the penitent's past sins that had already been specifically forgiven in a previous Confession, and only those sins that had been committed with sufficient understanding and full consent of the will. A person who is truly ignorant about the sinfulness of some thought, word, action, or omission cannot incur grave guilt and, since only serious sins need to be confessed, we don't know why a priest would mention sins "you are ignorant of."

Q. The enclosed article from a parish bulletin says that "recently, theologians have observed that the recital of each mortal sin [in Confession] is a law of the Church and not a law of God. (They point out that it is not required in Eastern churches whose rite of reconciliation is accepted by Rome.)" Does Rome have a double standard or are theologians blowing the devil's smoke again? — A.J.S., Pennsylvania

A. First of all, there is no dichotomy between Church law and God's law since God gave the Church the authority to make laws in His name (cf. Matthew 16:19 — "Whatever you declare bound on earth shall be bound in heaven").

Second, neither is there any double standard since the recital in Confession of each and every mortal sin of which a penitent is aware has long been required for worthy reception of the sacrament of Penance. In the words of the Council of Trent:

"All mortal sins of which penitents after a diligent self-examination are conscious must be recounted by them in confession, even if they are most secret and have been committed against the last two precepts of the Decalogue; for these sins sometimes wound the soul more grievously and are more dangerous than those which are committed openly."

The reason why mortal sins must be confessed in kind and in number was explained by Pope John Paul II in his apostolic exhortation *Reconciliation and Penance*:

"The confession of sins is required, first of all, because the sinner must be known by the person who in the sacrament exercises the role of judge. He has to evaluate both the seriousness of the sins and the repentance of the penitent; he also exercises the role of healer, and must acquaint himself with the condition of the sick person in order to treat and heal him.

"But the individual confession also has the value of a sign: a sign of the meeting of the sinner with the mediation of the Church in the person of the minister; a sign of the person's revealing of self as a sinner in the sight of God and the Church, of facing his own sinful condition in the eyes of God" (n. 31).

Q. Our new pastor has some of us confused with his procedure in the confessional. He says "Hi" when we enter, tells us to say an Act of Contrition outside the confessional "if you have time," says "I absolve you" and a few more words that I couldn't understand, and at the end says, "Have a good day." Is all of this valid? — Name Withheld, Arizona

A. The *Rite of Penance* includes four basic parts: (1) contrition or sorrow for the sins committed along with the intention of sinning no more, (2) confession of specific sins to the priest, (3) expiation or satisfaction for sins committed through an act of penance, usually prayers or acts of self-denial or charity, and (4) absolution or pardon for one's sins.

As for the procedure described by our reader from Arizona, the rite says that "the priest should welcome penitents with fraternal charity and, if need be, address them with friendly words" (n. 16). "Hi" is certainly a friendly word, but it strikes us as a little too folksy for the sacrament.

Second, the penitent is supposed to say an act of contrition or prayer of sorrow before being granted absolution (n. 19), not at some later time. Third, the absolution formula is as follows (n. 46): "God, the Father of mercies, through the death and resurrection of his Son has reconciled the world to himself and sent the Holy Spirit among us for the forgiveness of sins; through the ministry of the Church may God give you pardon and peace, and I absolve you from your sins in the name of the Father, and of the Son, and of the Holy Spirit." The penitent responds, "Amen."

The essential words are "I absolve you from your sins in the name of the Father, and of the Son, and of the Holy Spirit." If these words are omitted or changed, the sacrament is not valid. If the other words in the formula are omitted, changed, or added to, the conferring of the sacrament would be illicit, but not invalid. If the "few more words" your priest said, but which you could not understand, were "in the name of the Father, and of the Son, and of the Holy Spirit," then the sacrament was validly administered.

Finally, the rite suggests several ways of dismissing the penitent, none of which is, "Have a good day." The priest might say, for instance, "The Lord has freed you from your sins. Go in peace." Or "Blessed are those whose sins have been forgiven, whose evil deeds have been forgotten. Rejoice in the Lord, and go in peace" (n. 47).

Q. In our parish, the priest said that in the sacrament of Reconciliation, saying the Our Father along with him takes the place of the Act of Contrition. Is he right?— G.B., Wisconsin

A. After one's confession of sins and acceptance of a penance, says the *Rite of Penance*, there is "a prayer for God's pardon" by which "the penitent expresses contrition and the resolution to begin a new life. It is advantageous for this prayer to be based on the words of Scripture" (n. 19).

The rite later lists a number of possible prayers that the penitent might recite, but the Our Father is not one of them. Most of the prayers (cf. nn. 85-92) are taken from Scripture, but the first one (n. 45) sounds somewhat like the traditional Act of Contrition that many of us learned as children:

"My God, I am sorry for my sins with all my heart. In choosing to do wrong and failing to do good, I have sinned against you whom I should love above all things. I firmly intend, with your help, to do penance, to sin no more, and to avoid whatever leads me to sin."

Q. The priests at my parish do not give penances to adults at Confession. But when my young son made his First Confession, he was told to go home and clean the bathroom. This seemed strange that no prayers were included. What's going on? — S.A.D., Georgia

A. According to the *Catechism*, penance or satisfaction for sins is very important. While absolution takes away sin, says the *Catechism*, it does not make up for all the harm caused by sin. It says that the sinner cannot recover his "full spiritual health" unless he does "something more to make amends for the sin," and that something is called "satisfaction" or "penance" (n. 1459).

The penance the confessor imposes, says the *Catechism*, "must take into account the penitent's personal situation and must seek his spiritual good. It must correspond as far as possible with the gravity and nature of the sins committed" (n. 1460). Thus, penance "can consist of prayer, an offering, works of mercy, service of neighbor, voluntary self-denial, sacrifices, and above all the patient acceptance of the cross we must bear" (*Ibid.*).

If these kinds of penances are given, says the *Catechism*, they can help "configure us to Christ, who alone expiated our sins once for all" (*Ibid.*). So the priests in your parish should be following these guidelines for those coming to the sacrament of Penance. And, by the way, there was nothing wrong with assigning your son a good deed to do instead of a prayer to say.

Q. At my parish, children go through the formal program for First Confession in fourth grade. Although second and third graders are allowed to participate, the fact is that they aren't invited (notices are sent out only to fourth-grade students). It seems that the parish feels

canon 914 is only a recommendation, not a law. I've enclosed a copy of a letter sent to me by the vicar general. After receiving it, I feel like a pharisee who's only interested in the law and being critical of those who do not follow it. Should I just concentrate on my own faults and leave the "crusading" to others? — D.L.O., Minnesota

A. Canon 914 says that "it is the responsibility, in the first place, of parents and those who take the place of parents as well as of the pastor to see that children who have reached the use of reason are correctly prepared and are nourished by the divine food as early as possible, preceded by sacramental confession."

According to the letter from D.L.O.'s vicar general, "the standard canonical interpretation of canon 914 is that young people and their parents should be trained for First Penance, offered every opportunity to participate in First Penance, and encouraged to avail themselves of the sacrament prior to receiving Communion. Since actual celebration of the sacrament is a matter of the internal forum, most canonists hold that it is not possible to require the actual completion of the celebration of the sacrament before a public act, such as the reception of First Communion, can take place."

Contrary to what "most canonists hold," the official Church interpretation of canon 914 is stated in n. 1457 of the *Catechism*: "Children must go to the sacrament of Penance before receiving Holy Communion for the first time [cf. CIC, can. 914]."

What does the Church say? She says that children *must* go to Confession before First Communion. That seems pretty clear, and no amount of "standard canonical interpretation," or intimidation by pastors and directors of religious education, should keep parents from having their children receive First Penance before First Communion (children with special needs would be an exception).

There are good reasons for having First Penance in the second grade: (1) Children at that age know right from wrong and can commit sins, particularly in a culture that glorifies sin. (2) It is much easier to get them in the habit of Confession when they have only venial sins to tell rather than to wait until they are older and have committed more serious sins. (3) Those whose Penance is delayed beyond First Communion sometimes don't get to the sacrament of Reconciliation at all, either because they have moved to another parish, or they have stopped coming to religion classes.

You may not discover that some children have never been to Confession until you begin preparing them for Confirmation in the ninth or tenth grade. One cannot truly appreciate the Church's insistence on First Penance before First Communion until one tries to persuade a 15-year-old to go to Confession for the first time.

Speaking as a religion coordinator who has prepared many second graders for First Penance, and who makes sure that they continue to receive the sacrament at least twice a year, we can say that it is a joyful experience. With the proper instruction and training, the children approach the sacrament with an understanding of how they have failed to love God and others, and with an appreciation for the love and mercy of God.

At First Penance, we focus on such parables as the Good Shepherd and the Prodigal Son (which might be more aptly titled the Forgiving Father) and have the children hold lighted candles signifying the light and life of Christ within us. They (and their parents) are told to keep that light burning brightly throughout their lives, and if sin should extinguish that light, there is the sacrament of Penance or Reconciliation to obtain Christ's forgiveness and rekindle the flame.

So, to D.L.O. we say, "Keep crusading!"

Q. Your reply about Catholics not being able to receive Holy Communion if they are "conscious of grave sin" and have not had such sin forgiven in Confession was incomplete. Catholics must also go to Confession and Communion at least once during the Easter season (cf. *Catechism of the Catholic Church*, n. 2042). — B.R., Florida

A. The section of the *Catechism* cited, which deals with the first three precepts of the Church, refers the reader in two footnotes to canons 920 and 989 of the Code of Canon Law. Canon 920 says that Catholics are obliged to receive Holy Communion "at least once a year. This precept must be fulfilled during the Easter season unless it is fulfilled for a just cause at some other time during the year."

Canon 989 says that "after having attained the age of discretion, each of the faithful is bound by an obligation faithfully to confess serious sins at least once a year." There is no mention of doing this during the Easter season, although annual Confession has been linked in the minds of Catholics with the obligation to receive Communion during the Easter season since, presumably, a person receiving Communion only once a year might have some serious sins to confess.

But the operative word here is "serious." While the Church recommends that Catholics also confess venial sins (canon 988.2), one is obliged only to confess mortal sins and, if a person is not conscious of having committed any mortal sins during the year, he is not required to receive the sacrament of Penance.

It goes without saying that Catholics in the state of grace ought to receive the Holy Eucharist at least weekly and ought to take advantage of the sacrament of Penance at least monthly whether they have committed mortal sins or not.

"The frequent and careful celebration of this sacrament is also very useful as a remedy for venial sins," says the *Rite of Penance.* "This is not a mere ritual repetition or psychological exercise, but a serious striving to perfect the grace of Baptism so that, as we bear in our body the death of Jesus Christ, his life may be seen in us ever more clearly. In confession of this kind, penitents who accuse themselves of venial faults should try to be more closely conformed to Christ and to follow the voice of the Spirit more attentively" (n. 7).

Q. The Church often counsels us to make an act of perfect contrition, especially when death seems imminent. What constitutes such an act? And can we be certain that God will accept it, given the fact that we usually do things imperfectly? — J.A.W., Pennsylvania

A. Perfect contrition means sorrow for sins because they offend God; imperfect contrition means sorrow for sins because we fear the punishment of Hell. The *Catechism* says (n. 1452) that perfect contrition "arises from a love by which God is loved above all else," and it obtains forgiveness of mortal sins "if it includes the firm resolution to have recourse to sacramental confession as soon as possible [cf. Council of Trent (1551): DS 1677]."

It says that imperfect contrition "is born of the consideration of sin's ugliness or the fear of eternal damnation and the other penalties threatening the sinner (contrition of fear)" (n. 1453). By itself, however, the *Catechism* says, "imperfect contrition cannot obtain the forgiveness of grave sins, but it disposes one to obtain forgiveness in the sacrament of Penance [cf. Council of Trent (1551): DS 1678; 1705]."

If we truly give our best effort in making a act of perfect contrition, we can be sure that God will accept it.

Q. What are the true limitations of the "seal of Confession"? I ask this because I have recently seen two movies that deal with the issue in what seems a rather implausible way. The first is *Priest,* the most anti-Catholic film I've ever seen, in which a priest is supposedly forced to permit a child to continue being molested by her father after the child, in the confessional, asks the priest for help. We are expected to believe that the priest is powerless to go to the authorities even after the girl's father candidly admits and defends his crimes to the priest. The other movie is Hitchcock's *I Confess,* less farfetched but still improbable, or so it appears to me. — F.B., Maryland

A. Talking about the confidentiality of Confession, canon 983 of the Code of Canon Law says that "the sacramental seal is inviolable; therefore, it is a crime for a confessor in any way to betray a penitent by word or in any other matter or for any reason." Canon 1388 says that "a confessor who directly violates the seal of confession incurs an automatic (*latae sententiae*) excommunication reserved to the Apostolic See; if he does so only indirectly, he is to be punished in accord with the seriousness of the offense."

This secrecy is essential because, if a penitent thought that a priest could reveal something he heard in Confession, the penitent would either stay away from the sacrament or be tempted to conceal grave sin. The seal of Confession binds the priest because he would know nothing about a person's sins unless he heard them in his role as a confessor. The penitent tells the sins for the good of his soul, not for any wordly considerations, and thus the priest must behave toward the world as if he had never heard those sins.

A *direct violation* of the seal would involve not only mentioning the penitent's name and the sin, but also revealing circumstances which would allow someone to know who the penitent was and the sin that was committed. An *indirect violation* would involve things said or done by the confessor that would allow others to know the sin confessed and the identity of the sinner.

Not having seen either of the movies mentioned, we don't know the exact situations portrayed. If the girl in *Priest* asked for help in the confessional, the priest could advise her to report her father to some trusted person or to the police, but he could not notify the authorities himself. If the father confessed that he had molested his daughter, the priest, before giving him absolution, would have to warn the father that he must have the firm resolve not to commit this sin again. He would also have to instruct the man to make reparation for the harm he had done to his daughter, and perhaps to move out of the home and to seek professional counseling.

But the bottom line remains that the priest cannot reveal to anyone, by word or behavior, or for any reason, what the penitent told him for the purpose of obtaining absolution. He can use only knowledge that came to him in the ordinary way that any person might obtain such knowledge, say, if a neighbor or teacher reported that the child was being molested.

Editor's Note: In response to questions in the past, we have stated that it is not permissible to confess one's sins over the telephone, nor can one fulfill the Sunday Mass obligation by watching the Mass on television. For the record, this has been confirmed by the National Conference of Catholic Bishops' Committee on the Liturgy in its statement that there must be a "physical presence" between a member of the faithful and the bishop, priest, or deacon celebrating the sacrament.

Writing in the May-June 1999 issue of the committee's newsletter, executive director Fr. James P. Moroney said:

"Electronic communication via telephone, television, video conference, or Internet is not sufficient for the celebration of the sacraments. The celebration of the sacrament of Penance via telephone, participation in Mass via television, or the celebration of the sacrament of Confirmation via video conference have on occasion been proposed. The liturgy, however, requires a full, conscious, active participation which demands the presence of the whole person in contact with the reality — not merely an image or concept — of the saving presence of Christ. A 'live' telecast of an event allows a limited kind of 'presence' for the viewer, but the viewer is very aware that he or she is not 'really there' in the same manner as those physically present at the event."

Q. A friend questions worship on Sunday. He also questions whether Christ was crucified on Good Friday. He states that John 19:31 shows that the Passover feast was to be eaten on that Friday, and the Jews would not have had Christ crucified on that day. How can I convince him otherwise? — D.H., Indiana

A. Since apostolic times, the Catholic Church has celebrated the Lord's Day on Sunday, the first day of the week (Acts 20:7) and the day after the Jewish Sabbath. The Church was given the authority to change the day of the Lord from Saturday to Sunday by Christ: "Whatever you declare bound on earth shall be held bound in heaven, and whatever you declare loosed on earth shall be held loosed in heaven" (Matthew 18:18).

In *Dies Domini*, Pope John Paul II explained the change:

"Because the Third Commandment depends upon the remembrance of God's saving works and because Christians saw the definitive time inaugurated by Christ as a new beginning, they made the first day after the Sabbath a festive day, for that was the day on which the Lord rose from the dead" (n. 18).

The article sent by D.H., which contends that biblical references to the first day of the week "do not give any evidence whatsoever of Sunday being a day of worship," is not only wrong in its understanding of Scripture, but it also ignores many important statements from the early centuries of the Church that confirm what the Bible says about celebrating the Lord's Day on Sunday. For example, St. Justin in the second century said:

"We all gather on the day of the sun, for it is the first day [after the Jewish Sabbath, but also the first day] when God, separating matter from darkness, made the world; and on this same day Jesus Christ our Savior rose from the dead."

Two centuries later, St. Jerome echoed Justin when he said:

"The Lord's Day, the day of Resurrection, the day of Christians, is our day. It is called the Lord's Day because on it the Lord rose victorious to the Father. If pagans call it the 'day of the sun,' we willingly agree, for today the light of the world is raised, today is revealed the sun of justice with healing in its rays."

As for the Holy Week objections, John 19:31 says that "since it was the Preparation Day, the Jews did not want to have the bodies left on the cross during the sabbath, for that sabbath was a solemn feast day." This does not say that the crucifixion occurred on the Passover, but rather on the Preparation Day for the Sabbath, which would make it a Friday.

This is confirmed by the three Synoptic Gospels, which leave no doubt that Christ was crucified on a Friday. Matthew 27:62 calls it "the Day of Preparation," Mark 15:42 calls it "Preparation Day, that is, the eve of the sabbath," and Luke 23:54 says that it was "the Day of Preparation, and the sabbath was about to begin."

Q. Would you please comment on the enclosed article by a syndicated columnist and tell me if his view is that of the Church? — S.A.M., Maryland
A. The columnist was asked if it were a serious sin to miss Mass while traveling on vacation. After noting the seriousness of the obligation to participate in the Mass on days of obligation and "the central importance of the Eucharist in Catholic life," he said that vacation travel can be a legitimate reason for missing Mass. He said that one who takes the Mass obligation "seriously and fulfills it faithfully otherwise, and misses Mass because of a pleasure trip, can surely do so in good conscience."

But in his apostolic letter *Dies Domini*, Pope John Paul said that "pastors should remind the faithful that when they are away from home on Sundays they are to take care to attend Mass wherever they may be" (n. 49). We would agree with the columnist that vacation travel can be a valid excuse for missing Mass, but we wish he had added the Holy Father's admonition that vacationers are to make an effort to attend Mass. They ought to shape their travel plans, if possible, to include being near a Catholic church on Saturday afternoon or Sunday morning. There is even a web site (www.masstimes.org) listing all the Catholic churches in the United States and the times of Masses.

If Catholics are going to be far removed from a church on Sunday, say, because they are in a country where the opportunities for attending Mass are few and far between, or they are backpacking in some remote area, then, suggests moral theologian Germain Grisez, they could request from their pastor a dispensation from their obligation or the substitution of a Mass on a weekday (*Living a Christian Life*, p. 148).

Q. I have been a priest for 55 years, and I am sometimes confused by the changes in the celebration of the sacraments. Did I do wrong when I anointed the hands and feet of a priest on his deathbed? He asked me if I would be so kind as to do it. — C.S., Kentucky

A. No, Father, you did not do anything wrong. The *Rite of Anointing Outside of Mass* says that the priest anoints with oil the forehead and hands of the sick person and, "depending upon the culture and traditions of the place, as well as the condition of the sick person, the priest may also anoint additional parts of the body, for example, the area of pain or injury" (n. 124).

Q. Does the worthy reception of the Anointing of the Sick remit the temporal punishment for sins in Purgatory? What effect does it have on a comatose patient? — T.F.G., Texas

A. Yes, worthy reception of the Anointing of the Sick does indeed remit at least some of the temporal punishment due to forgiven sins. According to the document *Pastoral Care of the Sick: Rites of Anointing and Viaticum* (n. 6):

"This sacrament gives the grace of the Holy Spirit to those who are sick; by this grace the whole person is helped and saved, sustained by trust in God, and strengthened against the temptations of the Evil One and against anxiety over death. Thus the sick person is able not only to bear suffering bravely, but also to fight against it.

"A return to physical health may follow the reception of this sacrament if it will be beneficial to the sick person's salvation. If necessary, the sacrament also provides the sick person with the forgiveness of sins and the completion of Christian penance."

As for those who are comatose, the document says that "the sacrament of Anointing is to be conferred on sick people who, although they have lost consciousness or the use of reason, would, as Christian believers, have at least implicitly asked for it when they were in control of their faculties."

Excluded from the sacrament, says the document, are those sick persons who remain "obdurately in open and serious sin" (n. 15).

Q. During the Old Covenant times, God used priests as the go-between for Him and man. The Old Law, and all that was part of it, including the priesthood, were nailed to the cross with Jesus and done away with forever. In all the pages of the New Testament, not a single time do we find anyone serving as a priest for God, such as the now-

in-force Roman Catholic priesthood. So where did the Roman Catholic priesthood come from? — R.E.M., Florida

A. Why from the Lord Jesus Himself, who instituted the priesthood at the Last Supper when, after consecrating the bread and wine, He told the Apostles to "do this as a remembrance of me" (Luke 22:19).

The priesthood of Aaron and the service of the Levites in the Old Testament, says the *Catechism*, were "a prefiguring of the ordained ministry of the New Covenant" (n. 1541). Or as St. Thomas Aquinas said: "Christ is the source of all priesthood: the priest of the old law was a figure of Christ, and the priest of the new law acts in the person of Christ."

As for their being no mention in the New Testament of anyone serving as a priest for God, that is not true. It might help to know, however, that every time you see in the New Testament the Greek word *presbuteros*, from which the English words "priest" or "presbyter" are derived, it is referring to one involved in priestly work.

For example, Paul and Barnabas "installed presbyters" in each church that they established (Acts 14:23). Timothy was ordained to the priesthood when "the presbyters laid their hands" on him (1 Timothy 4:14), just as men are ordained today when the bishop lays hands on them. Paul said that "presbyters who do well as leaders deserve to be paid double, especially those whose work is preaching and teaching" (1 Timothy 5:17).

We also find men carrying out the sacramental functions of priests in the Letter of James, where he says: "Is there anyone sick among you? He should ask for the presbyters of the church. They in turn are to pray over him, anointing him with oil in the Name [of the Lord]" (James 5:14).

And of course on the first Easter Sunday night, we see Jesus giving the Apostles the power to forgive sins, a power that has from the time of Christ been recognized as belonging to the Catholic priesthood. Jesus did not say to the Apostles, "If *I* forgive men's sins, they are forgiven them," but rather, "If *you* forgive men's sins,/ they are forgiven them" (John 20:23).

Q. My parish priest has told the congregation on two occasions that its members share as fully in the priesthood as he does, and that they were concelebrating the Mass with him. I would appreciate your comments. — J.F.S., New York

A. Your priest is confusing the ministerial priesthood, which he received through Holy Orders, and the common priesthood of the faithful, which all the laity received at Baptism. By Baptism, said St. Peter, we have become "living stones, built as an edifice of spirit, into a holy priesthood" (1 Peter 2:5). He said that our Baptism gives us a share in the priesthood of Christ, explaining that we are " 'a chosen race, a royal priesthood, a holy nation, a people he [God] claims for his own to proclaim the glorious works' of the One who called you from darkness into his marvelous light" (1 Peter 2:9).

The common priesthood of the faithful differs in essence from the ministerial or hierarchical priesthood of bishops and priests, however. The essential difference, says the *Catechism*, is that "while the common priesthood of the faithful is exercised by the unfolding of baptismal grace — a life of faith, hope, and charity, a life according to the Spirit — the ministerial priesthood is at the service of the common priesthood" (n. 1547).

It says that "the ministerial priesthood is a *means* by which Christ unceasingly builds up and leads his Church. For this reason it is transmitted by its own sacrament, the sacrament of Holy Orders" (*Ibid.*).

The priest acts in the name of the whole Church when he offers the Eucharistic Sacrifice, the *Catechism* continues, but this "does not mean that priests are the delegates of the community. The prayer and offering of the Church are inseparable from the prayer and offering of Christ, her head; it is always the case that Christ worships in and through his Church" (n. 1553).

That is why "the whole Church ... prays and offers herself 'through him, with him, in him,' in the unity of the Holy Spirit, to God the Father." And that is why those in the Body of Christ who are God's special ministers "are called ministers not only of Christ, but also of the Church. It is because the ministerial priesthood represents Christ that it can represent the Church" (*Ibid.*).

Q. I hear conflicting stories about a crisis in vocations to the priesthood in the United States. Some dioceses seem to have very few, if any, seminarians, while other dioceses seem to have many men studying for the priesthood. What is the true situation? — M.H.T., Massachusetts

A. It depends on what diocese or religious order you are talking about. Priestly vocations are booming in places like Arlington, Virginia, Peoria, Illinois, Lincoln and Omaha, Nebraska, and

Denver, Colorado, and in religious orders like the Legionaries of Christ and the Priestly Fraternity of St. Peter. Why this is so was explained by Bishop Elden Curtiss of Omaha in the March 1999 issue of *Religious Life*:

"It seems to me that the vocation 'crisis' is precipitated and continued by people who want to change the Church's agenda, by people who do not support orthodox candidates loyal to the magisterial teaching of the Pope and bishops, and by people who actually discourage viable candidates from seeking priesthood and vowed religious life as the Church defines these ministries.

"I am personally aware of certain vocation directors, vocation teams, and evaluation boards who turn away candidates who do not support the possibility of ordaining women, or who defend the Church's teaching about artificial birth control, or who exhibit a strong piety toward certain devotions, such as the rosary."

When there is a determined effort to discourage orthodox candidates from entering priesthood and religious life, said Bishop Curtiss, "then the vocation shortage which results is not caused by a lack of vocations but by deliberate attitudes and policies which deter certain viable candidates. And the same people who precipitate a decline in vocations by their negative actions call for the ordination of married men and women to replace the vocations they have discouraged. They have a death wish for ordained priesthood and vowed religious life as the Church defines them. They undermine the vocation ministry they are supposed to champion."

He said that a successful vocation strategy must include "loyalty to the Pope and bishop; a vocation director and team who clearly support a male, celibate priesthood and religious communities loyal to magisterial teaching; a presbyterate that takes personal ownership of vocation ministry ... more and more parents who encourage their children to consider a vocation to priesthood and religious life; Eucharistic devotion in parishes with an emphasis on prayer for vocations; and vocation committees in most of our parishes which focus on personally inviting and nourishing vocations."

Q. I was thinking about establishing a vocations committee in my parish/deanery both to encourage vocations

and to invigorate and enliven local parish priests. **Have you any guidelines for establishing such a committee where there is none and where the priests are very laissez-faire? Also, can you tell me where to get a copy of** *Religious Life***? I would be interested in the issue with the article by Archbishop Elden Curtiss and also in obtaining his address. — C.L., Connecticut**

A. Archbishop Curtiss can be reached at the Archdiocese of Omaha Chancery Office, 100 N. 62nd St., Omaha, NE 68132. *Religious Life* is published by the Institute on Religious Life, P.O. Box 41007, Chicago, IL 60641. Back issues are $1 each and there are associate membership dues each year. The Institute would be a very good source of information on getting a vocations committee started. You can contact it by mail or visit its web site at www.religiouslife.com.

Q. What dioceses and groups in the U.S.A. have large enrollments in their seminaries? By groups I mean the Priestly Fraternity of St. Peter. Do you have the number of men enrolled in each diocese? — J.R., Michigan

A. You are correct in saying that priestly vocations are booming in such religious orders as the Priestly Fraternity of St. Peter and the Legionaries of Christ. The reason is that these orders are loyal to the magisterial teaching of the Pope and the bishops in communion with him, and they offer young men an opportunity to become "other Christs," and not glorified social workers.

As for the total number of seminarians in each of the 175 archdioceses and dioceses in the United States, we don't have those figures immediately at hand, but you could do some homework yourself and look up the numbers in the latest *Official Catholic Directory*, which is published by P.J. Kenedy & Sons.

However, we do know that, according to the Vatican's *Statistical Yearbook for 1997*, for example, there were 35,000 seminarians in the United States, up from 22,000 in 1978. Worldwide, there were 108,517 men studying for the priesthood in 1997, a 70 percent increase over 1978, when there were 63,882 men preparing for the priesthood.

The pendulum is finally swinging the other way, after the downturn following the Second Vatican Council, so keep up your prayers for more vocations to the priesthood and the religious life.

Q. I seem to recollect a directive from the Vatican that all priests and religious must wear their clerical garb as a statement to the world of their consecration to Jesus Christ and service to His Church. Can you give me the full text of this directive? — G.F.M., Florida, and G.D.W., Pennsylvania

A. Actually, there are several statements about this matter. Vatican II's *Decree on the Appropriate Renewal of Religious Life* said that "since they are signs of a consecrated life, religious habits should be simple and modest, at once poor and becoming. They should meet the requirements of health and be suited to the circumstances of time and place, as well as to the services required by those who wear them. Habits of men and women which do not correspond to those norms are to be changed" (n. 17).

Thus, Vatican II did not abolish habits, but said that they could be modified to meet certain conditions of health, time, place, and occupation.

The Code of Canon Law promulgated in 1983 said in canon 284 that "clerics are to wear suitable ecclesiastical garb in accord with the norms issued by the conference of bishops and in accord with legitimate local custom," and in canon 669 that "religious are to wear the habit of the institute made according to the norm of proper law as a sign of their consecration and as a testimony of poverty. Clerical religious of an institute which does not have its own habit are to wear clerical dress according to the norm of can. 284."

Q. Pope John Paul has stated in *Ordinatio Sacerdotalis* that the Catholic priesthood is restricted to males and that he has no authority to confer the priesthood on other than males. This should end the discussion, but there does seem to be the impression in this country that, once John Paul is gone, another Pope might change this situation. Is this a possibility? Have authoritative papal statements been repudiated in the past, or completely changed in meaning and effect? — P.A.L., Illinois

A. No, authoritative papal statements on matters of faith and morals have never been repudiated, and there is no more possibility of a future Pope allowing the ordination of women to the priesthood than having some future Pontiff reverse the Church's ban on artificial contraception, as some wishful thinkers thought would happen once Pope Paul VI died. Statements by the Church's ordinary and universal magisterium can never change, and Popes frequently refer to the pronouncements of their predecessors in the Chair of Peter to show the continuity and immutability of Church teaching.

For example, in *Ordinatio Sacerdotalis*, John Paul quoted Paul VI as having said that the Church "holds that it is not admissible to ordain women to the priesthood, for very fundamental reasons." These reasons, said Paul VI, include "the example recorded in the sacred Scriptures of Christ choosing his apostles only from among men; the constant practice of the Church, which has imitated Christ in choosing only men; and her living teaching authority which has consistently held that the exclusion of women from the priesthood is in accordance with God's plan for his Church."

On November 18, 1995, eighteen months after Pope John Paul had declared that he had "no authority whatsoever to confer priestly ordination on women," the Sacred Congregation for the Doctrine of the Faith made clear that this teaching would never be reversed when it said that the pronouncement against the ordination of women had been "set forth infallibly by the ordinary and universal magisterium. Thus, in the present circumstances, the Roman Pontiff, exercising his proper office of confirming the brethren, has handed on this same teaching by a formal declaration, explicitly stating what is to be held always, everywhere, and by all, as belonging to the deposit of the faith."

Q. The Holy Father has forbidden further discussion about women priests, but what about women deacons? Deaconesses are mentioned in the Bible in Romans 16:1, where St. Paul sends greetings to "our sister Phoebe, who is a deaconess of the church of Cenchreae." Priests need the help of more deacons today, and not enough men are coming forward to fill this position, so wouldn't deaconesses be of help to the Church? — P. and J.S., California

A. First of all, the sacrament of Holy Orders has three levels: deacon, priest, and bishop and, while we are not aware of a specific Church prohibition against ordaining women as deacons, we would think that such a prohibition would flow logically from the ban on ordaining women as priests.

As for St. Paul's reference to Phoebe, he was referring to those holy women who without being ordained served the early Church by assisting the clergy in charitable works and in their sacramental ministry when appropriate, for example, in the baptism of female catechumens. That this was the case is indicated by writings from the early Church.

For instance, canon 19 of the Council of Nicaea in 325 said that "we have made mention of the deaconesses, who have been enrolled in this position, although, not having been in any way ordained, they are certainly to be numbered among the laity."

Some 50 years later, Epiphanius wrote in his *Panacea Against All Heresies*:

"It is true that in the Church there is an order of deaconesses, but not for being a priestess nor for any kind of work of administration, but for the sake of the dignity of the female sex, either at the time of baptism or of examining the sick or suffering, so that the naked body of a female may not be seen by men administering sacred rites, but by the deaconess."

This explanation was reiterated in *The Apostolic Constitutions* (A.D. 400), where it is written that "a deaconess does not bless, but neither does she perform anything else that is done by presbyters [priests] and deacons, but she guards the doors and greatly assists the presbyters, for the sake of decorum, when they are baptizing women."

Once the rite of baptism by immersion began to be replaced by infusion or pouring, the need for deaconesses declined and this non-sacramental office disappeared from the pages of Church history.

Women today and over two millennia, Pope John Paul noted in *Ordinatio Sacerdotalis*, have indeed been "true disciples, witnesses to Christ in the family and in society, as well as in total consecration to the service of God and of the Gospel," but they have done so, and will continue to do, as members of the laity, not the clergy.

Editor's Note: Following up on a recent reply about the ordination of women as deacons, three Vatican congregations issued a statement on September 17, 2001 saying that because the Catholic Church "does not foresee the possibility" of ordaining women deacons, "it is not licit to undertake initiatives which in some way aim at preparing female candidates for diaconal ordination."

Noting that the Vatican agencies have received "several signals regarding the planning or offering of courses directly or indirectly aimed at the diaconal ordination of women," the heads of the congregations for the Doctrine of the Faith, the Clergy, and the Sacraments said that such courses must be discontinued because they could "give rise to expectations lacking solid doctrinal soundness and could, therefore, generate pastoral disorientation."

The statement, which was approved by Pope John Paul II, said that "the authentic promotion of women in the Church ... opens other ample prospects for service and collaboration."

Q. Would you please comment on the enclosed Associated Press story, which cites the *Kansas City Star* as its source, about Catholic priests allegedly dying of AIDS-related illnesses at a rate four times greater than the general population? I assume this is a scandalous distortion of whatever modicum of truth might have inspired it. — J.H.Y., Alabama

A. Your assumption is correct, and we will rely on William Donohue of the Catholic League for Religious and Civil Rights to demonstrate the bias of this series of articles that first appeared in the *Kansas City Star*. The *Star* sent questionnaires to 3,000 of the 46,000 priests in the United States and received 801 responses, which represent less than two percent of the priests in the United States, hardly a comprehensive survey.

"An examination of the data," said Donohue, "shows that exactly one-half of one percent of priests have HIV or AIDS, and exactly 3.6 percent are critical of the way the Church has responded to this problem. What is striking about this is that the narrative offered in the series is written from the perspective that AIDS is rampant in the priesthood and that the clergy are furious with the way the Church has handled this problem. In essence, what could not be accomplished by citing the data had to be done by substituting anecdotal commentary drawn from a handful of angry priests *and* former priests."

Donohoe said "it is also striking that 70 percent of the priests said that changing the Church's teachings on homosexuality would not prove effective in dealing with this problem, and two-thirds said that changing the celibacy requirement would not prove effective either. Yet the narrative states that 'the Catholic Church's condemnation of homosexual acts, its requirement that priests be male, and its unique demand of celibacy make the issue all the more vexing for its followers.' However, this conclusion is not supported by the data."

Another example of the unscientific nature of the survey was the claim that AIDS-related deaths among priests are about four times the rate of the general population, which includes women and children. However, when the rate of AIDS-related deaths among priests is contrasted with the rate among *adult males*, which is the proper comparison to make, the rate is the same.

Are there priests with sexual problems? Yes, but there are far more priests living holy and chaste lives. Let us pray for all priests that they will be faithful to their vocation as other Christs.

Q. Do you have any comments on the sex abuse scandal involving priests in some dioceses? — K.R., New York
A. Yes, we do and here they are:

• Celibacy is not the problem; sin is. Why would anyone think that a priest who is attracted to children would be cured of his addiction by having a wife? Sexual abuse of children is more often perpetrated by mothers, fathers, aunts, uncles, brothers, sisters, grandparents, family friends, teachers, coaches, chaperones, and baby sitters — none of whom took a vow of celibacy.

• Penn State Professor Philip Jenkins, author of the book *Priests and Pedophiles*, said that his research over 20 years "indicates no evidence whatever" that Catholic clergy are more likely to be involved in misconduct or abuse than clergy of any other denomination. He said that "every Protestant denomination has had scandals aplenty, as have Pentecostals, Mormons, Jehovah's Witnesses, Jews, Buddhists, Hare Krishnas."

• Jenkins said that a study in the early 1990s of 2,200 priests who had served the Archdiocese of Chicago over the previous 40 years found that 46 priests (1.8 percent) were probably guilty of misconduct with minors at some point in their careers. Put another way, 98 percent of Chicago priests were *not guilty* of misconduct with minors.

• Most priests are good, holy, caring men, and the justified anger over the sinful and criminal actions of a few hundred of them should not turn people against the 46,000 innocent members of the clergy who have been faithful to the vow of celibacy and would never sexually abuse a child. We must pray for our priests and tell them that we love and support them.

• Some bishops relied too heavily on modern psychiatrists, who said the priests guilty of sexual abuse could be returned to parish work with children. We now know that pedophilia is incurable and that priests with this addiction should never be placed near children, but that fact was not known back then.

• The problem is not just pedophilia (abuse of prepubescent children), but also homosexuality (sex with teenagers and older persons). Homosexuality has been rampant in some seminaries for decades, and good, orthodox men who opposed homosexual behavior were kicked out of seminaries because they supported Church teaching on this and other moral evils.

• While some bishops failed to protect children from sexual abuse and tried to cover up for priests who were guilty of this awful sin, much tougher policies and standards have been in effect in most dioceses since the early 1990s.

• The answer to this scandal is holiness. We must — each one of us — become more holy through prayer, fasting, Confession, and the Holy Eucharist. While there are sinners in the Church, the Church herself is always holy because it is the Body of Christ on earth. Jesus promised that the gates of Hell would never prevail against His Church, and we must remain loyal to the Church, while being outraged at those who have blackened her name.

Prayer for Priests

Keep them, I pray Thee, dearest Lord,
    Keep them, for they are Thine —
Thy priests whose lives burn out before
    Thy consecrated shrine.
Keep them, for they are in the world,
    Though from the world apart.
When earthly pleasures tempt, allure,
    Shelter them in Thy heart.
Keep them, and O remember, Lord,
    They have no one but Thee,
Yet they have only human hearts,
    With human frailty.
Keep them as spotless as the Host
    That daily they caress,
Their every thought and word and deed
    Deign, dearest Lord, to bless.

Chapter 9

The Holy Eucharist

Q. Can you tell me what the Council of Trent said about Jesus being completely present — Body, Blood, Soul, and Divinity — in both the consecrated Host and the consecrated Wine? — D.C.D., South Dakota

A. In the section (n. 1374) on the presence of Jesus in the Holy Eucharist, the *Catechism* quotes two statements from the Council of Trent. The first says that "in the most blessed sacrament of the Eucharist 'the body and blood, together with the soul and divinity, of our Lord Jesus Christ and, therefore, *the whole Christ is truly, really, and substantially* contained' [Council of Trent (1551): DS 1651]."

In paragraph 1376, the *Catechism* offers the following summary from Trent of Catholic faith in the Eucharist:

"Because Christ our Redeemer said that it was truly his body that he was offering under the species of bread, it has always been the conviction of the Church of God, and this holy Council now declares again, that by the consecration of the bread and wine there takes place a change of the whole substance of the bread into the substance of the body of Christ our Lord and of the whole substance of the wine into the substance of his blood. This change the holy Catholic Church has fittingly and properly called transubstantiation [Council of Trent (1551): DS 1642; cf *Mt* 26:26 ff.; *Mk* 14:22 ff.; *Lk* 22:19 ff.; 1 *Cor* 11:24 ff.]."

As to whether Jesus is fully present under each species, the *Catechism*, without mentioning Trent, says this is true and that Communion under the species of bread alone makes it possible to receive all the fruit of Eucharistic grace. It says that for pastoral reasons this manner of receiving Communion has been legitimately established as the most common form in the Latin rite, but adds (n. 1390) that " 'the sign of communion is more complete when given under both kinds, since in that form the sign of the Eucharistic meal appears more clearly' [GIRM 240]."

Q. During a conversation with an evangelist team that came to my door, they agreed that our Lord said we must "eat of my Body and drink of my Blood," but said that was cannibalism. I do not know a reasonable rebuttal to that argument. Can you help? — J.A.J., California

A. In their booklet *Beginning Apologetics 3: How to Explain and Defend the Real Presence of Christ in the Eucharist*, Fr. Frank Chacon and Jim Burnham offer this rebuttal:

"It was precisely this misunderstanding that led the unbelieving Jews and disciples in John 6 to reject Jesus when he said they must eat his body and drink his blood. They thought Jesus was commanding them to consume him in a bloody, cannibalistic way. However, the believing disciples were rewarded for their faith at the Last Supper. Jesus revealed that they would receive his true body and blood *sacramentally* (present in a hidden way).

"In the sacrament of the Eucharist, Christ's body and blood are truly present, but not with their normal physical properties. Jesus' body isn't spread out in space; its normal condition is hidden under the appearance of bread and wine. While the apostles truly consumed Christ's real body and blood, it wasn't cannibalism because Christ wasn't in his natural condition. They didn't bite off pieces of Christ's arm, for example, or swallow quantities of his blood; instead they received Christ whole and entire — body, blood, soul, and divinity — under the appearance of bread and wine. Receiving Christ's real, but sacramental, presence in the Eucharist has nothing to do with cannibalism or drinking blood" (pp. 16-17).

By the way, this 40-page booklet is one of six by Chacon and Burnham on the Catholic faith. They are very well done and are available from San Juan Catholic Seminars, P.O. Box 5253, Farmington, NM 87499.

Q. I am in a quandary after reading in our parish bulletin the following statement: "After five years of praying before the Real Presence, we've come to affirm and be truly conscious of the Real Presence in ourselves and, if in ourselves, then certainly in one another." When I showed this to a Eucharistic minister, he said, "Oh, yes, we're divine, we are God, the Real Presence, the Blessed Sacrament." I cannot accept this answer. — E.F., Florida

A. We can't accept that answer either. While Jesus can be present to us in different ways, His presence in the Eucharist is unique, and while He "humbled himself to share in our humanity" so that we might come to share in His divinity when we are made perfect in Heaven, that does not make us God or the Blessed Sacrament.

At their June 2001 meeting in Atlanta, the U.S. Bishops issued a document entitled *The Real Presence of Jesus Christ in the Sacrament of the Eucharist: Basic Questions and Answers*. Among other things, the Bishops said:

"The Catholic Church professes that in the celebration of the Eucharist, bread and wine become the body and blood of Jesus Christ through the power of the Holy Spirit and the instrumentality of the priest. Jesus said: 'I am the living bread that came down from Heaven; whoever eats this bread will live forever; and the bread that I will give is my flesh for the life of the world .... For my flesh is true food, and my blood true drink' (Jn. 6:51-55).

"The whole Christ is truly present, body, blood, soul, and divinity, under the appearances of bread and wine — the glorified Christ who rose from the dead after dying for our sins. This is what the Church means when she speaks of the Real Presence of Christ in the Eucharist. This presence of Christ in the Eucharist is called real not to exclude other types of his presence as if they could not be understood as real (cf. *Catechism of the Catholic Church*, 1374). The risen Christ is present in his Church in many ways, but most especially through the sacrament of his body and blood."

Q. Does our Lord leave the Eucharist if it is being profaned, say, at a "Black Mass"? — T.H., New Mexico

A. It is Catholic teaching that Jesus remains present in the Holy Eucharist as long as the appearances of bread and wine remain. So if satanists were able to procure a consecrated Host for their hellish rituals, and the Host had not been digested or dissolved and still retained the appearance of bread, Jesus would still be present in the Host, even while it was being profaned. If Jesus were no longer present in the species, then no profanation could occur.

Canon 1367 states that "a person who throws away the consecrated species or who takes them or retains them for a sacrilegious purpose incurs an automatic excommunication reserved to the Apostolic See." There would be no need to excommunicate someone who abused a piece of bread, but to abuse or desecrate that which is holy and sacred, i.e., the Body and Blood of the Lord, would warrant the penalty of excommunication.

Q. If a priest has committed a mortal sin, can he still receive Communion while he is celebrating Mass? — J.K., Pennsylvania

A. Only for a "grave reason" (cf. canon 916) and if he has been unable to get to Confession first but makes an act of perfect contrition with the intention of confessing his sin as soon as possible afterwards. The Council of Trent put it this way:

"If it is not fitting for anyone to approach any sacred functions except in a state of holiness, then certainly to the extent that the holiness and godliness of this heavenly sacrament is more and more known to the Christian, all the more must he take care that he does not come to receive it without great reverence and holiness, especially because of the fearful words of the Apostle which we read: 'A person who eats and drinks without recognizing the body of the Lord is eating and drinking his own condemnation' (1 Cor. 11:29). Thus the following precept should be recalled to the one desirous of receiving Holy Communion: 'Let a man so examine himself' (1 Cor. 11:28).

"Ecclesiastical custom declares that the proving of one's self is necessary, so that no one, conscious of having committed mortal sin, though considering himself contrite, should approach the Holy Eucharist without first having made a sacramental confession. This holy Synod declares that this must perpetually be observed by all Christians, even by priests, whose duty it is to celebrate Mass, as long as there is an availability of confessors. If in the case of urgent necessity a priest will have celebrated without previous confession, he is to make a confession as soon as possible."

Q. Regarding what constitutes invalid matter for the Eucharist, my questions are: (1) What are the consequences for the Catholic receiving invalid matter, believing it to be consecrated? (2) Should a Catholic attend a Mass if he knows the matter is invalid? — L.L., Virginia

A. (1) A Catholic who unknowingly receives invalid matter obviously does not receive the Body of Christ, but since he is invincibly ignorant of this fact, he has done nothing wrong and will not suffer any consequences. We are sure that the Lord will impart graces to this person since he came to Mass with the sincere intention of receiving Jesus in the Eucharist.

(2) A Catholic most definitely should not attend a Mass if he knows that invalid matter will be used. If it's a case of a recipe for the bread that clearly makes the matter invalid, the person should first approach his pastor and, if his concerns go unheeded, he should then inform his bishop.

Q. At a Mass for our parish school, the Communion was small, uniform squares that looked like rye bread. It was disturbing to see all the Eucharistic ministers digging in a salad bowl to get Communion for their stations. After Communion, there were many Hosts not consumed, so they passed them down the rows of people to be consumed.

When I wrote to the pastor about this, I got a letter from the parish liturgist saying that passing the Hosts down the rows "is acceptable once the initial 'reception' has taken place." Is that true? — W.H., Missouri

A. No, it is not true. In the Sacred Congregation for the Sacraments and Divine Worship's "Instruction on Certain Norms Concerning the Worship of the Eucharistic Mystery" (*Inaestimabile Donum*), we find the following paragraph (n. 13):

"Even after Communion the Lord remains present under the species. Accordingly, when Communion has been distributed, the sacred particles remaining are to be consumed or taken by the competent minister to the place where the Eucharist is reserved."

Thus, the "competent minister" is responsible for consuming or reserving the Hosts remaining after Communion, not the people in the pews. The fact that the Hosts mentioned by W.H. were not reserved may have to do with the composition of them; the liturgist in her letter stated that the "bread bakers" in that parish "have studied many recipes and comply with the directive of no leavening agent."

She did not say, however, what ingredients *are* used in the recipe. In any case, here is some sound advice from liturgical expert Msgr. Peter J. Elliott:

"It is prudent always to use bread prepared professionally by those who observe Church law and custom rather than to allow others to bake bread according to 'recipes.' Wholemeal wheaten flour may be used to emphasize the food sign, but surely not the coarser forms of wholemeal where the grain is still largely intact. However, adding other kinds of flour, chemical colorings, oil, shortening, salt, sugar, honey, etc., renders the matter invalid or at least doubtful. No priest may use doubtful matter for the Eucharist" (*Ceremonies of the Modern Roman Rite*, n. 145).

Q. Enclosed is a recipe for Eucharistic bread being made for the parish of St. Mark in Virginia Beach, VA. My grandson will be making his First Communion there, and I am concerned about the validity of this bread. Please advise. — J.L.P., New York

A. The recipe that appears under the letterhead of the St. Mark Religious Education Office lists the following ingredients: 1/3 cup honey, 1/3 cup oil, 1 cup warm water, 1/2 cup milk, 2.5 cups whole wheat flour, 2.5 cups white flour, 2 tsp. salt, 3.5 tsp. baking powder, 1.5 tsp. baking soda.

The bread to be made from this recipe is certainly illicit, and probably invalid, matter, as can be seen from the following statements about the composition of bread for the Eucharist:

• Canon 924.2 of the 1983 Code of Canon Law says: "The bread must be made of wheat alone and recently made so that there is no danger of corruption."

• In *Inaestimabile Donum*, the Congregation for the Sacraments and Divine Worship says: "The bread for the celebration of the Eucharist, in accordance with the tradition of the whole Church, must be made solely of wheat and, in accordance with the tradition proper to the Latin Church, it must be unleavened .... No other ingredients are to be added to the wheaten flour and water" (n. 8).

• According to Fr. Nicholas Halligan: "The bread must be made from wheat, mixed with natural water, baked by the application of fire heat (including electric cooking), and substantially uncorrupted. The variety of the wheat or the region of its origin does not affect its validity, but bread made from any other grain is invalid matter. Bread made with milk, wine, oil, etc., either entirely or in a notable part, is invalid material" (*The Sacraments and Their Celebration*, p. 65).

If this recipe is used for your grandson's First Communion, he and his classmates will likely be receiving only bread, not the Body and Blood of Christ. The pastor of the parish should be asked about this immediately and, if there are no immediate assurances that invalid matter will not be used, then his bishop should be contacted and asked to forbid the use of such a recipe.

Q. Please comment on the use of table wine (or wine from liquor stores) for consecration at Mass. — Name and State Withheld

A. It is not appropriate to use table wines or wine purchased from liquor stores for consecration at Mass because those wines could be impure or adulterated in some way. "Priests should use only wine authorized by the bishops in accord with local Church law and custom," said Msgr. Peter Elliott in *Ceremonies of the Modern Roman Rite.* "Commercial wine in some countries is not 'natural and pure grape wine,' and no priest may use such doubtful matter" (p. 53).

He is echoed by Fr. Nicholas Halligan, who said in *The Sacraments and Their Celebration* (pp. 66-67):

"The Holy See has been insistent that sacramental or Mass wine come from sources beyond suspicion, since there are many ways in which wines can be vitiated or adulterated, many methods which are actually used in this country to preserve, age, ameliorate wines. Wines should be purchased regularly only from reputable vendors of Mass wine or only when otherwise guaranteed to be pure and unadulterated."

Q. Please tell me what Vatican II document permitted non-ordained hands to touch the consecrated Host? — C.M.M., Mississippi

A. It was not a Vatican II document, but rather two documents issued after the Council ended in 1965. The first was *Memoriale Domini,* issued by the Sacred Congregation for Divine Worship on May 29, 1969. That document, noting a "desire to return to the ancient usage of depositing the Eucharistic Bread in the hand of the communicant," said that while the custom of placing the Host on the tongue "must be retained," two-thirds of the bishops of a country could petition the Holy See for permission to allow Communion in the hand.

Such permission might be granted, the Sacred Congregation

said, "in order to promote the common good and the edification of all" and provided that an adequate catechesis be given "so that the faithful will understand the significance of the action and will perform it with the respect due to the sacrament."

The second document was *Immensae Caritatis*, issued on January 25, 1973 by the Sacred Congregation for the Discipline of the Sacraments. This pertained, among other things, to allowing the laity to distribute Holy Communion "only for the spiritual good of the faithful and for cases of genuine necessity."

Q. After having a letter published in *The Commercial Appeal* about Mother Teresa's dislike for Communion in the hand (according to a quotation from your column), a dear friend sent me letters from Fr. George Rutler and the Missionaries of Charity (copies of both letters enclosed) saying that Mother Teresa had been misquoted. I must hear from you about this. — O.A.E., Tennessee

A. We first saw the alleged statement of Mother Teresa in an article in the *Homiletic & Pastoral Review*, which gave as its source a homily given in 1989 by Fr. Rutler at St. Agnes Church in New York City. However, the two letters sent by O.A.E. make clear that Mother Teresa was, in the words of Sr. M. Dominga, superior of the Missionaries of Charity house in the Bronx, "wrongly quoted," and we apologize for misleading our readers. We also pass along Fr. Rutler's comments:

"Several years ago I was misquoted in the press as having said that Mother Teresa opposed Communion in the hand. Mother said it made her sad to see people receive Communion irreverently, and she herself receives on the tongue, but she does not question the Church's permission for receiving in the hand. Whether on the tongue or in the hand is not the issue: the matter concerns the disposition of the heart.

"Mother Teresa was so concerned that anyone might think her critical of Communion in the hand that she asked me to correct this immediately. You can oblige her by doing the same."

Q. While serving as an extraordinary minister, I refused to give Communion to two persons who did not reply "Amen" when I held up the Body of Christ. I asked them if they were Catholic, and they replied, "No." So I told them to please pass on. After Mass, the priest said I was

wrong, that receiving Communion is between the receiver
and God, that I was to assume the person was approaching the altar in good faith, and that I should give them
Communion. Did I do the wrong thing? — J.F.O., Virginia

A. No, you did not. It would be wrong to presume that a person was in a state of mortal sin and thereby refuse to give him
Communion, but when a communicant appears to have no idea
of what to say or do, it is reasonable for the minister of the Eucharist to inquire if that person is a Catholic, or in the case of a
child if he or she has made First Communion. If the answer is
no, then Communion should not be given.

**Q. I know it's not right for a divorced and remarried
person to be giving out Communion at Mass, but can you
cite a specific Church statement against this? — P.H., New
Jersey**

A. As you imply in your question, common sense says that it
would not be right for a person living in sin, whose irregular
marriage situation prohibits him from receiving Communion, to
be an extraordinary minister of the Eucharist. While the following statement does not specifically mention the problem you
asked about, it does make clear that those given the privilege of
distributing the Body and Blood of the Lord ought to be persons
of high moral character. The statement is taken from *Immensae
Caritatis*, the 1973 document issued by the Sacred Congregation for the Discipline of the Sacraments.

"The person who has been appointed to be an extraordinary
minister of Holy Communion is necessarily to be duly instructed
and should distinguish himself by his Christian life, faith, and
morals. Let him strive to be worthy of this great office; let him
cultivate devotion to the Holy Eucharist and show himself as an
example to other faithful by his piety and reverence for this most
holy Sacrament of the altar. Let no one be chosen whose selection may cause scandal among the faithful."

**Q. On a recent trip to Cape Cod, my family and I at-
tended a Sunday morning Mass. As we approached the
altar at Communion time to receive our Lord on the
tongue, as is our preference, the priest clearly displayed
annoyance and shoved the Host into my mouth so hard
that he broke it in half. When I questioned a parishioner**

about this, she said that there is a movement in the Church to get Communion on the tongue discontinued because of "sanitary reasons." Do you know of such a movement? — M.T.S., New York

A. No, we know of no such movement, and the priest was completely wrong in giving you the Body of Christ in such an angry manner. It is up to the communicant, not the priest, to decide whether Communion should be received on the tongue or in the hand. Here is how Appendix 1 of the *General Instruction of the Roman Missal* for Catholics in the United States puts it:

"The practice must remain the option of the communicant. The priest or minister of Communion does not make the decision as to the manner of reception of Communion. It is the communicant's personal choice" (n. 240b).

Q. I always receive Communion on the tongue, but while attending Mass recently at a Benedictine abbey, the monk distributing Communion asked me to receive by intinction. I hesitated at first, but then received the Host on the tongue and drank the Precious Blood from the chalice. It is a general practice here in Quebec to receive the consecrated Host in the hand and then dip the Host in the chalice before consuming it. I know that self-intinction is forbidden by the Church, but do you have some information that I could show to this monk? — C.B., Quebec

A. First of all, you received under both species, not by intinction, since you first received the Host on the tongue and then drank the Precious Blood. You did not touch the Host with your fingers. Receiving the Body and Blood of Christ by intinction is permissible if the minister of the Eucharist dips the Host into the Precious Blood and gives it to the communicant. It is self-intinction when the communicant takes the Host in hand, dips it into the chalice, and then consumes the Eucharist.

In 1984, the U.S. bishops forbade self-intinction in the document *This Holy and Living Sacrifice: Directory for the Celebration and Reception of Communion under Both Kinds*. Here are the pertinent paragraphs:

"The chalice may never be left on the altar or another place to be picked up by the communicant for self-communication (except in the case of concelebrating bishops or priests), nor may the chalice be passed from one communicant to another. There shall always be a minister of the cup" (n. 46).

"However, if Communion is given by intinction, the communicant may never dip the Eucharistic Bread into the chalice. Communion under either the form of bread or wine must always be given by a minister with the usual words" (n. 52).

Q. After receiving the Blood of Christ recently, my husband was concerned because I had a cold that might spread to others who drank from the cup after me. I told him that my germs could in no way mix with the purity of the Blood of Christ and that Jesus would take care of any germs. Any thoughts on this? — K.J., Illinois

A. There are people who are much concerned about the spread of germs through drinking the Precious Blood from the cup at Mass, and those people will not receive our Lord under both species for that reason. While it is possible that germs might be spread in this fashion, we are not aware of any studies that show this having happened.

In fact, there are studies concluding that there is no increased risk of infection for those who receive Holy Communion under both species, even for those who receive every day.

The first study, published in 1943 in the *Journal of Infectious Diseases* and reprinted in 1965 in the Lutheran publication *Una Sancta*, was entitled "Survival of Bacteria on the Silver Communion Cup" and was prepared by William Burrows and Elizabeth S. Hemmens of the University of Chicago. That study, after noting that wiping the chalice with a purificator after each use reduced the bacterial count on the chalice rim by more than 90 percent, came to this conclusion:

"Evidence is presented which indicates that bacteria swabbed on the polished surface of the silver chalice die off rapidly. Experiments on the transmission of test organisms from one person to another by common use of the chalice showed that approximately 0.001% of the organisms are transferred even under the most favorable conditions; when conditions approximated those of actual use, no transmission could be detected.

"Only small numbers of bacteria from the normal mouth could be recovered from the chalice immediately after its use by four persons. It is concluded that in practice the silver communion cup is not an important vector of infectious disease."

The other study, published in the July/August 1997 issue of the *Journal of Environmental Health*, was prepared by Anne LaGrange Loving, Assistant Professor of Microbiology at Felician College in New Jersey, and Lisa F. Wolf. This study, entitled "The Effects of Receiving Holy Communion on Health," was based on a 10-week-long survey of 681 individuals.

It compared illness rates among three groups: those who receive Communion, those who go to church but do not receive, and those who do not attend Christian services. After noting that concern about the possible spread of disease through shared Communion cups dates back to 1887, the article said:

"The results of this study indicate that fears from the last century, like those of Dr. Howard S. Anders, should not be of concern to individuals who attend church and receive Holy Communion. No significant differences were found in the rates of illness among Christians who receive Holy Communion, Christians who attend church but do not receive the sacraments, and people who do not attend Christian services."

Professor Loving also looked into whether those involved in religious life had a higher incidence of reported illness. Her finding: "These individuals attended church and received the sacraments as often as daily, and some consumed the 'dregs' of the consecrated Wine after all parishioners had sipped from the chalice. For all categories of health problems, no significant differences were found between participants with religious vocations and other respondents."

Q. Our deacon and his wife use our personal names when giving out Communion, such as "Betty, the Body of Christ." Sometimes I feel like saying, "Frank, Amen." Are there guidelines on this? — W.R., Pennsylvania

A. Those giving out Communion are supposed to say, "The Body of Christ" — period. Using the names of people they know takes away from the reverence due to Christ and could be hurtful to those who are not addressed by their first names.

Q. Parishioners from a nearby church tell me their new pastor requires that they state their names to him as they receive Holy Communion and also in the confessional. Is this liturgically correct? — P.A.R., Virginia

A. While it is commendable for the new pastor to want to learn the names of his parishioners as quickly as possible, in no way is it liturgically correct for him to ask people to state their names while receiving Communion or confessing their sins. The only thing the communicant says upon being shown the Body of Christ is "Amen." Penitents also have the right to anonymity when receiving the sacrament of Penance (that's why a screen is provided for those who do not wish to confess face to face), so it would be highly imprudent for a priest to require a penitent to identify himself by name.

We might note, however, that in Eastern Rite Catholic churches, it is permissible to ask the communicant's name so as to complete the phrase the priest says aloud before dispensing Holy Communion. The phrase is: "The Servant of God (name of the person) partakes of the Holy Body and Blood of Christ Jesus!"

Q. A priest has informed me that a document was issued some time ago which requires a person to observe the Eucharistic fast for only 15 minutes before Communion if he is taking medication for any reason. Have you heard of such a document? — J.V., California

A. No, we have not heard of such a document, but we do know that since 1953, there has been no required fast from medicine at all before receiving Holy Communion. Canon 919 of the 1983 Code of Canon Law says that "one who is to receive the Most Holy Eucharist is to abstain from any food and drink, with the exception only of water and medicine, for at least a period of one hour before Holy Communion."

Note that the fast is one hour before *Communion*, not one hour before Mass begins, but since the canon says "at least" one hour, it would be good to fast from the beginning of Mass and even longer than one hour to show one's appreciation for the privilege of receiving Christ in the Holy Eucharist.

The traditional total fast from midnight the night before, prescribed in the 1917 Code of Canon Law, was reduced to a three-hour fast in 1957 and to a one-hour fast in 1964. Permission to take water or medicine anytime before reception of Holy Communion was granted in 1953. The medicine may be in solid or liquid form, and it need not be prescribed by a physician.

Q. As a convert who entered the Catholic Church in 1983, I have never heard a homily on the necessity of be-

ing in the state of grace before receiving our Lord in the Eucharist. If the lack of such homilies is widespread, which I suspect is so, is that why frequent Confession is so scarce, why there has been a radical decrease in belief in the Real Presence, and why there is so much careless dress and behavior before our Lord in church? Would clear and frequent homilies on this subject be a simple way to help our Church save souls? — D.N., Minnesota

A. The answer is a resounding yes to all your questions. If the Holy Eucharist is "the source and summit of the Christian life," as both the Second Vatican Council and the *Catechism of the Catholic Church* have told us, then there most certainly ought to be homilies and catechetical instructions on the conditions for receiving Holy Communion worthily.

In addition to having fasted from food and drink, with the exception of water and medicine, for at least one hour before receiving the Eucharist; and having the right intention for receiving our Lord, the *Catechism* says that "anyone who desires to receive Christ in Eucharistic communion must be in the state of grace. Anyone aware of having committed a mortal sin must not receive communion without having received absolution in the sacrament of penance" (n. 1415).

Homilies on the subject ought to include St. Paul's warning that "whoever eats the bread or drinks the cup of the Lord unworthily sins against the body and blood of the Lord. A man should examine himself first; only then should he eat of the bread and drink of the cup" (1 Corinthians 11:27-28).

These homilies also should stress the importance of a reverential demeanor on the part of the communicant, both coming from and going back to his seat. Tell your parish priest of your concerns and ask him to speak often about what the Holy Eucharist is and what is expected of Catholics who approach the altar to receive our Blessed Lord.

Q. At Communion time at Sonny Bono's funeral Mass, the priest announced, "All Catholics properly disposed may receive Communion and those not [properly disposed] may come forth for a blessing. Indicate this by putting your fingers to your lips or folding your arms across your chest." When people came forward, one woman took the Host out of the priest's hand and another bent her head over the Host after the priest placed it in her hand and ate it out of her hand. Some people received a blessing. Was it proper for the priest to make this announcement? — C.R., Pennsylvania

A. A big problem at weddings and funerals these days is the presence of nominal Catholics, i.e., those who rarely go to church and who have little or no idea of how to receive Communion. The actions mentioned by C.R. are commonplace not only at weddings and funerals, however, but even among some regular churchgoers who either have not been properly catechized or who have become careless in the way they receive the Lord. Priests need to remind people frequently about the proper way to receive the Host and about the reverence that ought to be displayed.

At weddings and funerals in particular, the celebrant must make some kind of announcement about who can receive Communion and under what conditions so as to avoid as far as possible sacrilegious reception of the Eucharist. He could include in his announcement the following guidelines for Catholics that can be found in the missals in the pews:

"In order to be properly disposed to receive Communion, participants should not be conscious of grave sin and normally should have fasted for one hour. A person who is conscious of grave sin is not to receive the Body and Blood of the Lord without prior sacramental Confession, except for a grave reason where there is no opportunity for Confession.

"In this case, the person is to be mindful of the obligation to make an act of perfect contrition, including the intent of confessing as soon as possible (Code of Canon Law, n. 916). A frequent reception of the sacrament of Penance is encouraged for all."

Q. Would you please comment on the enclosed article about giving Holy Communion to non-Catholic Christians under special circumstances? — A.M. and A.B., New York

A. The article announced new norms that would allow Christians from other churches to receive Communion at the wedding Mass of a Catholic and non-Catholic, at a Catholic funeral where close family members are present, or at hospitals, nursing homes, and prisons. "This is simply a local application, under limited circumstances, set by Catholic Church law," a spokesman for the diocese said.

The article said that the conditions under which non-Catholic Christians in the diocese will be able to receive Holy Communion will be that the person be validly baptized, believe in the Real Presence of Christ in the Eucharist, ask for the Eucharist freely, and be unable to have recourse to the sacrament otherwise.

But is this a proper application of Church law? For example, canon 844.4 says that intercommunion is possible only "if the danger of death is present or other grave necessity." The article makes no mention of these requirements, nor does it mention that the non-Catholic must be "properly disposed," i.e., free from mortal sin. Do the diocesan norms include these critically important requirements?

While we could see possible application of the conditions to persons in danger of death in hospitals, nursing homes, or prisons, no such application makes sense at weddings and funerals. Consider a typical mixed marriage where, say, the groom is a baptized non-Catholic. Intercommunion is usually suggested to avoid making the groom feel awkward in not being able to receive Communion at the same time as his Catholic bride, although the usual way around this is to have a wedding ceremony without a Mass.

But suppose that it has been determined that the groom is properly disposed, has asked for the sacrament on his own, shares Catholic belief in the Real Presence of Jesus in the Eucharist, and is unable to receive from his own minister (what if his own minister is standing right next to him at this ecumenical wedding, as if often the case?), there is still no danger of death, nor any grave necessity that we can see. And what about the groom's family and friends? Will they be invited to receive Communion, too, even though there is no possible way of determining whether all these people meet the conditions laid down in Catholic law?

The diocesan norms also fall short of the conditions spelled out in the 1993 *Ecumenical Directory*. Yes, the norms do include three of the conditions mentioned in the *Directory* (having no recourse to one's own minister, asking for the Eucharist on one's own initiative, and manifesting Catholic faith in this sacrament), but do they include the requirement that the person be "properly disposed" (n. 131)? Not according to the article. And the following paragraph (n. 130) from the *Directory* indicates still other problems with the guidelines:

"In case of danger of death, Catholic ministers may administer these sacraments [Eucharist, Penance, and Anointing of the

Sick] when the conditions given below (n. 131) are present. In other cases, it is strongly recommended that the diocesan bishop, taking into account any norms which may have been established for this matter by the episcopal conference or by the synods of Eastern Catholic Churches, establish general norms for judging situations of grave and pressing need for verifying the conditions mentioned below (n. 131)."

The problems are, first, all the conditions listed in paragraph 131 of the *Directory* are not mentioned in the article and presumably not in the norms. Second, the diocesan bishop is supposed to take into account "any norms which may have been established for this matter by the episcopal conference." The U.S. Bishops' Conference has established guidelines (they can be found in most missals used in Catholic churches), and those guidelines say that intercommunion with other Christians must conform with the provisions of canon 844.4.

Third, even if no danger of death is present and a diocesan bishop is free to establish norms "in other cases," the *Directory* says that the norms can be invoked only in "situations of grave and pressing need." We can't conceive of weddings and funerals as constituting situations of grave and pressing need.

So if the article accurately reflects what the guidelines say, we see no justification for issuing such norms.

Q. I recently attended an Episcopal memorial service at which the priest invited everyone to receive communion. I did not, but I observed several practicing Catholics do so. I think they were wrong, but I can't find information in the *Catechism of the Catholic Church*. Can you help? — J.M., Massachusetts

A. As we have noted in the past, the Code of Canon Law (c. 844.2) has this to say about Catholics receiving Communion in non-Catholic churches: "Whenever necessity requires or genuine spiritual advantage suggests, and provided that the danger of error or indifferentism is avoided, it is lawful for the faithful for whom it is physically or morally impossible to approach a Catholic minister to receive the sacraments of Penance, Eucharist, and Anointing of the Sick from non-Catholic ministers in whose churches these sacraments are valid."

Your fellow Catholics who received at the Episcopal service were wrong on several counts:

(1) There was no necessity or genuine spiritual advantage in what they did.

(2) There was the danger of error and indifferentism since their action implied that there was no difference between receiving the Body of Christ in a Catholic Church and ordinary bread in the Episcopal Church.

(3) Receiving the Eucharist from non-Catholic ministers is permitted *only in churches which have valid sacraments* (such as the Orthodox Church), and that is not true of the Episcopal Church.

Q. At a memorial Mass I attended, the pastor invited all the congregation, Catholics and non-Catholics, including the non-Catholic husband of the deceased person, to receive Holy Communion. He said, "I'm sure the Lord welcomes everyone." I was shocked. What is your comment on his actions? — A.B., California

A. The pastor violated the U.S. Catholic Bishops' *Guidelines for the Reception of Communion*, which can be found in the missals used in many churches. Those guidelines permit reception of Communion only by Catholics who have fasted for one hour and are not conscious of having committed grave sin, and by fellow Christians who meet the "exceptional circumstances" spelled out in canon 844, which we are quite sure did not apply to the situation witnessed by A.B.

Someone should remind the pastor of the words of St. Paul:

"Whoever eats the bread or drinks the cup of the Lord unworthily sins against the body and blood of the Lord. A man should examine himself first; only then should he eat of the bread and drink of the cup. He who eats and drinks without recognizing the body eats and drinks a judgment on himself" (1 Corinthians 11:27-29).

Q. What are the regulations for Orthodox and Polish National Catholics to receive Communion, Penance, and the Sacrament of the Sick in Catholic churches? — W.F.H., Rhode Island

A. The U.S. Bishops' guidelines mentioned in the previous questions also state that "members of the Orthodox Churches, the Assyrian Church of the East, and the Polish National Catholic Church are urged to respect the discipline of their own churches. According to Roman Catholic discipline, the Code of Canon Law does not object to the reception of Communion by Christians of these churches" (canon 844.3).

Canon 844.3 says that Catholic ministers may licitly administer these sacraments to members of those churches "if they ask on their own for the sacraments and are properly disposed."

On March 13, 1996, Bishop Oscar H. Lipscomb, chairman of the Bishops' Committee for Ecumenical and Interreligious Affairs, issued the following additional comments:

"While the law of the Roman Catholic Church (canon 844.3) makes generous provisions, it should be kept in mind that these cases are seen as exceptional, not the norm. Normally, Polish National Catholics, it is expected, will seek sacraments from their own bishops and priests, and only on certain occasions approach Roman Catholic sacramental ministers.

"Out of respect for individual consciences and sensitivity to individual spiritual needs, cases should be responded to on an individual basis. General public invitations to communicate are not appropriate."

Q. There is some controversy in a neighboring parish about a little girl with Celiac Disease who is unable to receive Holy Communion under the form of bread. When the pastor and Cardinal Law both said that the Church could not substitute a rice host for one made from wheat flour, the parents of the girl left the Catholic parish and joined a Methodist church. An article in the *Boston Herald* was headlined, "Unbending church forces family to rethink its faith." What can the Church do for people with this disease? — M.K., Massachusetts

A. The same thing the Church has for a long time done for Catholics with Celiac Disease — let them receive Jesus under the form of wine, i.e., the Precious Blood. In fact, the Church recommends providing a separate chalice for the Communion of persons with Celiac Disease because there could be a problem from the particle of the Host that the priest breaks into the regular chalice, or from Hosts dipped into the Precious Blood for Communion by intinction.

By way of background, Celiac Disease is an allergic reaction to the gluten in wheat that damages the digestive system and predisposes its victims to osteoporosis, neurological illnesses, and lymphoma. While a bishop can grant permission for priests to use low-gluten altar breads after presentation of a medical certificate (Bishops Committee on the Liturgy *NewsLetter*, July 1995, p. 25), some Celiac sufferers contend that even a low-gluten Host is dangerous.

A gluten-free host produced in England, which substitutes a binder such as xanthum gum for the gluten, has been imported on occasion by Celiac groups in the United States. However, the introduction of this ingredient makes those hosts invalid matter for the Eucharist in the Catholic Church. This means that those hosts can never become the Body of Christ.

Although the mother of the little girl said that she knew of some Catholic priests who use hosts made from rice flour, such hosts are also invalid matter and may never be lawfully used at a Catholic Mass. In a letter to the family involved, Bernard Cardinal Law, the Archbishop of Boston, explained that "the law of the Church is extremely explicit. In keeping with the Last Supper narrative found in the Gospels, the bread must be made of wheat alone."

A major omission in the *Herald* article was the failure to mention the alternative of receiving Jesus in the Precious Blood. In a conversation this writer had with the columnist, he admitted that leaving out that information was a big mistake. He added, however, that the mother of the child had implied to him that receiving under the species of wine could also be harmful to her daughter.

So we contacted the Celiac Sprue Association in Omaha, Nebraska, and asked about consumption of altar wine by Celiac victims. We were told that altar wine was not a problem for Celiac sufferers and were sent a copy of page 11 of the 5th edition (May 2000) of the *Cooperative Gluten-Free Commercial Product Listing*. Under the heading of "Beverages" were these words:

"Wines and brandies without preservatives (or with preservatives that are tolerated, i.e., sulphites) and most added dyes are considered appropriate for the clinical diet. Celiacs appear to do better on white wines, such as the Chableaus and Zinfandels."

A shorter version of this statement can be found in Leon H. Rottmann's book *A Case for the Gluten-Free Diet*, which was published by the Celiac Sprue Association in September 2000.

Two final points: (1) The mother in question told the *Herald* columnist that she felt Jesus would give her daughter "the bread she needs and not make her feel different from all the other children. I believe He'd love her enough to do that." Apart from the fact that the child's disease unfortunately has already made her different from her peers, this argument sounds very much like the one advanced by those who remarry after divorce and say that Jesus would want them to be happy.

True happiness, however, cannot come from circumventing the teachings of Jesus, but only from following Jesus totally, accepting everything He said even if we don't understand it and even if it means going to the cross with Him.

Following Jesus completely also means following the Church that He established on earth, gave the authority to make decisions ("bind and loose") in His name, and promised to be with all days, until the end of the world. The same Church that St. Paul said was the "pillar and bulwark of truth" (1 Timothy 3:15).

(2) The other point is the irony that, in leaving the Catholic Church, the daughter (and her mother) will still not be able to receive the Body of Christ since ministers in the Methodist Church do not have the power to confect the Eucharist. She may receive a non-gluten wafer, but it will be nothing more than a non-gluten wafer.

We hope that Catholic priests will use this incident as a teachable moment for their parishioners to remind them that the Holy Eucharist is not just a piece of bread, but really is the Body and Blood, Soul and Divinity, of Jesus Christ, the second Person of the Blessed Trinity, and that when the priest pronounces those words of Christ ("This is my Body .... This is my Blood"), "the bread and wine have ceased to exist after the Consecration, so that it is the adorable Body and Blood of the Lord Jesus that from then on are really before us under the sacramental species of bread and wine" (Pope Paul VI, *Credo of the People of God*).

Q. I have had the occasion to observe extraordinary ministers of the Eucharist distributing consecrated Wine by handing a cup to communicants while standing in a carpeted area of a modern church. Since there are bound to be accidents, does the Church prescribe a dignified way of handling spills on a carpet? — S.J.C., Illinois

A. "If any of the Precious Blood spills," says the *General Instruction of the Roman Missal*, "the area should be washed and the water poured into the sacrarium" (n. 239). Msgr. Peter Elliott, in his *Ceremonies of the Modern Roman Rite*, explained further:

"A purifier or larger towel should be carefully placed on the area affected so that the Sacred Species is gradually absorbed. This is then reverently taken away and allowed to soak for some time in an ample quantity of water. Then it may be hung out to dry before it is washed as usual. A damp towel should be applied to the place where the accident happened, and this is also soaked in water before it is washed" (n. 853).

Q. At a local parish I overheard a minister of Communion ask the congregation after Mass if they wanted to consume more of the consecrated Wine as he hated to pour it down the drain. I know this act is wrong, but can you give me the specific rules covering this act so I can pass the information on? — J.S., Illinois
A. It is indeed a grave abuse and a profanation of the Blood of Christ to pour the contents of the chalice down the sacrarium, the special sink in the sacristy that is used for the disposal of water that was used for cleansing the sacred vessels or linens. On November 1, 1984, the U.S. Catholic Bishops issued a document entitled *Directory for the Celebration and Reception of Communion Under Both Kinds*. The document states:

"In those instances when there remains more consecrated Wine than was necessary, the ministers shall consume it immediately at a side table before the prayer after Communion, while the vessels themselves may be purified after Mass. The amount of wine to be consecrated should be carefully measured before the celebration so that none remains afterward" (Norm 36).
"It is strictly prohibited to pour the Precious Blood into the ground or into the sacrarium" (Norm 38).

As for inviting members of the congregation to consume the Blood of Christ reverently if there is a large quantity remaining, that is permitted (cf. Msgr. Peter J. Elliott, *Liturgical Question Box*, p. 121), provided that there is too much for the celebrant, or any deacon or extraordinary ministers assisting him, to consume.

Q. In our sterile, modern, sometimes concert hall, sometimes community center, sometimes church, the taber-

nacle is located out in left field. After daily Mass, there is usually an assault upon the tabernacle by attendees armed with pyx, change purse, or whatever, and with a diverse display of deference or none at all. Then there is a pattern, more common than not: lengthy conversations within a few feet of the tabernacle or in the parking lot or the parish office complex. Some even stop for breakfast en route to the Communion calls. What happened to a sense of the sacred? Are there no ground rules apart from belief in the Real Presence? Does anybody care? — T.D., Florida

A. The loss of the sense of the sacred is deplorable, as we have pointed out for years. About the only thing people don't do in church these days is genuflect. Certainly there are ground rules, some of them common sense, others imposed by the Church, governing reverence for the Real Presence and the conduct of extraordinary ministers of the Eucharist. We wonder sometimes if some of these irreverent folks even hold a belief in the Real Presence; they sure don't act as if they do.

Bringing Communion to the sick and to shut-ins is an admirable work of charity, but this service demands a reverential demeanor. The proper container for the sacred Host is a pyx, not a change purse. There should be no conversations near the tabernacle, those carrying the Body of Christ should not engage in any unnecessary chitchat in the parking lot or parish office complex, and persons carrying the Holy Eucharist should never stop for breakfast.

Speak out against these abuses, and pray that Catholics will once again demonstrate that same awe and wonder in the Real Presence that was shown in the fourth century by St. Tarcisius, the Roman martyr who was murdered for refusing to surrender the Blessed Sacrament to a pagan mob on the Appian Way.

Q. One of my neighbors noticed that the priest left the key in the tabernacle door after depositing the Hosts there. She said something to him, but he just smiled and gave no reply. Is there a rule that the tabernacle be locked and the key removed? — P.C., New Jersey

A. The *General Instruction of the Roman Missal* says that the tabernacle should be kept "locked so that the danger of desecration is avoided as much as possible" (n. 314). What we don't know from the question is why the priest left the key in the door. Was he planning to return a few moments later, say, after locking the church, to get some Hosts to bring to the sick? Or was he on his way to the rectory and might not return for some time? If the latter, he was wrong; if the former, what he did was all right, although it might be more prudent to keep the key in his pocket.

Q. The Blessed Sacrament is exposed in a monstrance in a chapel where there is perpetual adoration. This chapel is not part of a church building and, while it does have a tabernacle, I'm not certain whether there are consecrated Hosts therein. Would it be appropriate to have a sanctuary light indicating the Real Presence of our Lord in the vicinity of the monstrance? — W.F.H., Rhode Island

A. Canon 940 of the Code of Canon Law says that "a special lamp to indicate and honor the presence of Christ is to burn at all times before the tabernacle in which the Most Holy Eucharist is reserved." So, yes, it would also be appropriate to have a special lamp in the vicinity of the monstrance in which the Lord Himself is exposed for perpetual adoration.

Q. I would appreciate it very much if you would share with me the directives for the exposition of the Holy Eucharist once a week for several hours. — R.T.K., Florida

A. These directives can be found in the document *Holy Communion and Worship of the Eucharist Outside Mass*, particularly paragraphs 82-100. Among other things, the directives say that four to six candles are lighted and incense is used when the Blessed Sacrament is exposed in the monstrance; that the ordinary minister for exposition is a priest or deacon who should be vested in an alb, or a surplice over a cassock, and a stole; that a song may be sung when the minister comes to the altar; that there should be prayers, songs, readings, and religious silence during adoration.

The directives say that toward the end of adoration, the priest or deacon goes to the altar, kneels, and incenses the Blessed Sacrament while a hymn is sung; that the priest or deacon sings or says a prayer, puts on the humeral veil, genuflects, and makes the Sign of the Cross over the people with the monstrance in silence; and that after the blessing, the priest or deacon replaces the Blessed Sacrament in the tabernacle, genuflects, and leaves while the people sing or say an acclamation.

Chapter 10

The Sacred Liturgy

Q. How do I refute the following statement: Since the first Mass took place at the Last Supper and plays such an important part in the Catholic Church, how come not even one of the Gospel writers ever mentions celebrating Mass or attending Mass? — A.G., North Carolina

A. Just because a particular teaching or word or ritual is not specifically mentioned in the Gospels does not mean that it did not exist at the time or that it never happened. For instance, the words "Trinity" and "Purgatory" do not appear anywhere in the Bible, but there is plenty of evidence that those doctrines were taught by the early Church.

Furthermore, the Gospels focus primarily on the resurrected Lord's appearances during the six weeks between the Last Supper and the Ascension, although the two main segments of the Mass (the Liturgy of the Word and the Liturgy of the Eucharist) are recognizable in Jesus' appearance to the two men on the road to Emmaus (cf. Luke 24:13-35).

So while Matthew, Mark, and Luke all mention the institution of the Holy Eucharist at the Last Supper, it is in the Acts of the Apostles and the writings of St. Paul that we find mention of the early Christians taking part in the "breaking of bread" or the "Lord's Supper," both of which refer to the Holy Sacrifice of the Mass. One of the four evangelists, Luke, in the Acts of the Apostles, his other New Testament book, describes attendance at Mass by the early Christians in these words:

"They devoted themselves to the apostles' instruction and the communal life, to the breaking of bread and the prayers .... They went to the temple area together every day, while in their homes they broke bread" (Acts 2:42-46).

Luke also says later in Acts that this breaking of bread took place on Sunday, "the first day of the week" (Acts 20:7). And St. Paul, in one of his letters, condemns the deplorable conduct of those attending the celebration of the "Lord's Supper" years later in the city of Corinth (cf. 1 Corinthians 11:17-34).

So even if the Gospels do not specifically mention attendance at Mass, other New Testament books do, and so do writings from the early Church. For example, the *Didache*, a collection of apostolic teachings from the first century, tells Catholics of the time:

"Assemble on the Lord's Day and break bread and offer the Eucharist, but first make confession of your faults, so that your sacrifice may be a pure one."

One of the clearest descriptions of the Mass was written by Justin Martyr in the middle of the second century. He talks about gathering on "the day we call the day of the sun," listening to someone read "the memoirs of the Apostles and the writings of the prophets," offering prayers "for ourselves and for all others," exchanging "the kiss," bringing bread and water and wine "to him who presides over the brethren," saying "Amen" at the conclusion of the prayers and thanksgivings, and letting "deacons give to those present the 'eucharisted' bread, wine, and water and take them to those who are absent" (cf. *Catechism of the Catholic Church*, n. 1345).

Q. I would like to know what book on Church history I could read to find out when the Mass was said in Latin and what language it was in before. — H.M., Louisiana

A. We can suggest two sources: Joseph A. Jungmann, S.J.'s book *The Mass of the Roman Rite*, which traces the origins and development of the Mass, and Fr. Jovian Lang's *Dictionary of the Liturgy*, especially appendix 3, which is entitled "Select Chronology of Major Events in the History of the Liturgy."

According to that chronology, Jewish Christians first celebrated Mass in Aramaic, and Hellenistic Christians conducted the liturgy in the Greek of the people, known as "Koine." The language of the Mass changed from Greek to Latin in the fourth century and remained in Latin until 1964, when the Mass in English, and other languages, was introduced.

Q. Where in the Vatican II documents can I find a *de fide* definition of a Catholic Mass, and can this definition be squared with the one at Trent? — W.N., Rhode Island

A. Yes, it can, and the definition you are looking for can be found in paragraph 47 of Vatican II's *Constitution on the Sacred Liturgy*:

"At the Last Supper, on the night when He was betrayed, our Savior instituted the Eucharistic Sacrifice of His Body and Blood. He did this in order to perpetuate the sacrifice of the Cross throughout the centuries until He should come again, and so to entrust to His beloved spouse, the Church, a memorial of His death and resurrection: a sacrament of love, a sign of unity, a bond of charity, a paschal banquet in which Christ is consumed, the mind is filled with grace, and a pledge of future glory is given to us."

The Council of Trent, in its 22nd session on September 17, 1562, said of our Lord Jesus Christ:

"... At the Last Supper, on the night He was betrayed, that He might leave to His beloved spouse, the Church, a visible sacrifice, such as the nature of man requires, whereby that bloody sacrifice once to be accomplished on the cross might be represented, the memory thereof remain even to the end of the world, and its salutary effects applied to the remission of those sins which we daily commit, declaring Himself constituted *a priest forever according to the order of Melchizedek*, offered up to God the Father His own Body and Blood under the form of bread and wine, and under the forms of those same things gave to the apostles, whom He then made priests of the New Testament, that they might partake, commanding them and their successors in the priesthood by these words to do likewise: *Do this in commemoration of me*, as the Catholic Church has always understood and taught.

"For having celebrated the ancient Passover which the multitude of the children of Israel sacrificed in memory of their departure from Egypt, He instituted a new Passover, namely, Himself, to be immolated under visible signs by the Church through the priests in memory of His own passage from this world to the Father, when by the shedding of His blood He redeemed and *delivered us from the power of darkness and translated us into His kingdom*.

"And this is indeed that clean oblation which cannot be defiled by any unworthiness or malice on the part of those who offer it; which the Lord foretold by Malachi was to be great among the Gentiles, and which the apostle Paul has clearly indicated when he says that they who are defiled by the partaking of the table of devils cannot be partakers of the table of the Lord, understanding by table in each case the altar. It is, finally, that [sacrifice] which was prefigured by various types of sacrifices during the period of nature and of the law, which, namely, comprises all the good things signified by them, as being the consummation and perfection of them all."

Q. Where in the *General Instruction of the Roman Missal* does it state that the Mass is a propitiatory sacrifice? I hear that the Mass is a sacrifice of praise and thanksgiving, but never that the Mass is a propitiatory sacrifice. — W.E.N., Rhode Island

A. In the introduction to the *GIRM*, you will find the following paragraphs about the Mass as sacrifice:

"The sacrificial nature of the Mass was solemnly proclaimed by the Council of Trent in agreement with the whole tradition of the Church. Vatican Council II reaffirmed this teaching in these significant words: 'At the Last Supper our Savior instituted the eucharistic sacrifice of his body and blood. He did this in order to perpetuate the sacrifice of the cross throughout the centuries until he should come again and in this way to entrust to his beloved Bride, the Church, a memorial of his death and resurrection.'

"The Council's teaching is expressed constantly in the formularies of the Mass. This teaching, in the concise words of the Leonine Sacramentary, is that 'the work of our redemption is carried out whenever we celebrate the memory of this sacrifice'; it is aptly and accurately brought out in the eucharistic prayers. At the anamnesis or memorial, the priest, addressing God in the name of all the people, offers in thanksgiving the holy and living sacrifice: the Church's offering and the Victim whose death has reconciled us with God. The priest also prays that the body and blood of Christ may be a sacrifice acceptable to the Father, bringing salvation to the whole world.

"In this new Missal, then, the Church's rule of prayer (*lex orandi*) corresponds to its constant rule of faith (*lex credendi*). This rule of faith instructs us that the sacrifice of the cross and its sacramental renewal in the Mass, which Christ instituted at the Last Supper and commanded his apostles to do in his memory, are one and the same, differing only in the manner of offering and that consequently the Mass is at once a sacrifice of praise and thanksgiving, of reconciliation and expiation" (n. 2).

Q. Since most of us have experienced deviations from the rubrics of the Mass, two questions come to mind: (1) To whom does the Mass belong, and (2) If the rubrics are altered, does the priest commit a sin of disobedience? — R.S., Wisconsin

A. (1) The Mass belongs to the whole Church, bishops, priests, and laity, and all of us have a right to a liturgy that is celebrated according to the laws of the Church. In the introduction to *Inaestimabile Donum*, the Congregation for the Sacraments and Divine Worship said:

"The faithful have a right to a true liturgy, which means the liturgy desired and laid down by the Church, which in fact has indicated where adaptations may be made as called for by pastoral requirements in different places or by different groups of people. Undue experimentation, changes, and creativity bewilder the faithful."

The supervision of the sacred liturgy, says canon 838 of the Code of Canon Law, "depends solely on the authority of the Church which resides in the Apostolic See and, in accord with the law, with the diocesan bishop." Canon 846 says that "the liturgical books approved by the competent authority are to be faithfully observed in the celebration of the sacraments; therefore, no one on personal authority may add, remove, or change anything in them."

(2) A priest who celebrates Mass in a manner contrary to the norms laid down by the Church, says *Inaestimabile Donum*, "is guilty of falsification." While such a priest may think that he is celebrating Mass in a more effective way, said Pope John Paul in *Dominicae Cenae*, "objectively it is always a betrayal of that union which should find its proper expression in the sacrament of unity."

The Holy Father also said that "every priest who offers the Holy Sacrifice should recall that during this sacrifice it is not only he with his community that is praying but the whole Church, which is thus expressing in this sacrament her spiritual unity, among other ways by the use of the approved liturgical text" (n. 12).

So, yes, a priest who on his own personal authority adds, changes, or removes anything in the liturgy commits a sin of disobedience. He goes against the vow he made at ordination, when he promised "respect and obedience" to his bishop and when he expressed his resolve "to celebrate the mysteries of Christ faithfully and religiously as the Church has handed them down to us for the glory of God and the sanctification of Christ's people" (*Rite of Ordination*, nn. 15, 16).

Q. I have read that there were five or six Protestant "advisors" at the meetings re the revision of the Mass at Vatican II. Can you provide information on who these advisors were and what religions or denominations they represented? — R.W., Texas

A. Representatives from various religions, including some Protestant denominations, were present during the four sessions of the Second Vatican Council (1962-1965), but they were there as observers, not as advisors. They had been invited because one of the chief purposes of the Council was to bring about unity among Christians.

Those who raise this issue either imply or insist that these half-dozen "advisors" exerted such influence over the 2,500 Catholic bishops who participated in the Council that they were able to "Protestantize" the liturgy and water down Church teachings on the Eucharist. But that isn't true, as a reading of the Council documents will demonstrate.

Sure, the language of some sections in the 16 documents needs to be carefully studied and interpreted, but there is nothing that was promulgated by Vatican II that contradicts any of the Church's previous 20 ecumenical councils or any of its magisterial teachings. Ralph McInerny tells us why in his book *What Went Wrong with Vatican II* (Sophia Institute Press):

"Whatever problems may be posed by the documents of Vatican II, contradictions of earlier councils cannot be one of them. It is the Pope who calls an ecumenical council into session; he monitors the work of the assembled bishops; and he promulgates the documents expressing the judgment of the bishops. When he does that, those documents become the measure of our faith.

"That which makes Vatican II valid is what made Vatican I, the Council of Trent, and every other council valid. To accept one council is to accept them all; to reject one council is to reject them all; we cannot have pick-and-choose conciliarism. I do not, therefore, defend the Second Vatican Council against those who think it is suspect and in contradiction to earlier councils or to solemnly defined teachings of the Church. On the contrary, I take as a necessary premise the fact that we are bound by the teachings of the Second Vatican Council" (pp. 14-15).

Q. In one of your "Catholic Replies," R.W. from Texas has reference, I believe, to the Protestant advisors whom Archbishop Bugnini called in to get their input on the New Order of the Mass. This, of course, was after Vatican II. — C.A., Arizona

Q. I can't believe your reply about the six Protestant ministers who contributed to the formulation of the *Novus Ordo* mess. The teaching of the Popes prior to John XXIII and the councils prior to Vatican II were set aside and ignored by the Rhineland modernist heretics who gained control of the Council and the Consiliums after the Council to implement their own distortions of the Catholic faith. This brought about "the spirit of Vatican II." — R.F., Pennsylvania

Q. My humble disagreement with your answer. The Second Vatican Council was not a dogmatic Council and therefore its teachings, which are contrary to any of the teachings of all the previous councils or which require interpretation, are certainly invalid. — A.S.E., New York

Q. Those Protestant advisors did not have to present their ideas since Catholics did their bidding for them. There can be no doubt that the new Vatican Council Mass liturgy is more Protestant than Catholic, as evidenced by the fact that Protestant ministers can now use the new Mass liturgy without any qualms of conscience. The fact is, Vatican II was not a dogmatic Council; only pastoral. — W.J. H., Illinois

A. First of all, six Protestants were invited after Vatican II to participate in the work of a Consilium to implement the liturgical reforms called for by the Vatican Council. What was their role? According to Archbishop Annibale Bugnini, the secretary of the Consilium, they were only "observers" who never intervened in the discussions and never asked to speak.

However, Canon Ronald Jasper, one of the observers, told author Michael Davies in 1977 that, while they were not allowed to join in the official debates of the Consilium, the Protestants were allowed to comment and make suggestions at the informal meetings with the *periti* (experts) who prepared the draft documents for the Consilium to consider.

Were these Protestants responsible for the liturgical chaos of the past three decades? No, because whatever the Consilium produced had to be approved by Pope Paul VI and, as the Holy Father said, correctly, in a general audience on November 19, 1969, "nothing of the substance of the traditional Mass has been altered."

He also expressed the wish that the liturgical reform would put "an end to uncertainty, arguments, and misguided experiments." Unfortunately, his wish did not come true, but this was the fault, not of Protestant advisors, but of Catholics with their own illicit liturgical agenda who were not slapped down by their bishops.

This failure to discipline the liturgical termites was acknowledged in 1980 by Pope John Paul II, who asked forgiveness in a letter to the world's bishops — "in my own name and in the name of all of you, venerable and dear brothers in the episcopate — for everything which, for whatever reason, through whatever human weakness, impatience, or negligence, and also through the at-times partial, one-sided, and erroneous application of the directives of the Second Vatican Council, may have caused scandal and disturbance concerning the interpretation of the doctrine and the veneration due to this great sacrament [the Holy Eucharist]" (*Dominicae Cenae*, n. 12).

Later that same year, the Vatican document *Inaestimabile Donum* provided a litany of liturgical abuses and said that "we are face to face with a real falsification of the Catholic liturgy."

The blame for that sad state of affairs, it is clear, belongs to national and diocesan liturgical commissions which have blatantly ignored or rejected numerous ecclesiastical documents calling for a faithful implementation of Vatican II.

That's where the problem lies, not with half a dozen Protestant advisors, and the problem will be solved when those commissions are staffed by persons who are faithful to the magisterium of the Church and to its liturgical norms.

As for the contention that we don't have to pay attention to Vatican II because it was a pastoral council, not a dogmatic council, that is not true. First of all, pastoral means giving guidance to the faithful in spiritual matters. It doesn't exclude dogmatic statements. In fact, two of the sixteen documents issued by Vatican II were entitled "Dogmatic Constitutions." And even the only document with the word "pastoral" in its name (*Pastoral Constitution on the Church in the Modern World*) made some rather dogmatic statements.

For example, "abortion and infanticide are unspeakable crimes" (n. 51). The same document also condemned murder, genocide, euthanasia, mutilation, torments inflicted on body or mind, subhuman living conditions, arbitrary imprisonment, deportation, slavery, prostitution, selling of women and children, and disgraceful working conditions (n. 27).

Here are some other examples of dogmatic statements made by the Second Vatican Council:

• "For it is through Christ's Catholic Church alone, which is the all-embracing means of salvation, that the fullness of the means of salvation can be obtained" (*Decree on Ecumenism*, n. 3).

• "This sacred Synod professes its belief that God himself has made known to mankind the way in which men are to serve him, and thus be saved in Christ and come to blessedness. We believe that this one true religion subsists in the catholic and apostolic Church, to which the Lord Jesus committed the duty of spreading it abroad among all men" (*Declaration on Religious Freedom*, n. 1).

• "Holy Mother Church has firmly and with absolute constancy held, and continues to hold, that the four Gospels just named, whose historical character the Church unhesitatingly asserts, faithfully hand on what Jesus Christ, while living among men, really did and taught for their eternal salvation until the day he was taken up into heaven" (*Dogmatic Constitution on Divine Revelation*, n. 18).

• "This sacred Synod turns its attention first to the Catholic faithful. Basing itself upon sacred Scripture and tradition, it teaches that the Church, now sojourning on earth as an exile, is necessary for salvation .... Whosoever, therefore, knowing that the Catholic Church was made necessary by God through Jesus Christ, would refuse to enter her or to remain in her could not be saved" (*Dogmatic Constitution on the Church*, n. 14).

But whatever word is used to describe Vatican II, Catholics are obliged to accept its teachings because it has the same authority as all previous ecumenical councils, beginning with Nicaea in A.D. 325. There is nothing heretical in the documents of the Second Vatican Council, nor could there be, since that would mean that the gates of Hell had prevailed against the Church, something that Jesus promised would never happen.

Q. What is the purpose of the altar railings and when did they come into being? — J.B.C., New Jersey

A. The altar rail derives from the rood screen that was first erected in large churches served by monastic bodies and also visited by large numbers of pilgrims. It completed the choir enclosure so that the Office and the Mass could be celebrated in relative tranquillity while throngs of visitors circulated around the screened area. People could assist at Mass and receive Communion through a grille or doors in the screen.

The screen later took on the function of a barrier, dividing the space of the clergy (the sanctuary) from that of the laity (the nave), and was subsequently replaced with just an altar rail.

Q. Our church has a Communion railing in front of the altar where we kneel to receive Communion. However, with the possible expansion of the church or possibly the construction of a new church, we are afraid that they will eliminate the Communion railing. Someone said that such railings are against Church law. Can that be true? — A.P., Connecticut

A. There is nothing in any Vatican II or post-Vatican II Church document that calls for elimination of Communion railings. The railings began disappearing in the early 1970s, at the instigation, we are sure, of so-called liturgical experts, and you are most fortunate to have had one in your church all these years. If anyone tries to take it away from you, ask him to produce an official Church document that specifically mandates elimination of these railings.

Q. In time of war or persecution, is it obligatory that the priest offer the whole rite of the Mass, or because of such extreme circumstances can he only consecrate bread and wine to consume himself or to distribute to the faithful? — A.C. Pennsylvania

A. Under conditions of war, persecution, or imprisonment, priests may consecrate bread and wine without celebrating the entire rite of the Mass. For example, in his *Memoirs* Jozsef Cardinal Mindszenty of Hungary recalled being brought back to his room shortly after his arrest and interrogation by the Communists on December 26, 1948:

"Utterly exhausted, I lay down on the battered couch and turned toward the wall. Then I noticed a small glass of wine on the stand. So even in this place of horror there was still a humane person who considered what a blessing Holy Mass is for a priest in such a situation. I took a small piece of bread I was brought for breakfast and concealed it. When the guards left me alone for a moment, I poured half of the wine into my water glass, spoke the words of consecration over the bread and wine, and communicated. In this way I was able to celebrate Mass twice. Thereafter no more wine was put out for me" (pp. 102-103).

Q. Are the laity "co-presiders" at the Mass? — G.G.M., Texas

A. No, they are not. The priest is the visible presider, or celebrant, at Mass, representing Christ, the invisible presider. The role of the laity is to join in the liturgy by actively praying, singing, and responding at the appropriate times. Here is how the *Catechism* explains the roles of priest and faithful:

"Christians come together in one place for the Eucharistic assembly. At its head is Christ himself, the principal agent of the Eucharist. He is high priest of the New Covenant; it is he himself who presides invisibly over every Eucharistic celebration. It is in representing him that the bishop or priest acting *in the person of Christ the head* (*in persona Christi capitis*) presides over the assembly, speaks after the readings, receives the offerings, and says the Eucharistic Prayer. *All* have their own active parts to play in the celebration, each in his own way: readers, those who bring up the offerings, those who give communion, and the whole people whose 'Amen' manifests their participation" (n. 1348).

Q. I have been told that Rome sent a letter to all Bishops, asking them to establish the Tridentine Latin Mass somewhere in their dioceses. I have been unable to find the letter or anything like it. Does it exist? — T.H., Florida

A. Actually, this request to the bishops has been made in several Vatican documents and letters. On October 3, 1984, the Sacred Congregation for Divine Worship issued *Quattuor abhinc annos* in which the Holy Father granted to diocesan bishops "the possibility of using an indult whereby priests and faithful ... may be able to celebrate Mass by using the Roman Missal according to the 1962 edition."

Four years later, Pope John Paul II, in the apostolic letter *Ecclesia Dei*, said that "respect must everywhere be shown for the feelings of those who are attached to the Latin liturgical tradition, by a wide and generous application of the directives already issued some time ago by the Apostolic See, for the use of the Roman Missal according to the typical edition of 1962."

The wishes of the Holy Father have since been reaffirmed by Augustin Cardinal Mayer, the first prefect of the Ecclesia Dei Commission, in a 1991 letter to the Bishops of the United States; by Msgr. Camille Perl, secretary of the Commission, in a 1995 letter; by Cardinal Mayer in another letter in 1997; and twice by the Holy Father himself: on September 28, 1990 to the monks of Sainte-Madeleine at le Barroux in France, and on October 26, 1998 to pilgrims who had traveled to Rome to mark the tenth anniversary of *Ecclesia Dei*.

For a good summary of all these documents and letters and discourses, with extensive quotations from them, see Peter A. Kwasniewski's article "Introibo Ad Altare Dei" in the May-June 2000 issue of *The Catholic Faith* magazine.

Q. The enclosed church bulletin offers for sale copies of a Liturgical Calendar that "is in harmony with the 1962 edition of the Roman Missal, which we are required to follow in keeping with the papal indult to offer the Traditional Latin Mass. This calendar lists every feast day accurately, as well as the fast and abstinence days in accordance with the fasting regulations in effect in 1962." Does this mean that those using the 1962 Missal do not acknowledge any persons canonized or beatified since then, such as Maximilian Kolbe, Padre Pio, Francisco, or Jacinta? — C.P. and P.M., Minnesota

A. No, it does not mean that, and the Fraternity of St. Peter has published a *Liturgical Ordo and Directory* that contains a supplement of feasts in the United States and Canada that can be used with the 1962 Roman Missal. Some of the feasts mentioned are those of Sts. Elizabeth Seton, John Neumann, and Junipero Serra.

Q. Is it mandatory for a priest to say Mass each day? Was this mandatory prior to Vatican II? — W.E.N., Rhode Island

A. No, priests were not mandated to celebrate Mass daily by the 1917 Code of Canon Law, nor are they mandated to do so by the 1983 Code. However, it is strongly recommended that they say Mass every day. Here is canon 904 of the 1983 Code:

"Remembering that the work of redemption is continually accomplished in the mystery of the Eucharistic Sacrifice, priests are to celebrate frequently; indeed daily celebration is strongly recommended since, even if the faithful cannot be present, it is the act of Christ and the Church in which priests fulfill their principal function."

And canon 276.2 says that priests "are to nourish their spiritual life from the twofold table of Sacred Scripture and the Eucharist; priests are therefore earnestly invited to offer the sacrifice of the Eucharist daily."

Q. Our diocese forbids Masses without a congregation, and this bothers my former pastor, who is retired. Can a a priest celebrate a Mass without a congregation? — C.A.T., Arkansas; C.S., Kentucky; J.J.W., North Carolina

A. According to canon 906, "a priest may not celebrate without the participation of at least some member of the faithful, *except for a just and reasonable cause.*" This alters the discipline of the 1917 Code of Canon Law, says the commentary in the Paulist Press edition of the 1983 Code, in that "the requirement that there be serious necessity for a priest to celebrate alone is changed to a just and reasonable cause. Such a cause would be demonstrated whenever a member of the faithful is unavailable and when the priest is unable to participate in a communal celebration, e.g., as result of illness, infirmity, or travel. A just and reasonable cause would not be the mere convenience of the priest or his preference for celebrating alone."

At a general audience on June 9, 1993, Pope John Paul II recalled that the Second Vatican Council (*Decree on the Ministry and Life of Priests*, n. 13) had earnestly recommended "daily celebration [of the Eucharist], which is an act of Christ and the Church, even if it is impossible for the faithful to be present." He said that "although everything possible should be done to gather the faithful for the celebration, it is also true that, even if the priest is alone, the Eucharistic offering which he performs in the name of Christ has the effectiveness that comes from Christ and always obtains new graces for the Church."

The Holy Father repeated these sentiments on May 21, 1998 at an ad limina meeting with bishops from Michigan and Ohio, saying that because "the celebration of the Eucharist is the most important moment of the priest's day ... priests should be encouraged to celebrate Mass every day, even in the absence of a congregation, since it is an act of Christ and the Church."

Q. I understand that the Congregation for Divine Worship and the National Conference of Catholic Bishops have strictly forbidden dancing during the sacred liturgy. But in the enclosed letter from my bishop, he says that "the 1975 ruling of the Congregation for the Sacraments and Divine Worship does not preclude all liturgy. These sacred dances of prayer and worship have the permission of the local bishops in the various dioceses where they are performed. The bishops of Idaho have accepted these dances as in conformity with liturgical law."

This reply confuses me. Can a bishop on his own initiative change the Vatican norm? — R.I., Idaho, and D.M., Maine

A. While the bishop is the chief teacher and liturgist in his diocese, he cannot sanction something that has been forbidden by the Vatican congregation concerned with liturgical matters. In its 1975 document *Religious Dance: An Expression of Spiritual Joy*, the Congregation said that dancing "has never been made an integral part of the official worship of the Latin Church," that if it did take place it was always "outside of liturgical services," and that "conciliar decisions have often condemned the religious dance because it conduces little to worship and because it could degenerate into disorder."

While religious dance is permitted in those cultures where it is "still reflective of religious values and becomes a clear manifestation of them," the document said, such is not the case in the western culture, where "dancing is tied with love, with diversion, with profaneness, with unbridling of the senses. Such dancing, in general, is not pure. For that reason, it cannot be introduced into liturgical celebrations of any kind whatever."

If religious dancing is to be made welcome in the West, the Congregation said, it must be found "outside of the liturgy, in assembly areas which are not strictly liturgical. Moreover, the priests must always be excluded from the dance."

Returning to the topic again in 1994 (*Instruction on Inculturation and the Roman Liturgy*), the congregation said:

"Among some peoples, singing is instinctively accompanied by handclapping, rhythmic swaying, and dance movements on the part of the participants. Such forms of external expression can have a place in the liturgical actions of these peoples on condition that they are always the expression of true communal prayer of adoration, praise, offering, and supplication, and not simply a performance" (n. 42).

Q. Would you please advise me about the position of Pope John Paul in reference to altar girls? — M.F.D., Maryland, and G.B., Ohio

A. On March 15, 1994, the Sacred Congregation for Divine Worship and the Discipline of the Sacraments sent a letter to the conferences of bishops throughout the world, saying that each bishop, in his own diocese, could make a "prudential judgment" to allow girls to serve at the altar. That change, which was approved by the Holy Father, came after the Pontifical Council for the Interpretation of Legislative Texts ruled that canon 230.2 of the 1983 Code does not bar females from being altar servers.

"The permission given in this regard by some bishops can in no way be considered as binding on other bishops," the letter said. "In fact, it is the competence of each bishop, in his diocese, after hearing the opinion of the episcopal conference, to make a prudential judgment on what to do, with a view to the ordered development of liturgical life in his own diocese."

The letter said that "the Holy See respects the decision adopted by certain bishops for specific local reasons on the basis of the provisions of canon 230.2. At the same time, however, the Holy See wishes to recall that it will always be very appropriate to follow the noble tradition of having boys serve at the altar. As is well known, this has also led to a reassuring development of priestly vocations. Thus, the obligation to support such groups of altar boys will always continue."

If on the basis of canon 230.2, the congregation continued, a "bishop permits that, for particular reasons, women may also serve at the altar, this decision must be clearly explained to the faithful in the light of the above-mentioned norm. It shall also be made clear that the norm is already being widely applied by the fact that women frequently serve as lectors in the liturgy and can also be called upon to distribute Holy Communion as extraordinary ministers of the Eucharist and to carry out other functions, according to the provisions of the same canon 230.2."

Editor's Note: The following letter was sent to us by the Most Rev. Edward J. O'Donnell, bishop of Lafayette, Louisiana:

"In [a 'Catholic Replies' dated September 18, 1997], you replied to two persons who asked about the position of the Holy Father in reference to altar girls. Your reply is helpful and factual, but I think that it omits an important consideration, especially since the writers specifically asked about the position of the Holy Father.

"At an audience at Castelgandolfo on September 3, 1995, Pope John Paul II said: 'Today I am appealing to the entire Church community to favor in every way women's participation in its internal life. In large part that participation would include simply implementing existing roles open to women, including the teaching of theology, approved forms of liturgical ministry, including service at the altar, pastoral and administrative councils in various Church institutions, curias, and tribunals.'

"Since the Pope expressed his words as 'an appeal,' I think they should be part of any response inquiring about his position."

In a more recent ruling on this matter, the Sacred Congregation for Divine Worship said that a diocesan bishop cannot oblige his priests to admit women and girls to service at the altar. In a letter dated July 27, 2001, Jorge Cardinal Medina Estevez, prefect of the congregation, said that while a diocesan bishop, "in his role as moderator of the liturgical life in the diocese entrusted to his care, has the authority to permit service at the altar by women within the boundaries of the territory entrusted to his care," such an authorization "may not, in any way, exclude men or, in particular, boys from service at the altar, nor require that priests of the diocese make use of female altar servers."

The letter reiterated the Church's belief that "indeed, the obligation to support groups of altar boys will always remain, not least of all due to the well-known assistance that such programs have provided since time immemorial in encouraging future priestly vocations."

Q. A nun at our church has been planning activities for the school's sixth-grade religion class, including a "clown liturgy." Is this appropriate? — M.O., Michigan

A. No, it is not appropriate. On February 27, 1987, the Congregation for Divine Worship said that "it is strictly forbidden that any form of clowning should take place in a church at any time. The Bishops' Committee on the Liturgy (U.S.A.) has already issued a statement forbidding such behavior during the liturgy."

The same goes for priests wearing clown vestments. "The beauty and nobility of a vestment should derive from its material and design rather than from lavish ornamentation," says the *General Instruction of the Roman Missal*. "Representations on vestments should consist only of symbols, images, or pictures portraying the sacred. Anything out of keeping with the sacred is to be avoided" (n. 344).

Q. At a recent meeting in our newly built church, the priest explained the absence of the tabernacle by saying that many bishops and theologians felt that there would be confusion between the presence of Christ in the tabernacle and His presence at the Consecration of the Mass. He also stated that Pope Pius XII told the bishops that the Mass should be celebrated with an empty tabernacle so that there would be no confusion. Have you heard of this remark of Pius XII? — Name and State Withheld

A. Not only did Pius XII *not* make such a remark, he said *exactly the opposite* in an address to the International Congress on Pastoral Liturgy on the Liturgical Movement (*Praesentia Christi*) on September 22, 1956. While the Holy Father agreed that one can distinguish between the sacrifice taking place on the altar and the presence of Jesus in the tabernacle, he insisted that "an awareness of their unity is more important than a realization of their differences. It is one and the same Lord who is immolated on the altar and honored in the tabernacle, and who pours out his blessings from the tabernacle."

He said that "a person who was thoroughly convinced of this would avoid many difficulties. He would be wary of exaggerating the significance of one to the detriment of the other."

To those who contend that having the tabernacle near the altar of sacrifice only confuses the faithful, Pius XII said:

"There is question, not so much of the material presence of the tabernacle on the altar, as of a tendency to which we should like to call your attention, that of a lessening of esteem for the presence and action of Christ in the tabernacle. The sacrifice of the altar is held sufficient, and the importance of Him who accomplishes it is reduced.

"Yet the person of our Lord must hold the central place in worship, for it is His person that unifies the relations of the altar and the tabernacle and gives them their meaning..... To separate tabernacle from altar is to separate two things which by their origin and their nature should remain united."

Q. Does the cross in the front of the church have to have the *INRI* sign on it? — W.F.S., Arizona

Q. My pastor worked for two years with an artist in deciding what type of cross to place in the sanctuary. The result was a cross with a resurrected Christ, but doesn't the new *General Instruction* call for a "cross with the figure of Christ crucified upon it"? — J.M., Louisiana

A. While the cross does have to have the figure of Christ crucified on it (*General Instruction*, nn. 117, 122, 308), there is no liturgical requirement that it carry the letters of the sign that was placed over the head of Christ on Calvary. Those letters, by the way, stand for *Iesus Nazarenus Rex Iudaeorum*, which means "Jesus of Nazareth, King of the Jews."

Q. The main altar used to have a relic embedded under the surface, and the priest would kiss that spot. The modern table does not have a relic, so why does the priest kiss it and, when there are several priests concelebrating, why do they all kiss the altar in different places? — A.S.E., New York

A. Both the *General Instruction* (n. 302) and the Code of Canon Law mandate a relic under the surface of the altar. Here is canon 1237.2: "The ancient tradition of keeping the relics of martyrs and other saints under a fixed altar is to be preserved according to the norms given in the liturgical books." So the main altar in your church should have a relic under it.

But even if an altar did not have a relic, the priest would still venerate it because it is the altar of sacrifice upon which the Second Person of the Blessed Trinity will become really and truly present and the holy table for the Eucharistic banquet by which we are nourished by the Body and Blood of the Lord.

If several priests are concelebrating Mass, it is more orderly for them to kiss the altar in different spots at the same time, rather than have each one of them venerate the altar at its central point. It is not necessary to kiss the precise spot where the relic is imbedded.

Q. We have a church in Buffalo that has put in what I consider scandalous windows. They portray, among other things, a Buddha, an Egyptian fire god, a Hindu goddess, Martin Luther King, and two priests who were murdered during a robbery in the rectory. I thought only saints could be portrayed in church windows. — G.B., New York

A. "In keeping with the Church's very ancient tradition," says the *General Instruction*, "images of the Lord, the Virgin Mary, and the saints may be displayed in sacred buildings for the veneration of the faithful, and may be so arranged that they guide the faithful to the mysteries of the faith which are celebrated there" (n. 318). This would surely apply to stained-glass images, too, so the portrayals that you have mentioned are clearly contrary to the very ancient tradition of the Church.

It is true that church windows often include non-saints, such as Pontius Pilate and his soldiers in a Passion window, but including Budda and a Hindu goddess will never guide the faithful to the mysteries of the Catholic faith.

Q. I donated a beautifully framed picture of Our Lady of Perpetual Help to my pastor with the hope that it would be hung in the church or the church lobby. I was told that there can be only one image of a particular person, and since an image of Mary as Our Lady of Guadalupe already hangs in the church, and an image of her as the Immaculate Heart hangs in the lobby, my picture cannot be used. My feeling is that this rule does not apply when dealing with the various images of Mary. Could you shed some light on this? — R.R., Maryland, and E.M., Wisconsin

A. According to the *General Instruction*, "care should be taken" that the number of religious images displayed in church "not be increased indiscriminately, and that they are situated in such a way that they do not distract the faithful's attention from the celebration. There is to be only one image of any given saint as a rule" (n. 318).

The phrase "as a rule" indicates that there is some latitude here, and Michael Rose, in *The Renovation Manipulation*, contends that the rule "does not apply to crucifixes and multiple images of our Lord, or even our Lady insofar as she appears under her various titles. Were this the case, both St. Peter's in Rome and the Shrine of the Immaculate Conception in Washington, D.C., would have to undergo thorough overhauls" (p. 83).

Q. Recently I'm noticing that our parish priests begin Mass to the left and towards the front of the altar. During the readings, they remain seated there until the reading of the Gospel. Then they return to their place at the altar. They also sit to the left of the altar after Communion and return to the altar for the concluding prayers. Is there anything in the rubrics which spells out anything against this? — E.B., New York

A. No, this is perfectly acceptable conduct for the celebrant of the Mass. In *Ceremonies of the Modern Roman Rite*, Msgr. Peter Elliott, speaking of where the priest sits during Mass, said:

"The presidential chair should be located behind or near the altar, in a convenient place and at a height where the celebrant may be seen to preside over the assembly. Taking into account the size and plan of the church, the chair should be arranged so that the priest presides without dominating. A truly beautiful and dignified chair should be designed or chosen, in harmony with the style of the church, nor should the comfort of the celebrant be forgotten. It must not resemble a throne" (p. 20).

Msgr. Elliott added, however, that "in a cathedral, the cathedra is a throne reserved for bishops. The cathedra should be raised on steps so that the bishop is clearly visible when he presides in his own church. A separate chair must be provided for a priest who is the celebrant at the main altar of a cathedral" (*Ibid.*).

Q. Some communities are using paper purificators at Mass. These have a cross on them and are of heavier pa-

per. After use, I am told, they are thrown into the trash. Are these permitted? — J.T., Michigan

A. The purificator is a small piece of white absorbent linen, about eight by sixteen inches, folded in thirds lengthwise, and marked with a cross in the center. It is used to wipe the lip of the chalice after the reception of the Precious Blood and to dry the chalice after it is washed following Communion or after Mass.

If paper purificators do exist and are damp with Precious Blood, it would be a sacrilege to throw them into the trash. In *Ceremonies of the Roman Rite*, Msgr. Peter Elliott described the proper care of linen purificators after Mass:

"Soak them for some time in water, which is then poured down the sacrarium, or down the drain of the font, or onto the garden. Then they may be hung out to dry before they are washed as usual" (p. 314).

How one could go through this careful and respectful process with paper purificators, we don't know. Nor do we know how one could dispose of them in an appropriate way.

Editor's Note: In one of our replies, we said that we did not know of any Church rule against playing taped music during Mass. Now, thanks to several readers, we do know of such a rule. The only exception to the general prohibition against using recorded music for the liturgy would be in Masses with children. Here are the pertinent paragraphs from *Liturgical Music Today*, a 1982 document of the U.S. Bishops' Committee on the Liturgy:

"The liturgy is a complexus of signs expressed by living human beings. Music, being preeminent among those signs, ought to be 'live.' While recorded music, therefore, might be used to advantage outside the liturgy as an aid in the teaching of new music, it should, as a general norm, never be used within the liturgy to replace the congregation, the choir, the organist, or other instrumentalists [n. 60].

"Some exceptions to this principle should be noted, however. Recorded music may be used to accompany the community's song during a procession out-of-doors and, when used carefully, in Masses with children [*Notitiae* 127 (February 1977), 94; Congregation for Divine Worship, *Directory for Masses with Children* (1 November 1973), 32]. Occasionally it might be used as an aid to prayer, for example, during long periods of silence in a communal celebration of reconciliation. It may never become a substitute for the community's song, however, as in the case of the responsorial psalm after a reading from Scripture or during the optional hymn of praise after Communion [n. 61].

"A prerecorded sound track is sometimes used as a feature of contemporary 'electronic music' composition. When combined with live voices and/or instruments, it is an integral part of the performance and, therefore, is a legitimate use of prerecorded music" [n. 62].

Q. The song "Bread of Life" by Rory Cooney is a favorite of our choir director because he has the choir sing it frequently at Mass. The melody is not bad, but the words send out the wrong message. People are confused enough about the Real Presence of Jesus in the Eucharist. Why make it worse? What can I do about this? If I speak to our choir director or pastor, nothing will happen as they are not open to suggestions. — R.M.S., California

A. There isn't much you can do about the music in your parish if the pastor and the choir director are not open to suggestions, except pray for a change of heart or a change of personnel. As for the song, here are the words that troubled R.M.S.:

"I myself am the bread of life. You and I are the bread of life, taken and blessed, broken and shared by Christ that the world might live."

The first line repeats the words of Jesus from John 6:35 and, if the song were sung as the words of the Lord Himself, there wouldn't be a problem. For instance, there is another Communion song that begins, "I am the Bread of Life, you who come to Me shall not hunger .... And I will raise you up on the last day."

But the Cooney song has the people calling themselves the bread of life and equating themselves with Christ, and we agree that undermines belief in the Real Presence.

Q. Please identify each layer of attire the priest wears to say Mass, and explain the origin and symbolism of each. — P.J.P., South Dakota

A. Beginning with the inner garments and working outward, the priest usually wears the following vestments:

Amice — an oblong white linen cloth worn over the neck and shoulders and secured by two tapes. Its purpose is to cover the priest's secular clothes and may be eliminated if the collar of the alb or chasuble is so made as to take the place of the amice.

Alb — a full-length white linen garment worn over the cassock or habit. It is based on the Greco-Roman tunic and symbolizes the purity of soul with which the Mass should be offered.

Cincture — a lengthy cord symbolizing chastity that is meant to garner and control the flowing alb around the waist. This can be eliminated if the alb is form-fitting.

Stole — a long, narrow band of material worn around the neck by priests and bishops at Mass (and at the left shoulder like a sash by deacons), during the celebration of the sacraments (including Confession) and sacramentals, and at ceremonies involving the Blessed Sacrament. It is worn under the chasuble and symbolizes the authority of the priest or bishop to carry out his liturgical functions. It is usually the same color as the chasuble.

Chasuble — the sleeveless, tent-like vestment worn over all the other vestments and usually the color of the liturgical season. It is the distinctive sign of the priestly office, symbolizing the yoke of Christ. "The chasuble," says Msgr. Peter Elliott in his book *Liturgical Question Box,* "is *the* eucharistic vestment par excellence, reserved for those ordained into the sacrificing priesthood of Jesus Christ. It signifies the charity with which He clothes our weakness at the altar, when indeed we do act *in persona Christi*" (p. 47).

Q. When I attend Mass, it is becoming frequent that the priest begins with the comment, "Welcome to the celebration of the Eucharist," or words to that effect. My question is, What has become of what I have always understood to be the Holy Sacrifice of the Mass? Your comments would be appreciated. — J.H., New Jersey

A. While the confecting of the Holy Eucharist by the priest at the time of the Consecration is indeed the high point of the Holy Sacrifice of the Mass, it is not incorrect to refer to the Mass itself as the celebration of the Eucharist. All the things that we do at Mass — the prayers, the Scripture readings, the offertory, the rituals — point to the Eucharist, which Vatican II and the *Catechism* (n. 1324) have called " 'the source and summit of the Christian life' [*LG* 11]." The parish church, says the *Catechism,* is "the place where all the faithful can be gathered together for the Sunday celebration of the Eucharist" (n. 2179).

This sacrament is so inexhaustible in its richness, says the *Catechism*, that we call it by many different names, each one revealing a different aspect of the Eucharist. The word itself means "an action of thanksgiving to God" (n. 1328), but the celebration is also known as the Lord's Supper, the Breaking of Bread, the Eucharistic assembly, the memorial of the Lord's Passion and Resurrection, the Holy Sacrifice of the Mass, the Holy and Divine Liturgy, the Sacred Mysteries, Holy Communion, and Holy Mass (cf. the *Catechism*, nn. 1328-1332).

While some in the Church have downplayed the sacrificial aspect of the Mass, that is not the mind of the Church, as one can learn from paragraphs 1362-1372 of the *Catechism*. For example, paragraph 1365 says that "the sacrificial character of the Eucharist is manifested in the very words of institution: 'This is my body which is given for you' and 'This cup which is poured out for you is the New Covenant in my blood' [*Lk* 22:19-20]."

In the Eucharist, the *Catechism* continues, "Christ gives us the very body which he gave up for us on the cross, the very blood which he 'poured out for many for the forgiveness of sins' [*Mt* 26:28]." So "the Eucharist is thus a sacrifice because it *represents* (makes present) the sacrifice of the cross, because it is its *memorial* and because it *applies* its fruit" (n. 1366).

Q. I believe that your answer in a recent column about the greeting at Mass ("Welcome to the celebration of the Eucharist") left out a very important point. Some priests make the Holy Sacrifice entirely too folksy and off the cuff by filling in their own greetings instead of using the biblical ones of the liturgy, e.g., "Hello, folks, welcome to our little celebration!" The Mass then becomes a get-together with the emphasis on a social rather than on giving honor and service to God and reliving our Redemption. Perhaps you could quote from the articles I have enclosed, which explain it much better than I can. — D.G.K., Oregon

A. The column referred to actually addressed a different point than the folksy greetings we often hear at the beginning of Mass these days, but since Fr. D.G.K. raises the issue we will take his suggestion and quote from an article by Mark R. Francis that appeared in the November-December 1994 issue of *Liturgy 90*, with the caveat that we prefer "priest" or "celebrant" to the over-used "presider":

"We often hear presiders — feeling perhaps that the rite begins in too abrupt a manner — change the initial greeting to something like 'Good morning. The Lord is with each and every one of you.' Sometimes, a presider will respond to the assembly's response, 'And also with you,' by saying 'Thank you.'

"Why is this inappropriate? First, to change the greeting to 'Good morning, the Lord is with you!' is to begin the celebration more like a news report than an invitation to the mystery of God's presence in prayer. Beginning with a secular greeting clearly indicates that the presider is uncomfortable with ritual language and somehow believes these words prevent communicating with the assembly. While one cannot dispute the fact that the Lord is with the assembly (since whenever two or more are gathered in Christ's name, Christ is there in their midst), the greeting is ritual language, not a mere statement of fact, like 'It sure is hot in here'....

"A banal 'thank you' on the part of the presider to such ritual language again reduces the dialogue to the level of small talk and underscores that what we are about is not all that singular or important — what we are doing is not ritual. It also seems to suggest that the presider must always have the last word. Surely no one who presides would want to give that impression. The introductory dialogue is best spoken as it is written."

Q. My parish has begun using hymn No. 848 of *Today's Missal* ("Gloria in Excelsis Deo") in place of the standard Gloria at Sunday Mass. Though No. 848 generally follows the Gloria, there seems to be more added to it. Is this an acceptable substitute for the Gloria? — M.S., Michigan

Q. During the last Christmas and Easter seasons, "Hark the Herald Angels Sing" and "Ode to Joy" were sung in place of the Gloria at Mass. Were these substitutions permissible? — J.W.K., Missouri

Q. Regarding your saying that it is all right to intersperse the long "Gloria in Excelsis Deo" from "Angels We Have Heard on High" at several places during the Gloria at Mass during the Christmas season, some years ago Rome specifically forbade the use of alternate words when singing any part of the Mass, with one exception, namely,

if necessary to fit the traditional musical score for that part. Obviously, the interspersing of 'Gloria in Excelsis Deo" or the more common, but equally incorrect, "Give glory to God in the highest," does not fit the exception. — R.S.H., New Jersey

Q. In my parish, instead of singing the traditional "Lamb of God," we sing, "Jesus, Lamb of God, broken for our sins, Jesus hear us. Hear our prayer, hear our prayer, through this Bread and Wine we share, let us be Your presence everywhere." Sometimes we use the words "Prince of Peace" and "Bread of Life." Are these variations allowed? — M.T., New York

A. First of all, the Gloria is an essential part of the Mass and should not be replaced by anything else. Here is what the *General Instruction of the Roman Missal* says:

"The Gloria is the ancient and venerable hymn in which the Church, assembled in the Holy Spirit, praises and entreats the Father and the Lamb. The text of this hymn is not to be replaced by any other" (n. 53).

Second, R.S.H. is correct in saying that the document *Music in Catholic Worship* allows alternate words in some sung parts of the Mass in order to adapt to the music. We are aware, however, that some liturgists have taken this permission to the extreme, and we want to quote some observations from the June 1999 issue of *Adoremus Bulletin*.

While these observations were addressed specifically to a question about substituting the words "Prince of Peace" and "Bread of Life" for "Lamb of God" in the Agnus Dei, the comments are pertinent to our discussion of the Gloria as well:

"The point has been very strongly made that no one, not even a priest, is permitted to alter the texts of the liturgy at all. However, according to a document called *Music in Catholic Worship*, if the texts are sung, the words may be altered for the sake of the music.

"Though it may not have been foreseen by those who approved *MCW*, some liturgists believe it gives blanket permission for changing almost any Mass text, so long as it is sung. This principle would have very serious implications if applied, for example, to the sung Eucharistic Prayer and other parts of the Mass special to the priest, and even when applied to parts sung by the people (the Kyrie, Gloria, Sanctus, Agnus Dei).

"It has now become very common for composers to change the words — sometimes substantially. This both weakens the authority of the approved texts and erodes the unity of worship."

In light of those comments, we would say that there are no acceptable substitutes for the Gloria, that additional words should not be interspersed into this ancient hymn, and that variations to the Agnus Dei, particularly the first one mentioned by M.T., go well beyond what *Music in Catholic Worship* allowed.

Q. I thought that only a bishop, priest, or deacon could read the Gospel, but I have attended Masses at different churches where the priest reads only the parts where Jesus speaks, while lay people read the other parts. Is this authorized? — G.H.L., New York

Q. After the priest read the Gospel at Mass, a nun got up and gave the homily. Doesn't this violate canon 767? — R.D.D., Washington, and E.F., Missouri

A. As we have noted in the past, canon law (c. 767.1) and the *General Instruction* (n. 66) restrict the reading of the Gospel to members of the clergy, except for Good Friday and Palm Sunday, when the laity may assist in the reading of the Passion of the Lord *(Paschales Solemnitatis*, nn. 33 and 66).

Canon law (c. 767.1) also restricts preaching of the homily to a priest or deacon, and this was reaffirmed in the 1997 Vatican instruction entitled *Some Questions Regarding Collaboration of Non-Ordained Faithful in Priests' Sacred Ministry.*

The instruction said that the laity may on special occasions (e.g., seminary days or days for the sick) give "personal testimonies" or explanations that would promote a greater understanding of the liturgy, but it stressed that "these testimonies or explanations may not be such so as to assume a character which could be confused with the homily."

The instruction also said that the non-ordained faithful may preach homilies "in non-Eucharistic liturgies" (e.g., a Sunday Communion service when there is no priest available for Mass), but "only when expressly permitted by law and when its prescriptions for doing so are observed." This means that the text of the homily would be prepared beforehand by or in consultation with a priest.

Q. Is there some rule that prevents the priest from incorporating doctrine into the Sunday homily? I seldom hear any mention of things "Catholic." — B.W., British Columbia

A. You know of course that there is no such rule and, in fact, canon law says that "in the homily the mysteries of faith and the norms of Christian living are to be expounded from the sacred text throughout the course of the liturgical year" (c. 767.1).

The problem to which you refer is one of bland and uninspiring homilies, e.g., those which seldom explain or defend doctrinal issues, such as the Real Presence, the authority of the Church, the reality of sin, death, and judgment, and the existence of Heaven, Hell, and Purgatory. Or if your priest talks about an important doctrine, such as the Immaculate Conception, he spoils it (as one of ours did) by calling Mary "an unwed mother" and Jesus a "lawbreaker" and a "hippie."

It is much more fashionable these days to talk about easy topics, such as poverty or peace or racism, rather than the tough issues, such as abortion, contraception, divorce, fornication, and homosexuality. Any priest worth his calling should talk about both the easy and the tough issues, reminding himself that his Sunday homily might be the only religious instruction his listeners will get that week.

Q. Is it permissible for the priest or liturgist to substitute the enclosed song ("We Believe, We Believe in God") by Carey Landry for the Apostles' Creed or the Nicene Creed at Mass? — M.E.B., Wisconsin

A. No, it is not permissible. The *General Instruction* says that "by professing the rule of faith in a formula approved for liturgical use, the great mysteries of the faith may be recalled and confirmed before their celebration in the Eucharist is begun" (n. 67). A "formula approved for liturgical use" means the Nicene Creed, although the Apostles' Creed may be substituted at children's Masses.

No other creeds, or versions of creeds, or songs with creedal statements may be used in place of the profession of faith. If the priest or liturgist want to use the Landry song, they can insert it at some other time in the Mass.

Q. When reciting the Creed, our priest says "and became human," instead of "and became man." Is this ap-

proved? Any suggestions for keeping recollected and prayerful during Mass, when our pastor's idea of a Mass seems to be a community gathering where the focus is more toward people than toward God? — A.M., Maine

A. No, your pastor's change of "man" to "human" is not permitted. If this keeps up, he will probably soon begin the Lord's Prayer with "Our Parent who art in Heaven...." All of this, of course, is an effort to be politically correct by using inclusive language.

But adapting the prayers of the Mass to one's own preferences was specifically forbidden by the Second Vatican Council's *Constitution on the Sacred Liturgy*: "Absolutely no other person, not even a priest, may add, remove, or change anything in the liturgy on his own authority" (n. 22).

As you say, it is not easy to be recollected when abuses occur during Mass. Our suggestion would be to offer up your discomfort to the Lord and pray that He will inspire those who stand in His place at the altar to celebrate the sacred mysteries according to the rules established by His Church.

Q. At the Offertory of the Mass in our parish, the priest adds a small amount of water to the wine in the chalice, as well as some water to the wine in the cruet, but some priests do not add water into both the chalice and the wine cruet. If the celebrant does not add water to the wine in the cruet, is there an element of matter missing?

Shouldn't the Precious Blood of Christ be placed in the most sacred vessel that we have, which is another chalice? Have we also added to our housekeeping chores since not only the chalices but also the wine cruet need to be purified after Communion is over? — J. and M.A.S., New Hampshire

A. (1) No, water does not have to added to the wine in the large container (which is more a flagon or decanter than a cruet) for that wine to become the Blood of Christ. If the flagon is on the corporal on the altar, the wine in it is consecrated along with the wine in the chalice.

(2) Regarding the vessel that holds the Precious Blood, Msgr. Peter Elliott said in his book *Ceremonies of the Modern Roman Rite* that because the chalice is "a unique sacred cup reserved for the Eucharist," it should be made of metal and gilded on the inside if it is subject to rust. He excluded glass or ceramic chal-

ices because they are easily breakable and said that when several chalices are needed, say at a concelebrated Mass, they should be of the same design and arranged at convenient points on the altar.

Consecrating wine in a flagon or decanter "does not seem to be a sound liturgical solution, both from a practical and a symbolic point of view," said Msgr. Elliott. He explained why in a footnote:

"(a) Practical advantages are offset by the problem of spilling the Precious Blood and of purifying the flagon. (b) Used with 'cups,' the flagon overemphasizes the meal dimension of the Mass, introducing a kind of repetition of the preparation of the gifts — pouring into cups at the fraction. The flagon was favored in some Reformation traditions, when it was perceived that the chalice is in itself a Catholic sign of offering sacrifice" (pp. 36-37).

(3) The number of vessels to be purified after Communion is not the problem, says Msgr. Elliott, but rather the material from which the vessels are made. Metal vessels with gilded interiors are easier to clean than those made of glass or ceramic.

Q. What is the purpose of the washing of the hands by a priest during the Mass? I have watched priests touch their beard, mouth, and nose during Mass and later shake hands with the people, and I have seen concelebrating priests not wash their hands at all. It is not very hygienic to serve Communion to the faithful with unclean hands. — F.P.C., Florida

A. The washing of the hands by the priest at Mass has nothing to do with hygiene, although it did in the early centuries of the Church when the priest accepted as gifts from the people food and even animals. The ritual today, explains the *General Instruction*, is "an expression of his desire to be cleansed internally" (n. 76). Thus, while the water is poured over his hands, the priest says, "Lord, wash away my iniquity; cleanse me from my sin."

It should be added, however, that the priest or deacon, and any Extraordinary Ministers who will be distributing Communion, ought to have washed their hands carefully before Mass and ought to be conscious during Mass of keeping their hands as clean as possible

Q. Please read the underlined section from the enclosed parish bulletin and tell me if this is correct theology or liturgy. I thought that only an ordained priest could consecrate the bread and wine at the Mass. — M.A.P., Illinois

A. The questionable section reads: "Beginning today and for the rest of the liturgical year the Eucharistic prayer will be enhanced musically, with chant, response, and instrumental accompaniment. Most often it seems that the Eucharistic prayer is the priest's monolog, giving the impression that the priest does the consecration. But actually it is the prayer of thanksgiving of all the church."

Contrary to this statement, it is the priest, and only the priest, who "does the consecration." While it is true that the faithful join with the priest in offering the Eucharist to the Father, there would be no offering, and no consecration, without the priest.

"The ministerial priest, by the sacred power he enjoys, molds and rules the priestly people," said Vatican II's *Dogmatic Constitution on the Church.* "Acting in the person of Christ, he brings about the Eucharistic Sacrifice, and offers it to God in the name of all the people. For their part, the faithful join in the offering of the Eucharist by virtue of their royal priesthood" (n. 10).

In his apostolic exhortation on the formation of priests (*Pastores Dabo Vobis*), Pope John Paul stated this more bluntly:

"For priests, as ministers of sacred things, are first and foremost ministers of the Sacrifice of the Mass. The role is utterly irreplaceable because without the priest there can be no Eucharistic offering."

Q. During Mass, the deacon seems to say the words of consecration to himself. He is not audible, but one can see his lips moving. He also touches the chalice, giving the impression that this is a co-consecration. Is this proper behavior for a deacon? — A.J.M., Florida

A. Deacons who assist a bishop or priest at Mass have certain legitimate functions to perform, but they are not to say the words of consecration, audibly or inaudibly, while the priest is saying them because they are not concelebrants. Nor are they to touch the chalice during this part of the Mass. In fact, deacons would not be in a position to do this if they followed the instructions of the *Ceremonial of Bishops*, which say that "deacons remain kneeling from the epiclesis to the elevation of the cup" (n. 155).

The epiclesis is the prayer just before the Consecration that asks God to send the Holy Spirit to change the bread and wine into the Body and Blood of Christ.

It is permissible for the deacon to hold up the chalice at the end of the Eucharistic prayer, when the priest holds up the Host and says, "Through him, with him, in him, in the unity of the Holy Spirit, all glory and honor is yours, almighty Father, for ever and ever" (cf. *General Instruction*, n. 180).

Q. Can a priest break the Host into two pieces before he says the words of consecration? — J.C., New Jersey

A. No, the priest is supposed to break the Host into two pieces during the Agnus Dei (*General Instruction*, nn. 83, 155), not during the Consecration. This part of the Mass is called the "fraction rite." Msgr. Peter Elliott explains why the breaking of the bread should take place then in *Liturgical Question Box*, p. 91:

"The eucharistic action of our Roman Rite clearly and graciously extends what appears to take place in a few moments at the Last Supper. Therefore, the Liturgy of the Eucharist unfolds in these four stages: (1) Jesus Christ *took bread and wine* (the preparation of the gifts); (2) He *gave thanks* and so blessed the bread and wine (the Eucharistic Prayer); (3) He *broke the bread* now transformed into His Body (the fraction); (4) He *gave* His Body and Blood to the apostles (the Communion Rite)."

Q. A fellow priest in Alcoholics Anonymous has permission to use grape juice for Mass, but I hesitate to drink from his chalice and would prefer that a separate chalice with wine be consecrated. But he says, "Why, don't you believe the Blood of Christ is in my chalice?" I presume that he is right, but what should I do? — C.J.S., Kentucky

A. Priests suffering from alcoholism may obtain their bishop's permission to use mustum instead of wine for the consecration. Mustum is fresh juice from grapes or juice preserved by suspending its fermentation by means of freezing or other methods which do not alter its nature.

Yes, the AA priest's chalice does contain the Blood of Christ if he uses mustum, but he is forbidden to preside at a concelebrated Mass, except under certain circumstances, and if he does preside at a Mass with special circumstances, a chalice with normal wine must be consecrated for the other celebrants.

Here is the pertinent section of a letter on this subject that was distributed on June 22, 1994 by Joseph Cardinal Ratzinger of the Sacred Congregation for the Doctrine of the Faith:

"In general, those who have received permission to use mustum are prohibited from presiding at concelebrated Masses. There may be some exceptions, however: in the case of a bishop or superior general; or, with prior approval of the Ordinary, at the concelebration of the anniversary of priestly ordination or other similar occasions. In these cases, the one who is to preside is to communicate under both the species of bread and that of mustum, while for the other celebrants a chalice shall be provided in which normal wine is to be consecrated."

Since the AA priest is apparently not celebrating Mass under these special circumstances, you should not concelebrate with him. You should instead celebrate a separate Mass on your own or with concelebrants who do not suffer from alcoholism.

Q. Have you ever published an explanation of why the words of consecration of the wine were changed from "for many" to "for all"? I see priests changing the liturgy routinely, but I thought the words of consecration were carved in stone, like the Ten Commandments. The Gospels of Matthew and Mark also quote Jesus as saying "many" at the Last Supper, so why was the change made to "all"? — J.J.O., Florida; K.M., Indiana; R.S., New York; R.W.K., Ohio

A. It is true that the Latin words *pro multis* are more accurately translated "for many," but translating them "for all" does not affect the validity of the Mass since Jesus did shed His blood for all men (cf. 1 Timothy 4:10 and 1 John 2:2). Furthermore, as James Akin points out in his book *Mass Confusion* (Catholic Answers), "in biblical idiom, the term 'many' is often used as a synonym for 'all.' For example, when Paul says that 'by one man's [Adam's] disobedience many were made sinners' (Rom. 5:19), he means that all men were made sinners. The liceity of the translation 'for all' is not in question because it is part of a Church-approved text of the Mass" (pp. 120-121).

When asked if this change was justified, and if it superseded the teaching in the *Catechism of the Council of Trent*, the Vatican responded:

"The variant involved is fully justified:

a. According to exegetes the Aramaic word translated in Latin by *pro multis* has as its meaning 'for all': the many for whom Christ died is without limit; it is equivalent to saying 'Christ has died for all.' The words of St. Augustine are apposite: 'See what he gave and you will discover what he bought. The price is Christ's Blood. What is it worth but the whole world? What, but all peoples? Those who say either that the price is so small that it has purchased only Africans are ungrateful for the price they cost; those who say that they are so important that it has been given for them alone are proud' [*Enarr. in Ps.* 95, 5].

"b. The teaching of the *Catechism* is in no way superseded: the distinction that Christ's death is sufficient for all but efficacious for many remains valid

"c. In the approval of this vernacular variant in the liturgical text nothing inaccurate has slipped in that requires correction or emendation [*Notitiae* 6 (1970), 39-40, no. 28, *Documents on the Liturgy* 1445, n. RI 3]."

Q. At a recent Mass I attended, the priest, apparently distracted by a cold, stopped just before the words of consecration and then resumed the Mass without having said, "This is my Body ... This is my Blood." Were the bread and wine consecrated? Was it a valid Mass? Was the Sunday obligation satisfied? And did anyone present at that Mass receive valid Communion from the ciborium used by the priest? — C.M., Massachusetts

A. No, the bread and wine were not consecrated; no, it was not a valid Mass; yes, those in attendance who were invincibly ignorant of the lapse did satisfy their Sunday obligation; and no, those who received from the ciborium that the priest failed to consecrate did not receive valid Communion. If some received from a ciborium that was taken from the tabernacle at Communion time, which vessel presumably contained Hosts validly consecrated at a previous Mass, then they did receive the Body of Christ.

What could have been done? Having noticed the lapse by the priest, you could have gone up to him at the altar and told him quietly that he had forgotten to pronounce the words of consecration. Not an easy thing to do in front of the whole congregation, but such an action would have been much appreciated not only by the priest, but also by the people.

Q. It was not so long ago that the priest genuflected before and after consecrating the sacred Species. Today he may genuflect after consecrating them, he may only bow, or he may not do either. To do nothing seems to show an irreverence and a denial of the uniqueness of both the holy Species and the priesthood. I would appreciate your comments. — D.J.B., Massachusetts

A. Priests do not have the option of bowing or doing nothing after consecrating the Bread and Wine; they are required to genuflect, unless they are physically unable to do so. In the words of the *General Instruction*: "Three genuflections are made during Mass by the priest celebrant: after the showing of the Eucharistic bread, after the showing of the chalice, and before Communion" (n. 274).

The *GIRM* goes on to explain that "a genuflection, which is made by bending the right knee to the ground, signifies adoration, and for this reason is reserved to the Most Blessed Sacrament and to the Holy Cross" (n. 274), whereas "a bow is a sign of the reverence and honor given to persons or what represents those persons" (n. 275).

Thus, "an inclination of the head should be made when the three Divine Persons are named, at the name of Jesus, of the Blessed Virgin Mary, and of the Saint in whose honor Mass is celebrated." And "a bow of the body, or profound bow, is made toward the altar if there is no tabernacle with the Blessed Sacrament; during the prayers *Almighty God, cleanse* and *With humble and contrite hearts*; with the profession of faith at the words *was incarnate of the Holy Spirit ... made man*; in Eucharistic Prayer I (Roman Canon) at the words *Almighty God, command that your angel*. The same kind of bow is made by the deacon when he asks the blessing before proclaiming the Gospel reading. In addition, the priest bends over slightly as he says the words of the Lord at the consecration" (n. 275).

Q. When the Host and chalice are elevated after the consecration of the Bread and Wine, is one still allowed to say, "My Lord and my God," as recommended by Pope St. Pius X and other popes? — W.N., Rhode Island

A. We don't know any reason why not. We first learned that ejaculation in parochial school 50 years ago and still say it today at that part of the Mass. In doing so, we are simply repeating the words of Thomas the Apostle at the sight of Jesus after the resurrection (John 20:28). What could be wrong with quietly acknowledging that what the priest is showing to the people is truly our Lord and our God?

Q. Why is St. Joseph not mentioned in Eucharistic prayers 2, 3, and 4? Why is St. Joseph not honored as much as he should be? — M.N., Florida, and F.J.S., Wisconsin
A. Pope John the XXIII added St. Joseph to the Roman Canon in 1962, but the focus of the other Eucharistic prayers is on Mary, the Apostles as the foundation of the Church, the martyrs, and all the saints. Even in the *Catechism of the Catholic Church* St. Joseph is hardly mentioned. However, one person who has singled him out for praise is Pope John Paul. In his general audience on August 21, 1996, for example, the Holy Father said:

"Joseph's cooperation in the mystery of the Incarnation also includes exercising the role of Jesus' father .... While excluding physical generation, Joseph's fatherhood was something real, not apparent. Distinguishing between father and the one who begets, an ancient monograph on Mary's virginity — the *De Margarita* (fourth century) — states that 'the commitments assumed by the Virgin and by Joseph as husband and wife made it possible for him to be called by this name [father]; a father, however, who did not beget.' Joseph thus carried out the role of Jesus' father, exercising an authority to which the Redeemer was freely 'obedient' (Luke 2:51), contributing to his upbringing, and teaching him the carpenter's trade.

"Christians have always acknowledged Joseph as the one who lived in intimate communion with Mary and Jesus, concluding that also in death he enjoyed their affectionate, consoling presence. From this constant Christian tradition, in many places a special devotion has grown to the Holy Family and, in it, to St. Joseph, Guardian of the Redeemer. As everyone knows, Pope Leo XIII entrusted the entire Church to his protection."

Q. After the Consecration of the Mass, the priest says, "Let us proclaim the mystery of faith." I'm confused by the use of the word "the" since there are various responses. Wouldn't it be better to say "a mystery" or "this mystery"? — A.C.G., Illinois, and M.R., Texas
A. A mystery of our faith usually refers to a divinely revealed truth, such as the Trinity or the Incarnation, that we are not

fully able to understand but which we accept on the word of God, who can neither deceive nor be deceived. However, when the priest uses the term "mystery of faith" after the Consecration, he is referring to the Holy Eucharist. Here are the words of Pope Paul VI in his 1965 encyclical *Mysterium Fidei*:

"Fathers and doctors of the Church constantly professed and taught ... that the Eucharist is a very great mystery. In fact, properly speaking, and to use the words of the sacred liturgy, it is the Mystery of Faith. 'Indeed, in it alone,' as Leo XIII, our predecessor of happy memory very wisely remarked, 'are contained, in a remarkable richness and variety of miracles, all supernatural realities.'"

Q. Our pastor said that we should stand for the final doxology ("Through him, with him, in him, in the unity of the Holy Spirit, all glory and honor is yours, almighty Father, for ever and ever") at the end of the Eucharistic prayer. He said that this is "the more accurate posture for this action in the Mass," and that those who do not join with the community in theory "are not giving their support to what is being done in the Mass." Would you give us your views on this? — J.E.C., Pennsylvania

A. Our view is that of the National Conference of Catholic Bishops, which said in 1969 that Catholics in the United States should "kneel beginning after the singing or recitation of the Sanctus until after the Amen of the Eucharistic prayer, that is, before the Lord's prayer." In his book *Mass Confusion*, James Akin elaborated on this point:

"People are not to stand up *before* the Great Amen, nor are they to stand up *during* the Great Amen. The Great Amen is the climax of the congregation's participation in the Eucharistic Prayer, when it solemnly asserts, as a body, to what the priest has just prayed to God as their representative. This special solemnity is why, in America, the congregation remains kneeling *during* the Amen. Standing before the Amen is not permitted, and it is especially inappropriate to be changing postures *during* this most solemn moment" (p. 205).

Q. Recently while traveling I attended Mass where the priest, at the sign of peace, left the altar and shook hands

with at least 100 people and then returned to the altar. Without washing his hands, he then distributed Communion to the congregation. Isn't there a ruling that the priest is not to leave the altar during the offering of the Mass? — D.M., Wisconsin

A. The latest edition of the *General Instruction of the Roman Missal* (July 2000) says that "the priest may give the sign of peace to the ministers, always remaining in the sanctuary, lest the celebration be disrupted. He should do so likewise if, for a good reason, he wishes to offer the sign of peace to a few of the faithful" (n. 154).

Q. Years ago, after receiving Holy Communion, I could go to my pew, kneel down for a few minutes of silence, and have time for private meditation and prayer. Now, I am blasted with music from the organ and hymns from the choir. It is impossible for me to even repeat, mentally, memorized prayers of thanksgiving. Is there something wrong with me? — L.K., Colorado

A. No, there is nothing wrong with you, nor with having a brief period of silence after Communion to speak to the Lord. In fact, this is recommended by the Vatican document *Inaestimabile Donum*:

"The faithful are to be recommended not to omit to make a proper thanksgiving after Communion. They may do this during the celebration with a period of silence, with a hymn, psalm, or other song of praise, or also after the celebration, if possible, by staying behind to pray for a suitable time" (n. 17).

Q. You have probably answered this question before, but could you comment on the deplorable lack of reverence in church before and after Mass? It didn't used to be this way. What happened? — J.E., Nevada

A. The late Archbishop John Whealon of Hartford, CT once gave a good answer to this problem, and we would like to share it with our readers:

"Time was that Catholics at all times kept silent in church. All realized that the church is a house of prayer, that the Blessed Sacrament is there, and that it is not the place for talk. At least in many churches, a considerable and gradual change has taken place. Now some Catholics before and after Mass talk in church. This is a bad habit that has grown like crabgrass. It is contagious, and it is inconsiderate, impolite, even boorish.

"Why should you make it a personal rule not to talk in church? The first reason concerns your own prayer life. You believe that the church is a house of prayer, and you believe that in the tabernacle is Jesus Christ, present in the Blessed Sacrament, deserving your adoration and prayer. Your conduct in those minutes before Mass is a good test of your ability to pray privately.

"As a person of daily prayer, you should take holy water as a symbol that you are cleansing yourself of worldly interests and thoughts as you enter God's house. You should bend the knee in adoration to the Eucharistic Lord. You should then pray and prepare yourself for the Mass and Holy Communion. Certainly this is no time for talking to other human beings. The rest of the week, all the time outside church, is available to talk with people. This is the time for talking with God in God's own house, with Christ's special Eucharistic Presence.

"The second reason for keeping silent in church is simple consideration — elemental Christian charity to one's neighbor. If one follower of Christ is presently incapable of praying in church, that person should not talk and so distract others from praying."

As to the reason for this increasing lack of reverence and piety, Archbishop Whealon blamed it on a "decline in faith." He said that "prayer, that is, personal prayer, daily prayer, is indeed one sign of faith, and a decline in faith will lead to a decline in willingness to pray."

Q. I was surprised to hear various references to the Sunday before Easter as Palm Sunday and Passion Sunday. Since when was it permitted to call this Sunday by either name? — P.R.B, Connecticut

A. The fifth Sunday of Lent used to be called Passion Sunday, and the Sunday before Easter, Palm Sunday. Now the two names are used interchangeably for the Sunday that begins Holy Week because on that day the palms are blessed and distributed and the Passion of our Lord is read as we commemorate the entrance of Jesus into Jerusalem.

Q. This past Holy Thursday in my parish, several women were among those having their feet washed. Is this permissible? — M.S., Michigan

A. As we have noted in the past, the *Roman Missal* used in Catholic churches since 1970 contains the following rubrics for the Mass on Holy Thursday:

"Depending on pastoral circumstances, the washing of the feet follows the homily. The men who have been chosen are led by the ministers to chairs prepared in a suitable place. Then the priest (removing his chasuble if necessary) goes to each man. With the help of the ministers, he pours water over each one's feet and dries them."

You will find similar language in the *Ceremonial of Bishops*, n. 301, and there is also the following statement from the Vatican's Congregation for Divine Worship in 1988:

"The washing of the feet of chosen men which, according to tradition, is performed on this day, represents the service and charity of Christ, who came 'not to be served but to serve' [Matt. 20:28]. This tradition should be maintained, and its proper significance explained" (*Paschales Solemnitatis*, n. 51).

However, the U.S. Bishops in June 1996 approved as part of the revised Sacramentary a document entitled *Pastoral Introduction to the Order of Mass*. This document said that "those whose feet are washed should be chosen to represent various people who constitute the parish or community: the young and old, men and women."

Q. On Holy Thursday in our parish, we had hand-washing instead of foot-washing. During the homily, it was explained that in our culture, we do not wear sandals and therefore there is no need to wash feet. But we take care of the young and the elderly by washing their hands. I found this to be very inappropriate for Holy Thursday. What's a person to do? — J.H., Montana

A. It is indeed very inappropriate and, if your pastor won't pay attention to the quotations from Church documents in the previous reply, as well as the quotations below (and judging from the other abuses mentioned in your letter, he probably won't), then you should contact your bishop. Msgr. Peter Elliott, in his *Liturgical Question Box*, has remarked on the absurdity of washing hands:

"I cannot see the point of this practice. It can only satisfy the fastidious, who are not comfortable with Jesus, the Suffering Servant, kneeling to wash the feet of fishermen. In John 13:9 we read that one of them, St. Peter, objected, but once he saw what Our Lord was about, he wanted his hands and head washed as well; yet Our Lord insisted only on the humblest sign of washing feet. Hence, any substitute for this action only erases the radical sign of self-abasement and union with the Suffering Servant and His Covenant" (p. 177).

Msgr. Elliott also pointed out that "the only hand-washing recorded in the Passion accounts was the deplorable self-absolution of Pontius Pilate. I am sure no one would want that gesture to insinuate itself into the Sacred Triduum."

Q. I have been to a number of concerts in Catholic churches. The sanctuary lamp is always on, but the choir and the members of the audience behave as though they were in a concert hall. Does the Church have rules that cover this situation? — K.K., Massachusetts
A. Yes, and the rules were spelled out on November 5, 1987 by the Sacred Congregation for Divine Worship. The document, which was signed by Augustin Cardinal Mayer, O.S.B., the prefect of the congregation, said:

"The principle that the use of the church must not offend the sacredness of the place determines the criteria by which the doors of a church may be opened to a concert of sacred or religious music, as also the concomitant exclusion of every other type of music. The most beautiful symphonic music, for example, is not in itself of religious character.

"The definition of sacred or religious music depends explicitly on the original intended use of the musical pieces or songs, and likewise on their content. It is not legitimate to provide for the execution in the church of music which is not of religious inspiration and which was composed with a view to performance in a certain precise secular context, irrespective of whether the music would be judged classical or contemporary, of high quality or of a popular nature.

"On the one hand, such performances would not respect the sacred character of the church, and on the other would result in the music being performed in an unfitting context."

Noting that it is up to eccelesiastical authority "to regulate the use of churches in such a way as to safeguard their sacred character," the document says that the Ordinary can specify the following conditions for holding concerts in churches:

"a) Requests are to be made in writing, in good time, indicating the date and time of the proposed concert, the program giving the works, and the names of the composers.

"b) After having received the authorization of the Ordinary, the rectors and parish priests of the churches should arrange details with the choir and orchestra so that the requisite norms are observed.

"c) Entrance to the church must be without payment and open to all.

"d) The performers and the audience must be dressed in a manner which is fitting to the sacred character of the place.

"e) The musicians and the singers should not be placed in the sanctuary. The greatest respect is to be shown to the altar, the president's chair, and the ambo.

"f) The Blessed Sacrament should be, as far as possible, reserved in a side chapel or in another safe and suitably adorned place (cf. canon 938.4).

"g) The concert should be presented or introduced not only with historical or technical details, but also in a way that fosters a deeper understanding and an interior participation on the part of the listeners.

"h) The organizer of the concert shall declare in writing that he accepts legal responsibility for expenses involved, for leaving the church in order, and for any possible damage incurred."

Chapter 11

Christian Marriage

Q. What does canon law say about racially mixed marriages, say, between a white person and a black person? — P.P., Kentucky

A. Canon law doesn't say anything about marriages between persons of different races since all persons are of equal dignity in the eyes of God, and such things as race, color, or ethnic background are not obstacles or impediments to valid marriages in the Catholic Church. For as the *Catechism of the Catholic Church* (n. 1935) points out, " 'Every form of social or cultural discrimination in fundamental personal rights on the grounds of sex, race, color, social conditions, language, or religion must be curbed and eradicated as incompatible with God's design' [*GS* 29 § 2]."

Q. I recall reading that the United Church believes that there are biblical and theological grounds for recognizing same-sex "marriages." Can you shed some light on what those grounds might be? — E.J.T., Missouri

A. No, we can't because there are no such grounds. Oh, there may be "theologians" who claim to find such grounds in Scripture, but they are just turning the Bible on its head.

What Scripture does teach (cf. Genesis 19:1-29, Romans 1:24-27, 1 Corinthians 6:9, 1 Timothy 1:10, Jude 7) is that sexual relations between persons of the same sex are depraved. "They are contrary to the natural law," says the *Catechism*, because "they close the sexual act to the gift of life. They do not proceed from a genuine affective and sexual complementarity. Under no circumstances can they be approved" (n. 2357).

For more on this, see paragraphs 1601-1666, 2331-2336, and 2360-2400 of the *Catechism*.

Among other things, those paragraphs say that the vocation to marriage was written by the Creator in the very nature of man and woman, that the mutual love of man and woman is intended to be fruitful, that man and woman were created for one another, and that because it is not good for man to be alone,

God gave him woman as a helpmate and that is why "a man leaves his mother and father and clings to his wife, and the two of them become one body" (Genesis 2:24).

For a superb explanation of the Church's teaching on marriage, based on 129 homilies by Pope John Paul on "The Theology of the Body," see Christopher West's book *Good News About Sex & Marriage* (Servant Publications).

Q. I have noticed that when that reading about wives being submissive to their husbands comes up, lectors can use an alternate reading from Ephesians that leaves out the controversial passage. Wouldn't it be better to explain the real meaning of the passage? — T.L.D., Massachusetts

A. Of course it would, but either priests aren't sure of the real meaning or they're afraid of antagonizing the women in the congregation. The passage in question can be found in chapter five of Paul's letter, where the Apostle says:

"Wives should be submissive to their husbands as if to the Lord because the husband is head of his wife just as Christ is head of his body the church, as well as its savior. As the church submits to Christ, so wives should submit to their husbands in everything" (Ephesians 5:22-24).

There is no question that men over the centuries have used these verses to put women down and treat them as slaves, but they were wrong and sinful to do so. And Pope John Paul, in his 1995 *Letter to Women*, said that he was "truly sorry" for this mistreatment of women and that the time had come to set "women free from every kind of exploitation and domination" (n. 3).

But what about St. Paul's remarks? First of all, those who quote verses 22-24 seldom quote verse 21, which says that husbands and wives should defer or submit *to each other* out of reverence for Christ. So it's supposed to be a mutual submission of both spouses, not one lording it over the other. You might miss this point if you read the 1970 edition of the New American Bible because it puts the headline "Christian Wives and Husbands" after verse 21. Other Bible translations put verse 21 with the rest of St. Paul's remarks.

Second, as Christopher West points out in *Good News About Sex & Marriage*, we need to consider what the word "submission" means? "Sub" means "under" and "mission" means being sent out to perform some service. So when Paul says that wives should be submissive to their husbands, he is saying that wives should put themselves under the mission of their husbands, which is to serve them in the same way that Christ served the Church, i.e., by giving Himself up for her. Remember the words of Christ, who said that the Son of Man "has come, not to be served by others, but to serve, to give his own life as a ransom for the many" (Matthew 20:28).

If, as St. Paul says, husbands are to love their wives as Christ loved the Church, then husbands are supposed to have the same sacrificial love for their spouses that Christ had for the Church. "Husbands should love their wives as they do their own bodies," the Apostle said. "He who loves his wife loves himself. Observe that no one ever hates his own flesh; no, he nourishes it and takes care of it as Christ cares for the Church — for we are members of his body .... Each one should love his wife as he loves himself, the wife for her part showing respect for her husband" (Ephesians 5:28-33).

Echoing this thought in his apostolic letter on the Dignity and Vocation of Women (*Mulieris Dignitatem*), Pope John Paul II said that St. Paul knew that his way of speaking, "so proudly rooted in the customs and religious traditions of the time, is to be understood and carried out in a new way: as a '*mutual subjection out of reverence for Christ*' " (cf. Eph. 5:21).

He said that "this is especially true because the husband is called the 'head' of the wife *as* Christ is the head of the Church; he is so in order to give 'himself up for her' (Eph. 5:25), and giving himself up for her means giving up even his own life. However, whereas in the relationship between Christ and the Church the subjection is only on the part of the Church, in the relationship between husband and wife the 'subjection' is not one-sided but mutual" (n. 24).

The Holy Father went on to say that "the awareness that in marriage there is mutual 'subjection of the spouses out of reverence for Christ,' and not just that of the wife to the husband, must gradually establish itself in hearts, consciences, behavior, and customs. This is a call which from that time onward does not cease to challenge succeeding generations; it is a call which people have to accept ever anew....

"All the reasons in favor of the 'subjection' of woman to man in marriage must be understood in the sense of a 'mutual subjection' of both 'out of reverence for Christ.' The measure of true spousal love finds its deepest source in Christ, who is the Bridegroom of the Church, his Bride" (*Ibid.*).

In light of this, Christopher West asks: "What woman would not want to receive this kind of love from her husband? What woman would not want to be subject to her husband if he truly took his mission seriously to love her as Christ loved the Church? So often it's husbands who want their wives to take this Scripture passage to heart. I think it's we men who need to take it to heart first" (p. 62).

Q. A couple I know live together "without the benefit of clergy," but consider themselves married (they made vows to each other, they say). They contend that a marriage license is just "a piece of paper." Can you tell me how to answer them? — E.C., New York

A. You could ask them why they bothered with a high school or college diploma since those are just pieces of paper, too. And so is a teacher's certificate, or a nurse's license, or a driver's license. Yet all of these documents are essential for a person to get somewhere in our society today. They are signs that individuals, through study, commitment, and hard work, have achieved a level of competence in some area and, if they persevere, they have a good chance of being successful.

Marriage is also a career that requires study, hard work, commitment, and perseverance. The piece of paper that says two people are married to each other does not guarantee a successful marriage, but it does guarantee state recognition of the union and it protects the rights of the parties if the marriage fails.

From a moral and religious perspective, marriage was established by God at the beginning of the human race and was elevated by Jesus to the level of a sacrament through which spouses receive the grace to fulfill their marital and family obligations and lead each other to Heaven.

"This sacrament," Pope John Paul said during a visit to San Antonio, Texas, on September 13, 1987, "forms the stable basis of the whole Christian community. Without it, Christ's design for human love is not fulfilled. His plan for the family is not followed. It is precisely because Christ established marriage as a sacrament and willed it to be a sign of his own permanent and faithful love for the Church, that the parish must explain to the faithful why all trial marriages, merely civil marriages, free unions, and divorces do not correspond to Christ's plan."

You might tell this couple that not only does their "free union" lack the commitment and the divine assistance essential for a marriage to survive, it is also contrary to the plan of God and puts them on the road to Hell.

Q. My son has been living with a girl for five years. He calls it a "common-law marriage," but what does the Church say about this? I told him that fornication is a mortal sin and, if he died without being sorry, his soul would go to Hell. Can you give me some answers? — Name and State Withheld

Q. Recently I have met several couples in their sixties and seventies who are living together without marriage. They go to Mass weekly and all claim that their priests have given their blessing to this arrangement. Some say that they are married in the eyes of the Church and that priests have said that the Church does not require marriage for couples who cannot have children. I find their reasoning questionable, but as a non-Catholic I am unable to argue with their priests. Does your Church okay old-age "shack-ups"? — D.W., New York

A. No, the Catholic Church does not sanction "shack-ups" by young or old couples because their sexual relations objectively constitute the sin of fornication. That sin has been condemned by Jesus Himself (Matthew 15:19) as one of "the things that make a man impure" and by St. Paul (Galatians 5:19), who said that "those who do such things will not inherit the kingdom of God." Any priest who counsels couples otherwise is guilty of the grave sin of scandal since he is encouraging them to sin.

While an openness to children is a requirement for a valid marriage, the physical inability of a couple to have children, particularly in the case of those who are beyond the age of childbearing, does not eliminate the need for marriage if they intend to live together and enjoy the conjugal rights of married couples.

As for "common law marriages" or "trial marriages," Pope John Paul has rejected these arrangements as contrary to the "eternally faithful" symbolism of the union of Christ and His Church and as a cause of "grave scandal" and of such serious social consequences as "the destruction of the concept of the family; the weakening of the sense of fidelity, also towards society; possible psychological damage to the children; the strengthening of selfishness" (*Familiaris Consortio*, nn. 80-81).

What pastors and the Church community must do in these situations, said the Holy Father, is to "make tactful and respectful contact with the couples concerned, and enlighten them patiently, correct them charitably, and show them the witness of Christian family life in such a way as to smooth the path for them to regularize their situation."

Q. Reportedly many engaged couples are living together until marriage. They refuse to separate and are not contrite about it, so cannot receive the sacrament of Penance validly. Thus, they receive the sacrament of Matrimony in the state of mortal sin. Do they then commit a sacrilege? Does the officiating priest, by cooperating in their sinful wedding, also sin? This case assumes that the couple really is in the state of mortal sin, which probably happens not infrequently. — J.T., Michigan

A. Of the many examples that come under the definition of sacrilege, one involves the deliberate unworthy reception of a sacrament, which constitutes a mortal sin. So a couple that marries in a state of mortal sin objectively commits a sacrilege. Whether they are subjectively guilty of sacrilege would depend on whether they clearly understood the sinfulness of what they were doing and deliberately went through with the sacrament anyway.

As for the officiating priest, is he guilty of sin by cooperating in the sacrilege? We posed this question to six priests, some of whom have Licentiates in Sacred Theology. Their unanimous opinion is that a priest who officiates at the wedding of a couple whom he knows to be in a state of mortal sin formally cooperates in the sacrilege of the couple and is guilty of sin himself.

Some of these priests have in the past refused to marry couples in such a situation after determining that the couples saw nothing wrong with continuing to practice fornication and saw no reason to seek God's forgiveness in the sacrament of Penance.

What is a priest to do when faced with couples like these? Priests must try to explain to them that God expects them to live chaste and holy lives before and during marriage and that the marriage laws of the Church must be followed. Priests should also find out what these couples understand about the vocation of marriage, whether they know of its life-giving and love-giving purposes, whether they believe that marriage is permanent, and whether they plan to welcome children into their married life.

If couples do not answer these questions satisfactorily, if they appear to have little regard for the Church's teaching on marriage, then priests should refuse to marry them.

Q. My daughter and her fiance were married by a justice of the peace so that she could remain a resident of the state and pay less college tuition. Now she's pregnant and wants to get married before she starts showing too much, but the Catholic Church wanted her and her husband to separate until the marriage and take instructions. So she decided instead to get married in a Lutheran church.

She desperately wants her father to give her away, her practicing Catholic sister to be a bridesmaid, and other family members to participate in the wedding. My husband and I have told her that we cannot and will not attend the wedding, and our other children think we are wrong in our decision and that we should consult another priest for a second opinion. Could you please write something that would back us up and that we could show to the entire family? — Name and State Withheld

A. One troubling aspect of these situations is the absolute unwillingness of those who have made bad choices to grant those who disagree with them the right to disagree. It's okay for the party of the first part to go down a certain road, but the party of the second part is not supposed to exercise their own right to decide which road to travel. Those who object to the bad choices for very sound reasons are expected to cast those reasons aside and give their approval to something that is completely contrary to everything they have believed over many years.

So just from the viewpoint of logic and common sense, your daughter and her fiance have no right to demand your acquiescence in and support for their decision to marry in a Lutheran church. They are not willing to abide by your beliefs, so why should they expect you to abide by theirs?

But what can you say to them, and to other members of the family? We would begin by stating the reasons for what you believe, starting with something as basic as who God is and why we should listen to Him. As the inventor of marriage, God has the right to tell us what marriage is all about. He created us, male and female, in His own image; told us to "be fertile and multiply"; said that men and women need each other ("It is not good for the man to be alone. I will make a suitable partner for him .... That is why a man leaves his father and mother and clings to his wife, and the two of them become one body"); and said that marriage is forever ("Therefore, let no man separate what God has joined").

Jesus, who is also God, elevated marriage to the level of a sacrament so that God's grace would be available to help married couples be faithful to each other always. He also established a Church with the authority to set the rules and regulations for marriage ("Whatever you declare bound on earth shall be bound in Heaven"). Thus, the Catholic Church has the authority from God Himself to require her members to be married before a priest and two witnesses, or to obtain a dispensation from this form.

The Church's representatives also have the obligation, if they are to be faithful to their divine Founder, to ask couples to live apart and abstain from sex before their marriage (Jesus condemned fornication as a grave sin) and to take instructions on what marriage is all about in the eyes of God and His Church.

You and your husband believe firmly in what the Church teaches about marriage because you know that those teachings come directly from God the Father and His Son Jesus. For you to give approval to your daughter's plan to disregard these teachings would be to turn your back on God. It would be a violation of the First Commandment, which says that God must come first in everything — ahead of family members and friends who might say that they believe in God, but who live and act as if God did not exist.

You and your husband are undoubtedly aware of Jesus' warning that "whoever loves father or mother, son or daughter, more than me is not worthy of me." You know that if you expect to get to Heaven, you must follow Jesus faithfully, even carrying a cross as He did, in this case the cross of anger and frustration on the part of your children. But you, like your children and the rest of the human race, are called to be holy, to follow the way and be true to the One who said, "I am the Way, and the Truth, and the Life."

What kind of parents would give their child whatever she wanted, whether it was good for her or not? What kind of parents would willingly take part in a moral choice that puts their child on the road to Hell? You and your husband are understandably heartsick over this situation, but you are not responsible for the heartache; your daughter is. But you have to stand for what is right, no matter the heartache. Better pain and hurt feelings now than for all eternity.

Q. Considering that the procreative end of marriage is primary, is a marriage valid if the woman is already beyond the age of childbirth or for medical reasons cannot have children? Also, is it licit for such a couple to continue engaging in marital relations since children are impossible in these circumstances? — J.S.B., Utah

A. Marriage has two ends: the unitive or love-giving end, and the procreative or life-giving end. If a married couple is no longer able to conceive children, the husband and wife can still pursue the love-giving end of marriage and engage in marital relations. Pope Paul VI put it this way in *Humanae Vitae*:

"These acts, by which husband and wife are united in chaste intimacy, and by means of which human life is transmitted, are, as the [Second Vatican] Council recalled, 'noble and worthy,' and they do not cease to be lawful if, for causes independent of the will of husband and wife, they are foreseen to be infecund, since they always remain ordained toward expressing and consolidating their union" (n. 11).

Q. I am questioning the advice more than one priest gave my grandchild regarding a hasty wedding brought on by pregnancy and the need for medical coverage under the husband's insurance policy. He was told to marry now in a Protestant church, with the proper dispensation, and come back later to have the marriage blessed and the baby baptized in the Catholic Church.

One of the priests said, "Protestant ministers are permitted to witness marriages in the Catholic Church at times, so you just let a minister witness this one." We have held fast to the teaching of the Church on marriage, but it seems like the rug is being pulled out from under us. Is this now accepted Church practice? — C.F., Kansas

A. No, it is not accepted Church practice, although there are priests who give this kind of erroneous advice. The Church's teaching, as expressed in canon 1108 of the Code of Canon Law, is that a Catholic party can contract a valid marriage only in the presence of a Catholic bishop, priest, or deacon, who as the official witness of the Church must ask for and receive the consent of the parties in the name of the Church, and two other witnesses, whose function is to attest that the marriage actually took place.

In the case of a marriage between a Catholic and a Protestant, the local bishop of the Catholic party can dispense from these requirements "if serious difficulties pose an obstacle to the observance of the canonical form" (canon 1127.2), and he can permit the marriage to be celebrated in a Protestant church (canon 1118.2). However, these canons apply to marriages in which one of the parties is a baptized Catholic and not to marriage between *two* baptized Catholics, which appears to be the situation described by C.F.

It was dishonest for that priest to imply that having a Protestant minister witness the marriage of two Catholics is the same as having a minister witness the marriage of a Catholic and a non-Catholic after the proper dispensation had been obtained from the local bishop. We know that some priests suggest going to a minister or to a justice of the peace in situations in which the bride is pregnant in case the marriage ends in divorce because it would not be a valid ceremony in the eyes of the Catholic Church and that would make it much easier to enter into a future marriage.

However, this is a terrible way to counsel couples in these situations. Instead of calling upon them to face the consequences of breaking one of God's laws (the Sixth Commandment), they are told that it's all right to disregard a law of God's Church (canon 1108) in case they want to get off the hook later.

We are not suggesting, by the way, that marriage in the Catholic Church is always the right thing to do if a woman gets pregnant; in fact, it is a poor reason for marriage if the parties do not truly love each other and do not plan to remain faithful to each other for life. Better they should go their separate ways than to compound one bad choice with another one.

Q. If a baptized Catholic woman marries an unbaptized man with the proper dispensation, and the husband is later baptized, does their marriage become a sacrament then or must there be a formal act? Would the Catholic Church allow a validly married couple to separate if the wife wanted to enter the convent and the husband wanted to become a priest? — Name Withheld, Montana

A. Once the unbaptized spouse is baptized, the marriage becomes a sacrament. There is no need for a formal ceremony to complete the sacrament; a simple recommitment to the marriage covenant, such as an expression of each spouse's love for the other, would be enough.

There have been cases of married couples, with papal permission, entering religious life, but this dispensation from canon 643.2 is rare. The Holy See can also dispense (canon 1047.3) from the impediment marriage presents to Holy Orders (canon 1042.1), but this would be rare, too.

Q. My sister, a confirmed Roman Catholic, married a Jewish man. A priest and a rabbi were at the ceremony, which was performed at a catering hall. I was maid of honor and I believe I signed a piece of paper stating that I witnessed a Catholic marriage and that they would raise the children Catholic. A baby boy was recently born and they had a bris for him performed by a rabbi. Now they will have the baby baptized, and they intend to raise him in both religions simultaneously. Isn't this completely wrong? — C.G., New York

A. It's wrong on the part of your sister, who made a sincere promise to raise any children in the Catholic Church, and it shows why the Church is always concerned about a Catholic marrying a person of a different faith. Too often the Catholic party either drifts away from the Church, or joins the spouse's church, or the two of them decide to raise the child in both religions until he is old enough to choose for himself.

When your sister and her husband were preparing for marriage, they were presumably informed of canon 1125 of the Code of Canon Law, which states that the local Ordinary can grant a dispensation for a mixed marriage "if there is a just and reasonable cause" and if the following conditions have been fulfilled:

"(1) the Catholic party declares that he or she is prepared to remove dangers of falling away from the faith and makes a sincere promise to do all in his or her power to have all the children baptized and brought up in the Catholic Church;

"(2) the other party is to be informed at an appropriate time of these promises which the Catholic party has to make, so that it is clear that the other party is truly aware of the promise and obligation of the Catholic party;

"(3) both parties are to be instructed on the essential ends and properties of marriage, which are not to be excluded by either party."

As your sister's maid of honor (and perhaps godmother of the child), you have the duty to remind her of the promise she made. You might also remind her of canon 868.2, which states that one of the requirements for the licit baptism of an infant is that "there be a founded hope that the infant will be brought up in the Catholic religion; if such a hope is altogether lacking, the Baptism is to be put off according to the prescriptions of particular law and the parents are to be informed of the reason."

Q. I am a serious practicing Catholic married to an Evangelical Protestant. Prior to our marriage, my wife said that while she would probably never convert to Catholicism, she would not oppose baptizing our children in the Catholic Church and raising them as Catholics. But after our first child was born, she began demonstrating the most virulent anti-Catholicism imaginable and has since threatened me with divorce if I try to have our child baptized Catholic. What advice can you give me? — Name and State Withheld

A. This is a situation that can be handled only by a competent Catholic marriage counselor who is faithful to the Church's teaching on marriage. You should be able to get the name of a reliable counselor from the priest who married you, or from the family life bureau or the marriage tribunal in your diocese. We will ask all who read this to pray for you.

Q. If a wife in a lawful Catholic marriage divorces her husband, and the husband does not remarry, can he still receive the sacraments of Reconciliation and Holy Communion? — Name Withheld, New Mexico

A. Yes. It is remarriage after divorce, which usually constitutes a continuing state of adultery, that keeps one from obtaining absolution in Confession and, therefore, from being worthy to receive Communion.

Q. I was taught that divorced and remarried people were excommunicated, but in a recent story in the newspaper, Archbishop Tarcisio Bertone of the Sacred Congregation for the Doctrine of the Faith (SCDF) was quoted

as saying that such people are still in "ecclesial communion." Please explain. — G.F., New York

A. In 1884, the Council of Baltimore approved legislation which imposed excommunication on divorced Catholics who remarried. However, on October 22, 1977, Pope Paul VI authorized repeal of that law. So divorced Catholics who remarry are no longer excommunicated, although their remarriage puts them "in a situation that objectively contravenes God's law," said the SCDF in a letter to the world's bishops on October 14, 1994. "Consequently, they cannot receive Holy Communion as long as this situation persists" (n. 4).

The letter went on to say that "the faithful who persist in such a situation may receive Holy Communion only after obtaining sacramental absolution, which may be given only 'to those who, repenting of having broken the sign of the covenant and of fidelity to Christ, are sincerely ready to undertake a way of life that is no longer in contradiction to the indissolubility of marriage.'"

It said that "'this means, in practice, that when for serious reasons, for example, for the children's upbringing, a man and woman cannot satisfy the obligation to separate, they "take on themselves the duty to live in complete continence, that is, by abstinence from the acts proper to married couples."' In such a case, they may receive Holy Communion as long as they respect the obligation to avoid giving scandal" (*Ibid.*).

The interior quotations are from Pope John Paul's 1981 apostolic exhortation *Familiaris Consortio*, n. 84.

Q. I have been living in continence since I returned to the Catholic Church seven years ago. My husband, who was divorced, does not want to apply for an annulment. I have regularly received the sacrament of Penance, but have not been allowed to receive Communion. Your article [above] was a total shock to me and to my priest. He has since sent it to our diocesan officials to see what my situation is.

I now have a copy of *Familiaris Consortio* and would like very much to have a copy of the letter you mentioned from the Sacred Congregation for the Doctrine of the Faith. Are these documents magisterial, or just opinions? I have been trying so hard for years to understand my position in the Church, and have never found anyone who

had any answers. Can you help me? — Name Withheld, New York

A. We would be delighted to help you. The letter from the SCDF, which is entitled *Concerning the Reception of Holy Communion by Divorced-and-Remarried Members of the Faithful*, was published in the October 27, 1994 issue of *Origins*. It can be obtained from Catholic News Service, 3211 Fourth St., N.E., Washington, DC 20017.

Yes, both *Familiaris Consortio* and the SCDF letter are magisterial documents, not mere opinions. *Familiaris Consortio* was promulgated in 1981 by the supreme teacher of the Church himself, Pope John Paul II, and the letter was issued in 1994 by Joseph Cardinal Ratzinger, the prefect of the SCDF, the congregation that is charged with defending the Catholic faith.

In fact, Cardinal Ratzinger specifically mentioned in the letter (n. 4) the responsibility of the Church's "universal magisterium, in fidelity to Sacred Scripture and Tradition, to teach and to interpret authentically the *Depositum Fidei*" (Deposit of Faith) regarding whether divorced and remarried Catholics can receive Holy Communion.

Q. My sister was married in the Catholic Church and has since divorced and remarried civilly. If my sister and her new husband were to visit, should we allow them to stay in our home since, according to the Church, she is living in a state of adultery? — C.S., California

A. Since we have answered similar questions at length in the past (cf. the first *Catholic Replies* book, pp. 316-323), let us say briefly that you could allow your sister and her husband to stay in your home, but put them in separate rooms. This will sound incredibly out-of-date to those whose values are shaped by a steady diet of adulterous relationships on soap operas and sitcoms, not to mention in public life, with nary a hint that those engaging in these relationships have put themselves on the road to Hell. But just as you would not facilitate a couple seeking an abortion, so you should not facilitate those practicing adultery.

You should keep the lines of communication open to this couple, while continuing to indicate your disapproval of their sinful lifestyle. Or as Pope John Paul said in *Familiaris Consortio*, you should maintain "tactful and respectful contact with the couples concerned, and enlighten them patiently, correct them charitably, and show them the witness of Christian family life in such a

way as to smooth the path for them to regularize their situation"
(n. 81).

**Q. Is there any Church ruling prohibiting a faithful
Catholic from being matron of honor at the marriage of a
fallen-away Catholic? It is uncertain if the marriage will
be performed before a justice of the peace, but it will not
be before a priest. When I queried the matron of honor
about this, she replied: "I admire [the bride-to-be] for not
being a hypocrite." — Name Withheld, Maryland**
A. We don't know of any Church ruling that specifically prohibits a Catholic from being matron of honor at the marriage of
a fallen-away Catholic, but it would be wrong to take part in
what probably will be an invalid marriage. You don't mention
the religion of the prospective groom, but if both parties are baptized Catholics, and they get married before a justice of the peace
or a minister, the marriage is invalid. Or if the Catholic party
marries a non-Catholic (without a dispensation) before a justice
of the peace or a minister, the marriage is invalid.

A Catholic who knowingly and willingly takes part in such a
ceremony, say, as matron of honor, says by her actions that the
marriage laws of the Church founded by Jesus Himself have little
or no meaning to her. She can hardly be called a "faithful Catholic" if she finds it so easy to reject the teachings of her Church on
marriage. If you have any influence on the matron of honor, try
to talk her out of cooperating in this probably invalid wedding.

**Q. While I had hoped to meet a good Catholic man who
was serious about marriage and family life, I have instead
fallen in love with a Jewish man. He has just made his
intention of marriage known to me. I am so impressed by
his kindness, belief in God and moral values, and warmth
of character that I feel as if I am with the person I was
made for. He knows that I am a serious Catholic and he
admires this, but I have not discussed with him what
would happen should we marry because I'm not sure yet
how to proceed. Of course, I would love it if he became a
Catholic, but this is not a simple decision. Then there is
the question of children. What should I do next? — L.J.E.,
New York**
A. Any couple that is considering marriage, even if they are
both baptized Catholics, must reach agreement in at least the

following areas before they are married: the purpose and permanence of marriage, the place of God and religious practice in their lives, the number of children they hope to have and their religious and moral training, the standard of living they hope to achieve, the role of in-laws, and the pursuit of activities outside the home.

So the first step for a couple contemplating marriage is to discuss these matters thoroughly with each other. If they find themselves strongly disagreeing about some of these issues, and they cannot work out an amicable solution, then they should cancel their plans to marry each other.

Obviously, your situation is more complicated since you are thinking of marrying a person who has not been baptized. The Catholic Church actually discourages marriages between persons of different religions because studies have shown that a high percentage of Catholics who enter mixed marriages eventually stop practicing their faith. However, your bishop can grant permission for such a marriage "if there is a just and reasonable cause" and if the three conditions of canon 1125 mentioned on pages 355-356 are fulfilled.

The pastor of the parish where the marriage preparation is to take place is responsible for determining whether there is "a just and reasonable cause" for the mixed marriage. It is up to him to decide whether the maturity of the couple, their understanding of the ends and properties of marriage, and their commitment to their respective religions are strong enough to outweigh the presumed dangers of a mixed marriage.

So once you and your prospective spouse find that you agree on the points listed at the beginning of this reply, you should consult a priest who is faithful to the teachings of the Catholic Church on marriage and ask him to explain the three sections of canon law to both of you and to guide you through the marriage preparation process.

From what you have told us, your Jewish friend sounds as if he would not be opposed to your carrying out your responsibilities as a Catholic. However, you will have to discuss these responsibilities at more length with him.

You might, for example, ask him to read the section on the sacrament of Matrimony (articles 1601-1666) in the *Catechism*, Pope John Paul's apostolic exhortation on "The Role of the Christian Family in the Modern World" (*Familiaris Consortio*), and three solid books on marriage preparation: John Kippley's *Marriage Is for Keeps*, Frederick W. Marks' *A Catholic Handbook for Engaged and Newly Married Couples*, and Fr. Robert J. Fox's and Fr. Charles Mangan's *Until Death Do Us Part*.

Finally, you should pray constantly for divine assistance to help you make the right decision.

Q. The daughter of a friend had a civil wedding with the idea of getting married in the Church in the future. Now she has three children and wants to get married in the Church, but her husband will not agree to this. Are they living in sin, and is there anything she can do if her husband will not cooperate? — D.W., Illinois

A. Your friend's daughter is in a difficult situation. She apparently wants to make things right with God and the Church, but her husband refuses to cooperate. He may be good to his family in a material or social way, but he is not very good in a spiritual way if he won't agree to being married in the Church so that his wife can return to the sacraments. If he really loves his wife, he will do all that is necessary to quiet her conscience, give her peace of mind, and end their living in sin.

True love means putting the best interests of the other person first, but one wonders if he understands what's at stake here, namely, his salvation and that of his family? Has anyone tried to talk to him in these terms? If he's not willing to return to the practice of his faith, couldn't he at least make it possible for his wife to practice hers?

What can the wife do? First of all, she can engage in persevering prayer, for herself, for her husband, and for their children. Second, she can try to come closer to God herself through a fervent prayer life, Bible reading, works of charity, acts of sacrifice and penance, and attendance at Church, even though she is unable to receive the Eucharist. Perhaps, as St. Paul said, the unbelieving husband can be converted by his believing wife (1 Corinthians 7:14).

Third, she should ask her parish priest to help her petition for a "radical sanation" of the marriage. This healing of the marriage "at the root" can be granted by the diocesan bishop, and the husband's consent is not required. This is primarily a dispensation from canonical form that validates the original consent, and the invalid union becomes valid at the moment that the competent Church authority grants the favor.

The only proviso, assuming that there are no other impediments from which the Church cannot dispense, is that the marriage consent of this couple still exists, that is, that they intend to stay married.

Q. I have always heard that the Catholic Church stood for the permanence of marriage, but now I am not sure with so many Catholics getting annulments after their divorce that it seems merely a routine procedure. I have never heard of someone saying that the annulment was not granted. Can you tell me what percentage of annulments are granted compared to the number of people applying for them? — R.B., Michigan

A. According to Dr. Edward Peters, author of the book *100 Answers to Your Questions on Annulments* (Basilica Press) and a collegiate judge on the diocesan and appellate marriage tribunals in San Diego, "America's annulment picture ... is nothing to be proud of," but the "bad news should be kept in context."

Writing in the November 1996 issue of the *Homiletic & Pastoral Review*, Peters confirmed that declarations of nullity in the United States had mushroomed from about 300 a year in 1968 to about 60,000 a year then (the number was down to about 45,000 in 2000), but said that the reasons for this huge increase included procedural changes that were approved by the Holy See.

One such change allowed petitioners to file their nullity cases in the diocese where they were currently residing rather than in the diocese where the wedding took place or in the diocese where the other party (the respondent) was currently living. He said that the changes took on added significance when they were combined with canon 1095 of the 1983 Code of Canon Law, which allowed tribunal judges to take into account the impact of mental, emotional, personal, psychological, psychiatric, and chemical traumas suffered by persons attempting marriage.

More nullity petitions are adjudged on the basis of canon 1095, said Peters, than on all the other 15 or 20 possible grounds for nullity combined. He pointed out, however, that more than one-quarter of all annulments were based on violations of canonical form (the marriage was not contracted in the presence of a priest or deacon and two witnesses), and that tribunal judges have "virtually no discretion in the handling of canonical form cases; it is as close to an utterly objective type of case as canon law has."

While some petitioners never get beyond their local pastor,

and preliminary diocesan scrutiny weeds out still more potential petitions, Peters said that about 80 percent of those cases actually accepted for adjudication by diocesan tribunals are decided in the affirmative, compared to a 62 percent affirmative rate for the Roman Rota, the Vatican tribunal that handles annulment appeals from around the world.

But according to Robert H. Vasoli, author of *What God Has Joined Together* (Oxford University Press), U.S. tribunals granted annulments in about 97 percent of the cases heard in 2000. He also said that about 95-98 percent of U.S. annulments appealed to the Roman Rota were overturned.

Editor's Note: Over the years, Pope John Paul repeatedly expressed concern over the number of marriage annulments being granted and reminded tribunal judges of canon 1676, which says that before accepting a case, judges are "to use pastoral means to induce the spouses, if at all possible, to convalidate their marriage and to restore conjugal living." He said in 1990 that valid marriages cannot be annulled "without doing violence to the truth and undermining thereby the only solid foundation which can support personal, marital, and social life."

More recently, in an address to the Roman Rota on January 28, 2002, the Holy Father said that judges "cannot give in to the divorce mentality" and must vigorously uphold "the indissoluble nature of marriage."

He said that "an unjust declaration of nullity, opposed to the truth of the normative principles or the facts, is particularly serious, since its official link with the Church encourages the spread of attitudes in which indissolubility finds verbal support, but is denied in practice."

It may seem, said John Paul, "that divorce is so firmly rooted in certain social sectors that it is almost not worth continuing to combat it by spreading a mentality, a social custom, and civil legislation in favor of the indissolubility of marriage. Yet it is indeed worth the effort!"

He said that "actually, this good is at the root of all society as a necessary condition for the existence of the family. Its absence therefore has devastating consequences that spread through the social body like a plague — to use the term of the Second Vatican Council to describe divorce (cf. *Gaudium et Spes*, n. 47) and that have a negative influence on the new generations who view as tarnished the beauty of true marriage."

Q. Can a priest marry a couple after they apply for an annulment of a previous marriage if the annulment has not been officially granted? — Name Withheld, Minnesota

A. No. As long as there is the possibility that the decree of nullity might not be granted, the priest had better wait until it's official. In his book *Annulment: The Wedding That Was* (Paulist Press), Fr. Michael Smith Foster explains canons 1682-1684 of the Code of Canon Law:

"The Church declares a marriage null only after two concordant affirmative decisions. It is incorrect to state that a marriage has been declared null after the decision of only one court. Due process involves the decision of the First Instance Court (usually known as the diocesan tribunal) and the decision of an appellate level court (either provincial or Roman). A case is pending under procedural law until the Appellate Court's decision brings about a final judgment" (p. 182).

Q. Is there any provision in the annulment process for non-Catholics married to other non-Catholics? Is it possible for them to seek annulment without being members of the Catholic Church? I am not asking for myself, but I have a number of friends in this situation. It's hard not being free to offer them congratulations, and I honestly don't know what suggestions to make. — M.D., Wyoming

A. According to canon 1671 of the 1983 Code of Canon Law, it is possible for a non-Catholic to petition a Catholic tribunal for a decree of nullity. The commentary on that canon says:

"Although the Church claims the right, by this canon, to hear the cases of two Protestants, that right is in fact never exercised unless one of the parties wishes to marry a Catholic. By the same token, even though the Church, per se, has no right to hear the marriage cases of two unbaptized people, it will, in fact, hear such cases when petitioned by one of those unbaptized spouses (cc. 1476 and 1674.1 do not require that the spouse be baptized) who wishes to marry a Catholic."

However, since your non-Catholic friends apparently have no desire to marry a Catholic, would this exclude them from seeking marriage nullity from a Catholic tribunal? Dr. Edward Peters conceded in his book *100 Answers to Your Questions on An-*

nulments that most nullity petitions which come from non-Catholics "are prompted by the desire of one (or both) parties to enter the Church or to marry a Catholic," but said that "neither condition is a requirement for filing a nullity petition" (p. 61).

For a good survey of the annulment explosion in America over the past three decades, see Robert H. Vasoli's book *What God Has Joined Together* (Oxford University Press). Mr. Vasoli, a retired Associate Professor of Sociology at the University of Notre Dame, spent eleven years studying what he calls "the annulment crisis in American Catholicism" after his own marriage was declared null by a diocesan tribunal because of defective consent. He subsequently appealed the decree of nullity, and it was reversed by two panels of judges on the Roman Rota.

While emphasizing that "there are American tribunalists who struggle valiantly for honesty, restraint, and fidelity to Church teaching on the permanence and indissolubility of marriage" (p. 10), Vasoli concluded that "a well-oiled canonical assembly line is in operation, geared to provide apparent ecclesial and judicial legitimacy for divorce and remarriage .... The American Church suffers a runaway tribunal system, bent on making annulment as easy and painless as possible" (p. 200).

Q. On the question of divorce, why is divorce allowed in Matthew 5:32 and 19:9 for lewd or adulterous acts, but nowhere else in Scripture? Everywhere else in Scripture it says that what God has joined together, let no man put asunder. — M.G., Montana

A. First, here are the words of Christ in Chapter 5 of Matthew's Gospel (New American Bible): "What I say to you is: everyone who divorces his wife — lewd conduct is a separate case — forces her to commit adultery. The man who marries a divorced woman likewise commits adultery."

That Jesus was not permitting divorce in some circumstances is clear from his unequivocal condemnation of it elsewhere (cf. Mark 10:2-12 and Luke 16:18), and from St. Paul's equally clear statement:

"To those now married, however, I give this command (though it is not mine; it is the Lord's): a wife must not separate from her husband. If she does separate, she must either remain single or become reconciled to him again. Similarly, a husband must not divorce his wife" (1 Corinthians 7:10-11).

Note that Paul says that this command is not his own, but the Lord's. So how do we explain the so-called "Matthean exception"? The key is to look at the meaning of the word *porneia*, from which we get our word pornography. Depending on the Bible you consult, the word is translated as "adultery," "lewd conduct," "fornication," "unfaithfulness," "immorality," "unchastity," and "some terrible sexual sin" (International Student Bible).

Translating *porneia* as adultery makes no sense, first of all because the ordinary Greek word for adultery is *moicheia*, and second because it would make Jesus sound ridiculous in saying that everyone who divorces his wife for adultery forces her to commit adultery!

The other translations come closer to what Christ was talking about, which was an illicit sexual union, such as concubinage, which refers to the cohabitation of persons who are not legally married. Since those Jesus was talking about only appeared to be married, the question of divorce did not apply to them. Had they truly been married, they would have come under the prohibition of divorce that the Lord handed down in the Gospels of Mark and Luke.

Editor's Note: In a recent reply regarding the correct interpretation of Jesus' words about divorce in Matthew 5:32 and 19:9, particularly the meaning of the word *porneia*, we said that the Lord was referring to the cohabitation of persons who were not legally married, and therefore that divorce did not apply to them.

Now Marty Barrack, a convert from Judaism whose book *Second Exodus* describes his journey to Catholicism, has offered some valuable insights into those disputed passages, and we are pleased to share his thoughts with our readers.

"Perhaps my Jewish background can clarify why only Matthew mentioned the *porneia* exception. Leviticus 18 prohibits incestuous marriages. In Jesus' day, many Jews were in such putative marriages. Since they were forbidden by Torah, they were not valid marriages at all. Jesus was saying, as you correctly note, that no divorce is possible except where the marriage was merely putative rather than valid.

"Since only Jews were responsible for obeying Leviticus 18, Matthew had to make the distinction explicit. Leviticus 18 refers to 'uncover the nakedness' rather than to marriage, so that people could not say, 'Well, I can't marry her but I can have sex with her.' As you know, the Hebrew Scriptures always referred to the marital act delicately. Adam (Gn 4:1) 'knew Eve his wife.' Where the relationship was not covered by marriage, it was still described fairly delicately. Abraham (Gn 16:4) 'went into Hagar,' that is, entered her tent or bedchamber. Judah had said to Onan (Gn 38:8), 'Go into your brother's wife, and perform the duty of a brother-in-law.'

"The language became more explicit only when describing more sinful behavior. Consider the language of Gn 9:22 ('saw the nakedness'). The innocent reader might think that's all it was until he finds Gn 9:24 ('...and knew what his youngest son had done to him'). 'Uncover the nakedness' is comparable, used to describe sexual relationships that were not only non-marital but incestuous. We also find an angry description of King David's great sin when he (2 Sm 11:4) 'lay with' Bathsheba.

"I can think of only two places where Hebrew Scripture gets still more angrily explicit by describing the voluntary emission of seed, when Onan (Gn 38:9) 'spilled the seed on the ground' and when Ezekiel scathingly compared faithless Israel to a harlot who (Ez 23:20) 'doted upon her paramours there, whose members were like those of asses, and whose issue was like that of horses.'

"Hope this helps."

Q. What is the Catholic Church's teaching on the morality of using such medications as Viagra to correct problems of sexual dysfunction? Also, what kind of marital foreplay is permitted between a husband and wife? — D.C.D., Texas

A. Regarding the parameters of sexual intimacy between husband and wife, enclose a dollar in a stamped, self-addressed envelope, send it to the Couple to Couple League, P.O. Box 111184, Cincinnati, OH 45211, and ask for John Kippley's pamphlet *Marital Sexuality: Moral Considerations.*

As for the use of drugs like Viagra, we are indebted to Dr. Peter J. Cataldo, Director of Research at the National Catholic Bioethics Center in Boston (www.ncbcenter.org), for providing guidance on the morality of prescribing Viagra. His comments can also be applied to using the drug.

"In order to avoid formal cooperation in any possible intrinsically immoral acts by the patient as a result of using a Viagra prescription, the prescribing physician should prescribe Viagra only to married men with erectile dysfunction. Moreover, it should be prescribed on the assumption that the drug will only be used to assist the patient in the performance of conjugal acts with the patient's wife.

"If a physician has morally certain knowledge to the contrary regarding how the medication will be used, he or she cannot rightly prescribe it. Such moral certainty is not usually possessed by the physician. However, to prescribe Viagra to a patient knowing he will use the medication for the purpose of engaging in morally disordered activity is, it seems, to commit formal cooperation in those intrinsically immoral acts. To prescribe under these circumstances is to intend to help the individual perform an immoral act.

"The physician should inform the patient of all possible side-effects, as he or she should in any case. I do not think that the physician has a moral obligation to educate the patient about the moral ramifications of acting contrary to Catholic teaching on sexuality."

In short, then, the moral use of Viagra is restricted to a married man with erectile dysfunction, only for assisting in conjugal relations between this man and his wife, and only if there are no side effects from the drug that would be harmful to his health.

Q. I remember hearing at a Pre-Cana conference for engaged couples some years ago that sensual thoughts about someone other than one's married partner were not sinful prior to or during marital relations with one's spouse. I wonder how this can be reconciled with Christ's injunction against lust in the heart. — Name and State Withheld

A. If this is what you heard at a Pre-Cana conference, the person offering this opinion was encouraging marital unchastity and was speaking against the teaching of Christ and His Church. It is wrong for married couples to entertain sexual thoughts about another person, just as it is wrong for them to use pornographic materials to bring on sexual excitement, because such actions can arouse toward another person the adulterous sexual desire that Christ warned against. Here is how Christopher West explains this point in his book *Good News About Sex & Marriage*:

"Spouses must be faithful to each other not only in action but also in thought. For example, fantasizing about someone else while engaging in sexual relations with your spouse would be a blatant violation of fidelity. Right at the moment when spouses should be expressing their unyielding fidelity to each other, they would actually be committing 'adultery in their heart' (see Mt 5:28) with someone else. This is one of the reasons that the use of pornography is so devastating to a marriage. It does nothing but feed and foster this type of infidelity" (p. 91).

Recall, too, that Pope John Paul, in a general audience on October 8, 1980, warned that husbands and wives could even commit adultery in their hearts by looking lustfully at each other. You may remember the uproar this caused in the news media at the time. The media failed to grasp, however, that the Holy Father did not mean by this that spouses should not try to arouse each other by looks, but rather that they should not use each other "only as an object to satisfy instinct."

Q. My diocese has formed a Catholic Singles Group that puts single Catholics together for dancing, games, and dinners. The group is composed of single and divorced Catholics. Would it be an appropriate requirement for divorced Catholics to provide proof of annulments upon joining such a group since its purpose is to form relationships that could lead to marriage? — M.B., Colorado

A. It is laudable to want to help those whose marriage ended in divorce and who now find themselves alone and out of the social and cultural loop, so to speak. But it is not laudable, especially under Church auspices, to put divorced people in situations that could lead them to remarry outside the Church and thus enter into a permanent state of adultery.

In *Familiaris Consortio*, Pope John Paul expressed pastoral concern over the "loneliness and other difficulties" that are often the lot of the divorced. He went on to say, however, that such people, "being well aware that the valid marriage bond is indissoluble, [must] refrain from becoming involved in a new union and devote themselves solely to carrying out their family duties and the responsibilities of Christian life."

He said that "in such cases, their example of fidelity and Christian consistency takes on particular value as a witness before the world and the Church. Here it is even more necessary for the

Church to offer continual love and assistance, without there being any obstacle to admission to the sacraments" (n. 83).

Persons whose marriages have been irretrievably broken by divorce ought to look into whether they might be eligible for a decree of nullity before they become romantically involved with another person. The tendency today is to return to the dating scene, and even to make marriage plans, without any assurance that a first marriage will be declared null.

When a decree of nullity is not forthcoming, which does happen, the couple is faced with the choice of ending their relationship or attempting marriage outside the Church, and unfortunately the latter option is often the one chosen.

Chapter 12

On Human Life

Q. If scientists are successful in cloning human beings, will the Church consider them ensouled? If not, what moral status will the Church accord cloned human beings? — L.L., Ohio

A. If a cloned human being is alive, then he must have a human soul that was infused by God. The soul is the life-principle; without it we are dead, as is the person lying in the casket at the funeral home who just a day or two before was alive and well. What's missing from the dead person in the funeral home? His soul. If bodily death means the absence of a soul, then bodily life, even cloned life, means the presence of a soul.

In its 1987 document *Donum Vitae*, the Sacred Congregation for the Doctrine of the Faith said that "attempts or hypotheses for obtaining a human being without any connection with sexuality through 'twin fission,' cloning, or parthenogenesis are to be considered contrary to the moral law since they are in opposition to the dignity both of human procreation and of the conjugal union" (part 1, n. 6).

Q. In a column some time ago, you said that "if a cloned human being is alive, then he must have a human soul that was infused by God. The soul is the life-principle; without it we are dead." With all due respect, your major premise is taken for granted and therefore your conclusion could be incorrect. For example, using your reasoning, one could say if the soul is the life-principle and without it one is dead, then it follows that even cows, dogs, cats, and all animals that live have a soul. But we know that is not so. — L.V., Louisiana

A. But it is so. All living things have a life-giving principle. Plant life is characterized by such activities as growth and nourishment through soil and air. A rock cannot do these things because it is not alive. The sensitive life that is found in animals is characterized by growth and nourishment (the same as plants), but also by feeling, tasting, seeing, and hearing. Animals can do all that plants can, plus something more.

The rational and intellectual life that is found only in humans enjoys the same activities as plants and animals, plus the ability to think, to choose, and to love. Unlike the plant soul and the animal soul, the human soul is also immortal.

The *Catechism* (n. 363) says that in the Bible the term "soul" often refers "to human *life* or the entire human *person* [cf. *Mt* 16:25-26; *Jn* 15:13; *Acts* 2:41]," but it also refers to "the innermost aspect of man, that which is of greatest value in him [cf. *Mt* 10:28; 26:38; *Jn* 12:27; *2 Macc* 6:30], that by which he is most especially in God's image."

The *Catechism* (nn. 363, 366) teaches that "soul" signifies "the *spiritual principle* in man," that "every spiritual soul is created immediately by God — it is not 'produced' by the parents — and also that it is immortal: it does not perish when it separates from the body at death, and it will be reunited with the body at the final Resurrection [cf. Pius XII, *Humani Generis*: DS 3896; Paul VI, *CPG* § 8; Lateran Council V (1513): DS 1440]."

Q. I am a seminarian from Brunei studying in the United States. Can you explain to me what the controversy over stem cell research is about? Do we need to take stem cells from aborted babies or frozen human embryos in order to cure disease in adults? — R.L., Massachusetts

A. Wesley J. Smith, author of *Culture of Death: The Assault on Medical Ethics in America*, said in the Spring 2001 issue of *Human Life Review* that "stem cells are undifferentiated 'master cells' in the body that can develop into differentiated tissues, such as bone, muscle, nerve, or skin. Stem cell research may lead to exponential improvements in the treatment of many terminal and debilitating conditions, from cancer to Parkinson's to Alzheimer's to diabetes to heart disease."

He reported several recent scientific breakthroughs in experiments on animals, and noted that "none of these remarkable achievements relied on the use of stem cells from embryos or the products of abortion. Indeed, all of these experiments involved adult stem cells or undifferentiated stem cells obtained from other non-embryo sources."

According to Smith, umbilical cord blood is a "potentially inexhaustible source of stem cells since four million babies are born in the United States alone each year." So there is no need to destroy human embryos or get tissue from aborted babies to obtain vast quantities of stem cells.

Contrary to the popular wisdom, he said, fetal stem cells may actually constitute a danger to adults. For example, the *New England Journal of Medicine* reported on March 8, 2001 that the injection of fetal brain cells into the brains of Parkinson's disease patients had "utterly devastating" effects on the patients. These effects included writhing, twisting, head-jerking, arm-flailing, and constant chewing. One patient can no longer eat because of the treatment and required insertion of a feeding tube.

Smith also noted the warning of University of Pennsylvania bioethicist Glenn McGee, who told the MIT publication *Technology Review*: "The emerging truth in the lab is that pluripotent stem cells are hard to rein in. The potential that they would explode into a cancerous mass after a stem cell transplant might turn out to be the Pandora's box of stem cell research."

So why the aggressive campaign for federal funding for embryo and fetal research? And why do the media play down the good results from using adult stem cells, and virtually ignore the dangers of using fetal cells? Wesley Smith suggested three reasons: celebrities, abortion, and eugenics.

(1) The full federal funding of embryo research has been promoted by TV stars Michael J. Fox, who has Parkinson's disease; Mary Tyler Moore, who is afflicted with diabetes; and Christopher Reeve, who is paralyzed from the neck down.

(2) When pro-lifers express concern about destruction of human embryos, the pro-abortion side seizes the public relations high ground of compassionate concern for those suffering from disease and say that this proves pro-lifers don't care about people after they are born.

(3) But the ultimate purpose of this campaign, said Smith, "is to open the door to eugenic manipulations of the human genome. Once embryos can be exploited for their stem cells to promote human welfare, what is to stop scientists from manipulating embryos to control and direct human evolution?"

The proper course of action, said Smith, should not be to get caught up in the battle over federal funding, but rather to "focus our public resources with laser-like intensity on the incredible potential of adult and alternative sources of stem cells."

We also need to keep reminding people that the good end of curing disease can never be justified morally if it is achieved by the evil means of destroying human life.

Q. As the parents of nine children (ages five months to 14 years), how can we best reply when asked the questions: Were they all planned, and are we planning any more? And when our acquaintances make disparaging remarks about our large family, should we say something in defense or remain silent? — C.M., Michigan

A. Having been in exactly the same situation you are in now (our oldest was 14 when our ninth child was born), I can appreciate what you are going through. Shortly after our first child was born, my wife and I received a letter from Planned Parenthood congratulating us but at the same time urging us to limit the size of our family. We wrote back to PP, told it that we planned, with the help of God, to have a dozen children, and signed the letter, "Yours for a population explosion."

We never heard from them again.

What do you tell those who ask insensitive questions or make crude remarks? You tell them that children are a gift from God and you will accept as many gifts as the Lord sends you. Tell them that you are, in the words of Vatican II, "ready with stout hearts to cooperate with the love of the Creator and Savior, who through [you] will enlarge and enrich his own family day by day" (*Constitution on the Church in the Modern World*, n. 50).

And, really, that's what it's all about — cooperating with God in increasing the size of His family and giving more children the opportunity to know, love, and serve Him in this life so that they can be happy with Him forever in the next life.

Q. According to statistics, most married women today practice contraception. Since I am an orthodox Catholic man who is against contraception, what should be my attitude toward a prospective wife with no qualms about contraception, one who says that priests close an eye to it in the confessional and who refuses to practice Natural Family Planning? In short, would I be morally justified in having relations with her if she used contraceptives? — R.D.B., New York

A. It should be obvious that two people who intend to marry ought to be in total agreement about something as fundamental to the marriage covenant as procreation. A man and woman who are poles apart on the morality of contraception shouldn't get married until they can agree to live according to God's plan since a husband, or wife, who has marital relations with a spouse who practices contraception would be guilty of cooperating in sinful actions.

The prospective, or actual, spouse who recognizes contraception as evil must strive to educate his or her partner as to the reasons why the Church condemns contraception and recommends Natural Family Planning for those couples with serious reasons to space out the births of their children.

Some resources that would be helpful in this educational process would include Pope Paul VI's encyclical on human life (*Humanae Vitae*), Pope John Paul II's exhortation *Familiaris Consortio*, *Why Humanae Vitae Was Right: A Reader*, edited by Janet E. Smith (see also her excellent audio and video tapes on this topic), and John F. Kippley's book *Sex and the Marriage Covenant* (Couple to Couple League).

The Couple to Couple League also has some excellent pamphlets available on marital chastity and NFP, as well as a valuable newsletter (*CCL Family Foundations*) that is published six times a year and is sent to all those who contribute at least $18 a year.

Those interested in NFP should get a copy of John and Sheila Kippley's book *The Art of Natural Family Planning*, also available from the Couple to Couple League.

Q. With so many Catholics apparently practicing the sin of contraception and at the same time going to Holy Communion, and with so many priests apparently telling them that it is not a sin to engage in contraceptive behavior, aren't these priests also committing a sin when they give this counsel? — J.J.H., New York

A. We agree that polls show many Catholics not adhering to the Church's ban on contraception, and that some priests have told penitents in Confession that contraception is not sinful, but only God knows how many Catholics practicing contraception are in a state of mortal sin. None of us is competent to judge the state of a person's soul, nor should we attempt to do so.

Contraception is definitely objectively evil, but whether it's a mortal sin for a particular individual depends, as always, on whether the person sufficiently understands that this is grave matter and deliberately consents to practice it anyway. A person who engages in contraception on the advice of a priest, whom he or she sincerely believes to be stating the Church's teaching on the matter, may not be guilty of subjective mortal sin.

As for a priest who disagrees with the Church's teaching on contraception, and who misleads a penitent about the matter, he is guilty of scandal, of leading the penitent into sin. He is also guilty of flagrantly disregarding the command of Pope Paul VI in *Humanae Vitae* "to expound the Church's teaching on marriage without ambiguity" (n. 28). The Holy Father continued:

"To diminish in no way the saving teaching of Christ constitutes an eminent form of charity for souls. But this must ever be accompanied by patience and goodness, such as the Lord himself gave example of in dealing with men. Having come not to condemn but to save, he was intransigent with evil, but merciful toward individuals. In their difficulties, may married couples always find, in the words and in the heart of a priest, the echo of the voice and the love of the Redeemer" (n. 29).

Editor's Note: Following up on Pope Paul's statement about the obligation of priests to present the Church's teaching on marriage "without ambiguity," John Kippley reminded us of an even stronger statement by Pope Pius XI in his 1930 encyclical on Christian marriage *(Casti Connubii)*. After declaring that "any use whatsoever of matrimony exercised in such a way that the act is deliberately frustrated in its natural power to generate life is an offense against the law of God and of nature, and those who indulge in such are branded with the guilt of a grave sin," Pius XI said:

"We admonish, therefore, priests who hear confessions and others who have the care of souls, in virtue of our supreme authority and in our solicitude for the salvation of souls, not to allow the faithful entrusted to them to err regarding this most grave law of God; much more, that they keep themselves immune from such false opinions, in no way conniving in them.

"If any confessor or pastor of souls, which may God forbid, lead the faithful entrusted to him into these errors or should at least confirm them by approval or by guilty silence, let him be mindful of the fact that he must render a strict account to God, the Supreme Judge, for the betrayal of his sacred trust, and let him take to himself the words of Christ: 'They are blind and leaders of the blind: and if the blind lead the blind, both fall into the pit' " (nn. 56-57).

Q. Prior to his *Humanae Vitae* encyclical, Pope Paul VI convened a commission to study the contraception question. I have never understood or heard why he did this. If contraception has always been taught by the Church to be a mortal sin, why didn't the Pope just issue a statement to that effect? Surely he was not contemplating a change in Church teaching? — B.B., Ontario

A. First of all, it was Pope John XXIII who convened the Papal Commission for the Study of Problems of the Family, Population, and Birth Rate. After John's death in 1963, Pope Paul asked the Commission to continue its work and eventually increased its membership to more than 60 persons, including cardinals, bishops, doctors, married couples, and experts on population matters.

There is no official statement as to why the Commission was convened, although its name suggests some reasons for its existence. In her book *Humanae Vitae: A Generation Later*, Dr. Janet E. Smith offered this explanation:

"Its original purpose seemed to have been a rather broad study of the Church's teaching on marriage but came to focus on contraception. It seems possible that Paul VI never really questioned the prohibition against contraception but that he did have doubts about the status of the Pill and wanted a more updated defense of the Church's teaching in light of contemporary problems, such as population" (p. 13).

In the first six paragraphs of *Humanae Vitae*, Paul VI said that the purpose of this latest Church statement on human life, and presumably that of the Commission itself, was to address such matters as rapid population growth, the economic and educational concerns of those with large families, the person of the woman and her place in society, the meaning of conjugal love, and whether the "principle of totality" could be applied here by excusing individual acts of contraception if the totality of married love was open to new life.

That Paul VI was not contemplating a change in the Church's ban on contraception is indicated by his intervention in 1965, three years before *Humanae Vitae*, in the final version of Vatican II's *Pastoral Constitution on the Church in the Modern World*, particularly the insertion of footnote 14.

Following the statement that "sons of the Church may not

undertake methods of regulating procreation which are found blameworthy by the teaching authority of the Church in its unfolding of the divine law," the footnote cited Pius XI's *Casti Connubii*, which, as noted earlier, called any deliberate act of contraception "an offense against the law of God and of nature and ... a grave sin."

Janet Smith quoted Bernard Haering as saying that when he was invited to join the Commission, "I received from officials on all levels of the Holy Office unequivocal instructions and warnings that I was to keep precisely within the framework of *Casti Connubii*. However, efforts to restrain freedom of speech were only partially successful" (p. 14).

Q. When someone on the radio said that contraception was not condemned in the Bible, I called in and pointed out that the sin of Onan (Genesis 38:9) was coitus interruptus, that he intended this as a form of birth control, and that God promptly struck Onan dead. The fellow on the radio said that "all the theologians today" believe that God struck Onan dead for violating the Levirate law [requiring a man to marry his brother's widow if the brother died before they had children] and failing to fulfill his duty as Tamar's brother-in-law, not for practicing contraception. What do you say? — J.C., Illinois

A. In his book *Sex and the Marriage Covenant*, John Kippley devoted eight pages (309-316) to refuting the opinion of "all the theologians today." He noted, first of all, that "for centuries the most common form of contraceptive behavior was coitus interruptus, and Onanism was the general term for all forms of contraception. He said that the anti-contraception interpretation of the Onan account was challenged during the birth control debate in the mid-1960s by those who wanted to see the Church change her teaching to allow contraceptive actions.

While one ought to read Kippley's full discussion of this matter, let us mention briefly his points that "there is utterly no support for the Levirate-only interpretation either in Scripture or Tradition"; that the anti-contraception interpretation has been upheld by St. Augustine, John Calvin, Martin Luther, and dozens of Protestant theologians (cf. Charles Provan's book *The Bible and Birth Control*); and that two other persons who violated the Levirate — Onan's father Judah and his brother Shelah — were not struck dead.

"When three people are guilty of the same crime but only one of them receives the death penalty from God," says Kippley, "common sense requires that we ask if that one did something the others did not do. The answer is obvious: Only Onan went through the motions of the covenantal act of intercourse but then defrauded its purpose and meaning; only Onan engaged in the contraceptive behavior of withdrawal."

Q. I remember reading that Mahatma Gandhi, the Hindu leader, made some strong statements against birth control. Is this true? — C.C., Michigan
A. Yes, it is true. "Self-control is the surest and the only method of regulating birth," Gandhi said. "Birth control by contraceptives is race suicide" (*Young India*, September 16, 1926). He said that "contraceptives are an insult to womanhood. The difference between a prostitute and a woman using contraceptives is only that the former sells her body to several men, the latter sells it to one man" (*Harijan*, May 5, 1946).

Gandhi ridiculed the notion that "the use of contraception will be restricted to the mere regulation of progeny. There is hope for a decent life only so long as the sexual act is definitely related to the conception of precious life. This rules out perverted sexuality and to a lesser degree promiscuity. Divorce of sexual act from its natural consequence must lead to hideous promiscuity and condonation, if not endorsement, of natural vice" (*Harijan*, October 3, 1936).

But what about the population problems faced by countries like India? In a letter sent on March 20, 1924 to the Bombay Birth Control League, Gandhi said:

"If it is contended that birth control is necessary for a nation because of overpopulation, I dispute the proposition. It has never been proved. In my opinion, by a proper land system, better agriculture, and a supplementary industry, this country [India] is capable of supporting twice as many people as there are in it today.

"I am totally opposed to artificial means of controlling the birthrate, and it is not possible for me to congratulate you or your co-workers on having brought into being a league whose activities, if successful, can only do great moral injury to the people. I wish I could convince you and your co-workers to disband the league and devote your energy to a better purpose. You will pardon me for giving my opinion in a decisive manner" (*The Collected Works of Mahatma Gandhi*, volumes 2 and 4, quoted on pp. 290-291 of Brian Clowes' book *The Facts of Life*).

Q. In a recent column, you explained that contraceptive practices are intrinsically evil regardless of intentions or circumstances. My question is this: my husband has herpes and when he experiences the symptoms we use a condom to avoid infection to myself. Is such an act intrinsically evil if the purpose is not to prevent conception? — Name Withheld, California

A. Reliable Catholic moral theologians, such as Germain Grisez, contend that using a condom in marital intercourse is wrong, even if the intention is not contraceptive. In his book *Difficult Moral Questions*, Grisez said that " 'intercourse' with a condom is not truly intercourse, and so cannot be marital intercourse, even if the intention is, not to prevent conception, but to prevent the transmission of disease" (p. 160).

Furthermore, said Grisez in replying to a question about whether a parent should advise a teenager to practice so-called safe sex, condoms are notoriously unreliable in protecting a person from a venereal disease. He compared them to umbrellas:

"Umbrellas often keep you from getting soaked when you must go out in a heavy rain. But they don't keep the rain off you entirely, and sometimes the wind blows them around, despite your best efforts to hold them steady, and they tear or turn inside out, and you do get soaked. If your life depended on not getting rained on, I wouldn't tell you: 'Don't go out in the rain without your umbrella.' No, I'd just tell you: 'Never go out in the rain!'

"Now, when people engage in sexual intercourse and try to protect themselves by using a condom, their lives may well depend on its working perfectly. But condoms are like umbrellas. They sometimes break, tear, leak, or slip off entirely. So, nobody should imagine that condoms make risky sex safe" (p. 103).

Q. In the past you have said that while contraception is objectively wrong, whether it's a mortal sin for the particular individual "depends on whether that person sufficiently understands that contraception is grave matter and deliberately consents to practice it. A person who

practices birth control on the advice of a priest, whom he sincerely believes to be stating the Church's position on the matter, may not be guilty of subjective mortal sin." Can you give me the names of magisterial documents where I may find such teaching? — J.A.D., Virginia

A. On the conditions for a mortal sin, see nn. 1857-1860 of the *Catechism*, and particularly n. 1857, which says: " 'Mortal sin is sin whose object is grave matter and which is also committed with full knowledge and deliberate consent' [*RP* 17 § 12]."

Paragraph 2370 of the *Catechism* quoted from *Humanae Vitae*, which described as intrinsically evil "every action which, whether in anticipation of the conjugal act, or in its accomplishment, or in the development of its natural consequences, proposes, whether as an end or as a means, to render procreation impossible [*HV* 14]."

This clear teaching of the Church was reiterated on March 1, 1997 by the Pontifical Council for the Family in a document entitled a *Vade Mecum for Confessors Concerning Some Aspects of the Morality of Conjugal Life*. According to the introduction, the purpose of the document was to offer confessors "some practical guidelines for the confession and absolution of the faithful in matters of conjugal chastity." This is necessary, the Pontifical Council said, because "a certain void has been forming with regard to implementing these teachings in pastoral practice."

The Vatican body went on to say that "priests, in their catechesis and in their preparation of couples for marriage, are asked to maintain uniform criteria with regard to the evil of the contraceptive act, both in their teaching and in the area of the Sacrament of Reconciliation, in complete fidelity to the magisterium of the Church. Bishops are to take particular care to be vigilant in this regard, for not infrequently the faithful are scandalized by this lack of unity, both in the area of catechesis, as well as in the Sacrament of Reconciliation" (n. 16).

We do not know of a magisterial statement that says a person who practices contraception on the faulty advice of a dissident priest or theologian may not be subjectively guilty of a mortal sin, but we think that is a reasonable conclusion based on the magisterial statements quoted above.

Q. (1) Pope John Paul II has called contraception a "grave" sin. Is this the same thing as what we used to call a mortal sin? (2) If a person is practicing contraception,

knowing that it is wrong, can any number of good works make up for that practice? — C.M.C., Indiana

A. (1) Yes, grave sin is mortal sin (cf. the *Catechism*, nn. 1855 and 1857), and the *Catechism* (n. 2370) calls methods of birth regulation that render procreation impossible, such as artificial contraception, "intrinsically evil [*HV* 14]."

Pope John Paul reiterated this moral judgment on many occasions. For example, on September 17, 1983, he told a group of priests that "contraception is to be judged objectively so profoundly unlawful as never to be, for any reason, justified. To think or to say the contrary is equal to maintaining that, in human life, situations may arise in which it is lawful not to recognize God as God."

(2) If a person is deliberately practicing contraception, knowing that it is a grave moral evil, no amount of good works can make up for or cancel out repeated mortal sins. The person must sincerely repent of his sins and obtain forgiveness through the Sacrament of Penance before he can receive the graces that flow from good works.

Q. It is my understanding that *Humanae Vitae* not only nixed artificial birth control, but also taught that recourse to Natural Family Planning (NFP) is only permitted for "grave reasons." What does the Church mean by "grave"? Do Catholics have a moral obligation to have as many children as possible, relying on God's providence to care for them? — G.L., Virginia

A. In *Humanae Vitae*, Pope Paul VI said that married couples could use NFP when "there are serious motives to space out births, which derive from the physical or psychological conditions of husband and wife, or from external conditions" (n. 16). Note that the Holy Father said "serious" not "grave" motives.

What might these serious motives be? Vatican II's *Pastoral Constitution on the Church in the Modern World* explained that married couples "will thoughtfully take into account both their own welfare and that of their children, those already born and those which may be foreseen. For this accounting they will reckon with both the material and the spiritual conditions of the times, as well as of their state in life. Finally, they will consult the interests of the family group, of temporal society, and of the Church herself" (n. 50).

Pope John Paul also spoke about the meaning of responsible

parenthood on many occasions. For example, in his homily on the Washington Mall on October 7, 1979, the Holy Father said:

"Decisions about the number of children and the sacrifices to be made for them must not be taken only with a view of adding to comfort and preserving a peaceful existence. Reflecting upon this matter before God, with the graces drawn from the sacrament [of Matrimony], and guided by the teaching of the Church, parents will remind themselves that it is certainly less serious to deny their children certain comforts or material advantages than to deprive them of the presence of brothers and sisters, who could help them to grow in humanity and to realize the beauty of life at all its ages and in all its variety."

On December 14, 1990, John Paul told a group of NFP instructors that in cooperating with the divine plan of the Creator, spouses "are called, out of respect for the objective moral order established by God, to an obligatory *discernment of the indications of God's will concerning their family*. Thus, in relationship to physical, economic, psychological, and social conditions, responsible parenthood will be able to be expressed 'either by the deliberate and generous decision to raise a large family, or by the decision, made for serious moral reasons and with due respect for the moral law, to avoid for the time being, or even for an indeterminate period, another birth.' " (The interior quotation is from *Humanae Vitae*, n. 10).

For a fuller discussion of this subject, see pages 59-75 of John Kippley's book *Sex and the Marriage Covenant*.

Q. I have heard it said that the difference beween contraception and Natural Family Planning is that contraception involves taking deliberate steps before, during, or after the marital act to prevent pregnancy, while NFP involves no marital act at all, that contraception means doing something, while NFP means doing nothing. This is incorrect since couples using NFP do do something — they deliberately abstain from sex relations during the fertile period, and this is just as positive an act as using a contraceptive. — J.P.W., Delaware

A. In his apostolic letter on the family (*Familiaris Consortio*), Pope John Paul offered a lengthy explanation of the difference between contraception and NFP. Here is what he said:

"When couples, by means of recourse to contraception, separate these two meanings [unitive and procreative] that God the Creator has inscribed in the being of man and woman and in the dynamism of their sexual communion, they act as 'arbiters' of the divine plan and they 'manipulate' and degrade human sexuality — and with it themselves and their married partner — by altering its value of 'total' self-giving.

"Thus the innate language that expresses the total reciprocal self-giving of husband and wife is overlaid, through contraception, by an objectively contradictory language, namely, that of not giving oneself totally to the other. This leads not only to a positive refusal to be open to life, but also to a falsification of the inner truth of conjugal love, which is called upon to give itself in personal totality.

"When, instead, by means of recourse to periods of infertility, the couple respect the inseparable connection between the unitive and procreative meanings of human sexuality, they are acting as 'ministers' of God's plan and they 'benefit from' their sexuality according to the original dynamism of 'total' self-giving, without manipulation or alteration.

"In the light of the experience of many couples and of the data provided by the different human sciences, technological reflection is able to perceive and is called to study further the difference, both anthropological and moral, between contraception and recourse to the rhythm of the cycle: It is a difference which is much wider and deeper than is usually thought, one which involves in the final analysis two irreconcilable concepts of the human person and of human sexuality. The choice of the natural rhythms involves accepting the cycle of the person, that is, the woman, and thereby accepting dialog, reciprocal respect, shared responsibility, and self-control.

"To accept the cycle and to enter into dialog means to recognize both the spiritual and corporal character of conjugal communion, and to live personal love with its requirement of fidelity. In this context the couple comes to experience how conjugal communion is enriched with those values of tenderness and affection which constitute the inner soul of human sexuality, in its physical dimension also.

"In this way sexuality is respected and promoted in its truly and fully human dimension, and is never 'used' as an 'object' that, by breaking the personal unity of soul and body, strikes at

God's creation itself at the level of the deepest interaction of nature and person" (n. 32).

In other words, the Holy Father is saying that NFP requires the loving cooperation of both parties, rather than putting all the burden on one spouse, usually the woman, who endangers her health by taking powerful drugs or using dangerous devices. The dialogue between a husband and wife using NFP can enhance the respect, increase the affection, and deepen the love that they feel for one another, which helps to explain why NFP couples have a divorce rate of only two percent, far below that of contracepting couples.

For more on this issue, see Christopher West's book *Good News About Sex & Marriage*.

Q. Can you please tell me what is the morally acceptable procedure to prevent pregnancy after rape ? — M.S., State Unknown

A. This question was answered in the document *Ethical and Religious Directives for Catholic Health Care Services*, which was issued in 2001 by the United States Conference of Catholic Bishops. Directive No. 36 reads as follows:

"Compassionate and understanding care should be given to a person who is the victim of sexual assault. Health care providers should cooperate with law enforcement officials, offer the person psychological and spiritual support as well as accurate medical information. A female who has been raped should be able to defend herself against a potential conception from the sexual assault. If, after appropriate testing, there is no evidence that conception has occurred already, she may be treated with medications that would prevent ovulation, sperm capacitation, or fertilization. It is not permissible, however, to initiate or to recommend treatments that have as their purpose or direct effect the removal, destruction, or interference with the implantation of a fertilized ovum."

A footnote recommends that "a sexually assaulted woman be advised of the ethical restrictions that prevent Catholic hospitals from using abortifacient procedures."

Q. Please comment on the enclosed article in which Dominican moral theologian Fr. Kevin D. O'Rourke said

that Catholic moral theology approves the use of the drug Ovral to prevent conception by victims of rape. But isn't Ovral an abortifacient, and on what sound moral grounds may an abortifacient be used? — R.P. New York

A. There are no sound moral grounds that would permit the use of an abortifacient to prevent conception following a sexual assault. Writing about recourse to pregnancy preventive medications in the event of rape in the November 1998 issue of *Ethics & Medics*, Msgr. Jeremiah J. McCarthy and Fr. Richard B. Benson said that "there is widespread consensus among Catholic moralists that such measures are permissible and can be used if it is clear that they are contraceptive, that is, 'preventive,' and not 'abortifacient.' By 'abortifacient' we mean a medication that achieves its effect by destroying the fertilized ovum rather than by preventing the union of sperm and ovum."

Since rape violently breaks "the indispensable linkage between the unitive and procreative meanings of human sexuality," the two priests said, "it is morally permissible to intervene, on the basis of self-defense, to prevent the undesired pregnancy. The difficulty is that, until now, no clear medical evidence has been available to support the view that medications such as Ovral are exclusively contraceptive."

They noted that a long search of medical literature by Fr. Luke Dysinger, a Benedictine priest, medical doctor, and theologian, "could find no conclusive evidence that Ovral functioned in an exclusively contraceptive manner. That is, the evidence is not clear that Ovral does not also function as an 'abortifacient.' Since this abortifacient effect cannot be conclusively ruled out, Ovral is not a morally safe option."

Q. In your book *Catholicism and Ethics*, you state that it is morally permissible to remove a tubal pregnancy to save the mother's life, even though the baby will die. Can you cite any Church teaching to back this up? — C.K., Wisconsin

A. We are not aware of a specific Church statement on the morality of removing a fallopian tube containing an ectopic pregnancy, but reliable Catholic moralists have long held that this does not constitute a direct abortion since the intention of the operation is not to kill the baby but to save the life of the mother, and that therefore such surgery is morally permissible under the principle of the double effect.

According to that principle, an act having both a good and bad effect can be performed under four conditions: (1) The act must be morally good or at least morally neutral. (2) The good effect must come directly from the act itself and not as a result of the bad effect. (3) The good must be willed and the evil merely allowed or tolerated. (4) The good effect must be at least equivalent in importance to the bad effect.

Applying these conditions to the case in question, we see that removal of the tube is a good act, that saving the mother's life results from this act and not from the death of the baby, that the life-saving surgery is willed and the death of the baby is merely tolerated, and that saving the life of the mother is equal in importance to the unfortunate death of the child.

Let us quote from two Catholic moral theologians noted for their fidelity to the magisterium. First is Fr. Heribert Jone, who in his 1961 book *Moral Theology* (TAN Books) said that indirect killing of an unborn child may be permitted for grave reasons. "In case of an ectopic pregnancy which endangers the mother's life," he said, "the pathological formation may lawfully be removed, even though the foetus will be removed together with it, provided, however, one cannot otherwise save the mother and surgical intervention can no longer be postponed" (p. 138).

Echoing Jone in a 1993 book, *Living a Christian Life* (Franciscan Press), Germain Grisez said that sometimes the baby's death may be accepted to save the mother if four conditions are simultaneously fulfilled: "(i) Some pathology threatens the lives of both a pregnant woman and her child, (ii) it is not safe to wait or waiting surely will result in the death of both, (iii) there is no way to save the child, and (iv) an operation that can save the mother's life will result in the child's death" (p. 502).

Grisez went on to say that "if the operation was one of those which the classical moralists considered not to be a 'direct' abortion, they held that it could be performed. For example, in cases in which the baby could not be saved regardless of what was done (and perhaps in some others as well), they accepted the removal of a cancerous gravid uterus or of a fallopian tube containing an ectopic pregnancy. This moral norm plainly is sound since the operation does not carry out a proposal to kill the child, serves a good purpose, and violates neither fairness nor mercy."

He added in a footnote that "if the embryo could be transplanted from the tube to the uterus and both persons saved, it hardly would be fair to allow the baby to die."

Q. Please discuss the morality of the surgical separation of the twin sisters in England. — W.C.S., Connecticut

A. Before getting to the morality of the surgery, here is the background. Twin girls Jodie and Mary (not their real names) were joined together at the abdomen at birth. While Jodie had a functioning heart and lungs, Mary's heart functioned at only 10 percent, her lungs did not work at all, and she was entirely dependent on Jodie.

The Catholic parents of the twins refused to consider surgery, saying that they were opposed to killing one twin in order for the other to survive and that they were willing to accept the deaths of both children as "God's will." The doctors, however, went to court, obtained a ruling that overrode the wishes of the parents, and performed the operation that resulted in the expected death of Mary. Jodie is still doing well as these words are written many months after the surgery.

As for the morality of the separation of the conjoined twins, Catholics came down on both sides of the case. For example, an editorial in *The Pilot*, the Boston archdiocesan newspaper, said that the surgery was "both medically and morally acceptable" under the principle of the double effect because the operation "was good in itself and was directly productive of the good effect (saving Jodie's life). The circumstances were good, the intentions of the surgeons were good, and the reasons for the surgery were proportionally serious to the probable but unintended bad effect — the death of little Mary."

The Pilot editorial added that "this 'principle of the double effect,' however, never justifies using evil means to achieve an apparent good."

On the other side was the National Catholic Bioethics Center, also located in Boston, which agreed that "it might be possible to perform an operation on one conjoined twin, even though it would be foreseen that the other twin might indirectly die from the procedure. However, it would be wrong to kill one twin in the operation in order to save the other; we may never do evil to achieve good."

The problem in this case, the NCBC said in a press release, is the difficulty in determining whether in the actual surgery "one child is being assaulted to save the other or whether the operation is actually being performed on the one child for its benefit with the unintended and indirect but foreseen death of the other. Obviously other factors must be brought to bear as well before such a procedure can go forward, such as whether there is a reasonable hope of benefit for the child upon whom the operation is performed."

The NCBC noted that the Linacre Centre, a Catholic bioethics group in London that advises the Catholic hierarchy of Great Britain, had opposed the surgery because "it did in fact, in the Centre's opinion, constitute a non-beneficial, intentional mutilation of Mary in order to save Jodie. The Centre based this judgment on the medical information which was available to it."

Also at stake, said the NCBC press release, was "the right of parents to decide what is in the best interests of their children. No one denied that the operation on the twins would be risky and extraordinary, and there was no guarantee of success for Jodie. Indeed, the surgery lasted 20 hours. The parents did not want to subject the children to such a difficult procedure, which in many respects was experimental, without more certitude that Mary would not be directly killed in the process and that Jodie herself would survive it. The parents were more confident in the loving mercy of God toward their children than they were of the actions and intentions of the medical technicians. Yet the English courts overrode the parents' judgment, setting a dangerous precedent for the usurpation of parental rights by the state."

Based on all the information available to us, and after conversations with several reliable Catholic ethicists, we find ourselves siding with the NCBC and the Linacre Centre in concluding that the separation of the twins was morally wrong because it constituted more a direct surgical attack on Mary than a beneficial operation on Jodie that only indirectly led to Mary's death. But at the same time we can see how morally sound Catholics could find themselves on opposite sides in this heartrending case.

Q. If we know that a woman is carrying a baby that is grotesquely deformed, or does not have a brain, can she have the baby removed by abortion? Could the baby be given conditional Baptism? — M.A.M., Alabama

A. If we admit that God is the Author of all life, even life that is grotesquely deformed or brainless, and that all life is precious because it is created in His image and likeness, then we cannot give anyone the right to take the life of another person because that person is not perfectly formed or in possession of all his organs. Abortion is a terrible evil and can never be tolerated for any reason, medical, social, financial, or convenience.

Conditional Baptism usually refers to a person who is entering the Catholic Church but is not certain whether he was previously baptized, or to a person who appears to be dead but in whom there might still be a spark of life. A child in the womb cannot be baptized, but must at least have his head outside the mother so that water can be poured on it. If a child were delivered alive, any Baptism that is performed would be a real, not a conditional, Baptism.

Q. A non-Catholic relative has pointed out that our Holy Father, in the one place in *Evangelium Vitae* where he speaks *ex cathedra*, states that "by the authority which Christ conferred upon Peter and his successors, and in communion with the bishops of the Catholic Church, I confirm that the direct and voluntary killing of an innocent human being is always gravely immoral." My relative's point is that the word "abortion" is not mentioned and, if it should ever be proved that the unborn is not a human being, the Church would have to change its position on abortion. This relative believes that the Pope is being ambiguous and leaving the door open for a change in the Church's position on abortion. Can you help me answer this charge made by a man with a Ph.D. in philosophy? — T.R.B., Connecticut

A. We won't even get into your relative's foolish statement that someone, someday might prove that unborn children are not human beings (has he ever heard of an unborn child who became something other than a human being at birth?). But to answer your question, you didn't read far enough into *Evangelium Vitae*. The statement about the grave immorality of killing the innocent appears in paragraph 57. Later in that same paragraph, the Holy Father, without using the word "abortion," certainly refers to it when he says that "nothing and no one can in any way permit the killing of an innocent human being, *whether a fetus or an embryo,* an infant or an adult, an old person, or one suffering from an incurable disease or a person who is dying."

Five paragraphs later, however, John Paul, after noting that the Church has condemned abortion from the first century through the 20th century, and that he was speaking with the same authority which Christ had conferred on Peter and his successors, used the same solemn language in proclaiming the evil of abortion that he had used in paragraph 57:

"I declare that direct abortion, that is, abortion willed as an end or as a means, always constitutes a grave moral disorder, since it is the deliberate killing of an innocent human being. This doctrine is based upon the natural law and upon the written word of God, is transmitted by the Church's tradition and taught by the ordinary and universal magisterium" (n. 62).

Q. In Roger Pearson's book entitled *Shockley on Eugenics and Race*, Shockley says, "...Thomas Aquinas' conclusion that abortion of an early foetus is not murder...," and again, "that the foetus in a pregnant woman does not become a human being before several months of life," was startling to me. If what Shockley says is true, how are we as Catholics to reconcile this with Church teaching? — R.L.H., Missouri

A. We can reconcile it by pointing out that while St. Thomas, relying on the biology of Aristotle, thought that the soul was not infused into the body until forty days after conception, he always taught that abortion was a grave evil. And that has been the constant teaching of the Church for two millennia. In its 1974 *Declaration on Procured Abortion*, the Sacred Congregation for the Doctrine of the Faith offered this summary of early Church teaching against abortion:

"In the course of history, the Fathers of the Church, her Pastors, and her Doctors have taught the same doctrine — the various opinions on the infusion of the spiritual soul did not cast doubt on the illicitness of abortion. It is true that in the Middle Ages, when the opinion was generally held that the spiritual soul was not present until after the first few weeks, a distinction was made in the evaluation of the sin and the gravity of the penal sanctions.

"In resolving cases, approved authors were more lenient with regard to that early stage than with regard to later stages. But it was never denied at that time that procured abortion, even during the first days, was objectively a grave sin. This condemnation was in fact unanimous.

"It is enough to cite some from among the many documents. The First Council of Mainz in 847 reconsiders the penalties against abortion which had been established by preceding Councils. It decided that the most rigorous penance would be imposed 'on women who procure the elimination of the fruit conceived in their womb.' The Decree of Gratian reports the following words of Pope Stephen V [885-891]: 'That person is a murderer who causes to perish by abortion what has been conceived.' St. Thomas [Aquinas], the Common Doctor of the Church, teaches that abortion is a grave sin against the natural law" (n. 7).

Q. How is a Catholic to vote when the choice is between two candidates, one of whose views are against everything the voter holds dear, while the other holds views that generally reflect the voter's views with the exception of abortion? This latter candidate supports the anti-life position, but not partial-birth abortion. Can a person vote for the lesser of two evils, or should he vote for a right-to-life candidate if there is one? — J.F.S., New York

A. Relying on such documents as Pope John Paul's encyclical on *The Gospel of Life* and Archbishop John J. Myers' pastoral letter on *The Obligations of Catholics and the Rights of Unborn Children*, we would answer this way:

(1) If all candidates for an office support abortion equally, one should refrain from voting for that particular office. (2) If one candidate is less supportive of abortion than another, one could vote for that candidate with the intention of helping to prevent the election of someone whose pro-abortion position is more extreme and, in so doing, perhaps save the lives of some babies. (3) If there is a third-party or independent candidate who is pro-life, one could vote for that person, even if he or she has no realistic chance of winning. (4) A Catholic may never vote for a candidate, even partially because of his or her pro-abortion stance, since that would make the voter complicit in the abortions that the election of this candidate would make possible.

So while a Catholic could vote for the less objectionable of two pro-abortion candidates, Notre Dame Law Professor Emeritus Charles E. Rice said that he should not because "any candidate who believes that the law should treat any innocent human beings as non-persons by tolerating their execution is unworthy to hold any public office, whether President of the United States or trustee of a mosquito abatement district." In his book *The Winning Side* (St. Brendan's Institute), Rice explained:

"The compromise tactic of voting for the less objectionable of two pro-abortion candidates is a tactic of incremental surrender.

That approach in practice has mortgaged the pro-life effort to the interests and judgment of 'the great human scourge of the twentieth century: the professional politician.' The politicians half-heartedly endorse marginal pro-life proposals in exchange for pro-life endorsement of their re-election campaigns. And pro-life activists give the politicians a veto power over the pro-life agenda by advancing only those proposals likely to get the approval of the politicians.

"Solely concerned with re-election, the politicians know they can placate the pro-lifers with small-change rhetoric and guarded endorsements of peripheral bills without arousing the focused opposition of the pro-abortion camp. The 'practical' pro-lifers are so devoted to politics as 'the art of the possible' that they risk becoming professional politicians themselves."

Professor Rice said that "the political pro-life movement will be counterproductive until it stops playing politics and stands firm on the truth that the law can never validly tolerate the intentional killing of innocent human beings. Our only chance to succeed is through fidelity to the truth ... whether it brings political success or not." He quoted Charles Colson as saying that "when our goal becomes success rather than faithfulness, we lose the single-minded focus of obedience and any real power to be successful" (pp. 257-258).

Q. Are Catholic politicians who facilitate the crime of abortion, and who have knowledge of the penalty of excommunication that is attached, automatically excommunicated? If so, then how can people like Senator Ted Kennedy receive Holy Communion? — J.F.G., New Jersey
A. We turn for help on this question to Msgr. William B. Smith, the respected moral theologian. In his question-and-answer column in the August/September 2000 issue of *Homiletic & Pastoral Review*, Msgr. Smith said that the pro-abortion voting record of Ted Kennedy and others is "a scandal to the faith and is radically inconsistent with being a 'practicing Catholic.' It is not, however, an automatic excommunication."

He explained that "the canonical penalty of excommunication is carefully delineated in Church law and purposely limited in application. In fact, it is a general principle of canon law that penalties of law and the restriction of rights are to be interpreted strictly (cn. 18), that is, narrowly."

While noting that canon law imposes automatic excommunication on the "one who actually procures an abortion," as well as on those necessary cooperators "without whose assistance" the abortion would not be done, Msgr. Smith did not include pro-abortion legislators under this penalty. He said it may well be that a number of abortions performed would not have occurred without the votes of lawmakers like Kennedy, "but since it 'may be' so and is not patently clear causal participation in an actual abortion, then it seems to me this is outside the scope of cn. 1329, #2 and does not engage the penalty of excommunication."

This does not mean that pro-abortion legislators are "off the hook," the Monsignor said. He said "we must never forget that abortion is the direct killing of a moral innocent (i.e., morally, it's murder). By every moral standard, every direct and deliberate act of that kind (murder) is an objective offense against the natural law and divine positive law, from which no one on this planet is exempt. By definition, this is grave scandal and incompatible with being a practicing Catholic. Those who promote, sustain, and expand abortion cannot disentangle themselves completely from this grave sin and objective injustice."

As for how pro-abortion Catholic politicians like Ted Kennedy can receive Communion, only one who knows their subjective state of mind could answer that question. Objectively speaking, their actions should exclude them from the Eucharist, but only God knows the true state of their souls and whether their Communions are worthy or sacrilegious.

Q. Is it ethical for a Catholic to invest in U.S. Treasury bonds since the U.S. Government spends large sums of money funding abortion agencies? What about investing in certificates of deposit, even though the bank probably takes the money for the CDs and puts it into Treasury bills? — T.L.M., Michigan

A. As we have noted in the past, there is not always a clear moral answer to this type of question. Obviously, one cannot cooperate formally in evil, i.e., to will or share in the evil intention by, say, giving money directly to Planned Parenthood or buying or continuing to hold a large number of shares in a company that is actively supporting immoral activities.

But there is also material cooperation, in which a person does not will or intend the evil but knows that some of his funds could be used for evil activities. The morality of this cooperation depends on how close one is to the immoral action (proximate or remote) and whether there is a proportionate reason for the co-operation. The more necessary one's material cooperation is to the act, the graver must be the reason to justify it morally. Since the government can still accomplish its immoral activities without the assistance of T.L.M.'s investments, then his cooperation would be remote and only an ordinary or slight reason would be sufficient to justify buying government securities.

In his book *Difficult Moral Questions,* moral theologian Germain Grisez listed four conditions that must be met for acceptable material cooperation in purchasing or holding stocks in companies or mutual funds (pp. 502-507). The four conditions do not apply exactly to investments in government bonds or Treasury bills, but some of his advice, adapted to the latter situation, is worth considering.

For example, he said that one must have a justified need for investing in some way and must have concluded, after a reasonable investigation, that government securities are the only form of investment necessary to meet that need or that investing in any adequate alternative would be at least as problematic.

Second, one should steer clear of investments that are heavily tainted with immoral activities, and we know that the U.S. Government contributes millions of dollars to anti-life agencies like Planned Parenthood or to the shipment of contraceptives and abortifacients to Third World nations.

Third, one must resist the temptation to take into account the profitability of certain investments if that profitability depends on something immoral.

This leads us to conclude that a Catholic who wants to avoid any cooperation in morally tainted activities should refrain from investing in government securities, but that investing in certificates of deposit at the local bank, even if they are put into Treasury bills, would constitute such a remote type of material cooperation as to be morally allowable.

Q. Can you give me some good reasons to convince some friends of mind that assisted suicide is wrong? — M.H., Massachusetts

A. Here is a list of reasons that was prepared by the Massachusetts Catholic Conference for legislative hearings on a bill that would permit doctors to prescribe lethal drugs so that terminally ill patients could commit suicide:

• Because assisted suicide entails direct killing of persons.

• Because residents of Massachusetts already have the legal right to refuse any treatment they don't want.

• Because with competent medical care no one needs to die in unrelenting pain; doctors should kill the pain, not the patient.

• Because the legal permission to die can easily become the duty to die.

• Because the elderly, disabled, and poor will be put at risk.

• Because dying is not "undignified"; it is rather part of being human.

• Because doctors who cure and heal should not be agents of death.

• Because in the Netherlands, where assisted suicide is allowed, doctors kill patients who never requested death.

• Because assisted suicide means an unfair loss of protection for lives that the state decides are not worth living.

• Because killing is incompatible with caring.

Q. I recently read an article about the removal of a feeding tube from Hugh Finn. What is wrong with removing a feeding tube from a comatose person? Is this necessarily a part of ordinary care? I ask this because I don't have availability to a priest to answer this kind of query and you have a good knack of explaining complicated issues clearly. — D.A.P., South Korea

A. Hugh Finn was a Virginia man left comatose after an automobile accident in 1995. He died in October 1998 after doctors removed a tube that had provided him with food and water. The tube was removed following a Virginia court ruling that "withholding and/or withdrawal of artificial nutrition or hydration from Hugh Finn, a person in a persistent vegetative state, merely permits the natural process of dying and is not mercy killing or euthanasia."

In deciding on the use of various means of sustaining life, Catholic moral teaching has long distinguished between ordinary and extraordinary means, that is, we are held to use ordinary means to sustain life, but not extraordinary means in every case. The Vatican's 1980 *Declaration on Euthanasia* refined this principle by stating that medical therapy or technology need not be used if they are excessively burdensome or provide no benefit to the patient.

Reliable Catholic moralists hold that food and water are not primarily forms of therapeutic medical treatment because of and by themselves they do not overcome disease or restore health. Rather, they are basic means of sustaining life, and a person will die without them. Thus, nutrition and hydration should be provided as part of a patient's natural care, unless or until the benefits of such care are clearly outweighed by a definite danger or burden, or they are clearly useless in sustaining life.

If we understand the facts of the Hugh Finn case correctly, he was in an unconscious but non-dying condition. Taking food and water away from him did not "merely permit the natural process of dying," it hastened his death by starvation and dehydration. If the withdrawal of nutrition and hydration was intended to hasten or cause his death, then it was euthanasia, and that is morally impermissible. The New Jersey Catholic Conference has summarized the ethical principles that apply in this situation:

"In the unconscious, non-dying patient, nutrition and hydration should be supplied. Feeding is not useless because it sustains a human life. There is no indication that the person is suffering, nor is there any clear evidence that the provision of nutrition and hydration is an unreasonable danger or burden. In such a case, the withdrawal of nutrition/hydration brings about death by starvation and dehydration. Absent any other indication of a definite burden for the patient, withdrawal of nutrition/hydration is not morally justifiable."

Q. What is the responsibility of a person in her 90s regarding extraordinary means, such as resuscitation, when one has a variety of health problems — diabetes, high blood pressure, cholesterol — none of which keeps one bedridden, but all of which make getting places burdensome? Must one be ready at all times to be rushed to an emergency hospital, or may one put that aside and not have to worry about it? I have been a faithful Catholic to the best of my ability during my long life. — Name Withheld, Arizona

A. You would be completely within the parameters of Catholic teaching if you were to refuse extraordinary means to keep you alive at your age and with your health problems. If you do not already have an advance medical directive or health-care proxy, you should get and sign one, expressing your wishes about end-of-life treatment and designating a trusted family member or friend to act as your health-care agent should you be unable to make medical decisions yourself.

Included in the document should be a "do not resuscitate" order, indicating your wish not to have heroic measures used to bring you back to life once your heart stops. This a perfectly legitimate moral choice for you to make. In the words of Pope John Paul II: "To forgo extraordinary or disproportionate means is not the equivalent of suicide or euthanasia; it rather expresses acceptance of the human condition in the face of death" (*Evangelium Vitae*, n. 65).

Q. Is there any reason why an older person, with his family all gone, cannot pray to God to take him soon? I am not talking about a person in ill health. Nor am I talking about a person thinking of suicide. Would that be a sin? — J.S., Michigan

A. No, longing for Heaven is not a sin. St. Paul expressed that same longing on different occasions. For example, he told the people of Corinth: "Indeed we know that when the earthly tent in which we dwell is destroyed, we have a dwelling provided for us by God, a dwelling in the heavens, not made by hands but to last forever. We groan while we are here, even as we yearn to have our heavenly habitation envelop us" (2 Corinthians 5:1-2).

And he told the people of Philippi: "To me, 'life' means Christ; hence dying is so much gain. If, on the other hand, I am to go on living in the flesh, that means productive toil for me — and I do not know which to prefer. I am strongly attracted by both: I long to be freed from this life and to be with Christ, for that is the far better thing; yet it is more urgent that I remain alive for your sakes" (Philippians 1:21-24).

To be sure, it can be lonely when one's family is gone, but God has kept you on earth this long for a reason; He must still have some work for you to do. While you should never stop yearning for Heaven, ask God to help you discern His will for you in your remaining years. Perhaps, like Paul, it is more urgent that you remain here.

Are there friends or neighbors that you could help with chores or shopping or letter-writing? Do you have skills that you could teach to others? Are there children whom you could tutor? Could you volunteer time at your parish visiting the sick or helping with the parish census? Could you give time at a local shelter or food pantry? Could you cheer up fellow seniors and help prepare them to meet the Lord? The possibilities of acting as God's instrument (cf. the Prayer of St. Francis) are many. Be open to what God has in mind for you.

Q. Catholic hospitals here have "advance medical directives," whereby a person may declare what treatment he wants when helpless or unconscious. Where can one get official Catholic teaching about such things as "do not resuscitate" orders and whether food and hydration can be refused in a terminal state? — W.C., New York
A. You can start with sections 2278 and 2279 of the *Catechism* and sections 64-66 of Pope John Paul's encyclical on *The Gospel of Life*. Then you should look at the Pontifical Council for Pastoral Assistance's *Charter for Health Care Workers* and the National Conference of Catholic Bishops' *Ethical and Religious Directives for Catholic Health Care Services*.

You might also want to look at two books: *Catholicism & Ethics* (C.R. Publications) by Hayes, Hayes, Kelly and Drummey, and *Catholic Bioethics and the Gift of Human Life* (Our Sunday Visitor) by William E. May.

Q. I have a friend who belongs to the Hemlock Society and actively counsels the elderly in the Hemlock way. He is an otherwise devout Catholic and feels that he exercises his Hemlock Society membership as a form of Catholic charity. I have read that the Hemlock Society provides a do-it-yourself suicide booklet which, among other things, tells how to mix a lethal dosage of barbiturates in applesauce. My friend denies this. Where can I get information to refute him? And may a Catholic be a member of the Hemlock Society? — M.A.M., Alabama
A. Several years ago, when Bishop Fabian Bruskewitz of Lincoln, Nebraska, warned members of his flock that they faced excommunication unless they severed all ties with organizations whose principles and policies are "totally incompatible with the Catholic faith," one of the organizations he mentioned was the Hemlock Society. So in answer to your second question, no Catholic can in good conscience be a member of the Hemlock Society.

This organization was founded in 1980 by Derek Humphry, who helped his first wife to kill herself and later hounded his second wife into taking her life. Hemlock believes that every person has a right to take his own life and that euthanasia should be administered to any person who requests it. If there is a suicide booklet, you ought to be able to obtain a copy from Hemlock.

As for your friend who thinks that he is practicing Christian charity in supporting an organization devoted to killing the old and the sick, we recommend that you urge him to read Pope John Paul II's encyclical *The Gospel of Life*, in which the Holy Father said:

> "*I confirm that euthanasia is a grave violation of the law of God* since it is the deliberate and morally unacceptable killing of a human person. This doctrine is based upon the natural law and upon the written word of God, is transmitted by the Church's tradition and taught by the ordinary and universal magisterium. Depending on the circumstances, this practice involves the malice proper to suicide or murder" (n. 65).

The Pope also said that "even when not motivated by a selfish refusal to be burdened with the life of someone who is suffering, euthanasia must be called a false mercy and indeed a disturbing 'perversion' of mercy. True 'compassion' leads to sharing another's pain; it does not kill the person whose suffering we cannot bear" (n. 66).

Q. What is a morally acceptable definition of death? With the possibility of an organ transplant sometime next year, I am concerned because I understand organs begin to decay immediately upon death and that patients considered terminal are sometimes killed to get their organs. What is the morality of receiving an organ transplant? — K.S., New Hampshire

A. First of all, an organ transplant done in an ethically acceptable manner is not only a good thing, but Pope John Paul once equated it with "an everyday heroism made up of gestures of sharing, big and small, which build up an authentic culture of life" (*Evangelium Vitae*, n. 86). And second, the *Catechism of the Catholic Church* has spelled out the ethical guidelines for such transplants:

> "*Organ transplants* are in conformity with the moral law if the physical and psychological dangers and risks to the donor are proportionate to the good that is sought for the recipient.

Organ donation after death is a noble and meritorious act and is to be encouraged as an expression of generous solidarity. It is not morally acceptable if the donor or his proxy has not given explicit consent. Moreover, it is not morally admissible directly to bring about the disabling mutilation or death of a human being, even in order to delay the death of other persons" (n. 2296).

So organs can only be harvested from the dead, not from the dying, and the Church has long encouraged medical scientists to pursue research and studies in order to determine as precisely as possible the exact moment and the indisputable sign of death. For then one would know at what point it would be morally permissible to remove an organ for transplanting and to guarantee the best chance for a successful outcome.

In a speech on August 29, 2000 to the International Congress on Transplants, Pope John Paul discussed the question of when a person could be considered dead with complete certainty. He first noted that death is a single event that results when the life principle (or soul) separates from the body, but added that no scientific technique or empirical method can identify this event directly.

However, the Pontiff continued, certain biological signs, such as cessation of heart and respiratory function, have long been recognized as indicating that a person has died, but now, he said, the emphasis has shifted from "the traditional cardio-respiratory signs to the so-called 'neurological' criterion. Specifically, this consists in establishing, according to clearly determined parameters commonly held by the international scientific community, the complete and irreversible cessation of all brain activity (in the cerebrum, cerebellum, and brain stem)."

Using this criterion "does not seem to conflict with the essential elements of a sound anthropology," said John Paul. "Therefore, a health worker professionally responsible for ascertaining death can use these criteria in each individual case as the basis for arriving at that degree of assurance in ethical judgment which moral teaching describes as 'moral certainty.'

"This moral certainty is considered the necessary and sufficient basis for an ethically correct course of action. Only where such certainty exists, and where informed consent has already been given by the donor or the donor's legitimate representatives, is it morally right to initiate the technical procedures required for the removal of organs for transplant."

While some respected Catholics in the field of medicine remain skeptical of brain death criteria, the Holy Father said that it is morally legitimate to use these criteria if they are applied in a rigorous and responsible manner. It is also important to bear in mind that he was speaking of total loss of brain activity, and not the partial-loss standard that some in the medical field have advocated.

Chapter 13

Christian Morality

Q. I have heard that there are nine ways that we can be an accessory to sin. Do you know what they are? — I.N., Iowa

A. Once listed in missals and prayer books as part of an examination of conscience, here are the nine ways, along with examples of each:

(1) By counsel (I would recommend you get an abortion.)

(2) By command (You must get an abortion.)

(3) By consent (You're going to get an abortion? Good idea.)

(4) By provocation (I'll make this person angry if I keep nagging him this way.)

(5) By praise or flattery (You look sexy in that low-cut dress.)

(6) By concealment (I'll fix the books to cover your theft.)

(7) By partaking (The two of us can rob this company blind.)

(8) By silence (I know you took the money, but I'll keep quiet.)

(9) By defense of the ill done (He took the computer, but he needed it to help his children, and the company won't miss it.)

Q. In the first letter of John (5:16-17), he speaks of "deadly sin." Is this the seven deadly sins of avarice, lust, etc., or is it the sin against the Holy Spirit that will not be forgiven in this life or the next? Also, would you please give some examples of things that are intrinsically evil? And against which of the Ten Commandments does the use of artificial contraception offend? — R.D., Texas

A. (1) St. John says that we should petition God to forgive the person whose sin is not deadly, which presumably means mortal sin because he says that "life will be given to the sinner." But when he also says that we should not pray for those in deadly sin, he is probably talking about final impenitence, the rejection of God's love and mercy at the moment of death.

(2) Intrinsically evil means something that is always and everywhere wrong in itself, regardless of intentions or circumstances. The Church has traditionally included in this category

such sins as abortion, adultery, blasphemy, contraception, euthanasia, fornication, genocide, idolatry, murder, sexual perversion, and voluntary suicide (cf. *Veritatis Splendor*, nn. 80-81).

(3) Contraception offends against both the Sixth Commandment, since it is a grave violation of marital chastity, and the Fifth Commandment, since it is also hostile to new life, and this is particularly true if the so-called contraceptive being used is actually an abortifacient.

Q. Where can I obtain a book on the Ten Commandments that tells which specific sins follow under each of the Commandments? A friend of mine says that reading pornography is not a sin. Can you give me specific information on this issue? — J.E.K., Pennsylvania

A. For a discussion of the Ten Commandments and which sins come under which commandment, see the *Catechism of the Catholic Church*, nn. 2084-2557. A popularly written summary of the Commandments can be found in the book *Catholicism & Life* by Hayes, Hayes and Drummey, which is available from C.R. Publications Inc., 345 Prospect St., Norwood, MA 02062, or call toll-free 877-730-8877.

Pornography "offends against chastity," says the *Catechism*, "because it perverts the conjugal act, the intimate giving of spouses to each other. It does grave injury to the dignity of its participants (actors, vendors, the public), since each one becomes an object of base pleasure and illicit profit for others. It immerses all who are involved in the illusion of a fantasy world. It is a grave offense. Civil authorities should prevent the production and distribution of pornographic materials" (n. 2354).

Addressing the Religious Alliance Against Pornography on January 30, 1992, Pope John Paul called pornography a "plague" on society and said that "by its very nature, pornography is immoral and ultimately anti-social precisely because it is opposed to the truth about the human person, made in the image and likeness of God.

"By its very nature, pornography denies the genuine meaning of human sexuality as a God-given gift intended to open individuals to love and to sharing in the creative work of God through responsible procreation. By reducing the body to an instrument of gratification of the senses, pornography frustrates authentic moral growth and undermines the development of mature and healthy relationships. It leads inexorably to the exploitation of individuals, especially those who are most vulnerable, as is so tragically evident in the case of child pornography."

Some years ago, the Attorney General's Commission on Pornography, after holding hearings in six American cities and hearing testimony from more than 1,000 persons, concluded that pornography is addictive, that it progressively corrupts its addicts, and that it desensitizes men's attitudes toward women.

Ted Bundy, the serial killer whose addiction to hard-core pornography fueled his sexual fantasies and inspired him to murder perhaps as many as two dozen young women, said that "you reach that jumping-off point when you begin to wonder if actually doing it would give you that which is beyond just reading about it or looking at it."

The day before his execution in Florida, Bundy said that porn users "are not some kind of inherent monsters. We are your sons and we are your husbands. Pornography can snatch a kid out of any home today."

Q. I am enclosing an article from *Catholic Digest* that quotes St. Thomas Aquinas as saying, "It is better to die excommunicated than to violate the conscience." Did Aquinas say this, and what is the teaching of the magisterium on conscience? — E.S., Arizona

A. Yes, Aquinas did say this, but in the context of a time when excommunication was used much more widely than today. Nevertheless, the teaching of the magisterium is that "a human being must always obey the certain judgment of his conscience. If he were deliberately to act against it, he would condemn himself" (*Catechism*, n. 1790).

In *Veritatis Splendor*, Pope John Paul, after describing the judgment of conscience as "a judgment which applies to a concrete situation the rational conviction that one must love and do good and avoid evil" (n. 59), said that "the judgment of conscience also has an imperative character: man must act in accordance with it. If man acts against this judgment or, in a case where he lacks certainty about the rightness and goodness of a determined act, still performs that act, he stands condemned by his own conscience, *the proximate norm of personal morality*" (n. 60).

The reason why this is so, as explained by William E. May in his book *An Introduction to Moral Theology* (Our Sunday Visitor), is that "this judgment of conscience is the final judgment that a person makes about the moral goodness or badness of the alternatives possible for him or her. If one were willing to act contrary to this judgment, one would be willing to do what one had personally judged one ought not choose to do. One would thus be willing to be an evildoer if one were willing deliberately to act contrary to one's own best judgment" (p. 36).

Having established that, however, it must be noted that the *Catechism*, the Holy Father, and Dr. May all insist that a person must seek the truth in forming his conscience. "A well-formed conscience is upright and truthful," says the *Catechism*. "It formulates its judgments according to reason, in conformity with the true good willed by the wisdom of the Creator. Everyone must avail himself of the means to form his conscience" (n. 1798).

Pope John Paul included in *Veritatis Splendor* the following quotation from Vatican II:

"In forming their consciences the Christian faithful must give careful attention to the sacred and certain teaching of the Church. For the Catholic Church is by the will of Christ the teacher of truth. Her charge is to announce and teach authentically that truth which is Christ, and at the same time with her authority to declare and confirm the principles of the moral order which derive from human nature itself" (n. 64).

Because our own judgments about moral decisions can be erroneous, said May (p. 37), we have a "serious obligation" to seek the truth. He said that "our obligation is to conform our judgments of conscience to objective norms of morality, norms that have as their ultimate source, as *Dignitatis Humanae* put it, 'God's divine law — eternal, objective, and universal.'"

He then quoted the following passage from *To Live in Christ Jesus*, the U.S. Bishops' 1976 pastoral letter on the moral life:

"We must have a rightly informed conscience and follow it. But our judgments are human and can be mistaken; we may be blinded by the power of sin in our lives or misled by the strength of our desires. 'Beloved, do not trust every spirit, but put the spirits to a test to see if they belong to God' (1 John 4:1).

"Clearly then, we must do everything in our power to see to it that our judgments of conscience are informed and in accord with the moral order of which God is Creator. Common sense requires that conscientious people be open and humble, ready to learn from the experience and insight of others, willing to acknowledge prejudices and even change their judgments in light of better instruction."

Q. Since sin never seems to be part of a Sunday homily, and it has been years since the Ten Commandments were mentioned, might a casual observer wonder if talking about sin has gone out of style? My pastor even said that the Commandments can be the subject for a homily only once every three years. Is that true? — J.C.F., Montana

A. Recent Popes have lamented the loss of a sense of sin among Catholics, and certainly part of the reason for that loss is the failure of priests to talk about sin in their homilies. This is contrary to the wishes of Pope John Paul, who said in his 1984 apostolic exhortation *Reconciliation and Penance*:

"The sense of sin can only be restored through a clear reminder of the unchangeable principles of reason which the moral teachings of the Church have always upheld."

Nine years later, in *Veritatis Splendor*, the Holy Father specifically listed, in paragraphs 13, 49, 80, 81, 100, and 101, numerous mortal sins that are very prevalent in society today and that ought to be the subject of many homilies.

To suggest that a priest can mention the Ten Commandments only once every three years is ludicrous. The readings from Scripture over a three-year cycle provide opportunities galore for homilies on the Commandments. Referring to Jesus' conversation with the rich young man (Matthew 19:16-22), in which our Lord quoted five of the Ten Commandments and said that "if you wish to enter into life, keep the commandments," Pope John Paul said:

"From the very lips of Jesus, the new Moses, man is once again given the Commandments of the Decalogue. Jesus himself definitively confirms them and proposes them to us as the way and condition of salvation" (n. 12).

If Jesus, the Holy Father, and the *Catechism* (cf. n. 2072, which talks about the *"grave* obligations" imposed on us by the Commandments) consider the Ten Commandments so essential to the moral life that one who deliberately violates them cannot get to Heaven, how can a pastor say that the Church expects priests to preach on them only once every three years?

Q. I would like to know why the priests of today are afraid to talk about venial sins or mortal sins. Are they afraid they'll lose people attending Mass? I've gone to several different churches and it's the same type of sermon (do good and love your neighbor) every Sunday. I would appreciate your view on this. — A.M., Minnesota

A. Our view is the same as yours. Week after week, the Scripture readings at Mass offer great opportunities to preach against sinfulness in general and mortal and venial sins in particular, but the homilies are for the most part bland and innocuous.

For instance, in one Sunday's (NAB 1986 NT) first reading, St. Peter said: "Repent, therefore, and be converted, that your sins may be wiped away" (Acts 3:19). In the second reading, St. John said that "I am writing this to you so that you may not commit sin" (1 John 2:1). And in the Gospel, Jesus said that He had to suffer and rise from the dead so that "repentance, for the forgiveness of sins, would be preached in his name to all the nations, beginning from Jerusalem" (Luke 24:47).

Here was a chance to talk about sin, to define what the term means, to give examples of sins that require repentance and forgiveness from Christ, and to mention that forgiveness is available in the Sacrament of Penance. It would be so easy to take some of the outrageously sinful actions we hear about every day in the media, explain why they are sinful, and call those in the pews to repentance in their own lives and to holiness.

The priests that we know are good and holy men who celebrate Mass reverently, have a devotion to our Lady, encourage Eucharistic adoration, are loyal to the Holy Father, and are disturbed at the cavalier attitudes of those who come for marriage preparation for themselves or for sacramental catechesis for their children, while at the same time living as if God did not exist.

These priests give good homilies as far as they go, but, in our opinion, they could sound a more certain trumpet that would be heard not only by those in church, but eventually by those on the outside as well. Let the word go out that Father said it was a mortal sin to miss Mass deliberately on Sunday, to live together before marriage, to engage in masturbation, fornication, and adultery, to practice contraception by taking pills or using devices, to procure or help procure an abortion, etc., and perhaps more people would see the need for repentance and Confession, and some who have been away from the Church might even come back to hear the message of Christ preached in its entirety.

The only way that this will happen is if we pray for our priests, encourage them in their often difficult vocation, pat them on the back when they do things well, and offer them suggestions for the kinds of homilies mentioned above. Yes, some parishioners might be offended to be told that their lifestyle is contrary to the teaching of Christ and His Church, but God will be more offended with priests who water down His message and fail to teach and preach the whole Gospel.

Q. I have a chronic pain condition and sometimes take advantage of a televised Mass in order to meet my Sunday obligation. Is this right? — D.B., Indiana

A. You are not obliged to attend Sunday Mass if your chronic pain condition prevents you from doing so. Illness has always been considered a legitimate reason for not fulfilling the Sunday Mass obligation.

For the record, one cannot satisfy the Sunday obligation by watching Mass on television. It is certainly laudable for a person who for a good reason is unable to get to Mass at his parish church to watch the televised Mass (the purpose of such Masses is to bring the Holy Sacrifice to the sick and to shut-ins), but one must be physically present at Mass to fulfill this precept of the Church.

Q. I am shocked at the attitude my pastor takes in the enclosed bulletin about the responsibility of fulfilling our Easter duty. Please comment. — W.C.M., Michigan

A. In the bulletin, the pastor says that the Easter duty "is a concept from years ago and we who are older like to remember those 'things' of the past from time to time. Remembering them often makes them seem so unreal in the light of the present, but there you are — a past that our youth cannot even believe could have happened."

Contrary to what your pastor said, fulfilling the Easter duty is not a thing of the past, but a very current obligation of every Catholic. Canon 920 of the Code of Canon Law says:

"All the faithful, after they have been initiated into the Most Holy Eucharist, are bound by the obligation of receiving Communion at least once a year. This precept must be fulfilled during the Easter season unless it is fulfilled for a just cause at some other time during the year."

This obligation is also stressed as a precept of the Church in section 2042 of the *Catechism*.

Q. It was my understanding that under the 1917 Code of Canon Law, a trip of over 50 miles dispensed one from attending Mass on Sunday. More recently I have heard that 200 miles is now the distance which dispenses from the Mass obligation. Is there a Church document that mentions these numbers? — J.W.M., New Jersey

Q. Are people in their 80s and 90s obliged to walk to church on Sundays if their church is a couple of miles away? — J.T., New Jersey

A. We are not aware of any Church document or precept, in the 1917 or 1983 Codes of Canon Law or anywhere else, with a mileage limit that would dispense from attending Sunday Mass, nor do we think such a limit could exist. After all, canon law is written for the whole world, for those who go to church on a donkey and those who travel in a BMW. A physically able person could live a mile from the church and not be able to attend Mass because of unsafe streets or severe weather conditions.

All the 1983 Code says is that "on Sundays and other holy days of obligation the faithful are bound to participate in the Mass" (canon 1247). The Church leaves it up to faithful Catholics to make a reasonable judgment as to how far they can safely or prudently travel to fulfill their Mass obligation.

This applies to those in their 80s and 90s, too. They are not obliged to walk two miles to church if they are physically unable to do so. They might, however, inquire of their pastor about the possibility of having some parishioner provide them with transportation to church.

Q. During a trip to Alaska last summer, we stopped at a church with a scheduled 10 a.m. Mass, only to find that Sr. So-and-So would be conducting a Communion service because no priest was available for Mass. She said that this would fulfill our Sunday obligation. Does this mean that if we had a choice, we could fulfill our obligation by attending a Communion service instead of Mass? Or that if we did not go to the Communion service we would have committed a serious sin? — S.M., Michigan

A. Canon 1247 of the Code of Canon Law says that "on Sundays and other holy days of obligation the faithful are bound to participate in the Mass." Canon 1248 says that, "if because of a lack of a sacred minister or for other grave cause participation in the celebration of the Eucharist is impossible, it is specially recommended that the faithful take part in the liturgy of the word if it is celebrated in the parish church or in another sacred place according to the prescriptions of the diocesan bishop, or engage in prayer for an appropriate amount of time personally or in a family or, as occasion offers, in groups of families."

And Pope John Paul, in his apostolic letter *Dies Domini* ("The Day of the Lord"), had this to say about Sunday celebrations without a priest:

"In situations where the Eucharist cannot be celebrated, the Church recommends that the Sunday assembly come together even without a priest, in keeping with the indications and directives of the Holy See which have been entrusted to the episcopal conferences for implementation. Yet the objective must always remain the celebration of the sacrifice of the Mass, the one way in which the Passover of the Lord becomes truly present, the only full realization of the Eucharistic assembly over which the priest presides *in persona Christi*, breaking the bread of the word and the Eucharist.

"At the pastoral level, therefore, everything has to be done to ensure that the sacrifice of the Mass is made available as often as possible to the faithful who are regularly deprived of it, either by arranging the presence of a priest from time to time, or by taking every opportunity to organize a gathering in a central location accessible to scattered groups" (n. 53).

In light of this, we would say that if there is no priest available on Sunday, obviously there would be no way of fulfilling one's obligation to attend Mass, and no sin would be attached to missing Mass under those circumstances. While the Church does not oblige attendance at a Communion service when there is no Mass, it does especially recommend that Catholics gather together for such a service. Strictly speaking, this would not fulfill the Sunday obligation of participating at Mass, but it would assist Catholics in keeping the Lord's Day holy.

Q. If the statistics are true that Sunday Mass attendance has plummeted from 70 percent of Catholics in the 1960s to 25 percent today, does it follow that on any given

Sunday 75 percent of American Catholics are in the state of mortal sin (excepting of course those who have legitimate reasons for missing Mass)? The *Catechism* says that "those who deliberately fail in this obligation commit a grave sin" (n. 2181). Why is this obligation not preached from the pulpit and placed in parish bulletins and newsletters? — J.L.S., Minnesota

A. The key words in the *Catechism* are "deliberately fail." To commit a mortal sin by missing Mass, one must know that it is a grave obligation to attend Mass every Sunday and must deliberately stay away from Mass without a good reason, such as illness or the care of infants.

While some Catholics who deliberately miss Mass on Sundays are surely guilty of mortal sin because they know what they are doing, we would guess that many Catholics who stay away from Mass are not subjectively guilty of mortal sin because they don't have a clue about the seriousness of this obligation. They either never heard the obligation preached or taught when they were going to Mass or to religion classes, or they were led to believe by some priest, nun, or lay teacher that you only have to go if you feel like it or if you get something out of it.

Two priests in the same parish told us recently that since they started talking about sin, the number of people going to Confession has increased. Well, of course it has. If people don't think they are sinners, why would they feel the need for Confession? But if good and holy priests and catechists remind people that we are all sinners, and some of us serious sinners, in need of God's mercy and forgiveness, then people will respond by returning to the Sacrament of Penance.

Similarly, if the word gets out to those deliberately skipping Mass on Sundays and holy days of obligation, that they are jeopardizing their souls, not to mention missing out on that great source of strength in the Holy Eucharist, then perhaps we will see increasing numbers of Catholics returning to Church. That is why Pope John Paul wrote *Dies Domini*, to remind Catholics that "it is crucially important for the life of faith that they should come together with others on Sundays to celebrate the Passover of the Lord in the sacrament of the new covenant."

He said that "it is the special responsibility of the bishops, therefore, 'to ensure that Sunday is appreciated by all the faithful, kept holy, and celebrated as truly "the Lord's Day," on which the Church comes together to renew the remembrance of the

Easter mystery in hearing the word of God, in offering the sacrifice of the Lord, in keeping the day holy by means of prayer, works of charity, and abstention from work' " (n. 48).

We can't think of a better time to spread this message than on Christmas and Easter, when there are many more people in church than on a typical Sunday. Priests ought to remind these once- or twice-a-year Catholics that their absence from church during the rest of the year makes them unworthy to receive Holy Communion when they do come on Christmas or Easter.

Q. I know that it is a mortal sin to miss Mass deliberately on Sunday, but can you give me some additional reasons for going to Mass that might convince people who no longer attend? — M.H.D., New York

A. Here are ten reasons why we should be at Mass every Sunday and holy day:

(1) Because the night before He died a horrible death on the cross for our sins, Jesus said that we should do this in His memory. It would be very selfish of us not to honor Jesus' command just before He shed His blood for us. God gives us 168 hours each week. How difficult is it to spend one hour with Him on Sunday? Do you want to stand before the Lord on Judgment Day and try to explain to the One who sacrificed His life for you that you didn't have time to worship Him because you played golf on Sundays or liked to sleep and relax all day?

(2) Because the Mass is a sacrifice (reminding us of the sacrifices of the Jewish people in the Old Testament and the perfect sacrifice of Jesus on the cross) and a banquet (reminding us of the Last Supper and the banquet that we will enjoy in Heaven at the end of the world).

(3) Because the four ends of the Mass are adoration, thanksgiving, petition, and reparation. *Adoration*: The main reason for going to Mass is to adore, worship, and give glory to the God who created us and who watches over us. *Thanksgiving*: We should express gratitude to God for all the blessings in our life. *Petition*: We should ask God for the things we need or that others need. *Reparation*: We should try to repair or make up for the damage caused by our sins and the sins of the world by offering to God all our prayers, works, joys, and sufferings.

(4) Because we can hear the Word of God read from the Bible and strive to apply these readings to our daily lives. A person who goes to church every Sunday for three years will hear 7,000

verses from the Bible and learn how God wants us to live so that we can get to Heaven.

(5) Because we can profess our belief in God, Jesus Christ, the Holy Spirit, and the Catholic Church in the Creed or Profession of Faith. We need to remind ourselves just what beliefs we hold.

(6) Because we can join with our fellow Catholics in praying for our needs and concerns in the General Intercessions or Prayers of the Faithful.

(7) Because we can offer to God, through the priest, our gifts of bread and wine so that the priest can change them into the Body and Blood of Christ during the Eucharistic Prayer.

(8) Because we can say together the only prayer that Jesus taught us — the Our Father, in which we praise God, pray that His kingdom will come and His will be done, ask for our daily bread and other needs, promise to forgive others so that God will forgive us, and ask God to protect us from the Evil One.

(9) Because, most importantly, we can receive Jesus in Holy Communion and get the spiritual food we need to be holy people so that we can one day be with Jesus in Heaven. Remember the words of Christ: "If you do not eat the flesh of the Son of Man/ and drink his blood,/ you have no life in you./ He who feeds on my flesh/ and drinks my blood/ has life eternal/ and I will raise him up on the last day" (John 6:53-54).

(10) Because we can leave the church filled with God's life and love, which will enable us to be apostles and witnesses for Jesus in a world that is far removed from His teachings.

Q. I have always heard that obedience to one's superiors in a religious order is very important, but how does one handle a situation in which the superior asks someone to do something that is sinful? — A.C.G., Illinois

A. By refusing to do what is sinful. Regarding the obedience that children owe their parents or other lawful authorities under the Fourth Commandment, the *Catechism* says that children should ordinarily "obey the reasonable directions" of parents and teachers, "but if a child is convinced in conscience that it would be morally wrong to obey a particular order, he must not do so" (n. 2217).

The same is true of orders from a religious superior or from civil and political authorities if their demands are "contrary to those of an upright conscience" (*Catechism*, n. 2242). As St. Peter said: "Better for us to obey God than men!" (Acts 5:29).

Q. Regarding the issue of capital punishment, the revised *Catechism* says that the death penalty can be imposed when it is the only possible way of effectively defending human lives against an unjust aggressor. It adds,
however, that such situations are virtually nonexistent
(cf. n. 2267). I conclude from this that the state can execute a criminal for defensive reasons only.

But I have seen a statement from Pope Pius XII in 1952,
in which he said that "the state does not dispose of the
individual's right to live" for defensive reasons but "in
expiation of his crime" since by his crime "he has already
deprived himself of the right to live." Did Pius XII say
this, and can you help me reconcile what appears to be
two contradictory teachings? — C.T., New Jersey

A. Yes, Pius XII did make such a statement, but we don't believe that his statement is irreconcilable with what the *Catechism*
said. If you look at paragraph 2266 of the 1997 edition of the
Catechism, you will note it says that "legitimate public authority has the right and duty to inflict punishment proportionate to
the gravity of the offense. Punishment has the primary aim of
redressing the disorder introduced by the offense. When it is
willingly accepted by the guilty party, it assumes the value of
expiation."

So the revised *Catechism* talks about expiation, just as Pius
XII did, and it talks in paragraph 2267 about the state still having the right to execute an offender when there is no other possible way of protecting society from him. But the *Catechism* goes
a step beyond Pius XII and urges every effort to give the guilty
party what Pope John Paul II called "an incentive and help to
change his or her behavior and be rehabilitated" (*Evangelium
Vitae*, n. 56).

This new way of looking at the death penalty, John Paul said,
"must be viewed in the context of a system of penal justice ever
more in line with human dignity and, thus, in the end, with God's
plan for man and society" (*Ibid.*). Restricting the death penalty
to only the rarest of cases is not a repudiation of what Pius XII
said; it is rather a legitimate development of the Church's doctrine on capital punishment and its reasonable application to
the circumstances of today.

Q. The abortionist and the pregnant girl that aborts
her baby, are these my neighbor? — V.A., Illinois

A. Absolutely. Our neighbor is everyone in need of our love, assistance, and prayers (cf. the parable of the Good Samaritan in Luke 10:25-37). Didn't Jesus command us to love even our enemies and to pray for our persecutors? He said that "this will prove that you are sons of your heavenly Father, for his sun rises on the bad and the good, he rains on the just and the unjust. If you love those who love you, what merit is there in that? Do not tax collectors do as much? And if you greet your brothers only, what is so praiseworthy about that? Do not pagans do as much? In a word, you must be made perfect as your heavenly Father is perfect" (Matthew 5:45-48).

Q. I was saddened to learn that a local Catholic church allowed a Mass of Christian Burial for a man who was killed in the commission of a robbery during which he killed two patrons. Aren't armed robbery and murder mortal sins and, if so, why a Mass of Christian Burial for this man? — J.J.O., Pennsylvania

A. According to canon 1184 of the Code of Canon Law, the following are to be deprived of the Church's funeral rites unless they have given some signs of repentance before their death:

(1) notorious apostates, heretics, and schismatics;
(2) persons who had chosen the cremation of their own bodies for reasons opposed to the Christian faith;
(3) other manifest sinners for whom ecclesiastical funeral rites cannot be granted without public scandal to the faithful.

A commentary on section 3 says that "a manifest sin is one for which there are eyewitnesses who can give testimony about it. If there is no public scandal, the right of burial is not to be denied even to manifest sinners. The local Ordinary should always be consulted if there is any doubt about the appropriateness of denying Christian burial. This is to protect persons against possibly arbitrary pastoral discretion at the local level."

We don't know whether there were any signs of repentance on the part of the robber before he died and lacking such signs it would seem that he should have been denied Christian burial.

Q. A person in our parish committed suicide and was given a Catholic burial. Is this right? I always thought that suicide was the worst sin. — M.M.R., Texas

A. Once upon a time, the Church would not celebrate a funeral Mass for a suicide victim on the grounds that taking one's life was such a grave sin that a Mass of Christian Burial would be of no value to the person. Today, however, the Church does offer Mass for the soul of the deceased, and for his or her family, on the grounds that we cannot know for certain the state of the person's soul at the time of death.

Since killing oneself is so contrary to human nature, there is the presumption that the victim was not rational and was therefore incapable of the sufficient reflection and full consent of the will necessary to commit a mortal sin that would send one to Hell.

You might want to look at paragraphs 2280-2283 of the *Catechism* for further explanation of the teaching on this matter. While noting that suicide is "gravely contrary" to the just love of self, to love of neighbor and ties of solidarity with family and friends, and to love for God, the *Catechism* says that "grave psychological disturbances, anguish, or grave fear of hardship, suffering, or torture can diminish the responsibility of the one committing suicide" (n. 2282).

Therefore, says the *Catechism*, "we should not despair of the eternal salvation of persons who have taken their own lives. By ways known to him alone, God can provide the opportunity for salutary repentance. The Church prays for persons who have taken their own lives" (n. 2283).

Q. Is the sin of smoking too much (intemperance) a grave enough matter to prevent one from receiving Communion? — R.D., Texas

A. When deciding whether smoking too much constitutes grave matter that would keep us from receiving Communion worthily, we need to remember that our bodies are gifts from God. We do not own our bodies, but rather are stewards of them with the obligation of taking proper care of them. Therefore, any action that seriously harms our health or our life — driving recklessly, consuming too much alcohol, or smoking too much, etc. — violates our obligation to be good stewards of the life given to us by God.

Presuming that these actions constitute grave matter, and respected moral theologians such as Germain Grisez argue that heavy use of tobacco, as opposed to occasional or light use, is grave matter (cf. *Difficult Moral Questions*, pp. 601-602), whether they are mortally sinful would depend on whether we had given these actions sufficient reflection and understood them to be grave matter and whether we had nevertheless committed them with full consent of the will.

Medical findings are clear about the health hazards of smoking and it seems unlikely that any intelligent person, i.e., one who can and has read the warning label on a package of cigarettes, could be unaware of these hazards. But the seriousness of the sin for an individual could be diminished by such things as compulsion and habit, which affect a person's ability to give full consent.

But if all three conditions for a mortal sin (grave matter, sufficient understanding, and full consent of the will) are in place, then, yes, that would keep one from receiving Holy Communion worthily.

Q. My husband wants to get a vasectomy, but I told him that sterilization is a mortal sin. He went to his mother for advice, and she admitted to him that she had had a hysterectomy after the ninth child so as to have no more children. Now my husband is more convinced than ever to have the vasectomy. Did his mother commit a mortal sin by revealing her own sin and not discouraging him from having the surgery? He views her as a good Catholic. — Name and State Withheld

A. The *Catechism* says that anyone who uses his power to lead others to commit sin "becomes guilty of scandal and responsible for the evil that he has directly or indirectly encouraged" (n. 2287). It recalls the warning of Jesus, who said that "temptations to sin are sure to come, but woe to him by whom they come" (Luke 17:1 NAB 1986 NT).

The *Catechism* defines scandal as "an attitude or behavior which leads another to do evil. The person who gives scandal becomes his neighbor's tempter. He damages virtue and integrity; he may even draw his brother into spiritual death. Scandal is a grave offense if by deed or omission another is deliberately led into a grave offense" (n. 2284).

When your mother-in-law told your husband about her hysterectomy, and did not advise him against the vasectomy, she at least indirectly encouraged him to do evil. How serious her sin was would depend on whether she sufficiently understood what she was doing and whether she fully consented to her action.

Q. I have always understood it to be Church teaching that cohabitation of unmarried persons is sinful if sex is involved, but I can't find anything in the *Catechism* that makes this clear. Can you help? — M.K., New York

A. Try section 2353, which says that *"fornication* is carnal union between an unmarried man and an unmarried woman. It is gravely contrary to the dignity of persons and of human sexuality which is naturally ordered to the good of spouses and the generation and education of children. Moreover, it is a grave scandal when there is corruption of the young."

Q. Which is the greater sin — adultery or masturbation? — A.J.M., Illinois

A. Both actions are grave offenses against chastity, and both involve a misuse of the sexual faculty given to us by the Creator. However, we would judge adultery to be the greater sin because it harms not only the individual and his relationship with God, but other persons as well. In fact, in the early Church adultery was ranked (ahead of other sexual sins) with murder, apostasy, and blasphemy as the four most serious sins.

The *Catechism* says that adultery is a grave evil because "he who commits adultery fails in his commitment. He does injury to the sign of the covenant which the marriage bond is, transgresses the rights of the other spouse, and undermines the institution of marriage by breaking the contract on which it is based."

It says that the adulterer "compromises the good of human generation and the welfare of children who need their parents' stable union" (n. 2381).

Q. According to the *Catechism*, judging the moral guilt of a person who masturbates involves taking into account such factors as "conditions of anxiety or other psychological or social factors that can lessen, if not even reduce to a minimum, moral culpability" (n. 2352). In light of this, if your spouse has had a hysterectomy for medical (not birth control) reasons and has lost the desire for sexual relations, would masturbation for the other spouse be acceptable?

The state of marriage is the joining of two people for love, companionship, and friendship, and not just for sex. But you did not enter marriage to lead a celibate life. — Name Withheld, Florida

A. Section 2352 of the *Catechism* says that masturbation is an "intrinsically and gravely disordered action" [CDF, *Persona humana* 9] that is contrary to the essential purpose of the sexual faculty, which is to be used only in a relationship between married persons " 'in which the total meaning of mutual self-giving and human procreation in the context of true love is achieved' [CDF, *Persona humana* 9]."

Thus, in the objective realm, masturbation is always and everywhere wrong; in the subjective realm, one's moral guilt can be lessened, if not reduced to a minimum, due to certain emotional or psychological factors. However, one cannot deliberately use these factors as an excuse to sin, and sincere efforts must be made to overcome these conditions through prayer and the sacraments and the advice of a good confessor.

So the answer to your question is no, masturbation would not be an acceptable or moral solution for a person whose spouse is unable or unwilling to have sexual relations. It is true that you did not enter marriage to lead a celibate life, but circumstances sometimes require celibacy of married couples, e.g., during pregnancy or illness, when a spouse is away from home, or when a spouse becomes physically or psychologically incapable of marital relations. It is then that we fall back on those essential ingredients of marriage that you mentioned: love, companionship, and friendship.

This is not a rare situation for married couples, and it can be a cross for one or both spouses. But the Lord calls us to shoulder our crosses with humility, to share them with Him who made the ultimate sacrifice on the cross, and to offer them up for our own spiritual well-being or for that of someone else. We cannot do this on our own, but only with the help of the God who said:

"Come to me, all you who are weary and find life burdensome, and I will refresh you. Take my yoke upon your shoulders and learn from me, for I am gentle and humble of heart. Your souls will find rest, for my yoke is easy and my burden light" (Matthew 11:28-30).

Q. Our priest informs us that he has approved the selection of the Benziger Family Life series to better prepare parents in dealing with sex education for their children. Is this a suitable selection? If not, what would you recommend? — J.L.M., Indiana

A. No, the Benziger Family Life sex education series is not suitable for giving Catholic children a correct understanding of the Church's teaching on sexuality because it contradicts many of the principles stated in *The Truth and Meaning of Human Sexuality*, which was issued in 1995 by the Pontifical Council for the Family. This very important document is available from the U.S. Catholic Conference Publishing Services, 3211 Fourth Street, N.E., Washington, DC 20017.

The problems with the Benziger series were spelled out by Catholics United for the Faith, who can be reached at 827 N. Fourth St., Steubenville, OH 43952. Among other things, CUF said that the Benziger material is designed for use in a coed setting, which violates a child's privacy and modesty; that it impinges on a child's "years of innocence" by presenting explicit sexual information to which older children, let alone younger ones, should not be exposed; that it is deficient in its presentation of Catholic doctrine on original sin and fails to treat mortal and venial sin at all; and that it offers an ambiguous treatment of official Church teaching on marriage and family, especially with regard to artificial contraception.

For a reliable K-8 supplement for teaching the virtues (with chastity emphasized in grades 6-8), write to the Couple to Couple League, P.O. Box 111184, Cincinnati, OH 45211 and ask for information about their *New Corinthians Curriculum*.

Editor's Note: In a recent reply about reliable materials on sex education, we recommended the *New Corinthians Curriculum (NCC)* that is published by the Foundation for the Family, an affiliate of the Couple to Couple League. The *Curriculum* consists of a 330-page book, with five lessons for each year from kindergarten through eighth grade, and a 50-page *Parent-to-Child Instruction on Human Sexuality* that parents can use to explain Catholic teaching on human sexuality to their children.

Several readers have since taken strong issue with our recommendation and sent along two lengthy critiques of the *NCC*. The first, "New Corinthians Exposed," was published by Mothers' Watch (P.O. Box 2780, Montgomery Village, MD 20886) in the fall of 1996. Among other things, it called the *NCC* "dirty sex education" and said that the program "is very heavily laced with the poison of the sex education/values clarification methodology."

The second critique, "A Closer Look at The New Corinthians K-8 Curriculum," was written by Lisa M. Contini and published in 2000 by Aletheia Press (P.O. Box 577, Massena, NY 13662). In summary, Mrs. Contini said that the *NCC* "is alarmingly similar to existing secular and Catholic programs which offend modesty, utilize values clarification techniques, damage conscience, usurp the God-given rights of parents, and bear some alarming similarities to certain Planned Parenthood methodologies."

The Foundation for the Family, in the persons of Keith Bower and John F. Kippley, have responded at length to both critiques and their responses are available from the FFF at the Couple to Couple League address in the previous reply. In brief, Bower and Kippley called the Mothers' Watch allegations "highly erroneous" and Mrs. Contini's objections false or distorted. "For the most part," said Kippley, "her objections can best be labeled NHW, Not Her Way." He did, however, credit Mrs. Contini with raising several valid points and promised changes in the next edition.

Having read the statements of both sides on this issue, and having read the *NCC* itself, we stand by our earlier recommendation of this program as one of the best tools we have seen for educating children in the virtues, and particularly the virtue of chastity. We do not think that the charges made against the *NCC* are credible. The inflammatory language of the critics ("dirty sex education" and "Planned Parenthood methodologies") is not supported by the content of the *NCC*.

But don't just take my word for it. Read all of the pertinent material yourself, especially the *NCC*, and then decide whether you think that this program is suitable for Catholic families. As the father of nine children and a religious educator for more than 30 years, I think it is suitable and that it would prove very helpful to parents looking for assistance in this vital area.

Q. In section 2357 of the *Catechism*, it says: "Basing itself on Sacred Scripture, which presents homosexual acts as acts of grave depravity [cf. *Gen* 19:1-29; *Rom* 1:24-27; 1 *Cor* 6:10; 1 *Tim* 1:10], tradition has always declared that 'homosexual acts are intrinsically disordered' [CDF, *Persona humana* 8]." In number 2358, however, it says that homosexual men and women "do not choose their homosexual condition; for most of them it is a trial."

Does this mean that homosexual acts are no sin at all since those who commit them did not choose their condition and do not have the full consent of the will? — D.D., South Dakota

A. No, that is not what the sentence means, and perhaps to clarify the point the second edition of the *Catechism* (1997) changed the latter sentence to read: "This inclination, which is objectively disordered, constitutes for most of them a trial." The point is that all homosexual acts, like all heterosexual acts that are contrary to God's divine plan, are objectively sinful.

Whether they are subjectively sinful for the person committing them depends on whether the person fully consents to them, and moral theologians have long recognized that a person's responsibility for his actions can be lessened by such factors as ignorance, habit, and compulsion.

Those seeking solid insights into these issues ought to read two books by Fr. John Harvey, who has been involved for more than 20 years in the pastoral counseling of persons with a homosexual inclination. The books are *The Homosexual Person* and *The Truth About Homosexuality*, both published by Ignatius Press. In the latter volume (pp. 141-142), Fr. Harvey said:

"It seems that in this question of personal responsibility for homosexual acts one should avoid two extreme attitudes: first, that a person cannot help acting out his homosexual tendencies — it is impossible for such persons to be sexually abstinent; and second, that a person has full freedom to get rid of homosexual fantasies, feelings, and actions.

"My experience leads me to believe that many persons have suffered a loss of full freedom because of family background, childhood sexual abuse, ignorance of the moral law, lack of education concerning chastity during the formative years, and various other factors.

"This is not to mention the all-pervading erotic culture proclaiming that one must have physical sex to be normal. While a person with homosexual tendencies may not be compulsive, he may still have greater difficulty in remaining chaste than the ordinary heterosexual person.

"As I said in *The Homosexual Person*, the noncompulsive person is generally not able to share his feelings and desires with those around him for fear of rejection, and that kind of secrecy makes temptations all the stronger. It also creates an interior loneliness and a strong desire to be with other homosexual people."

Despite all these difficulties, said Fr. Harvey, "such a person remains responsible for his actions. The point is that it is generally more difficult for such a person to remain chaste than it is for the ordinary heterosexual man or woman."

The *Catechism* also reminds us that, like everyone else, "homosexual persons are called to chastity." It says that they can "gradually and resolutely approach Christian perfection" by self-mastery, prayer and the grace of the sacraments, and the support of disinterested friends (cf. n. 2359).

Q. A priest discussing lying gave us this scenario: You are at home and someone knocks at your door. You send your child to see who it is. The child comes back and lets you know the person wants to see you. You tell your child to tell the visitor that you are not at home. The priest said that this is not a sin because you are not there for that person. He used some term that sounded like "justification" to describe the situation. Is this a lie or not? — R.P., Georgia

A. He probably used the term "mental reservation," which means using words that can be understood in a true sense, but which will probably be understood by the hearer in another sense. To say that a parent is not home when he is home means in this scenario that he is not home to the visitor. A better way of putting it might be to have the child tell the visitor that the parent is not available, a phrase that people commonly understand to mean that he is not available to talk to you at this time.

Obviously, mental reservations must be used prudently and only for a very good reason lest they create such an atmosphere of mistrust and uncertainty that people are not sure what to believe. And parents ought to explain this distinction to children so they won't think it's okay to lie.

Q. Is lying ever not a sin? Is it ever necessary or justified? I'm wondering about circumstances, such as during World War II when Hitler's soldiers asked, "Are there Jews in your house?" Would a lie have been justified in that situation? Similarly, was our beloved Pope Pius XII in sin when he issued fake baptismal certificates to Jews to save them from death? — M.D., Illinois

A. "The *right to the communication* of the truth is not unconditional," says the *Catechism*. "Everyone must conform his life to the Gospel precept of fraternal love" (n. 2488). It says that this requires those in concrete situations to decide whether or not it is appropriate to reveal the truth to the person who is asking for it.

The *Catechism* (n. 2489) goes on to explain that "charity and respect for the truth should dictate the response to every *request for information or communication*. The good and safety of others, respect for privacy, and the common good are sufficient reasons for being silent about what ought not be known or for making use of a discreet language. The duty to avoid scandal often commands strict discretion. No one is bound to reveal the truth to someone who does not have the right to know it [cf. *Sir* 27:16; *Prov* 25:9-10]."

Relating these comments to the situations raised by M.D., one can see that Nazis seeking to arrest and execute Jews had no right to the truth about where Jews might be found. Concealing the truth from the Nazis by silence, use of discreet language, and falsified baptismal certificates was done for the good and safety of others and for the common good, and was done out of fraternal love. Therefore, no sin was involved.

For an example of the use of discreet language, there is a story of the time St. Athanasius was being pursued in a boat by his enemies. When he told the pilot of his boat to turn around and face his enemies, the skipper of the enemy craft shouted, "Have you seen Athanasius?" The pilot of the saint's boat replied, "Just a short time ago he passed this very spot, going up river."

Q. Can you explain about rash judgment, what would be a serious sin and what would be a venial sin? — B.F.S., Arizona

A. The *Catechism* (n. 2477) says that a person is guilty of rash judgment if he, "even tacitly, assumes as true, without sufficient foundation, the moral fault of a neighbor." In other words, it is the willingness to believe, without sufficient evidence, that a person is guilty of some evil. We might also call it "jumping to conclusions" or "judging a book by its cover."

An example would be a person who saw a neighbor coming and going at odd hours of the night and assumed that the neighbor was involved in some illegal or immoral activity, when in fact the neighbor was attending Nocturnal Adoration services at a church in the next town.

Rash judgment is always a sin against justice both because of the hasty imprudence with which the faulty judgment is made and because this judgment diminishes in our own mind the reputation of the person involved. For the sin to be a grave one, the matter in question must be important, there must be a firm conviction that the judgment is correct, the judgment must be made with full deliberation, and there must be no sound reasons for the judgment.

Jesus Himself, who was often rashly judged for associating with persons perceived to be sinners, offers this advice to us:

"If you want to avoid judgment, stop passing judgment. Your verdict on others will be the verdict passed on you. The measure with which you measure will be used to measure you. Why look at the speck in your brother's eye when you miss the plank in your own? How can you say to your brother, 'Let me take that speck out of your eye,' while all the time the plank remains in your own? You hypocrite! Remove the plank from your own eye first; then you will see clearly to take the speck from your brother's eye" (Matthew 7:1-5).

Chapter 14

Miscellaneous Matters

Q. In two different anthologies of Catholic poetry, I've come across a verse by Irish poet Joseph Mary Plunkett entitled "I See His Blood Upon the Rose." I would like to know where I could get more information about him and read more of his poetry. — P.K.T., West Virginia

A. Joseph Mary Plunkett (1887-1916) was an Irish poet and patriot who was executed by the English for signing the Proclamation of the Irish Republic during the Rising in 1916. The son of Count George Plunkett, Joseph attended the Catholic University School, Belvedere College, and Stonyhurst College. He was briefly the editor of the *Irish Review*, a literary journal, and the author of an astonishing number of poems in his 28 years of life.

The two published volumes of his poetry are *The Circle and The Sword* and *Occulta*. His poetry can be read on the Internet at www2.localaccess.com/elizabeth/bio2.htm. "I See His Blood Upon the Rose" is a particular favorite of this writer. Here are the words:

"I see His blood upon the rose/And in the stars the glory of His eyes./His body gleams amid eternal snows,/His tears fall from the skies./I see His face in every flower;/The thunder and the singing of the birds/Are but His voice — and carven by His power,/Rocks are His written words./All pathways by His feet are worn,/His strong heart stirs the ever-beating sea./His crown of thorns is twined with every thorn,/His cross is every tree."

Q. Can you help me find a beautiful and inspirational poem entitled "No One Needs Thee More Than I," author unknown? — B.G., California

A. Several readers were kind enough to send copies of the poem and here it is:

"Dearest Jesus, all Thy creatures/Are more worthy of Thy grace/Than the vile and wretched sinner/Who now kneels before Thy face;/Yet one claim have I upon Thee,/Which Thou never will deny:/In the bounds of Thy creation/No one needs Thee more than I!

"Other souls have been more faithful,/And have served Thee better far,/Many spotless hearts more fitting/For Thy gracious Presence are;/Many lips devout a greeting/Far more fervent can supply,/But, dear Master, well Thou knowest/No one needs Thee more than I!

"Many loving hearts have carried/Richer offerings to Thy shrine,/Many generous hearts have loved Thee/With a purer love than mine;/These, Thy chosen ones, approach Thee/As the doves to covert fly,/Although utterly unworthy,/No one needs Thee more than I!

"Sins unnumbered unatoned for/Have made havoc in my soul,/And against me stands as witness/Thy recording angel's roll;/All untilled has been my vineyard,/And its soil is hard and dry,/O my God! my only refuge,/No one needs Thee more than I!

"For without Thee I am helpless,/Fast in sin's strong fetters caught,/Blinded by my evil passions,/Swayed by impulses untaught;/I could do no good unaided,/It were worse than vain to try;/Come Thyself to me, sweet Jesus,/No one needs Thee more than I!

"Thou didst leave the Father's bosom/To reclaim and save the lost,/Thou didst take upon Thee freely/Our Redemption's awful cost;/Thou Thyself hast called to Thee,/Thou wilt hearken to my cry:/In the bounds of Thy creation/No one needs thee more than I!"

Q. I have this poem in my head from an old prayer card. I am not sure who wrote it, but here are some lines that I remember. Can you help? — B.M., Louisiana

A. The prayer/poem is entitled "Lo! There He Hangs," by an unknown author, and here are the lines:

"Lo! there he hangs, ashened figure — pinioned to the wood./God grant that I might love Him — even as I should./I draw a little closer — to touch that face divine./And then He leans to whisper — 'Ah, foolish child of mine./If now I should embrace you — my hands would stain you red./And if I leaned to kiss you — the thorns would pierce your head.'/'Twas then I learned in meekness — that love demands a price./'Twas then I knew that suffering — is but the kiss of Christ."

Q. For years I have been trying to find a poem entitled "Rabboni" that was supposedly composed by Mary Magdalen. Here are the first few lines. Can you help? — M.C., Illinois

A. The poem was written by Fr. Joseph Shea, S.J., and here is one version of it:

"When I am dying,/How glad I shall be/That the lamp of my life/Has been burned out for Thee./That sorrow has darkened/ The pathway I trod,/That thorns — not roses/Were strewn o'er its sod./That anguish of spirit/Full often was mine,/Since anguish of spirit/So often was Thine./My cherished Rabboni!/How glad I shall be/To die with this hope/Of a welcome from Thee."

Q. There is a child's bedtime prayer that goes, "Now I lay me down to sleep./I pray the Lord my soul to keep./If I should die before I wake,/I pray the Lord my soul to take." There are two more lines that I can't remember. Can you supply those lines? — J.M., Tennessee

A. The most common form of this prayer, which appeared in *The New England Primer* in 1784, is the four lines quoted above, but two additional lines are: "If I should live another day,/I pray the Lord will guide my way."

Some readers concerned about not frightening children suggested the ending: "Guide me safely through the night,/And wake me with the morning light," or "Angels watch me through the night,/And keep me safe 'til morning light."

Another version goes like this: "Now I lay me down to sleep./ I pray the Lord my soul to keep./Four corners to my bed,/Four angels there o'erspread,/One to watch and one to pray,/Two to bear my soul away./Matthew, Mark, Luke, and John,/Bless this bed that I lie on."

And finally, this version: "Matthew, Mark, Luke and John,/ Bless the bed that I lie on./Before I lay me down to sleep,/I give my soul to Christ to keep./Four corners to my bed,/Four angels there a-spread,/Two to foot and two to head,/And four to carry me when I'm dead./I go by sea,/I go by land,/The Lord made me by His right hand./If any danger come to me,/Sweet Jesus Christ, deliver me./He's the branch and I'm the flower,/Pray God send me a happy hour./And if I should die before I wake,/I pray that Christ my soul will take."

Sweet dreams, everyone!

Editor's Note: To those who asked whether CARE for the Child, which is part of the CARE organization, promotes birth control, family planning, and abortion, we have received an answer from the March/April 1997 issue of *The Caleb Report*, which is published by Life Decisions International in Washington, DC.

According to Douglas R. Scott, president of LDI, the leaders of the international relief agencies Save the Children, CARE, and World Vision signed a letter to Congress in support of the Clinton Resolution, which would fund population control activities overseas. Scott said that World Vision subsequently issued another letter favoring "Mexico City" language in the law that would prohibit sending these funds to organizations that perform or promote abortion as a method of family planning.

The leaders of CARE and Save the Children, however, refused to back such language and "made it clear that the separation between family planning and abortion is merely lip service, and no amount of reasoning was going to change their position," said Scott. He urged pro-lifers to give second thoughts to supporting CARE and Save the Children, adding that "if CARE and Save the Children support the Clinton Resolution and not the Mexico City policy, they are part of the abortion problem and should not be supported by child-loving Americans."

A flier issued by CARE listed seven reasons "why you should support CARE's family planning programs." The reasons are: "(1) Because family planning saves lives. (2) Because family planning helps children. (3) Because population growth puts stress on natural resources and the environment. (4) Because family planning responds to what women want. (5) Because you understand that education is half the battle. (6) Because family planning programs enhance CARE's other programs and help them work better. (7) Because we need to do more."

CARE has instituted family planning programs in 20 countries in Africa, Asia, and Latin America, according to the flier, but says that "there are still millions of families in developing countries who lack access to family planning services."

Q. Is Kwanzaa a pagan holiday? — S.P., New York

A. Kwanzaa — the name means "first fruits" — is not a religious holiday, but rather a cultural one that celebrates African-American traditions. It was created by Dr. Maulana Karenga of Long Beach State University in California, and is celebrated from December 26th to January 1st each year.

According to the movement's web site, "Kwanzaa was established in 1966 in the midst of the Black Freedom Movement and thus reflects its concern for cultural groundedness in thought and practice, and the unity and self-determination associated with this."

The holiday serves several functions, according to its promoters. The first is "to reaffirm and restore our rootedness in African culture." The second is "to strengthen community and reaffirm common identity, purpose, and direction as a people and a world community." The third is to introduce the seven principles of Kwanzaa: unity, self-determination, collective work and responsibility, cooperative economics, purpose, creativity, and faith.

Should African-American Catholics celebrate Kwanzaa? Not if it means honoring one's cultural traditions at the expense of one's religious traditions. Since Kwanzaa falls during the octave of Christmas, focusing on this cultural holiday would draw attention away from the birth of Jesus, which is the most important reason for the season.

Q. When I was boy, I remember the men in the parish marching into church and sitting together during the Holy Name Mass. But a priest told me recently that after Vatican II the Holy Name Society was replaced by other men's groups. Is the Holy Name still active, and how can I get information about it? — G.M., Massachusetts

A. Yes, the Holy Name Society is alive and well, although not to the degree it was 50 years ago. It has about five million active members today and holds national conventions each year.

Starting a Holy Name Society in your parish would be a great idea. For information on how to do so, write to the National Association of Holy Name Societies, P.O. Box 12032, Baltimore, MD 21281. By the way, women as well as men may be members with the permission of the local bishop and pastor.

Founded in 1274 by Blessed John Vercelli, master general of the Dominicans, to promote reverence for the Holy Name of Jesus, the Holy Name Society was introduced to the United States in 1870. The pledge that its members recite is one that all Catholics ought to say often:

"Blessed be God. Blessed be His Holy Name. Blessed be Jesus Christ, true God and true Man. Blessed be the Name of Jesus. I believe, O Jesus, that Thou are the Christ, the Son of the living

God. I proclaim my love for the Vicar of Christ on earth. I believe all the sacred truths which the Holy Catholic Church believes and teaches. I promise to give good example by the regular practice of my faith.

"In honor of His Divine Name, I pledge myself against perjury, blasphemy, profanity, and obscene speech. I pledge my loyalty to the flag of my country and to the God-given principles of freedom, justice, and happiness for which it stands. I pledge my support to all lawful authority, both civil and religious. I pledge my active support and prayers for the fulfillment of human rights for all my brothers and sisters in Christ, regardless of race, creed, or color. I dedicate myself to the honor of the Sacred Name of Jesus Christ and beg that He will keep me faithful to these pledges until death."

Q. I was at a charismatic conference and experienced what is called "holy laughter." Is this a new gift of the Holy Spirit? — C.A.L., New York

A. Several persons — J.M.B. of Maryland, R.F.K. of California, and P.T. of Georgia — were kind enough to send along some good material and to offer some valuable insights about the phenomenon of "holy laughter." According to Sylvia MacEachern, editor of the Canadian Catholic newsletter *The Orator*, "holy laughter" is also known as "the Toronto Blessing," "the Blessing," and "the Vineyard Experience." She said that people experiencing this phenomenon act and sound like animals, exhibiting what Vineyard literature, such as *God's Manifest Presence* by Mike Bickle and Michael Sullivan, says are the following signs:

"Shaking, jerking, loss of bodily strength, heavy breathing, eyes fluttering, lips trembling, oil on the body, changes in skin color, weeping, laughing, 'drunkenness,' staggering, travailing, dancing, falling, visions, hearing audibly into spirit realm, inspired utterances — i.e., prophecy, tongues, interpretation — angelic visitations and manifestations, jumping, violent rolling, screaming, wind, heat, electricity, coldness, nausea as discernment of evil, smelling or tasting good or evil presences, tingling, pain in the body as discernment of illnesses, feeling heavy weight or lightness, trances — altered physical state while seeing and hearing into the spirit world, inability to speak normally, disruption of natural realm — i.e., electrical circuits blown."

MacEachern and others (e.g., Richard M. Riss in an article

entitled "A History of the Revival of 1993-1995") have traced the movement's roots back to 1979, when an 18-year-old South African named Rodney Howard-Browne found himself "immersed in the liquid fire of the Holy Spirit" and, over a period of days, alternated among bouts of uncontrollable laughter, weeping, and tongues. He soon discovered the ability to "anoint" or "bless" people by knocking them over with a touch of his finger on their foreheads, pinning them to the floor for long periods of time and causing them to laugh uncontrollably.

Howard-Browne brought his "power" to the United States in 1987 and, in a series of revival meetings from 1993 to 1995, inspired pastors to take the "anointings" or "blessings" back to their own churches. He particularly impressed John Arnott, pastor of the Toronto Airport Vineyard in Ontario, Canada, whose church soon became a mecca for tens of thousands of pilgrims from all over the world seeking to experience the phenomenon. The pilgrims included four Catholic priests who brought "the Toronto Blessing" to Catholics in Ottawa. The movement has since spread to churches in many other countries.

But the phenomenon is not without its critics, as Paul Carden noted in the Winter 1995 issue of *Christian Research Journal*:

"Skeptics both within and without the charismatic camp in Britain and North America have wasted little time in condemning the renewal. They decry its near-total lack of scriptural support, tumultuous services in which preaching is rendered impossible, and the wide practical disregard for the guidelines in 1 Corinthians 12 and 14 and the premium the apostle Paul placed on self-control as a true mark of the Holy Spirit. Many scornfully attribute the manifestations to such human factors as mass hysteria and auto-suggestion or to demonic activity (drawing comparisons with similar ecstatic behavior, including 'holy laughter,' in Eastern and occult groups)."

P.T., a former charismatic Protestant pastor who converted to Catholicism in 1993, also offered these insightful comments:

"A few years back, several charismatic Protestant preachers found that sustained, irrepressible, and often intense laughter began erupting in the religious meetings where they preached and prayed for those attending. A pattern developed in which the laughter would typically begin with a few individuals and then spread throughout those assembled. Sometimes people laughed so hard and so long that they fell to the floor and were somewhat incapacitated until the phenomenon subsided."

He said that "the laughter was usually in response, not to what we normally consider to be humorous remarks or situations, but rather to a particular kind of interior experience, usually described by the one laughing as a sense of joy or liberation. Many of those present in such meetings have interpreted such 'holy laughter,' as they have dubbed it, as a freeing, cleansing 'gift' of the Holy Spirit, much as the Catholic tradition speaks of the 'gift of tears.'"

Noting that "others have been less certain of the phenomenon's divine origin," P.T. said that "they conclude instead that it's simply a rather harmless, if peculiar, illustration of common psycho-sociological dynamics. Laughter is notoriously contagious and the power of suggestion undoubtedly strong. When the expectation of laughter in a particular meeting has been firmly established, we shouldn't be surprised that a preacher with a reputation for sparking it would have little problem getting it started, or that the eruption of giggles or guffaws in one member of the audience would quickly spread throughout the whole gathering."

His conclusion is that "it's certainly possible for God to give Christians a 'gift' of laughter as a way of cleansing or freeing them from sadness, fear, or doubt; after all, the Scripture tells us that 'a cheerful heart is a good medicine' (Proverbs 17:22). On the other hand, I've also seen how the power of suggestion and expectation can press people in emotionally charged religious meetings to mimic those around them as an attempt to avoid feeling left out or appearing spiritually ungifted. When that happens, genuine spiritual feelings are replaced by religious hype, a situation that cheapens the spiritual life of the community and corrodes the soul of the individual.

"In short, I'd encourage folks to feel free to laugh in such a setting in response to a genuine sense of God's gift of joy. But I wouldn't assume that all laughter in such meetings is from the Holy Spirit, and I'd warn against any attempt to manufacture laughter artificially or to mimic others' laughter just to fit in."

Q. Can you give me any information on definitive ties between the liberal organization named Call to Action and a group known as Small Church Communities, which is promoted by Fr. Arthur Baranowski?— R.B., Minnesota

A. You might want to look at Brian Clowes' well-researched book *Call to Action or Call to Apostasy?* (Human Life International) for information on these Small Faith Communities, or Small Church Communities, and their ties with Call to Action. If the book is not available at your nearest Catholic bookstore, you can obtain a copy from HLI. On pages 71-73, Clowes points out that Call to Action dissenters "have invented the ideal mechanism" for weaning marginal Catholics away from the Church: Small Faith Communities or "house churches." He quotes Fr. Baranowski on the purpose of SFCs:

"We must begin again as church, reinvent the church, refound the church — with a different structure and leadership. Small faith communities are no longer an option but a necessity .... The refounded parish will be formed of clusters of communities relating regularly with the home church under the direction of parishioner leaders .... This new model of church is happening all over the world."

These small groups, says Clowes, gradually weaken their bond with the home parish and the Church, develop their own rituals and beliefs, and become a community "whose purpose is not to worship and glorify God, but to give a supportive environment to each of its members. It is entirely possible that such a 'house church' could be comprised solely of hard-core pro-abortionists who act as clinic escorts for a local abortuary, or promiscuous homosexuals who hold their meetings in a 'gay' bar. The people participating in such groups could adopt any morality or beliefs they liked, since they acknowledge no higher authority."

Q. Our parish is about to launch into a series of "faith communities." Our priests tell us that they are the "in thing" and have been very effective in parts of South America, but I have heard negative comments about them. Can you please give us an evaluation of them? — A.P., California

A. These faith communities, also known as basic or base communities, are small groups of parishioners who gather together on a regular basis for prayer, worship, Bible study, reflection, or acts of charity and social justice. They can be a "source of great hope for the Church" if they "really live in unity with the local Church and the universal Church," said the Sacred Congregation for the Doctrine of the Faith in its 1986 *Instruction on Christian Freedom and Liberation.*

However, some of these communities, particularly in Latin America, got caught up with Marxist ideologues whose methods of "liberating" people from poverty and injustice included promoting the class struggle and engaging in acts of terrorism and violence. Some of these groups arrayed themselves in opposition to the "institutional" Church and bitterly attacked the Church and its leadership.

Groups like these, said Pope Paul VI in his 1975 encyclical on evangelization (*Evangelii Nuntiandi*), "cannot in the true sense of the word be called ecclesial basic communities even though they claim that they remain within the unity of the Church, but yet in opposition to the hierarchy" (n. 58).

He said that the only ecclesial basic communities which can properly claim this title are those that:

• "draw their nourishment from the word of God and do not allow themselves to become the prisoners of extreme political factions or of popular ideologies...."

• "resist the ever-present temptation of offering a systematic challenge to the established order...."

• "are firm in their loyalty to the Church of the district in which they are established and to the universal Church."

• "maintain close and sincere relations with the pastors to whom the Lord has confided the Church and with the magisterium which the Spirit of Jesus has entrusted to them."

• "never entertain the illusion that the Gospel has been announced to them alone, that they alone have the task of proclaiming it or are its sole custodians."

• "make constant progress in their sense of responsibility, in their religious ardor, and in their solicitude and missionary zeal for others."

• "adopt an open attitude to all men, in no way favoring any special categories of people" (*Ibid.*).

Q. I am a physician's assistant who is interested in learning hypnotism, but I have heard that there may be a question of acceptance by our Church. If hypnotism is indeed against Church policy, I will drop the matter; otherwise I will pursue the learning of this art. Please advise. —L.C.L., Florida

A. The word "hypnosis" comes from a Greek word meaning "sleep" and may be defined as an artificially induced state resembling sleep, which is characterized by a particular type of rapport between subject and operator, in which the subject's awareness is narrowed and suggestibility is heightened. While hypnosis has been found useful in psychiatry, anesthesia, dentistry, obstetrics, gynecology, and in the treatment of asthma, migraine headaches, nervous tics, and pain relief, its use as entertainment is wrong because it could cause subjects to act in a foolish or sinful manner.

There is nothing wrong with L.C.L. learning hypnotism, but hypnosis can be used in good conscience only when the following conditions are fulfilled:

(1) There is a serious reason to hypnotize a subject.
(2) The permission of the subject has been obtained.
(3) The operator has proper training and sufficient skill.
(4) The operator is a person of good moral character.

Q. Is it true that the song "The Twelve Days of Christmas" was written in England after the Reformation as a kind of "secret catechism" for people to profess their beliefs and avoid persecution. — K.D., Massachusetts

A. Yes, it is true. The lines of the song have both a surface meaning and a hidden meaning known only to Catholic believers. Thus, when the song says, "On the first day of Christmas my true love gave to me," the words "my true love" refer to God and "me" refers to beleaguered believers. The meaning of the rest of the song is as follows:

The partridge in a pear tree is Jesus Christ. The two turtledoves are the Old and New Testaments. Three French hens stand for faith, hope, and charity. The four calling birds are the four Gospels. The five golden rings refer to the Pentateuch, the first five books of the Bible. The six geese a-laying stand for the six days of creation. The seven swans a-swimming represent the seven Sacraments or the seven gifts of the Holy Spirit. The eight maids a-milking are the eight beatitudes. The nine ladies dancing are the nine fruits of the Holy Spirit. The ten lords a-leaping are the Ten Commandments. Eleven pipers piping stand for the eleven faithful Apostles. Twelve drummers drumming refer to the twelve points of belief in the Apostles' Creed.

Q. What is Opus Dei? Why does it exist? Why do many parish priests and lay people often shy away from it and speak poorly of it? Is it a cult, as some people claim? Also, where could I read more about Opus Dei? — M.U., Illinois

A. Opus Dei (the name means "work of God") is a group that is dedicated to spreading the Gospel throughout society and calling people to holiness and Christian witness in the ordinary circumstances of daily living. Founded in Spain in 1928 by Msgr. Josemaria Escriva de Balaguer, who was beatified in 1982 and canonized in 2002, Opus Dei was raised to the status of a personal prelature by Pope John Paul II in 1982. This means a jurisdiction for special pastoral and missionary work according to statutes laid down by the Holy See.

The 2000 edition of the *Annuario Pontifico* said that the prelature had 1,734 priests, 344 major seminarians, 81,954 lay persons representing about 80 nationalities, and 1,654 churches and pastoral centers. Opus Dei also operates the Pontifical University of the Holy Cross in Rome and its courses of study include theology, philosophy, canon law, and social communications.

For more about Opus Dei, you can write to their information offices either at 99 Overlook Circle, New Rochelle, NY 10804 or at 655 Levering Ave., Los Angeles, CA 90024.

You would have to ask individual priests why they shy away from or speak poorly of Opus Dei, but we suspect that some of these priests are either ignorant of what the prelature is all about or they want no part of a group that is outstanding in its fidelity to the Holy Father and the magisterium.

The *New York Times* and other media giants have in the past attempted to portray Opus Dei as some kind of secret cult that poses a danger to society. But the *Times* is no more accurate in this assessment than it was when it portrayed Fidel Castro as the George Washington of Cuba.

Q. What is the Knights of Pythias and what is the Church's position on membership in this organization? — N.R.G., Florida

A. The Knights of Pythias was founded in 1864 by prominent Freemasons, and the *Catholic Encyclopedia* finds the following features of this organization objectionable:

"First, the oath of secrecy by which the member binds himself to keep secret whatever concerns the doings of the Order, even from those in church and state who have a right to know, under certain conditions, what their subjects are doing. Secondly, this oath binds the member to blind obedience, which is symbolized by a test. Such an obedience is against the law of man's nature, and against all divine and human law. Thirdly, Christ is not the teacher and model in the rule of life but the pagan Pythagoras and the pagans Damon, Pythias, and Dionysius."

We are not aware of a specific Church ban on Catholics joining the Knights of Pythias, but the Sacred Congregation for the Doctrine of the Faith, on November 26, 1983, said that Catholics are prohibited from joining "Masonic associations ... since their principles have always been regarded as irreconcilable with the Church's doctrine." The Congregation said that "Catholics enrolled in Masonic associations are involved in serious sin and may not approach Holy Communion."

We assume that "Masonic associations" include the Knights of Pythias.

Q. A friend of mine is an active member of the Rosicrucians. She also claims to be very Catholic and sees no contradiction in these two facts, asserting that the Rosicrucians are a noble body of purveyors of wisdom and virtue. She says that priests and nuns are in her group, but I always thought the Rosicrucians were like the Freemasons, that they are anti-Catholic and condemned by the Church. Who is right? — J.P.O, State Unknown

A. The Rosicrucians, also known as the Ancient Mystical Order Rosae Crucis (AMORC), are an occult group that resembles the ancient Gnostics, whose disciples believed that they possessed a special kind of secret knowledge, unavailable to ordinary humans, that would enable them to unlock the widsom of the universe and bring about a new paradise.

AMORC traces its lineage back to Christian Rosenkreutz, a fictitious person who supposedly lived about 600 years ago and who, during travels to the Holy Land, Egypt, Morocco, and Spain, acquired occult knowledge that was passed on to his disciples.

Modern Rosicrucianism was founded in New York City in 1915 by H. Spencer Lewis, an occultist. Its two major societies in the United States are located in Kingston, NY, and San Jose, CA. One of its formal published statements says that "because of its aggressiveness and growth, the Order Rosae Crucis of America, as well as in other countries, has been condemned by the Pope as destructive to the principles of Roman Catholicism." We don't know what Pope, if any, issued such a condemnation.

The general statutes of the order identify it as part of Freemasonry, and its strange mixture of Christian and non-Christian beliefs ought to preclude Catholics from getting involved with this group.

Q. I have heard that Fr. Richard P. McBrien's popular book *Catholicism* has been criticized by the Vatican for certain "inaccuracies." Can you tell me what these inaccuracies are? — R.S.J., Virginia

A. The criticism to which you are referring was compiled by the National Conference of Catholic Bishops' Secretariat for Doctrine and Pastoral Practices and was published in the April 18, 1996 issue of *Origins*. A copy of this issue is available from the Catholic News Service, 3211 4th St., N.E., Washington, DC 20017.

In general, the Committee on Doctrine said that the latest edition of *Catholicism* contained "inaccurate or misleading statements," put modern theological opinions on a par with magisterial teaching, and implied that "the past appears to be markedly inferior to the present." In particular, the review of McBrien's book said that he:

- maintained that Jesus could have sinned;
- questioned the virginal conception of Jesus;
- favored the view that Mary had "normal sexual relations after the birth of Jesus" and that Jesus had blood brothers and sisters;
- declared that contraception, homosexuality, and ordaining women are open questions, rather than settled Church teaching; and
- accused Popes of having "erred in matters of faith" and of having "come down on the side of a heretical position."

The Committee on Doctrine, which had raised similar concerns about the second edition of the book back in 1985, noted that not only were those "ambiguities" not corrected, but McBrien had introduced "additional problems" into the text of the third edition. Nevertheless, the book continues to be widely used in college theology courses and in religious education programs at the parish level.

Q. In a letter received from the bishop's office in my diocese, I was told that "Fr. Richard McCormick, S.J., is indeed a notable and respected Catholic moral theologian." I am confused. This does not coincide with information I have on Fr. McCormick. Do his views reflect the teachings of the Pope and the Church? — G.B., Ohio

A. No, Fr. McCormick's views do not reflect the teachings of the Pope and the magisterium of the Church. He is one of the most vocal dissenters from Church teaching on sexual morality and the most prominent proponent of the theory of proportionalism, which holds that persons can choose to commit an immoral act if the good effects proportionately outweigh the evil effects.

But Pope John Paul II said that such theories "are not faithful to the Church's teaching when they believe they can justify, as morally good, deliberate choices of kinds of behavior contrary to the commandments of the divine and natural law" (*Veritatis Splendor*, n. 76).

For more information on McCormick and his fallacious theory of proportionalism, see the Lawler, Boyle, May book *Catholic Sexual Ethics* (Our Sunday Visitor), pp. 79-88, and Germain Grisez's book *Christian Moral Principles* (Franciscan Herald Press), pp. 141-171.

Q. Could you tell me something about the comatose little girl in Worcester, Massachusetts in whose room a statue of the Blessed Virgin Mary cries bloody tears? — D.G., Pennsylvania

A. The girl's name is Audrey Santo and she has been in a non-speaking state since nearly drowning in 1987 at the age of three. Visitors to the home have reported oil oozing from statues of Jesus and the Blessed Mother, and blood stains on Communion hosts consecrated at Mass in the family's garage, which has been converted into a chapel. A diocesan commission that had been investigating the matter for 14 months said that tests of the blood showed that it was human blood, but it did not match the blood of any members of the Santo family.

At a news conference on January 21, 1999, Bishop Daniel P. Reilly of Worcester, who ordered the investigation late in 1997 and indicated that it will continue, said that "we are not yet able to confirm claims of miraculous events occurring at Audrey's home or as a result of a visit to Audrey, or from oils associated with

442 / Catholic Replies 2

her." He said he thinks that "there is a special presence of God in that home" and that Masses will continue to be celebrated there.

The Bishop cautioned, however, that "public prayer to Audrey is not acceptable in Catholic teaching," but "there can be private prayer." He also discouraged visits to the home "because they are disruptive to the family," and he urged people to "pray for Audrey, for her family, and for all those seeking healing and hope."

As for the oils reportedly oozing from statues, Dr. John P. Madonna, a psychologist who serves on the three-member commission, said that the panel "looked behind pictures and we picked up statues and we tried to determine what was really promoting the emission of fluids. And we found nothing that we could consider trickery." He said that "additional quantifiable study is needed to attempt to define the composition of the oil and to verify other claims, as well as to determine Audrey's ability to recognize and respond to outside stimuli."

Q. I would appreciate your comments on a magazine I received from the Most Holy Family Monastery in Fillmore, New York. It is entitled *A Voice Crying in the Wilderness* and contains several articles by a Brother Michael Dimond, O.S.B. I am disturbed by some of its extreme views about the Pope, the Mass, Natural Family Planning, and the possibility that Rome has become the "seat of the antichrist." — R.D., Michigan; R.D.P., New York; and R.B., Texas

A. You have good reason to be disturbed since the magazine is filled with outrageous nonsense. It contains literally hundreds and hundreds of statements which purportedly demonstrate that Pope John Paul II is "a blatant heretic and an enemy of the True Faith"; that "the New Mass is deadly"; and that "while all non-Catholics are lost to Hell, most Catholics also go to Hell."

We don't know who Brother Michael Dimond is, but many of the statements he makes in this 40-page magazine are absurd. One would have to spend thousands of hours checking the accuracy of his alleged quotations from numerous saints, popes, and councils, but we suspect that many of them are inaccurate or out of context. We know that many of his own statements are false, so we suspect that he has misrepresented his sources as well.

For example, Dimond says that when Pope Paul VI went to Fatima in October 1967, "he did not visit the shrine at the Cova da Iria," and "he refused to speak privately to Sr. Lucia, who is the only surviving visionary of Fatima." We have been to Fatima and have seen the pictures of Paul VI talking publicly with Sister Lucy (it is very likely that he spoke with her privately as well) and addressing more than one million pilgrims gathered at the Cova on October 13th of that year.

For another example, Dimond claims that Pope Pius XI's encyclical *Casti Connubii* "contains no explicit or implicit approval of regulating birth or allowing NFP [Natural Family Planning]." Here is what the Holy Father actually said in his encyclical: "Nor are those considered as acting against nature who in the married state use their right in the proper manner, although on account of natural reasons either of time or of certain defects new life cannot be brought forth" (n. 59). That's an endorsement of what we now call Natural Family Planning.

In summary, we cannot state too strongly that if this magazine finds its way to you, throw it in the nearest trash barrel. It is truly a danger to your Catholic faith.

Editor's Note: Regarding a recent reply about a Brother Michael Dimond and his magazine *A Voice Crying in the Wilderness,* several readers have written to take issue with our statements that Pope Paul VI spoke privately with Sister Lucia during a visit to Fatima in 1967 and that Pope Pius XI endorsed Natural Family Planning in his encyclical *Casti Connubii.*

There is probably little point in trying to reason with those who would give credibility to anything said by a man who called Pope John Paul "a blatant heretic," and ordinarily we would have let the matter rest with our advice to drop this magazine in the nearest trash barrel. But we would like to respond to the two points raised by our critics.

First, Dimond said that during his visit to Fatima on October 13th, the fiftieth anniversary of the miracle of the sun, Pope Paul "did not say one Hail Mary there [how on earth does Dimond know that?]. He did not visit the shrine at the Cova da Iria. He refused to speak privately with Sister Lucia, who is the only surviving visionary of Fatima."

The source for these statements is apparently a book entitled *Fatima: Prophecies of Tragedy and Triumph* by Frere Francois de Marie des Anges, excerpts from which were sent to us. According to that book, Paul VI commanded, not invited, Sister Lucia to leave her cloistered convent in Coimbra, against her wishes, and attend his Mass in front of the basilica in Fatima.

After the Mass, the book says, Lucia asked for a meeting alone with the Holy Father, but he told her to communicate her concerns to her bishop, who would pass them along to him. The cameras then recorded Lucia weeping, the story goes, and "the Pope did not see Sister Lucy again after that encounter at the podium after the Mass; he only saw her in public at the podium."

We are looking right now at a book about Fatima that has several pictures of Paul VI's 1967 visit. In one picture, he is shown praying at the foot of the statue of Our Lady in the Chapel of the Apparitions. The statue stands on the spot where the apparitions took place in 1917, so it is false to claim that Paul did not visit the shrine at the Cova da Iria.

Two other pictures show Lucia first kneeling before the Holy Father and later standing by his side and talking with him. There is no sign of tears in either picture, only a radiant smile on the nun's face.

Whether Sister Lucia met privately with Paul VI on that occasion, we have not been able to determine. But to suggest that the Pope spurned her alleged request or that she wept at the Holy Father's alleged rebuff is ridiculous. A more likely explanation for Lucia's presence on that October 13th is that Paul VI wanted to present her to the world and to show that he supported the role she had played so faithfully as a messenger of Our Lady for fifty years. For a reliable account of Paul VI's visit to Fatima, see Fr. Robert Fox's book *Fatima Today* (Christendom Publications), pp. 73-76 and 167-168.

Regarding our statement that Pope Pius XI endorsed Natural Family Planning in paragraph 59 of his 1930 encyclical, you don't have to take our word for it. Two experts on the Church's teaching on human life, John F. Kippley and Janet E. Smith, have clearly demonstrated this far better than we could.

See, for example, page 231 of Kippley's book *The Art of Natural Family Planning* (Couple to Couple League), which is co-authored by Sheila K. Kippley, and Smith's essay "The Moral Use of Natural Family Planning," which can be found in a book she edited entitled *Why Humanae Vitae Was Right: A Reader* (Ignatius Press), pp. 447-471.

Q. My husband and I are in our 70s and have a limited pension. We have tried to give a few dollars each month to various charities, but now we are bombarded with charitable requests. Some have heart-wrenching stories

and pictures that I think are geared to make us feel guilty if we don't contribute. We can't give to all these charities. Is there a list of legitimate charities that we can be sure are doing God's work? — I.K.G., New York

A. You are not alone in being bombarded with appeals for money from both religious and secular charities. We are sure that virtually every reader of this reply has been besieged in similar fashion. But unless you recently won millions in some lottery or sweepstakes, it is impossible to give to all of these charities, even though some of their fund-raising letters do indeed lay a guilt trip on you.

We don't know of any absolutely reliable list of Catholic charities, i.e., charities whose funds are directed only to individuals or groups whose needs and goals are completely in tune with Catholic teachings. There are some groups soliciting funds to support an agenda that is not that of the Church.

What can you do? Give first to local and diocesan charities where you can actually see what your money is accomplishing (e.g., the Society of St. Vincent de Paul). Second, give to those schools and religious orders, missionary societies, radio and TV apostolates, and organizations and publications that you know, from their literature or from the names of good people associated with them, are loyal to the magisterium of the Church.

Third, pick and choose, even among the good causes, since you cannot afford to give to all of them. Fourth, don't feel guilty if you are doing all you can to help the least of our brothers and sisters in need since you are doing what the Lord expects of you.

Q. Can you tell me anything about the movement known as Moral Rearmament? — T.L.H., Massachusetts

A. Founded in 1928 as the Oxford Group by a man named Frank Buchman (he renamed it Moral Rearmament in 1938), MRA attracted hundreds of thousands of followers in England and America in the 1940s and 1950s by calling people to change their hearts, and eventually the world, by living the four standards of honesty, purity, love, and unselfishness. It used various means of communication, including teaching, preaching, the media, and the theater, to spread its message.

MRA had two training centers, one in Mackinac Island, Michigan, and the other in Switzerland, and thousands of full-time workers who devoted their lives to the movement. One feature of MRA that caused considerable controversy was the public confession of one's personal sins. The Vatican's Holy Office, in 1951 and 1955, warned Catholics not to hold positions of responsibility in the movement because it promoted religious indifferentism, the idea that one religion is as good as another.

For additional information about this once-influential movement, see the book *Acts of Faith* (Ignatius Press) by Faith Abbott, who was born and raised in MRA and worked full time for it until she converted to the Catholic Church in 1954. Her memoir, written in the 1950s but not submitted for publication until 1994, is instructive for what it tells us about MRA, but it is also a beautifully written and moving conversion story.

Miss Abbott's detailed account of the instructions in the faith that she received from Fr. Eugene Clark is worth the price of the book and would make a good apologetics tool for prospective converts to the Catholic Church.

Q. When did the Church first officially and explicitly condemn slavery? — A.T., Rhode Island

A. Slavery was a legal and accepted part of Roman society when the Catholic Church came into existence in the first century, but the Church's exertions to better the lot of slaves by emphasizing their human dignity and working for their emancipation led to its virtual eradication by the fifth century.

Slavery surfaced again when the barbarians swept through Europe, but the Church's evangelizing and civilizing efforts were successful in almost eliminating the institution before it erupted again with the expeditions to the New World by Spain and Portugal in the 15th and 16th centuries. The Popes in those and succeeding centuries, including Eugene IV in 1435, Pius II in 1482, Paul III in 1537 (he imposed excommunication on those who took part in the slave trade), Urban VIII in 1689, Benedict XIV in 1741, and Gregory XVI in 1838, all condemned slavery.

The *Catechism of the Catholic Church* continued this long tradition in 1992 by saying that the Seventh Commandment forbids acts or enterprises that "lead to the *enslavement of human beings*, to their being bought, sold, and exchanged like merchandise, in disregard for their personal dignity" (n. 2414).

Q. I agree with warnings about not getting involved in yoga, but is it all right if one uses only the physical exercises of the yoga system to benefit one's health? — J.A.B., Oregon

A. Using yoga strictly as a way of exercising one's body would probably not pose a problem for Catholics, but one should definitely stay away from the religious elements of yoga since they could lead one into Hinduism and into accepting such false beliefs as reincarnation.

In his valuable book *Catholics and the New Age* (Servant Publications), Fr. Mitch Pacwa said that the word "yoga" is Sanskrit for "yoke" or "union," and that in Hinduism it describes "the general category of various kinds of disciplines meant to unite a person with the divine. Yoga can refer to physical (*hatha*), mental (*raja*), sexual (*tantra*), or other disciplines to achieve enlightenment" (p. 225).

Earlier in the book, Fr. Pacwa said that "the four main types of yoga are: knowledge or *jnana yoga*; love and devotion or *bhakti yoga*; work and effort or *karma yoga*; and psychological and physical exercises and meditation or *raja yoga*. Most New Agers are familiar with *raja yoga*, typically seen in exercises like sitting cross-legged in the 'lotus position,' or standing on one's head or shoulders, or in exercises requiring the flexibility of a contortionist" (p. 33).

He cautioned readers to remember that "Hindus did not devise these exercises for athletic limbering or muscle building. All were meant to lead the practitioner to enlightenment and the awareness of his or her inner divinity" (*Ibid.*).

Obviously, therefore, a Catholic should avoid getting involved in using yoga to seek enlightenment or an awareness of his "inner divinity" since it could lead him into New Age cults or activities. And perhaps a prudent Catholic ought to seek another type of exercise regimen that would be beneficial to his health.

Q. I have been given a book called *Stories From Heaven*, volume X, which purports to be the recordings of revelations from the saints, our Lady, and God to a woman named Frances Marie Klug in Southern California. What do you know about this book? — J.B., Wisconsin

A. Someone sent us four volumes (I, II, III, VI) of *Stories From Heaven* and, after looking at them, we would advise you to stay away from these books. While the publishers of these volumes claim that anyone reading them "will easily recognize the sound logic and sound direction the messages contain," we would suggest that the messages are unsound and contrary to Catholic teaching. For example, two of the "major revelations of significance" contained in the books are that "our Heavenly Mother is Part of the Divine, and St. Joseph is truly The Holy Ghost" (!).

While on this subject, let us caution readers not to accept as gospel private revelations and messages attributed to the Blessed Mother, the saints, and others unless these messages have been given official sanction by the Church. We get criticized from time to time for not relying on private revelations about the hidden life of Jesus and His mother. But we have no way of knowing if these accounts are accurate, and it would be unwise to accept them as factual.

As Catholics, we are obliged to believe only in public Revelation, which ended with the death of the last Apostle.

Q. As an orthodox Catholic, I almost always agree with your observations. However, I must disagree with your assumption that Vicka (one of the Medjugorje visionaries) was wrong in claiming that the Blessed Mother had endorsed *The Poem of the Man-God*. I know that Vicka would not lie about something the Blessed Mother said and, while I have great respect for Joseph Cardinal Ratzinger [who has questioned the reliability of *The Poem*], I think if there is any error, it is far more plausible to assume that it would be on the part of a human, rather than the Mother of God. — H.V.M., Kentucky

A. We agree with your last sentence and hasten to point out that since Vicka is human, she could very well be in error about what the Blessed Mother is alleged to have said. We never suggested that Vicka was a liar, only that she may have been mistaken in what she thought she heard.

Q. Your comments on *The Poem of the Man-God* leave me in a quandary. I refer you to the enclosed copy of a statement attached to the inside cover of volume 1 of the publication. It claims an imprimatur directly from Pope Pius XII. Your further comments would be appreciated. — R.J.M., Texas

A. According to the statement on the inside cover, Pius XII was given a typewritten copy of *The Poem* in 1947 and, in a private audience on February 26, 1948, told three priests:

"Publish this work as it is. There is no need to give an opinion about its origin, whether it be extraordinary or less. Who reads it will understand. One hears of many visions and revelations. I don't mean to say that they are all real, but there are some of which it can be said that they are real."

The statement claims that "this work by Maria Valtorta got its imprimatur directly from the Pope himself, which is strictly according to canon law of the Church (cf. amongst others, canon 218 in canon law 1917 and also canon 331 in canon law 1983)."

The two canons refer to the "supreme, full, immediate, and universal power" which the Pope is free to exercise in virtue of his office as Vicar of Christ and Pastor of the Church on earth. They say nothing about granting imprimaturs because Popes don't give imprimaturs; bishops do. According to canon 824, the power of granting imprimaturs resides with the "local Ordinary of the author or the Ordinary of the place in which the books are published."

Still on this subject, L.V. of Louisiana sent a copy of the Winter 1992 issue of *The Valtorta Newsletter*, which contained the following statement:

"Some object that *Il Poema's* English translation, *The Poem of the Man-God*, does not have the imprimatur. In fact, in 1965-1966, Pope Paul VI abrogated canons 1399 and 2318 of the 1918 [*sic*] Code of Canon Law, so that no book of the categories concerned by these canons need now have the imprimatur, and that includes *Il Poema* and all its translations."

The same argument has been used about other texts of alleged private revelations that are currently in circulation. But on December 4, 1996, the Sacred Congregation for the Doctrine of the Faith, in its "Notification on Vassula Ryden," made these statements:

"(1) The interpretation given by some individuals to a decision approved by Pope Paul VI on October 14, 1966 and promulgated on November 15th of that year, in virtue of which writings and messages resulting from alleged revelations could be freely circulated in the Church, is absolutely groundless. This decision actually referred to the 'Abolition of the Index of Forbidden Books,' and determined that — after the relevant censures were lifted — the moral obligation still remained of not circulating or reading those writings which endanger faith and morals.

"(2) It should be recalled, however, that with regard to the circulation of texts of alleged private revelations, canon 823.1 of the current code remains in force: 'The pastors of the Church have the ... right to demand that writings to be published by the Christian faithful which touch upon faith or morals be submitted to their judgment.'

"(3) Alleged supernatural revelations and writings concerning them are submitted in first instance to the judgment of the diocesan bishop and, in particular cases, to the judgment of the episcopal conference and the Congregation for the Doctrine of the Faith."

Q. I personally believe Medjugorje is fraudulent. But since I am convinced *Man-God* is authentic I find any linkage between them a kiss of death to Valtorta, and this is most unfortunate. I read Valtorta's works originally before I knew they had been Indexed, and we believers in Valtorta are not getting a fair shake. We have legitimate questions that are not being answered. Allow me to make some points. — D.V.S., Illinois

A. We do not have the space to treat all 11 of your points, but here are comments on three of them:

• "Did or did not Pius XII give *Man-God* his verbal (entirely acceptable) imprimatur? If he did, how could it be subsequently Indexed?"

Pius XII did not give *Man-God* an imprimatur.

• "If, as Cardinal Ratzinger said, *Man-God* could cause spiritual harm to those who read it, we are entitled to be told what the specific objections are. I've never seen any such evidence. I don't believe there is any."

We, too, would like to see the specific objections spelled out, but we would note that the Cardinal's original criticism of *The Poem* was toned down in 1993 when his congregation said that those who distribute *The Poem* must make clear that the "visions" and "dictations" of Maria Valtorta are literary forms used by her to narrate the life of Jesus, and they cannot be considered supernatural in origin.

• "It's extremely uncomfortable for us to be in seeming defiance of Cardinal Ratzinger and the Index. But we see the good Cardinal under tremendous constraints as regards Valtorta's writings. Christ's [alleged] comments about the Jews of His time and in the future are not conducive to ecumenical harmony. In fact, if the Church were to declare *Man-God* authentic, there would be a terrible rupture. Is Ratzinger being dishonest? No, but perhaps very, very prudent."

And this is what we advise all our readers to be — very, very prudent when it comes to private revelations that have not received the official approval of the Church. No matter how much one believes in these alleged revelations, it is spiritual folly to pit one's personal opinions against the authority of the Church.

Q. I have not seen any reference, good or bad, to a very wonderful Catholic author, Fr. Joseph F. Girzone, who, I believe, truly has the gift of the Holy Spirit in him when he writes. From what I have read, Fr. Girzone really does love the Catholic Church, but at the same time has seen firsthand the damage well-meaning persons have done to make people shy away from the Church and to keep us separate from other persons who believe in Jesus Christ.

I have included some long excerpts from two of Fr. Girzone's books, *Joshua and the Children* and *The Shepherd*, and would like to know what you think about his comments on priestly celibacy (Is his interpretation of Matthew 19:12 a fair one?) and optional worship services on Sunday. — D.A.C., Massachusetts

A. Regarding priestly celibacy, Fr. Girzone says, among other things, that "the priesthood and celibacy are two separate vocations. Demanding one as a requisite for the other does not mean that the Holy Spirit is going to cooperate and give them grace for both. The damage that attitude has caused is obvious to anyone with an open mind. In a situation as tragic as this is for all of Christianity, the words of Jesus stand out clearer than ever, 'The Sabbath was made for man and not man for the Sabbath. The law was made for man and not man for the law.'

"Where there is a human need, the law must bend. You don't insist on a law when it destroys people's lives and occasions unbelievable scandal to so many good people, and tears the Church apart, and attracts so many sick people into the priesthood. Jesus' advice on celibacy is short and to the point: 'Let him who can take it, take it' [Matthew 19:12]. He Himself made it optional. Insistence on observance of a law when it occasions so much human tragedy and scandal points out the wisdom of Jesus' philosophy."

It is true that Jesus did not make celibacy a prerequisite in His choice of the twelve Apostles, nor did the Apostles mandate it for those who presided over the first Christian communities (cf. 1 Timothy 3:2-5 and Titus 1:5-6), but it has been the approved practice of the Church founded by Christ since at least early in the fourth century (cf. Christian Cochini's book *The Apostolic Origins of Priestly Celibacy*).

Furthermore, we have the example of Christ Himself, who remained celibate during His life on earth and who commended those who were able to accept this special spiritual gift and to freely renounce sex "for the sake of God's reign" (Matthew 19:11-12). He also promised that "everyone who has given up home, brothers or sisters, father or mother, wife or children or property for my sake will receive many times as much and inherit everlasting life" (Matthew 19:29).

To say that "where there is a human need, the law must bend" is absurd on its face. That kind of logic could lead to Church approval of divorce, adultery, abortion, contraception, and a host of other evils. Celibacy is not the cause of damage and scandals in the Church; human sinfulness is. Celibacy is not forced on any candidate for the priesthood, but is freely chosen by those seeking to serve as other Christs after years of training, reflection, and prayer. And it is no more responsible for unfaithful priests than marriage is responsible for unfaithful husbands and wives.

We also strongly disagree with Fr. Girzone's opinion that the Holy Spirit is incapable of providing sufficient grace for priests to live a celibate life. Yes, some have failed in this regard, but what of the millions who have faithfully embraced this gift? In his encyclical letter on priestly celibacy (*Sacerdotalis Caelibatus*), Pope Paul VI showed the positive side of renunciation for the sake of the kingdom:

"There are still today in God's holy Church, in every part of the world where she exercises her beneficent influence, great numbers of her ministers — subdeacons, deacons, priests, and bishops — who are living their life of voluntary and consecrated celibacy in the most exemplary way. Nor can we overlook the immense ranks of religious men and women at their side, of laity and of young people too, united in the faithful observance of perfect chastity.

"They live in chastity, not out of disdain for the gift of life, but because of a greater love for that new life which springs from the paschal mystery. They live this life of courageous self-denial and spiritual joyfulness with exemplary fidelity and also with relative facility. This magnificent phenomenon bears testimony to an exceptional facet of the Kingdom of God living in the midst of modern society" (n. 13).

As for Fr. Girzone's view of attendance at Sunday Mass, characters in his book *The Shepherd* talk about people coming to Catholic Mass and not being fed. "Jesus spent his life teaching people they are family and that if they want to be close to God, they must find him in one another, not just in ritual," Joshua tells David.

He suggests letting "the people meet in smaller groups with their own leaders. God has called many more priests than are now recognized. Some may be married. That has never been an obstacle to God's call, so choose persons 'of tried and proven virtue.' They have already passed the test. They are stable and spiritual. They will be a credit and not a liability."

When David asks about the Sunday Eucharist, Joshua replies: "Jesus offered his Body and Blood as a gift, not a forced obligation on scheduled demand. Be open to change, David, if you want to respond to the needs of God's children. The law was made for them, not they for the law."

David went on to call his own candidates to the priesthood, bypassing the seminary, and he set up in every parish in the diocese "optional small communities where people met on Sundays for flexible liturgies and the Eucharist. When they felt the need, they could still go to the main church and worship with the large community. It worked well. People came to know one another and formed beautiful friendships."

Several comments come to mind. First, yes, we are supposed to find God in other people, but we are also to find Him in a special way in the Holy Eucharist. Second, ritual was very important to Jesus. Not only did He faithfully celebrate the Passover ritual, but He used that ritual to introduce the first Mass.

He also commanded that we celebrate Mass "in memory of Me." And the Church to which He gave the power to make laws in His name has made attendance at Sunday Mass obligatory for Catholics under pain of mortal sin.

Third, if some of David's "priests" were married, didn't come through Church-approved seminaries, and were not ordained by the bishop, where did they get the power to confect the Eucharist? Those attending these "flexible liturgies" may form beautiful friendships, but are they participating in the Holy Sacrifice of the Mass?

Fr. Girzone may love the Catholic Church, as D.A.C. suggests, but the church promoted by the characters in his books is not recognizable to us as the Catholic Church founded by Christ and presided over today by the Vicar of Christ.

Q. I would like to have more information about Serra International. — J.J.M., Nova Scotia

A. Serra International was founded in 1934 to foster vocations to the priesthood and the religious life and to train lay leaders for the Church. Located at 65 East Wacker Place, Chicago, IL 60601, it has more than 21,000 members in 35 countries and is formally affiliated with the Pontifical Society for Priestly Vocations.

Q. A column in our parish bulletin says that America "is not, and never was intended to be, a Christian nation." Is this correct? — F.C.D., Wisconsin

A. While not all the Founding Fathers of this country were Christians, and even those who were did not call specifically for the formation of a Christian nation, the 56 men who signed the Declaration of Independence certainly recognized the importance of God in their lives and in their momentous undertaking.

They mentioned God four times in that important document, referring to "the laws of nature and nature's God," acknowledging the "Creator" who endows everyone with certain unalienable rights, appealing to "the Supreme Judge of the world for the rectitude of our intentions," and beginning their historic quest for independence "with a firm reliance on the protection of Divine Providence."

Our founders may not have intended America to be a Christian nation, but Christianity has played a vital role in the growth of America (look at all the cities named after Catholic saints and Catholic doctrines) and one would have to be historically blind not to have noticed the amazing confluence (divinely inspired, in our opinion) of persons and events that led to the creation and expansion of what we still refer to as "one nation under God," although it might be hard to prove that claim today.

Nevertheless, we Catholics are continually called to Christianize this nation, to persuade others by our words and deeds that Christ remains the way, and the truth, and the life if we expect to attain everlasting joy and happiness in Heaven.

Q. Recent events involving the President of the United States have caused me to wonder if a Catholic, in good conscience, can become a member of the U.S. Secret Service. The Secret Service agents are to put their lives in the path of harm directed at the President, which can result in an agent giving his life. Would that be suicide?

There are reports that agents have been used to alert a President about his wife's approach while he skinny-dipped with women in the White House pool. Would it be wrong to cover for a President's immoral activities? — E.C.S., South Carolina

A. Of course it would be wrong to facilitate a President's sexual trysts or to help keep his wife and others from finding out about his sinful conduct. An agent with a properly formed conscience, who finds himself or herself constantly in that kind of immoral environment, ought to seek a transfer to another job in the Secret Service or, failing that, to find employment elsewhere in the government or the private sector.

We recognize that this would not be an easy decision to make, especially for a person who had entered the job with the highest of ideals and hopes for serving his country, and that it could invite political retaliation by the President or by those who are loyal to him. But if remaining in that situation would mean continually cooperating in another's sin, then a prudent and moral person ought to seek employment elsewhere.

As for an agent giving his life to protect the President, that would not be suicide, any more than in the case of the soldier who throws himself on a grenade to protect his comrades, or the police officer who dies while disarming a bomb, or the firefighter who gets trapped in a burning building while trying to rescue a child.

While each of these persons knew that the risks of their job included the possibility of dying in the line of duty, none of them entered their particular situation with the intention of dying. Their only intention was to save someone else's life, not to end their own, which is entirely different from the motivation of a suicide victim.

The words of Jesus would be appropriate in these cases:

"There is no greater love than this: to lay down one's life for one's friends" (John 15:13).

Q. Attached is a clipping from a recent issue of the *Catholic Voice*, which is published by the Oakland Diocese. The play "Late Nite Catechism" is being presented as a fundraiser by the Sisters of the Holy Family. Do you know anything about this play? Based on the title and the picture of the actress, it would not seem suitable for a Catholic group. — J.P.B., California

A. We have never attended a performance of "Late Nite Catechism," or any similar show, because we have too much love and respect for the wonderful religious sisters who by word and example instilled the Catholic faith in us in our formative years.

To patronize such performances, which we have heard evoke humor by presenting an exaggerated and ridiculous portrait of education in Catholic schools in years gone by, would, in our opinion, be a betrayal of the holy and committed religious women who helped us to come closer to God and to the Church. There have to be better ways of raising money than by caricaturing those dedicated nuns who taught the faith to so many of us.

Editor's Note: Regarding whether Catholics should patronize the show "Late Nite Catechism," our opinion has been corroborated by A.P. of Michigan, a volunteer usher at a recent performance of this play in her local community, who sent along a critique of the show.

The first part of the program contained much good humor and fun, said A.P., as "Sister," with a setting that resembled a Catholic school classroom, scolded members of the audience for talking or not sitting correctly. She also asked them questions and gave them a holy card if they came up with the right answer.

Further along in the program, however, "Sister" started talking about Adam and Eve and creation. She said that the Catholic Church did not oppose evolution and indicated that there were multiple "first couples." She said that the Adam and Eve story was a fable and, when asked who Lilith was, said that Lilith was Adam's first wife, but "Adam divorced her to marry Eve because Lilith was a feminist." Sister also said that married priests would be good and that the present Pope is a good man, but he will not be around forever.

A.P. said that the audience "reacted very favorably to the presentation, accepting all material and questioning nothing." One young girl who did raise a question was quickly but gently put down. A.P. got the impression that the audience did not know that what "Sister" said was not doctrinally correct.

By the way, there is no mention of a Lilith in the Book of Genesis, either as Adam's first wife or otherwise. The word "lilith" does appear in Isaiah 34:14 in reference to a demon who lives in the desert. It is in medieval Jewish demonology that Lilith is identified as the "first Eve."

She was allegedly created from the earth along with Adam, but refused to submit to him and now roams the earth looking to kill newborn babies. How fitting it is that pro-abortion feminists have adopted this mythical demon as one of their role models (cf. Donna Steichen's book *Ungodly Rage*, p. 94).

Q. Our parish men's study group has commenced using a video series on Vatican II. After viewing the first of the five videos (*The Faithful Revolution*) put out by Thomas More in Allen, Texas, we have become concerned about the orthodoxy of this series. Can you give us any information about it? — H.F.K., Ohio

A. We are not familiar with this video series, but two readers of our "Catholic Replies" column were kind enough to send along their comments.

W.C. of Massachusetts objected to "the strong bias — and I would have to say dishonesty — in the presentation of Church teaching. The assertion was made that Vatican II did not address contraception, followed by the implication that Pope Paul VI was imposing, via *Humanae Vitae*, a retrograde decision in opposition to the spirit of the Council. In fact, Vatican II did address contraception in *Gaudium et Spes*, n. 51, where the traditional teaching of the Church was reaffirmed."

W.C. also said that the video series slandered Pope Pius XII, "with hardly any account taken of the magnitude of the Church's lifesaving efforts undertaken at his direction. All of this is contrary to the praise given to Pope Pius XII after the war by many prominent rabbis throughout the world, various Jewish organizations, and Jewish political figures."

Furthermore, said W.C., Fr. Richard McBrien "was presented as a Catholic theologian, leading the unwary viewer to accept his opinions at face value. No mention was made of his years of public dissent via his columns and books. The bishops of Australia removed their imprimatur from his book *Catholicism*. His own bishop, of Hartford, CT, removed McBrien's column from the Hartford diocesan paper."

M.H.T. of West Virginia also found the five-part series "quite problematic." She said that the main problem was that "people like Fr. Andrew Greeley, Hans Kung, Fr. Francis X. Murphy ("Xavier Rynne"), Fr. Richard McBrien, and Fr. Charles Curran are interviewed time and time again on various topics, alongside people who uphold the magisterium. The aforementioned are identified merely as 'professor' or 'theologian,' etc., and people unfamiliar with their long history of liberalism and dissent could be easily misled and think their positions are acceptable."

For example, said M.H.T., "the conclusion after viewing this series would be something like: 'Birth control? Some Catholics think it's okay, some don't. Liberation theology? Looks pretty good. Women becoming pastoral administrators? Great!'

"Among many shocking remarks were that before Vatican II: (1) black Catholics were oppressed, (2) the Church had an 'imperious approach,' (3) Pope Pius XII was 'silent' about Naziism, (4) St. Augustine's teachings about matrimony need to be abandoned, (5) Opus Dei is a 'far-right group' whose founder came from 'fascist Spain,' and (6) the two 'most significant' Catholics since Vatican II are Philip and Daniel Berrigan."

In the final video, M.H.T. said that "Pope John Paul is described as 'dictatorial' because 'he grew up in a time of dictators.' Then the viewer is shown old film clips of Hitler, Stalin, and goose-stepping soldiers! It seemed inexcusably disrespectful to me."

Q. We have a new Religious Formation Director in our parish who has announced that the only book used in grades 6 to 8 will be the Bible. Anyone interested in teaching at this level must sign a form saying that they will not bring any outside material (like the *Catechism*?) into class. Some parents plan to teach religion to their children at home, but what will happen when it comes time for First Communion and Confirmation? How can parents protect their children from inaccurate teachings and still have them receive their sacraments? — J.J.C., Michigan

A. You raise a question that has troubled many parents throughout the country, and some answers were offered by Leon J. Suprenant Jr., president of Catholics United for the Faith, in the May 2001 issue of *New Oxford Review*. In an article entitled "Home-Schooling & Sacramental Preparation," Suprenant pointed out that the Church has long taught that parents are the primary educators, but not the sole educators, of their children in the faith, and that pastors are to assist parents in this vital work. Canon law puts it this way:

"It is the responsibility, in the first place, of parents and those who take the place of parents as well as of the pastor to see that children who have reached the use of reason are correctly prepared and are nourished by the divine Food as early as possible, preceded by sacramental Confession; it is also for the pastor to be vigilant lest any children come to the Holy Banquet who have not yet reached the use of reason or whom he judges are not sufficiently disposed" (c. 914).

While "the roles of parents and pastors are complementary, not conflicting, and in many cases these roles are being exercised harmoniously, to the benefit of all concerned — especially the children," said Suprenant, there are too many situations where diligent parents "have watched in horror as their efforts have been undermined by institutionalized dissent and moral laxity in some Catholic schools and catechetical programs."

So what are parents to do if the bishop or pastor mandates full participation by home-schooled children in the parish program, especially if there is a concern about what is being taught there? Suprenant cited guidelines issued by the Diocese of Pittsburgh as "clearly a good-faith attempt" to coordinate the efforts of parents and the local parish.

He said that "the Pittsburgh guidelines offer assistance, encouragement, and direction to home-schooling parents, but leave the decisions to the parents. For example, parents are free to decide whether the child is to receive the sacrament individually, with the family, or within a group. Parents are free to choose the catechetical materials they want, while the pastor or his delegate determines the readiness of the child for the sacrament. The guidelines explicitly provide that the child must not be denied a sacrament merely for failure to participate in the parish program."

Editor's Note: In a recent reply, we called attention to the home-school-friendly guidelines of the Diocese of Pittsburgh regarding the preparation of children for the Sacraments. However, T.G. of Florida wrote to say that guidelines issued by the Bishops of Florida for home-schooling parents are not as friendly. For example, the Florida guidelines state:

• "Parents/guardians who home school, together with their children, are to participate in all dimensions of the parish program for sacramental catechesis: catechetical, ritual, service, spiritual (retreats, etc.), and any other requirements for sacramental preparation as determined by the parish."
• "Parents/guardians who home school, together with their children, will use the catechetical text and supplementary catechetical resources established by the parish program."

T.G. wondered if these guidelines, which could force home-schooling parents to use materials that are deficient in presenting the Catholic faith (that's why these parents are leery of parish programs in the first place), might drive good parents out of the parish. That could very well happen, but we would suggest that before taking that step, home-schooling parents demand at a minimum that parish texts conform to the *Catechism of the Catholic Church*.

A list of those religion series which have been studied by the Bishops' Ad Hoc Committee to Oversee the Use of the Catechism and have been found to be in conformity with the *Catechism* can be obtained by writing to the Office for the Catechism, 3211 Fourth St., N.E., Washington, DC 20017.

The situation between home-schooling parents and their local parishes will vary from diocese to diocese, depending upon whether the catechetical authorities are in tune with the teachings of the Church, or whether they are part of the establishment that has made such a mess of Catholic education over the past three decades. We hope that more dioceses will imitate the Pittsburgh guidelines.

Bibliography

Akin, James. *Mass Confusion*
_____. *The Salvation Controversy*
Amorth, Gabriele. *An Exorcist Tells His Story*
_____. *An Exorcist: More Stories*

Baker, Kenneth, S.J. *Inside the Bible*
Balducci, Corrado. *The Devil: ..."alive and active in our world"*
Barrack, Martin K. *Second Exodus*
Behe, Michael. *Darwin's Black Box*
Bennett, Isaiah. *Inside Mormonism*
_____. *When Mormons Call*

Catechism of the Catholic Church
Catholic For a Reason. Edited by Scott Hahn and Leon J.
        Suprenant Jr.
Catholic For a Reason II. Edited by Leon J. Suprenant Jr.
Cavins, Jeff. *Life on the Rock*
Clowes, Brian. *Call to Action or Call to Apostasy?*
_____. *The Facts of Life*
Cochini, Christian. *The Apostolic Origins of Priestly Celibacy*
Crocker, H.W. III. *Triumph: The Power and Glory of the
        Catholic Church*
Cruz, Joan Carroll. *Relics*
Currie, David. *Born Fundamentalist, Born Again Catholic*

Daniel-Rops, Henri. *The Church in the Dark Ages* (2 vols.)
_____. *Daily Life in the Time of Jesus*
Demski, William A. *Intelligent Design*
Denton, Michael. *Evolution: A Theory in Crisis*
Dictionary of the Liturgy. Edited by Fr. Jovian P. Lang, O.F.M.
Documents of Vatican II, The. Edited by Walter M. Abbott, S.J.
Drake, Timothy. *There We Stood, Here We Stand*
Drummey, James J. *Catholic Replies*
Duggan, Michael. *The Consuming Fire*

Elliott, Peter J. *Ceremonies of the Modern Roman Rite*
_____. *Liturgical Question Box*
Evert, Jason. *Answering Jehovah's Witnesses*

Foster, Michael Smith. *Annulment: The Wedding That Was*
Fox, Fr. Robert J. *Fatima Today*
_____. and Mangan, Fr. Charles. *Until Death Do Us Part*
Freze, Michael. *The Making of Saints*
_____. *They Bore the Wounds of Christ*
Fuentes, Antonio. *A Guide to the Bible*

Graham, Henry. *Where We Got the Bible*
Grisez, Germain. *Christian Moral Principles*
_____. *Difficult Moral Problems*
_____. *Living a Christian Life*

Hahn, Scott, and Cavins, Jeff. *Our Father's Plan* (Video)
Halligan, Fr. Nicholas. *The Sacraments and Their Celebration*
Hardon, John A., S.J. *Modern Catholic Dictionary*
Harvey, John F. *The Homosexual Person*
_____. *The Truth About Homosexuality*
Hauke, Manfred. *Women in the Priesthood*
Hayes, Fr. Edward J., Hayes, Msgr. Paul J. and Drummey,
    James J. *Catholicism & Ethics*
_____. *Catholicism & Life*
_____. *Catholicism & Reason*
_____. *Catholicism & Society*

John Paul II, Pope. *Crossing the Threshold of Hope*
_____. *Dies Domini*
_____. *Evangelium Vitae*
_____. *Familiaris Consortio*
_____. *Misericordia Dei*
_____. *Ordinatio Sacerdotalis*
_____. *Reconciliatio et Paenitentia*
_____. *Veritatis Splendor*
Johnson, Philip. *Darwin on Trial*
Johnston, George Sim. *Did Darwin Get It Right?*
Jurgens, William A. *The Faith of the Early Fathers* (3 vols.)

Keating, Karl. *Catholicism and Fundamentalism*
Kellmeyer, Steve. *Bible Basics*
Kippley, John F. *Marriage Is for Keeps*
_____. *Sex and the Marriage Covenant*
_____. and Kippley, Sheila. *The Art of Natural Family Planning*

Kreeft, Peter. *Catholic Christianity*
____. *Everything You Ever Wanted to Know About Heaven*
____. *Making Sense Out of Suffering*
____. and Tacelli, Ronald K. *Handbook of Christian Apologetics*

Madrid, Patrick. *Any Friend of God's Is a Friend of Mine*
____. *Pope Fiction*
____. *Search and Rescue*
____. *Surprised by Truth*
____. *Surprised by Truth 2*
____. *Where Is That in the Bible*
Marchione, Margherita. *Pope Pius XII: Architect for Peace*
____. *Yours Is a Precious Witness*
Marks, Frederick W. *A Catholic Handbook for Engaged and Newly Married Couples*
May, William E. *An Introduction to Moral Theology*
____. *Catholic Bioethics and the Gift of Human Life*
McBride, Alfred. *The Second Coming of Jesus*
McInerny, Ralph. *The Defamation of Pius XII*
____. *What Went Wrong with Vatican II?*
McKenzie, John L. *Dictionary of the Bible*
Myers, John J. *The Obligations of Catholics and the Rights of Unborn Children*

Ott, Ludwig. *Fundamentals of Catholic Dogma*

Pacwa, Mitch, S.J. *Catholics and the New Age*
Paul VI, Pope. *Credo of the People of God*
____. *Humanae Vitae*
Peters, Edward N. *100 Answers to Your Questions on Annulments*
Pius XII, Pope. *Humani Generis*
____. *Mystici Corporis*
Pontifical Council for Promoting Christian Unity. *Principles and Norms of Ecumenism*

Ray, Stephen K. *Crossing the Tiber*
____. *Upon This Rock*
Rice, Charles E. *The Winning Side*
Robillard, Edmond. *Reincarnation: Illusion or Reality*
Rose, Michael. *Goodbye! Good Men*

_____. *The Renovation Manipulation*
_____. *Ugly as Sin*
Rychlak, Ronald. *Hitler, the War and the Pope*

Sacred Congregation for the Doctrine of the Faith. *Declaration on Certain Problems of Sexual Ethics*
_____. *Declaration on Euthanasia*
_____. *Declaration on Procured Abortion*
_____. *Instruction on Respect for Human Life in Its Origin and on the Dignity of Procreation*
_____. *Letter to the Bishops of the Catholic Church on the Pastoral Care of Homosexual Persons*
Shea, Mark. *Making Senses Out of Scripture*
Smith, Janet E. *Humanae Vitae: A Generation Later*
Smith, Wesley J. *Culture of Death: The Assault on Bioethics in America*
_____. *Forced Exit*
Steffon, Fr. Jeffrey J. *Satanism: Is It Real?*
Steichen, Donna. *Ungodly Rage*
Stravinskas, Fr. Peter M.J. *The Catholic Church & the Bible*
_____. *The Mass: A Biblical Prayer*
Suprenant, Leon J. Jr., and Gray, Philip C.L. *Faith Facts*

Thiede, Carston, and D'Ancona, Matthew. *Eyewitness to Jesus*
Thigpen, Paul. *The Rapture Trap*

Vasoli, Robert H. *What God Has Joined Together*
Vatican Council II: The Conciliar and Post Conciliar Documents. Edited by Austin Flannery, O.P. (2 vols.)

Walsh, John Evangelist. *The Bones of St. Peter*
Walsh, William Thomas. *Characters of the Inquisition*
Weigel, George. *The Courage to Be Catholic*
_____. *The Truth of Catholicism*
_____. *Witness to Hope*
Wells, Jonathan. *Icons of Evolution*
West, Christopher. *Good News About Sex & Marriage*
Why Humanae Vitae Was Right: A Reader. Edited by Janet E. Smith
Wrenn, Msgr. Michael J., and Whitehead, Kenneth D. *Flawed Expectations*

Index

IF YOU LIKED *CATHOLIC REPLIES 2*, YOU SHOULD ALSO HAVE A COPY OF THE FIRST *CATHOLIC REPLIES.*

In his first volume, nationally known author and speaker James J. Drummey also provided solid answers to another 800 questions about religion and morality. Questions that puzzle Catholics and which are often asked of Catholics, who sometimes are not sure what to say.

Questions such as why does God permit evil and suffering? How can the Pope be infallible? Do we still believe in Purgatory? Why should we confess our sins to a priest? Should a Catholic vote for a pro-abortion candidate for public office? Why can't women be priests? Where does the Church stand on the death penalty? What's wrong with homosexuality? What about predestination?

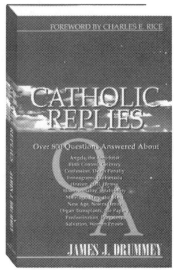

The answers to these and many other questions are backed up with quotations from the Bible, the *Catechism of the Catholic Church*, and the writings of saints and popes. If you are looking for something for the person who has everything, except a knowledge of the Catholic faith, give them this book, as well as *Catholic Replies 2*.

The first volume of *Catholic Replies* is available for $17.95, plus $5 for shipping by priority mail. You can order this 463-page book by writing to the address below, by calling toll-free (877) 730-8877, or by visiting the web site **catholicreplies.com**.

C.R. Publications Inc., 345 Prospect St., Norwood, MA 02062

✟ **HERE IS WHY SO MANY PEOPLE ARE** ✟
USING THE CATHOLICISM SERIES.

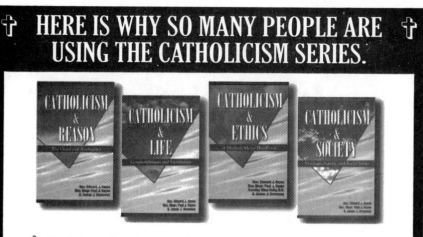

✟ The Series is informative, practical, solidly Catholic, and has excellent examples. -
Sister Carla Marie, SSND, *Bishop Sullivan High School,*
Baton Rouge, Louisiana

✟ Both as a teacher and as a program director, I have found these texts effective
in passing on the Faith by using apologetics as an important evangelical tool. -
Fr. David Mullen, *St. Brendan Parish, Bellingham, Massachusetts*

✟ Say goodbye to boring, empty religious education classes, and open the eyes
of youth to the truths of the Catholic Faith. -
Molly Gray, *Sacred Heart Parish, East Grand Forks, Minnesota*

✟ The Catholicism Series is thought-provoking but easy to read, sublime but
relevant; it provides an excellent, tangible study of Catholic apologetics. -
Bob Morrison, *St. Maurice School, Winnipeg, Manitoba*

✟ We are using the Series in our RCIA program, and the books are terrific. -
Fr. Walter Lawrence, *St. Mary Church, Barnesville, Maryland*

✟ We are using all four of your textbooks and highly recommend them to any
religious program. -
Ann M. Stock, *Mother of Dolors Church, Vandalia, Illinois*

Written by two priests and a layman, the series covers the Creed and Apologetics
(*Catholicism & Reason*), Commandments and Sacraments (*Catholicism & Life*),
Marriage, Family and Social Issues (*Catholicism & Society*), and Medical/Moral
Matters (*Catholicism & Ethics*). The books have been found to be in conformity
with the *Catechism of the Catholic Church* and are currently being used in dozens
of Catholic high schools and hundreds of parish religion programs (both with
teenagers and adults).

For information about prices and discounts, or for sample copies, contact:

C.R. Publications Inc., 345 Prospect St., Norwood, MA 02062
Toll free (877) 730-8877 or visit us at crpublications.com